ADVANCE PRAISE FOR
FINDING the FORCE OF the
STAR WARS FRANCHISE

"*Star Wars* is the most important franchise in the history of American popular culture, and Kapell and Lawrence's *Finding the Force of the Star Wars Franchise: Fans, Merchandise, and Critics* is the most important book about *Star Wars.* This collection of well-written and engaging essays examines the *Star Wars* phenomenon from a variety of important and revealing perspectives. It is a 'must have' for any *Star Wars* fan, or for anyone interested in the dynamic interplay of popular culture and society."

Gary Hoppenstand, Editor, The Journal of Popular Culture

"These essays place the dynamics of the twentieth century's most wide-reaching science fiction phenomenon in a meaningful cultural and political context."

Javier Martinez, Editor, Extrapolation

FINDING THE FORCE OF THE
STAR WARS
FRANCHISE

Toby Miller
General Editor

Vol. 14

PETER LANG
New York • Washington, D.C./Baltimore • Bern
Frankfurt am Main • Berlin • Brussels • Vienna • Oxford

FINDING THE FORCE OF THE
STAR WARS
FRANCHISE

FANS, MERCHANDISE, & CRITICS

EDITED BY
Matthew Wilhelm Kapell
& John Shelton Lawrence

PETER LANG
New York • Washington, D.C./Baltimore • Bern
Frankfurt am Main • Berlin • Brussels • Vienna • Oxford

Library of Congress Cataloging-in-Publication Data NOT IN YET

Finding the force of the Star wars franchise: fans, merchandise, and critics /
edited by Matthew Wilhelm Kapell and John Shelton Lawrence.
p. cm. — (Popular culture and everyday life; v. 14)
Includes bibliographical references and index.
1. Star Wars films. 2. Star Wars films--Collectibles. I. Kapell, Matthew. II. Lawrence, John Shelton.
III. Series: Popular culture & everyday life ; v. 14.
PN1995.9.S695F55   791.43'75—dc22   2006012617
ISBN 0-8204-8808-9 (hardcover)
ISBN 0-8204-6333-7 (paperback)
ISSN 1529-2428

Bibliographic information published by **Die Deutsche Bibliothek**.
Die Deutsche Bibliothek lists this publication in the "Deutsche
Nationalbibliografie"; detailed bibliographic data is available
on the Internet at http://dnb.ddb.de/.

Cover photograph by Stephanie J. Wilhelm

The paper in this book meets the guidelines for permanence and durability
of the Committee on Production Guidelines for Book Longevity
of the Council of Library Resources.

2006 Peter Lang Publishing, Inc., New York
29 Broadway, New York, NY 10006
www.peterlang.com

Printed in the United States of America

For

Jedi Master Zoe Blythe

And for those we traveled with on "some damn fool idealistic crusade"—

Robert Jewett   and   William G. Doty

With the greatest admiration.

Table of Contents

Myth

Religion

Sexuality and Gender

Genetics, Social Order, and Domination

Playtoys and Collecting

Evaluations

List of Illustrations

List of Tables

Acknowledgments

Each contributor to this volume went, in his or her own way, "above and beyond the call of duty" in reading each other's work, providing good copy on very limited schedules, and in other ways making this book much better than it might otherwise have been. We thank them all. Jonathan L. Bowen contributed his expert knowledge on the franchise. William G. Doty read a number of the essays that appear here and offered close readings and valuable insight. Lincoln Geraghty was generous in assisting with photography. Roger Kaufman helped with several crucial graphics issues. Marty Knepper was compulsively helpful as usual. Anthony Thompson at Signature Press helped with design questions. Our editor at Peter Lang, Damon Zucca, helped make this book possible in many ways. He, along with Sophie Appel and Bernadette Shade especially at Peter Lang, has our sincere thanks. The editor of this series, Toby Miller, offered insight from the time of the proposal for this volume up to the final product.

In the beginning there was merely *Star Wars* (1977). Its success permitted sequels and prequels as well as mountains of licensed merchandise. Consequently, a new way of naming the films was adopted. Imparting a sense of temporal chronology within a fictional universe (while winking at the serialized television of George Lucas's youth), Roman-numeraled episode names were attached to each film. The peculiar result was that twenty-two years after the first film's appearance, *Star Wars: Episode IV–A New Hope*, the plot-originating *Episode I* appeared. Then, after twenty-eight years, *Episode III–Revenge of the Sith* (2005) appeared, finally allowing audiences to fully understand the opening scenes of 1977's *Episode IV*.

Readers would find it cumbersome to read these scaled-up titles in every film reference, so we have adopted the stylistic convention of using an episode's descriptive title (along with its release year) for first occurrences within our chapters—as in *The Phantom Menace* (1999). Thereafter, our authors may or may not use acronymic initials in italics, as in *TPM*. They are guided by context, and, in situations where sequence matters, an author may use the episode number. We list here the official titles of principal films in the canon and their abbreviations. (A standard filmography that includes principal documentaries appears as an appendix.)

> *Star Wars: Episode I–The Phantom Menace* (1999); *TPM*
> *Star Wars: Episode II–Attack of the Clones* (2002); *AOTC*
> *Star Wars: Episode III–Revenge of the Sith* (2005); *ROTS*
> *Star Wars: Episode IV–A New Hope* (1977); *ANH*
> *Star Wars: Episode V–The Empire Strikes Back* (1980); *ESB*
> *Star Wars: Episode VI–Return of the Jedi* (1983); *ROTJ*

In discussing these six films, our contributors follow Lucasfilm's convention of treating all officially licensed material (novels, games, etc.) as part of the "Expanded *Star Wars* Universe" that helps to illuminate them. Such material has been carefully vetted for continuity and intent, often by George Lucas himself.

We also mention here that we use the Modern Language Association (MLA) system of embedded documentation. A Works Cited listing appears at the end of each essay, as do Endnotes for references within the chapter.

CHAPTER 1

Introduction: Spectacle, Merchandise, and Influence

John Shelton Lawrence

The *Star Wars* franchise stands as film history's greatest commercial and cultural success. From *A New Hope* (1977) to *Revenge of the Sith* (2005), the franchise spans twenty-eight years guided by a single creator, George W. Lucas, Jr. *ROTS*, the sixth and final film of the prequel series, set month-of-May attendance records like its older siblings. In addition to the U.S. screenings, *Variety* reported that *ROTS* opened in 105 foreign venues with more than 10,000 screenings its first week. French, German, and Spanish fans stood in line for hours to obtain tickets, with costumed Darth Vaders and Yodas saber slashing as they waited ("Force is with 'Sith'").

A steady surge of television ads, product tie-ins at restaurants, and themed merchandise flowed to toy counters. Diet Pepsi presented a television ad titled "Jedi Mind Trick" with Chewbacca and Yoda, with the little guru attempting to use the Force to move a can of soda toward himself. Pepsi also offered the Darth Dew Slurpee drink at the 7-Eleven franchise chain. In October of 2005, Amazon.com listed 3,980 *Star Wars* book titles, 84 music CDs, and 1,116 toys and games. Illustrating comprehensiveness in marketing, the Hasbro Company offered Mr. Potato Head Darth Tater, a bug-eyed, cuddly little fellow with a laser sword and shiny black helmet. ("Together we shall rule as father and spud," he remarks to little Luke Tater; see fig. 1). Lego also descended to the young children's market with Darth Vader's Transformation, a build-it-yourself surgical platform that allows the child to change the bloody Anakin into a slick black Vader (fig. 2). Meanwhile, at the U.S. Web site of eBay, 60,343 *Star Wars* items were for sale, including 4,125 Burger King Darth Vaders and 1,046 Darth Mauls.[1] One strains to imagine how any other franchise could surpass this commercial *everywhereness* of *Star Wars*.

Figure 1: Hasbro/Playskool's Mr. Potato Head adapted Darth Vader and Luke Skywalker with poseable, dressable Tater characters. According to the packaging, Darth Tater says to Luke Tater "Together we shall rule as father and spud." Advertised for ages 2+, the *Star Wars* franchise turns from melodrama to silliness in order to safely extend the drama of temptation and rejection to the littlest of tykes. Playskool also offers a "Spud Trooper," a less menacing Stormtrooper. Photography by Lincoln Geraghty.

The Commercial Achievement and Public Persona of George Lucas

Despite such relentless selling, George Lucas is hardly taken to be an anything-for-a-dollar huckster. Although he insists upon privacy, his public persona has emerged in rare appearances as that of a guru who generously shares insights on artistic creation, his technological innovations, and the life challenges of managing a global mythic franchise. Acknowledging his roles in filmmaking, technical innovation in film imagery and sound, philanthropy, and education, Lucas has received numerous honors, including a Lifetime Achievement Award from the American Film Institute in 2005. For the release of *The Phantom Menace* (1999), Lucas as philanthropist authorized charitable early screenings that raised $5.3 million in a dozen cities (Bowen 66). The grousing of exhibitors about Lucasfilm's demanding twelve-week contracts was buried in the trade papers ("Distribs 'Menace'" 3).

What more could a film auteur possibly attain? Seen against history's tapestry of grand creations, Lucas has woven himself in alongside Richard Wagner, who created his Ring of the Nibelungs cycle over an identical period of twenty-eight years (1848–1876). Wagner's innovations in staging and musical invention, combined with his ideas about destiny and passion, eventually made his venue at Bayreuth a cultural center for Germany and his philosophical ideas a potent force in the art world (Magee). Echoing Wagner's conception of his art as "Gesamtkunstwerk"—a totally encompassing, technologically refined blend of image and sound (Doty 10), Lucasfilm's *Within A Minute* (2005) documentary about *ROTS* demonstrates the artistic complexity of melding a mere forty-nine seconds of saber dueling on lava-drenched Mustafar. For this scene, Lucas synthesized twenty-six shots, 1,185 frames, drawing upon 910 artists who were reported to have worked 70,441 hours. Then an original music score by John Williams, performed by the London Symphony Orchestra, was overlaid into the complex sound track. A total work of art indeed!

For film historical perspective on the *Star Wars'* cultural achievement, re-call that *Citizen Kane* (1941), standing at #1 among the American Film Insti-tute's list of 100 Best Films, had no sequel or prequel. Its twenty-six-year-old director, Orson Welles, who produced, directed and acted in this highly re-garded masterpiece, received an Oscar for *Citizen Kane's* screenplay but never attained such distinction again. The film was regarded as innovative in its nar-rative technique, its unusual lighting and camera angles, and its ability to cre-ate and sustain its mood of angst. It regularly appears on lists of personal favorites or best films. Welles, despite other creations of considerable artistic merit, ended his career humbled by jobs such as narrating for the end times film, *The Late Great Planet Earth* (1979), and hawking for Paul Masson Winery in TV ads that promised "no wine before its time." One of his literary pinna-cles was a fifty-eight-page memo to Universal Studios complaining about cuts to his 1958 *Touch of Evil* (Heylin 316–20). The studio, thinking that it knew better how to finish a Welles film, had ignominiously booted him from the editing room. Today *Citizen Kane* is honored by a two-disc DVD set, several film history books, articles in film journals, and several dozen posters for sale on eBay. Belated admiration is certainly not the same as influence or wealth. Considering the puny scale of this legacy, who would deny that Welles was Old Hollywood, a frustrated genius who could hardly manage his assets as well as William Randolph Hearst—the butt whose excoriation earned the young di-rector's reputation as genius?

But even in the so-called New Hollywood, ever being redefined, "George Star Wars Lucas"[2] is something special. Indeed, Lucas early left the Los Angeles area to escape from the artistically challenged business men who thought that doing deals was making movies. Those tycoons, fortified by market studies, often tinker with product and become involved in accounting feuds with artists or corporate shareholders—yet collect huge compensation packages earned through contracts that reward failure as richly as success.[3] Reacting against this, George Lucas and Frances Ford Coppola created a kind of Rebel Alliance in the bucolic, Naboo-like Northern California, distant from the mechanized Coruscant, where the Greedos claimed bounties for capturing actors and directors in torturous contracts. After the Corporate Death Star destroyed the financing for their fledgling Zoetrope Studios, Lucas eventually removed himself to Marin County, California, eventually creating Lucasfilm at the rural Skywalker Ranch. As his enterprises expanded, he created a state of the art Letterman Digital Arts Center on the Presidio military preserve in San Francisco. There he has been celebrated as a model employer (Levy) and has provided the anchor for a growing complex of companies collectively called "Digiwood"—Industrial Light and Magic (a Lucas company), Lucas Arts Entertainment Company (creator of games), Skywalker Sound (a postproduction sound effects and editing company), Pixar Animation Studios (a Lucas spin-off), and PDI/Dreamworks, creators of *Antz* (1998) and *Shrek* (2001). And these are just the companies that have produced blockbusters to date (Straus).

Demonstrating that he remains an artist, Lucas appears on bonus tracks for the *Star Wars* DVDs as a confident, genial creator who fully understands how to synthesize films out of computer graphics and works as a peer among his helpers. In Lucas's more humane world there appear to be no casting couches, cigars, slick silk suits, or screaming fits to intimidate underlings. For the *Empire of Dreams* (2004) documentary on the history of the franchise, Lucas fingers himself as the powerful, Darth Vader figure within his own organization: "I have become the very thing I was trying to avoid" ("Saga Continues"). This demeanor as gentle and self-deprecating, saddened by his own power, repeatedly surfaces. It confirms the rumors that he began his career too shy, insecure, and inarticulate to be a director. Although he did not apply these words to himself, Lucas appears to be one of the little heroes that he defined in his television interview with Bill Moyers:

> Heroes come in all sizes, and you don't have to be a giant hero. You can be a very small hero. It's just as important to understand that accepting self-responsibility for the things you do, having good manners, caring about other people—these are heroic acts. ("Of Myth" 94)

Lucas has consistently conveyed this earnest responsibility for nurturing the relatively unknown actors and technicians who thrived within his businesses.

As much as Hollywood would love the consistent success and respect enjoyed by Lucasfilm Ltd., and George Lucas himself, it will not walk the conservative, craft-focused walk. Yet, because *Star Wars* is gold, Hollywood has stolen whatever it can from the Lucas approach to film content and marketing. Other studios and directors working today cannot be fully understood without recognizing the patterns they have acquired from the *Star Wars* franchise.

Myth

Long before Hollywood had Roman-numeraled sequels or prequels, there were genres that defined settings, character types, and plot paths along predictable comic or melodramatic arcs. *Star Wars* itself blended several genres including sci-fi, cowboy Westerns, World War II aerials, and Akira Kurosawa's samurai films. A discarded, but nonetheless significant poster for *ANH* pitched the retro aspect: "First, Buck Rogers. Then, Flash Gordon. Now, Luke Skywalker. It'll make you feel like a kid again" (Sansweet). The imprints of literary sources, such as Isaac Asimov's *Foundation* novels and Frank Herbert's *Dune*, are also apparent (Ebert 157–59). But the film's distinct new core lay in its mythological template, which artfully reflected archaic story patterns that other films could learn to mimic fairly easily.

As quickly as *ANH* was on the screen, scholars began to see the stamp of Joseph Campbell's classical monomyth, which he articulated in his *Hero with a Thousand Faces* (1949), a steady seller and cult classic since its early printings. Film scholar Andrew Gordon in 1978 mapped the monomythic story arc in a widely quoted article:

> *Star Wars* is a masterpiece of synthesis, a triumph of American ingenuity and resourcefulness, demonstrating, how the old may be made new again: Lucas raided the junkyards of our popular culture and rigged a working myth out of scrap. Like the hotrods in his previous film, *American Graffiti*, *Star Wars* is an amalgam of pieces of mass culture customized and supercharged and run flat out. He lifted parts openly and lovingly from various popular culture genres, but the engine that runs it is the "monomyth." (Gordon 73–4)

Other scholars, including Robert Jewett and myself, noted the American variants of the monomyth entailing Luke Skywalker's (Mark Hamill) sexual renunciation as the secret of his instinctually precise violence ("Pop Fascism in *Star Wars*").[4]

What was it in the archaic tales that inspired George Lucas? Chapter 2 of this book, "Joseph Campbell, George Lucas, and the Monomyth," offers Lucas's account of his discovery of and inspiration by the ancient story archetypes. The chapter also speculates about a later, unacknowledged departure from Campbell's schematic story modules. In his renowned *Hero* book,

Campbell had offered a metamyth, a condensed master plot that he claimed to derive from world myth and folklore.

> A hero ventures forth from the world of common day into a region of supernatural wonder: fabulous forces are there encountered and a decisive victory is won: the hero comes back from this mysterious adventure with the power to bestow boons on his fellow man. (30)

Campbell's energetic, tantalizing adventure takes readers through the alternate routes and stages of this master story pattern. He makes nuanced observations packed with compelling narrative ingredients: mentors, charms, dragon tests, captivities, sex with a goddess, apotheosis, etc. (245–46). Campbell's recipe-like enumerations offered up mythic story elements not only for *Star Wars* but also for the *Indiana Jones* series (Lucas served as writer and executive producer),[5] as well as *The Land Before Time* (1988) and *Willow* (1988), where Lucas also had a production hand. Other Hollywood blockbusters—*The Lion King* (1994), *The Matrix* trilogy (1999–2003), and *The Lord of the Rings* trilogy (2001–2003)—also reflect the monomyth-by-recipe on which Lucas built the franchise.

So enticing are Campbell's suggestively simplified enumerations that Christopher Vogler, a former script evaluator at Disney, has written *The Writer's Journey* (1998) that offers advice on creating Campbell monomythic-modeled tales—"With these tools you can construct a story to meet almost any situation, a story that will be dramatic, entertaining, and psychologically true. With this equipment you can diagnose the problems of almost any ailing plotline and make the corrections to bring it to its peak of performance" (1). Distilling Campbell's more complex mythic ingredients into twelve moments, Vogler offers to become your personal story trainer.

Such influences from *Star Wars* still remain in Hollywood, although the folk tale aspect in *Star Wars* diminished as Lucas outgrew the adolescent audience of his first trilogy and turned his attention to political economy, governing styles, and high-tech military trends. The Lawrence essay on Campbell and Lucas speculates about their personal encounters after the completion of the first trilogy; Campbell's fierce profession of political chastity, which forbade him as literary artist to take any position on a contemporary issue, probably struck Lucas as socially irresponsible. The films of the prequel thus move away from the classical archetypes toward a more explicit political discourse.

Sympathetic to this shift, John David Ebert's recent *Celluloid Heroes and Mechanical Dragons* (2005) looks at the United States through a Lucas-shaped lens and suggests that the nation is "like the robot army of the Trade Federation in *The Phantom Menace* which goes crashing through forests and destroying every living thing in its path" with "transnational corporations, in alliance with the military industrial complex ... threatening to turn the planet into a wasteland of indentured slavery, ruined topsoils, seas, and scarred strips of de-forested land swarming with refugee populations" (156). By the time of

ROTS's release, Lucas was frankly stating that his vision of decline from participative Republic to tyrannical Empire—while a generic map for collapsing civilizations—also fit his contemporary homeland alarmingly well. At the 2005 Cannes Festival, for example, he told CBS News that "the parallels between what we did in Vietnam and what we're doing in Iraq now are unbelievable" ("'Sith' Invites Bush Comparison"). The prequel films thus depart from Campbell's reductive vision of myth as follow-your-bliss New Age self-discovery and disclose Lucas as partisan artist.

Consistent with such a view of Lucas is Stephen McVeigh's treatment of the war theme in chapter 3, "The Galactic Way of Warfare." Critics from America's political left immediately complained about *ANH's* celebration of triumphal war as a fantasy that permitted recovery from the Vietnam War's moral contamination. Tom Engelhardt's *The End of Victory Culture* (1995) suggested that *ANH's* Rebel Alliance dramatically enacted a kind of ideological jiu-jitsu, in which America loses the shame of imperial oppression and becomes a country of "plucky underdogs."

> Once again, we could have it all: freedom *and* victory, captivity *and* rescue, underdog status *and* the spectacle of slaughter. As with the Indian fighter of old, advanced weaponry *and* the spiritual powers of the guerilla might be ours. (Engelhardt 267; author's italics)

Perhaps the founding narratives of the first trilogy did have this psychic benefit for American adults who felt national honor impaired by the Vietnam experience.

However, McVeigh suggests a flaw with this interpretation. He believes that, from the beginning, George Lucas meant to symbolically portray the United States as the Dreaded Empire, a mechanized force with overwhelming firepower that is used to subjugate the poor in distant places. He suggests that the deepening political-military-industrial alliance portrayed in the prequels points clearly at the Pentagon's Revolution in Military Affairs (RMA), a project launched in the early 1970s that aims to create a safer warfare for the American warrior by making it more lethal and more robotic. In McVeigh's words, the military theme "allows us to see *Star Wars* as a unique commentary on America's understandings of war over a thirty-year period."

Yet it would be a mistake to see Lucas as a pacifically inclined, articulate philosopher of democracy. In his most complex public utterance on governing, he revealed himself as a closet monarchist—indicating a spiritual affinity to the Old Republic's aristocracy. Responding to Orville Schell in a 1999 interview with the *New York Times*, he spoke the language of "rulers," as opposed to speaking of democracy as an opportunity for participation and shared responsibility. He offhandedly remarked that "a good despot" or "a benevolent despot who can really get things done" would be desirable, explaining himself this way:

> There's no respect for the office of the Presidency. Not that we need a king, but there's a reason why kings built large palaces, sat on thrones and wore rubies all over. There's a whole social need for that, not to oppress the masses, but to impress the masses and make them proud and allow them to feel good about their culture, their government and their ruler so that they are left feeling that a ruler has the right to rule over them, so that they feel good rather than disgusted about being ruled.... But there's probably no better form of government than a good despot. (Lucas 30)

Given an attraction to rulers who "wear rubies all over to impress the masses and make them proud," it is not surprising that Lucas brings a certain amount of controversy to the *Star Wars* franchise—if for no other reason than to strike back at an auteur who eschews populist rhetoric. But the success and the influence count too as lightning arrestors for critics.

In other ways, the mythic system of *Star Wars* reaches back toward archaic models, and this nurtured the sense that *ANH* gave aid and comfort to the religious impulse. It was called "a breath of fresh air" even by the liberal *Christian Century* (Siska). What experiences allowed Lucas to communicate with such apparent spirituality? Depressed by the glum catastrophe films and anti-Westerns of his contemporaries, George Lucas saw himself as a kind of revivalist who would bring some wholesome spiritual values back into American culture. But did he actually bring the theme of holy war, violence directed by a higher power? Some, like Frank Allnut, a former Disney publicist who wrote *Unlocking the Mystery of the Force* (1977), were thrilled by the divine/apocalyptic potential:

> The galactic wars in the movies are really religious wars. The people of the Alliance, who believe in and follow the ways of the Force, are pitted against the satanic emperor Palpatine, Darth Vader and all the other "fallen stars" of the Old Republic. The Bible tells us that there is a bitter conflict raging throughout the spiritual universe, and it's no secret to anyone that a fierce battle between the forces of good and the forces of evil is being fought on planet earth today. (Allnut 90)

As Allnut warms to his elaborate allegory, he likens the church to that "small band of Rebel forces led by Luke, Han, and Princess Leia on a mission to restore the former glory of the Alliance" (143). In the real, spiritual "star wars" that Allnut sees today, "Jesus has an even deadlier sword" than the light sabers, and he will use it "to strike down all the ungodly nations of the world" (169). Although never quite so explicitly Christian as an allegory of holy war, the theme of Force-assisted violence threads through *Star Wars* from the moment that Luke turns off his targeting computer in *ANH* to the final battle between Anakin (Hayden Christensen) and Obi-Wan (Ewan McGregor) on Mustafar in *ROTS*. In the novelization of *ROTS* that George Lucas himself edited, Matthew Stover writes of Obi-Wan that "He was only a vessel, emptied of self. The Force, shaped by his skill and guided by his clarity of mind, fought through him" (285). Celebrating Obi-Wan's transcendence of rationality and his surrender to the violence that the Force directs him to perform, Stover and Lucas write that, during his battle with General Grievous, "he had no need for a plan, no use for tactics. He had the Force" (122). This valorized violence, sanctioned by deities, runs deep in all cultures that have imagined themselves representing higher powers who authorize them to slaughter others in battle—whether it be Christian Crusaders in 1098 crying "Deus le volt" ("God wills it"), the *mission civilatrice* of French imperialism, America's *manifest destiny* as authorization for genocide of Native Americans,[6] or a Zen Buddhist–saturated assassin in 1930s Japan, such as Innoue Nissho who remarked in court "that I have no systematized ideas. I transcend reason and act completely on intuition" (Victoria 215).

Michelle Kinnucan's chapter 4 on "the pedagogy of the Force" picks up on this fervent apocalyptic theme and lays out "the myth of redemptive violence," a tale as old as the Babylonian story (1700–2000 BCE) of Marduk's slaying of his monstrous mother Tiamat. Through this telling, the violence of *Star Wars* achieves a righteousness, in which (quoting the theologian Walter Wink): "violence saves ... war brings peace ... might makes right." This critical reading of *Star Wars* as archaic myth of creation through destruction, which goes straight to the plot of blowing up the Death Stars (*ANH* and *Return of the Jedi*) and tossing Emperor Palpatine into the reactor core (*ROTJ*), differs from the more affirmative treatment of *Star Wars* as religion in the chapters by Jennifer Porter and Jonathan Bowen and Rachel Wagner. Juxtaposing their treatments with Kinnucan's illustrates the phenomenon of cultural polysemy, in which the same texts carry divergent meanings for audiences who bring differing backgrounds and expectations to their experience of popular film.

Religion

In his unsympathetic analysis of *Star Wars*' contribution to the contemporary blockbuster formula, film historian Thomas Schatz suggests that the

> one-dimensional characters and ruthlessly linear chase-film plotting are offset by a purposeful incoherence which actually "opens" the film to different readings (and readers), allowing for multiple interpretive strategies and thus broadening the potential audience appeal. (Schatz 23)

Rather than offering the particularity of classical Hollywood narrative, the new blockbuster that seeks ever larger markets employs the narrative of the generic that allows audiences to project into the film whatever they might be looking for. The essays on religion in this volume describe a process of religious discovery in which *Star Wars* functions as a sacred text for diverse religious traditions.

Jennifer Porter's chapter 6 frankly recognizes that "*Star Wars* is a commodity successfully sold to millions worldwide" but also suggests "that it has also

become the means by which some fans live, experience and express their spiri
tual lives." Working ethnographically with voices from the fans, she describes a
emerging Jedi faithful who align their spirituality with *Star Wars'* positive inspirational qualities. Similarly, Jonathan Bowen and Rachel Wagner's chapter
5 presents *Star Wars* as the text of a religion that symbolically maps the central
messages in Buddhism, Christianity, and Taoism. As they put it, "the films express the quest for meaning and purpose in a galaxy desperately needing balance." Focusing on Anakin Skywalker/Darth Vader, they argue convincingly
for deep complexity in this character whose life has been granted a remarkable
quantity of screen time over the twenty-eight-year cycle of the complete narrative. Such affirmative readings reflect a phenomenon in contemporary culture
can be identified as consumer-based religion, a spirituality liberated from
bricks-and-mortar churches, compulsory creeds, and demands for social con-
formity. Such adherents feel comfortable in identifying their inspirations in
copyrighted media products rather than revered traditional texts or spiritual
authorities that have earned their sacred status over centuries.

Sexuality and Gender

Gender and sexuality are muted topics in the *Star Wars* franchise, offering a
small sprinkle of assertive/erotic women to cope with a much larger cast of
men coded for heroic power. Philip Simpson's chapter 7 looks at the assertive
Leia (Carrie Fisher) and Padmé Amidala (Natalie Portman). His informative
metaphor suggests that the "narrative codes" present "their exercise of
autonomy as 'frigidity' ... placing both women in relationships that demand
not just 'thawing' but melting of their icy feminine royalty as the 'icy
princesses'" and their "stripping" as sexual partners for Han Solo (Harrison
Ford) and Anakin Skywalker (Hayden Christensen). He contends that their
subordination to biological bearing for Jedi lineage evinces three decades of
American cultural ambivalence about the conflicting roles of women as
leaders, lovers, and mothers.

Regarding the erotic component of *Star Wars*, George Lucas's initial targeting of the youth market meant that the first five films carried the PG rating,
which was merely a concession to the violence of chopped-off hands, the murder of Luke's parents on Tatooine, the bondage and abuse of Anakin's
mother, and other topics alarming to children. A kiss from Luke for Leia (in
The Empire Strikes Back, before they knew they were siblings) and Leia's golden
slave-bikini display for Jabba the Hutt (in *ROTJ*) seem as warm in heterosexual
eroticism as *Star Wars* could permit for the juvenile males whose parents had
to permit repeat film viewings. In chapter 8, Roger Kaufman opens up an
original way of understanding the limited heterosexual content by highlighting
a pronounced same-sex eroticism between the males. He suggests that several

physically restrained homosexual romances lie at the saga's passionate erotic heart—but it is a love that cannot name itself and must, in the end, punish itself. Anakin and Obi-Wan, who once loved each other, are doomed to hack away at one another in *ROTS*'s dreadful scene. Yet Kaufman's final judgment is one of hope regarding *Star Wars*' affirmative gay sexuality, where "the character of Luke Skywalker laudably represents in his portrayed psychological growth an inspiring movement toward the kind of homosexually creative and conscientiously individuated personhood so ethically and politically necessary for humanity's future."

Genetics, Social Order, and Domination

What are the sources of social order and leadership for the citizens of the galaxy in George Lucas's universe? Matthew Wilhelm Kapell's chapter 9 examines the biological basis for power in the Force (its midi-chlorian blood components, specifically), the use of clones, and the resonance of *Star Wars*' narrative as a revival of traditional eugenics. He finds a strong message of biological destiny: "Your destiny, like that of the Skywalker family, is a destiny determined by your lineage, by your midi-chlorians or genes. It is immensely entertaining, but it is not about merit or the insights that we ordinary people can attain." This reading reminds us that sustaining a narrative of more than thirteen hours may inadvertently combine disparate sets of messages about politics (ostensibly democratic) and social order (eugenic privileges at birth). Or these may simply reflect the latent contradictions in our own social order—an artistic necessity for pleasing a mass market.

Stephanie J. Wilhelm's chapter 10 helps us view the social and moral order within *Star Wars* through the lens of postcolonial theory, helping us understand how the costumes, the sets, the landscapes, represent the moral history of the characters and the very morality of the franchise:

> in the vast deserts of Tatooine, the frozen planet Hoth, the lush landscapes of Naboo, the murkiness of Dagobah, or the hustle and bustle of the metropolis Coruscant, Lucas reminds audiences that each of his characters has an origin rooted in the traditions of their home planets.

Those who "evade, adapt, and survive the machinations of the empire's evil forces" come from the distant places remote from the urban center.

Playtoys and Collecting

George Lucas was prescient enough to recognize that he might recover the investment costs for *ANH* by retaining control of any sequels and the merchandising rights.[7] By the time *ROTS* arrived in 2005, Lucasfilm had earned by its own reporting to the *Washington Post* "nearly $5.7 billion in worldwide box office sales, with toy and merchandise sales adding $9 billion more in revenue" (Ahrens E01). And what significance did of all those toys have for children who played with them and still remembered or collected the action figures as adults? In chapter 11, Jess Horsley describes his childhood encounters with *Star War* toys as an Iowa farm boy and is frank in acknowledging that "I wanted to be Luke Skywalker. Like Luke, I was a blonde-haired farm boy living in the middle of nowhere." The toys became his tools of that fantasy. In chapter 12, John Panton, another childhood action figure devotee, looks at the phenomenon of play developmentally, countering those critics like Tom Englehardt who have seen a malign or merely commercial influence in war-themed toys. Reviewing the extensive theoretical literature on children's play, Panton argues that "the perceived stereotypically male traits of battle and warfare in play must not be viewed as the entire scope and depth of male play"; he goes on to suggest the cognitive and social components that accompany action figure play. In chapter 13, Lincoln Geraghty examines the collecting phenomenon and concludes that becoming knowledgeable about artifacts is an important aspect of participation in the *Star Wars* toy world; the meaning of ownership changes significantly over time. He concludes "*Star Wars* toys have not only been 'played with' but have also been 'played up' in the day-to-day lives of people growing older."

Evaluations

A persistent focus of admiration and derision for the *Star Wars* franchise has been its advances in the technology of filmmaking. George Lucas almost single-handedly turned the Hollywood blockbuster toward computer-generated imagery (CGI) and, eventually, total digital production with so-called synthespians of the Jar Jar and Shrek kind. Some critics, like Dale Pollock, contend that Lucas became "more interested in his digital technology and advances than character and emotion" (Pollock "'Star Wars'"). As Pollock had explained earlier in his widely read biography of Lucas, "The actors never receive the entire script, only their individual scenes. All dialogue and text not directly related to the actor's role are deleted from the script pages. And those pages, numbered in indelible type, must be returned after every shooting day" (*Skywalking* 285). It's no surprise that some very fine actors like Liam Neeson as Qui-Gon in *TPM* strike viewers as bored or sullen on screen. He impulsively announced his retirement from film acting shortly after the shooting was done, complaining to *Redbook* magazine "Honest to God, I don't want to do it anymore. I'm not happy doing it. Film is a director's medium, it has nothing to do with actors. We are basically puppets, walking around, hitting marks, saying lines." Ewan McGregor, who had played Obi-Wan in all the prequel films, made similar complaints about the triviality of his acting moments in the digital film environment (Waxman C1).

Andrew Plemmons Pratt's chapter 14 looks beyond those blue screens that actors dread toward a closer, film theory-informed consideration of digital imagery's effect on point of view in narrative. His focus falls on "how CGI, which is central to Lucas's lifetime project, changes the way we have to think about the relationship between movie imagery and our familiar modes of interpreting the visible world. How do we understand the movie's references to a world outside the film based on what is present on or absent from the screen?" This question becomes increasingly important as the final two films, *Attack of the Clones* and *ROTS* were wholly produced using digital imagery. In his careful analysis of the pod race scene in *TPM*, he notices in digital rendition a subtler masking of an agenda to more seductively valorize a particular type of hero. In this way, the new in technology permits a more credible restatement of the familiar.

Mark McDermott in chapter 15 approaches the seminal *TPM* by looking at the reception of the totally CGI-synthetic Jar Jar Binks and the spoofing, ridiculing movement that has begun to change the understanding of copyright and the producer-fan relation. As he states the issue, "The creators of cultural texts have traditionally operated with the assurance that the process of creation is a one-way street: they publish or broadcast, and the fans consume." The response to *Star Wars* has decisively changed that. The best known expression of rebellious fan control of Lucasfilm's canonical texts is *The Phantom Edit*—a home-edited version of *TPM* that minimizes Jar Jar, discussions of midichlorian blood components, and other widely loathed film moments. In this region of fandom, the "textual poachers," defined by Michel de Certeau and Henry Jenkins, reign irreverently supreme.[8] Whether this type of poaching is merely a reaction against movies-by-template, it certainly rejects the traditionally conceived copyrights upon which the film industry depends. Whatever the ultimate direction, George Lucas himself has conceded the importance of "outlaw" creativity by making selections for the *Star Wars* Fan Film Awards. These honor amateur productions that use *Star Wars* characters and themes, sometimes in derogatory fashion ("Second").

Bruce Isaacs's chapter 16 comprehensively surveys U.S. critical receptions—the enthusiastic, the chilly, and the alarmed. Early popular assessments reflected thrill from the sights and sounds that came packaged with traditional values of faith and loyalty, committed to name and to destroy evil. Liberal-left reactions expressed fears of the film's stimulating influence upon those with dualistic views of conflict—such as those with political affinity for Reaganite conservatism. Critics of film art, such as Pauline Kael, David Thomson, Peter Biskind, and Thomas Schatz, were dismayed at the contagiousness of "kiddifying" films into plot-driven spectacles that hawk merchandise right there on the screen. From Lucas's status as the blockbuster king, they dourly predicted the dominance of less adult films—sometimes evoking an age of film paradise that was trashed by Lucas and Steven Spielberg. David Thomson, for example, has repeatedly attempted to sneer *Star Wars* into insignificance, mastering the invective art of the compound put-down: "Its excitement is never rooted in character or moral ordeal. There is no danger to the people on film, and no challenge to those watching. Its people are raised on junk food: they are pink, puffy, and anonymous" (538). "Oh dear!" as C–3PO might remark.

Savage attacks of this kind, well documented by Isaacs, have little effect on the franchise, but reading about them helps to account for Lucas's disappointment in the Fourth Estate. Isaacs's final judgment is conveyed in these words that reflect the incompatible points of view expressed by the authors in this volume: "The franchise eludes simplistic critical models and finds favor with critics of astonishingly varied political, ideological and cultural persuasions." Considering the diversity of opinion documented by Isaacs, we must expect the pattern to continue.

Conclusion

Star Wars has become a cultural juggernaut, and within the limits of one book it is impossible to consider more than a few aspects within American and world culture. Yet our authors will convince you that they have found important issues of value and culture in an ever-evolving text that often unpredictably writes itself. Within our pages we mostly explore *Star Wars'* so-called canon—the films of the two trilogies. But the canon, whose definition varies from fan to fan, may also include the so-called expanded universe, the licensed, best-selling novels and television series, such as *The Clone Wars*. This larger, official universe now includes "the essential chronology" of some 5,000 years that extends back to the most ancient of the Jedi Knights ("Essential Chronology") and has been compiled in written form (Anderson and Wallace). Will Brooker's book on *Star Wars* fans articulates the language of serious followers to whom such distinctions about "the canon" and the licensed expanded universe are important (105–9). There is also the "extended universe," in which unlicensed *Star Wars* storytellers occasionally spin out tales in ways quite offensive to those who wish to keep their imaginations within the canon's limits. One finds numerous "slash fiction" Web sites that serve as a gathering place for depictions of same-sex intercourse, frequently between Obi-Wan and Qui-Gon. Brooker's chapter "Slash and Other Stories" (129–71) carefully documents the phenomenon, but anyone can Google-cruise this alternative sexual galaxy and find the words, scenes, and passionate flesh that Lucasfilm would never display. These texts in the electronic imperium are part of the anti-canon described in Mark McDermott's chapter.

If we leave the canon-related questions and look at *Star Wars* in the larger political and business culture, we also find impudent trajectories of meaning. After Senator Ted Kennedy sought to ridicule Ronald Reagan's Strategic Defense Initiative (SDI) as "Star Wars," the label stuck. Critics liked the sound because of its association with fantasy, while advocates liked the heroic triumph of *ROTJ*. Edward Linenthal's study of the SDI showed how dozens of political cartoons adopted *Star Wars* imagery and motifs to make their points. George Lucas himself was unhappy about it and sued one advocate organization (High Frontier) and one critic organization (Committee for a Strong and Peaceful America) who had used the "Star Wars" name in television spots. Since the proposed orbiting weapons platforms resembled the infamous Death Stars, it is easy to understand why Lucas wanted to dissociate the trade name from a technology that genocidally destroyed the planet Alderaan (*ANH*) and threatened to destroy Endor (*ROTJ*). Federal District Court Judge Gesell ruled against Lucas: "Star Wars," the term, had acquired the cultural velocity to spin in its own orbit ("'Star Wars' Usage Is Upheld".) Lucasfilm did not bother to sue Enron in 2002 when it was disclosed that it had set up dummy companies called Kenobe Inc., Obi-1 Holdings, Jedi LP, and Chewco LP ("Lucasfilm Decries Enron's *Star Wars* Fixation"). But it complained in vain about the takings that mocked the ideals associated with *Star Wars*.

As Matthew Wilhelm Kapell points out so well in his conclusion, "we become not just those who experience the story, we become part of the story, itself." Having heard the story, we see its truths, love its seductions, and loathe its departures from what we think best. That is what it is to live myth. That is this book.

Figure 2: Lego participated in *Revenge of the Sith* merchandising by offering Darth Vader Transformation for the 6+ age group—including children normally advised not to attend theatrical screenings. Evoking the aftermath of Obi-Wan's duel with Anakin on Mustafar, the Transformation toy allows the child to build a rotating surgical platform. The medical droid allows the child to transform the bloody Luke to the bionic Darth. Horror is thereby reduced to motor skills in assembling and moving small parts. Photography by John Shelton Lawrence.

Notes for Chapter 1

1. View dates for Amazon.com and eBay were October 30, 2005.

2. George Lucas himself coined this phrase to describe his identity for *Star Wars* fans. See Soriano, "Lucas Rules Fans' Empire."

3. See James B. Stewart's *DisneyWar* or Edward Jay Epstein's *The Big Picture*.

4. The article "Pop Fascism in *Star Wars*" was absorbed into Jewett and Lawrence, *The American Monomyth* (2nd ed), and into Lawrence and Jewett, *The Myth of the American Superhero*.

5. *Raiders of the Lost Ark* (1981), *Indiana Jones and the Temple of Doom* (1984), and *Indiana Jones and the Last Crusade* (1989); Steven Spielberg directed the films.

6. See Jewett and Lawrence, *Captain America and the Crusade Against Evil*, for the theology of holy war and its manifestations in U.S. history.

7. Lucas himself tells the story in *Empire of Dreams*.

8. Both De Certeau, *The Practice of Everyday Life*, and Jenkins, *Textual Poachers*, describe fans as active meaning makers and transformers of popular culture.

Works Cited

Ahrens, Frank. " Final 'Star Wars' Caps Moneymaking Empire." *Washington Post* 14 May 2005: E01. 12 Sept. 2005 <http://www.washingtonpost.com/wp-dyn/content/article/2005/05 /13/AR2005051301512.html>.

Allnut, Frank. *Unlocking the Mystery of the Force: The Force of Star Wars*. Van Nuys, CA: Bible Voice, 1977.

Anderson, Kevin J., and Daniel Wallace. Star Wars: *The Essential Chronology*. New York: Del Rey, 2000.

Bowen, Jonathan. *Anticipation*. Lincoln, NE: iUniverse, 2005.

Brooker, Will. *Using the Force : Creativity, Community and Star Wars Fans*. London: Continuum, 2002.

Campbell, Joseph. *The Hero with a Thousand Faces*. 1949. Princeton, NJ: Princeton UP, 1968.

De Certeau, Michel. *The Practice of Everyday Life*. Berkeley: U of California P, 1984.

"Distribs 'Menace': Playtimes." *Variety* 2 Mar. 1999: 3.

Doty, William G. Introduction. *Jacking in to the Matrix Franchise: Cultural Reception and Interpretation*. Ed. Matthew Kapell and William G. Doty. New York: Continuum, 2004.

Ebert, John David. *Celluloid Heroes and Mechanical Dragons: Film as the Mythology of Electronic Society*. Christ Church, NZ: Cybereditions, 2005.

Empire of Dreams: The Story of the Star Wars Trilogy. Dirs. Kevin Becker and Edith Burns. Lucas Film Ltd./Fox Television Network/Prometheus Entertainment, 2004. 120 min.

Engelhardt, Tom. *The End of Victory Culture: Cold War America and the Disillusioning of a Generation*. New York, NY: BasicBooks, 1995.

Epstein, Edward Jay. *The Big Picture: The New Logic of Money and Power in Hollywood*. New York: Random House, 2005.

"The Essential Chronology." Star Wars *Official Web Site* 2 Mar. 2002. <http:// www.starwars.com/eu/lit/ref/f20000302/index.html>.

"Force is with 'Sith' across the Globe." *Variety* 30 May 2005.

Heylin, Clinton. *Despite the System: Orson Welles versus the Hollywood Studios*. Chicago, IL: Chicago Review P, 2005.

Gordon, Andrew. "Star Wars: A Myth for Our Time." *Literature/Film Quarterly* 6.4 (1978): 314-26.

Jenkins, Henry. *Textual Poachers: Television Fans and Participatory Culture*. New York: Routledge, 1992.

Jewett, Robert and John Shelton Lawrence. *Captain America and the Crusade Against Evil: The Dilemma of Zealous Nationalism*. Grand Rapids, MI: Eerdmans, 2003.

Jewett, Robert, and John Shelton Lawrence. "Pop Fascism in *Star Wars*, or Vision of a Better World?" *Des Moines Sunday Register* 27 Nov. 1977.

Lawrence, John Shelton, and Robert Jewett. *The Myth of the American Superhero*. Grand Rapids, MI: Eerdmans, 2002.

Levy, Dan. "Lucas Has Another Hit." *San Francisco Chronicle* 3 July 2005.

Linenthal, Edward. *Symbolic Defense: The Cultural Significance of the Strategic Defense Initiative*. Urbana, IL: U Illinois P, 1989.

"Lucasfilm Decries Enron's *Star Wars* Fixation." *Fox News Channel (Online)* 8 Feb. 2002. <http://www.foxnews.com/story/0,2933,44986,00.html>.

Lucas, George. "I'm A Cynic Who Has Hope for the Human Race." Interview with Orville Schell. *New York Times* 21 Mar. 1999: 28, 30.

Magee, Brian. "The Influence of Wagner." *Aspects of Wagner*. Rev., enlarged ed. Oxford: Oxford UP, 1988. 45–56.

"Of Myth and Men: A Conversation between Bill Moyers and George Lucas on the Meaning of the Force and the True Theology of *Star Wars*." *Time* 26 Apr. 1999: 90.

Pollock, Dale. *Skywalking: The Life and Films of George Lucas*. Updated ed. New York: Da Capo P, 1999.

——. "'Star Wars': George Lucas's Vision." *Washington Post Online* 19 May 2005.12 October 2005. <http://www.washingtonpost.com/wpdyn/content/discussion/2005/05/06/DI200 5050600821.html>.

"The Saga Continues." *Empire of Dreams: The Story of the* Star Wars *Trilogy* (TV show). *Star Wars Trilogy: Bonus Material* (disc 4). Digital Video Disc. Lucasfilm, Ltd., 2004.

Sansweet, Stephen J. Star Wars *Scrapbook: The Essential Collection*. San Francisco: Chronicle Books, 1998.

Schatz, Thomas. "The New Hollywood." *Film Theory Goes to the Movies: Cultural Analyses of Contemporary Films*. Ed. James Collins and Hilary Radner. New York: Routledge, 1993. 8–36.

"Second *Star Wars* Film Fan Awards." Star Wars *Official Web Site*. 3 Feb. 2003. 12 Sept. 2005 <http://www.starwars.com/community/fun/fanfilm/news20030203.html>.

Siska, William. "A Breath of Fresh Fantasy." *Christian Century* 20–27 July 1977: 66, 68.

"'Sith' Invites Bush Comparison." *CBS News (Online)* 16 May 2005. 12 Sept. 2005 <http://www.cbsnews.com/stories/2005/05/16/entertainment/cannes/main695449.shtml>.

Soriano, Cesar G. "Lucas Rules Fans' Empire." *USA Today (Online)* 25 Apr. 2005. 12 Sept. 2005 <http://www.usatoday.com/life/movies/news/2005-04-24-star-wars-convention_x.htm>.

"'Star Wars' Usage Is Upheld." *New York Times* 27 Nov. 1985: B8.

Stewart, James B. *DisneyWar*. New York: Simon & Schuster, 2005.

Stover, Matthew. *Revenge of the Sith* (novel). New York: Del Rey, 2005.

Straus, Tamara. "Reinventing Movies." *San Francisco* Nov. 2005: 132–45, 204–6.

Thomson, David. "George Lucas." *The New Biographical Dictionary of Film*. New York: Knopf, 2002. 537–38.

Victoria, Brian Zaizen. *Zen War Stories*. London: Routledge/Curzon, 2003.

Vogler, Christopher. *The Writer's Journey*. 2nd ed. Studio City, CA: Michael Wiese Productions, 1998.

Waxman, Sharon. "'Star Wars' Creator George Lucas Finds His Fantasy Come True." *Washington Post* 12 May 1999: C1.

Myth

CHAPTER 2

Joseph Campbell, George Lucas, and the Monomyth[1]

John Shelton Lawrence

It was very eerie, because in reading *The Hero with a Thousand Faces* I realized that I was following classical motifs.
—George Lucas on Joseph Campbell's book, which he read while struggling with the script for *A New Hope* (Larsen and Larsen 541)[2]

Well, my God, we had *Star Wars* in the morning, and we had *The Empire Strikes Back* in the afternoon, and we had *Return of the Jedi* in the evening. I tell you, I was really *thrilled.*
—Joseph Campbell on his screenings at Skywalker Ranch in 1984 (Campbell, *Hero's Journey* 181; emphasis in text)

The term *myth* has often carried disagreeable flavors of cultural falsehood, the masking of power relations, defective science, stories of local deities, or legends about national origins. *Star Wars* is not obviously any of these, yet it is mythic in the more honored sense of a narrative container of meaning that inspires its hearers. *A New Hope* (1977) was a fictional story portraying superheroic characters who liberate the oppressed and save themselves against overwhelming odds. Moreover, it offered an imaginative vision of relationships among humans, androids, and exotic aliens. The physical imagery was striking: Tatooine's desert and dwellings; the entrapment of Luke, Leia, and Han in a garbage compactor; Luke's training sessions with Obi-Wan and Yoda; the speeder bike duels in Endor's forest; and Luke's battle with the ice monster on Hoth.

These images of place, action, and character development became part of a generation's visual memory and play experiences. Most younger Americans in the 1970s and 1980s knew the imagery, and some even attended the films enough times to memorize the dialogue, which has offered widely recognized benedictions ("May the Force be with you"), jests ("the Jedi mind trick"), boasts ("Strong am I in the Force"), as well as the arch, syntactical imitations of Yoda's inverting grammar. Nor was *Star Wars* merely a phenomenon reflecting American mythic taste, a fact confirmed by consulting Internet Movie Database's reported earnings for the films in many of the world's countries.[3] The prequel films from 1999–2005 added richly to the first trilogy's image trove with Anakin's pod race in *The Phantom Menace* (1999), the arena battle with monsters in *Attack of the Clones* (2002), the smoking vision of Anakin's hacked and toasted body after the epic battle with Obi-Wan Kenobi in *The Revenge of the Sith* (2005), and many others. This is all the stuff of myth.

It is commonly believed that *Star Wars* derives its worldwide mythic appeal from a spiritual collaboration between George Lucas, the most successful film director of the twentieth century, and Joseph Campbell, the twentieth century's most successful writer on myth. (Stephen McVeigh's chapter 3 in this book reflects on the archetypal mythic appeals for Great Britain.) But what does the Lucas-Campbell relationship amount to when considering the entire arc of the franchise from 1977 through 2005? As the introduction to this book mentions, several scholars early recognized Joseph Campbell's mythic archetypes and narrative templates in *ANH*. Mainstream audiences who detected mythic impulses would eventually get confirming evidence through George Lucas's open acknowledgment of the classical monomyth's influence. Although it followed several years of interviews in which he made no mention of it, he began publicly to declare that the writings of Campbell had rescued him during his attempts to create his first *Star Wars* script. He singled out Campbell's *Hero with a Thousand Faces* (1949/1968) especially. In 1983, after the initial trilogy's completion, Lucas sought the personal acquaintance of Campbell, bringing him as a guest to his Skywalker Ranch for a screening of his films (Larsen and Larsen 542–43). Then Campbell came for days of shooting for the PBS *The Power of Myth* series in 1985 and 1986.[4] Affirming his closeness to Campbell at the National Arts Club in 1985, Lucas called him "my Yoda" (Campbell, *Hero's Journey* 180).

The merely book-based master-pupil relationship during the first trilogy's creation appears to be sincere and inspired discipleship, as evidenced by any listing of classical monomythic story elements (as shown below). Yet the admiration likely cooled somewhat after Lucas was fully exposed to Campbell's snobbish ignorance of most popular culture[5] and his arrested tastes in high culture, expressed by his refusal to advance past the modernists of the early twentieth century. Recognizing disappointment in the Lucas-Campbell relationship seems necessary to account for certain details in the evolution from the spiritualizing original trilogy, with its shaping by the classical monomyth, to the more overtly political discourses of the prequels. Perhaps the change in narrative interests, which plunge into some political issues and polemics of our own time, was Lucas's own mild form of oedipal rebellion, a type of moment that Campbell himself had exalted as a necessary step in the emergence of heroes. Lucas had earlier rebelled against the studios; perhaps he thought the time had come to outgrow the restraints of Campbell's limiting visions for a properly mythic art. To clarify this evolution of George Lucas as auteur of his saga, we must first explain more exactly what he found in Campbell's monomyth and then comment on his surpassing of its implied limits and the highly restrictive aesthetics of social quietism that came with it.

The First Trilogy—Making *Star Wars* Monomythic

George Lucas came to the challenge of *Star Wars* without first-hand knowledge of war. To conceive his master film, he distilled experiences from sources such as Frank Herbert's *Dune* novels, John Ford's *The Searchers* (1956), the films of Akira Kurosawa—especially *The Hidden Fortress* (1960)—and assorted World War II films and serialized television programs. Speaking to Stephen Zito in 1977 of "fantastic, surreal" forms of science fiction as a formative influence, Lucas remarked: "I grew up on it. *Star Wars* is sort of a compilation of this stuff, but it's never been put in one story before, never put down on film. There is a lot taken from Westerns, mythology, and samurai movies. It's all the things that are great put together" (47).

In Joseph Campbell the evangelically inclined Lucas had found a kindred spirit, since the younger man also felt a mythic decline that left youth drifting without the moral anchor sensed in the heroic genre films of his own youth. In the Zito interview, Lucas also remarked that he wanted "children to believe there is more to life than garbage and killing and all that real stuff like stealing hubcaps—that you could still sit and dream about exotic lands and strange creatures" (53). A decade later in an interview with John Seabrook, he averred that "it had seemed to me that there was no longer a lot of mythology in our society—the kind of stories we tell ourselves and our children, which is the way our heritage is passed down. Westerns used to provide that, but there weren't Westerns anymore" (205-6). Campbell, like Lucas, blamed the ills of American youth culture on the death of myth, the consequences of which he explained to Bill Moyers in *The Power of Myth* television series: "They are making up their own myths.... These kids have their own gangs and their own initiations and their own morality.... But they're dangerous because their own laws are not those of the city. They have not been initiated into our society" (8).

As his antidote for such drift, Campbell's *Hero* boldly mapped recurring themes and characters among the world's stories into a kind of schematic master plot that he called "the monomyth" (30). Campbell had taken a coined word from James Joyce to summarize important unities that he saw in world mythology. Scholars like Stith Thompson (1885–1976) and Vladimir Propp (1895–1970) had independently worked out vast catalogs of mythic motifs and typologies of narrative structure. Although Campbell ranged widely over world folklore and mythologies, he seemed less interested in advancing their comparative science of myth than in using selected aspects of myth to heal modernity's broken culture.

Speaking in his bardic culture-shaman's voice, Campbell ascribed divinity to revelations from older myths and suggested that their insights must be revived "so that through every act and detail of secular life the vitalizing image of the universal god-man who is actually immanent and effective in all of us may be somehow made known to consciousness" (Hero 389). He lamented the nearly total eradication of such truths about everyman's divinity that literalist religious dogmas had rendered unbelievable. He believed that skeptical scientific approaches had completed the wreckage of vital mythology in their attacks on the reality of spirit. The cultural result is that classical mythology's "timeless universe of symbols has collapsed" (Hero 387). For contemporaries, whose consciousness could be transported back into the ancient dream state, "myth is the secret opening through which the inexhaustible energies of the cosmos pour into human cultural manifestation" (3).

As a storyteller to young people, Lucas could never have succeeded if he had presented myth as this sort of abstract mystical theology. What Lucas found usable in the Hero book was the condensed formulation of the master plot that Campbell claimed to extract from world mythologies.

> A hero ventures forth from the world of common day into a region of supernatural wonder: fabulous forces are there encountered and a decisive victory is won: the hero comes back from this mysterious adventure with the power to bestow boons on his fellow man. (Hero 30)

This formulation is rather general, but later in his book Campbell offers a far more nuanced and script-suggestive statement that so much influenced Hollywood's plot designers.

> The mythological hero, setting forth from his common day hut or castle, is lured, carried away, or else voluntarily proceeds, to the threshold of adventure. There he encounters a shadow presence that guards the passage. The hero may defeat or conciliate this power and go alive into the kingdom of the dark (brother-battle, dragon-battle; offering, charm), or be slain by the opponent and descend in death (dismemberment, crucifixion). Beyond the threshold, then, the hero journeys through a world of unfamiliar yet strangely intimate forces, some of which severely threaten him (tests), some of which give magical aid (helpers). When he arrives at the nadir of the mythological round, he undergoes a supreme ordeal and gains his reward. The triumph may be represented as the hero's sexual union with the goddess-mother of the world (sacred marriage), his recognition by the father-creator (father atonement), his

own divinization (apotheosis), or again—if the powers have remained unfriendly to him—his theft of the boon he came to gain (bride-theft, fire-theft); intrinsically it is an expansion of consciousness and therewith of being (illumination, transfiguration, freedom). The final work is that of the return. If the powers have blessed the hero, he now sets forth under their protection (emissary); if not, he flees and is pursued (transformation flight, obstacle flight). At the return threshold the transcendental powers must remain behind; the hero re-emerges from the kingdom of dread (return, resurrection). The boon that he brings restores the world (elixir). (*Hero* 245-6)

To identify moments in the first trilogy that correspond to these narrative units is straightforward. And this was the appeal of *Star Wars* as a golden recipe of ingredients for other films.

Consider just a few intersections between the Lucas saga and Campbell's archetypes. R2-D2's holographic message from Leia to Luke is the lure to the "threshold of adventure" that is delivered to him in his "common day hut" on Tatooine. His Uncle Owen and Aunt Beru are the benign guardians who hold him back, while the Tusken Raiders are the vicious, "shadow presences" who threaten his life as he seeks to locate Obi-Wan Kenobi, who will eventually introduce him to "unfamiliar yet strangely intimate forces" that both "threaten him" and "give him magical aid." Campbell's book offers many such maps, each of which can be overlaid on the plot of *ANH* and its two successors in the first trilogy. For example, the encounter with Darth Vader is "father atonement," while his "divination" and "apotheosis" are his transitions to Jedi status through self-mastery and the rejection of the dark side. And, ultimately, Luke's journey has been "an expansion of consciousness," Campbell's preferred symbolic interpretation of heroism. Achievements beyond the ordinary, on this reading, are really a turning inward to find the divine within the self and its identity with the universe. In some concluding words of *Hero*, Campbell writes that "the essence of oneself and the essence of the world: these two are one. Hence separateness, withdrawal is no longer necessary" (386). Consistent with this notion that the hero explores self-consciousness rather than the resisting limits of an external world, the final moments of the entire *Star Wars* saga in *Return of the Jedi* (1983) present a Luke retreating from the battle for Endor's safety and the Empire's defeat to care for his father Vader's dead body. He does not show up at the victory celebration until he has conducted a lonely cremation ceremony.

Having completed his trilogy by aligning Luke with both the Force and his inner divinity as savior, Lucas continued to think about mythic underpinnings of the franchise. He sought out Campbell and offered personal friendship and screenings at Skywalker Ranch in 1985, where all three trilogy films were shown to him. Movies were a rare experience for Campbell. Harold Schechter and Jonna G. Semeiks report that, when sending a query "in 1979, soliciting a contribution to a collection on myth and popular art, Campbell replied that he had not 'seen a movie in some eight or ten years' and had 'no television set'" (179). For him, film as art had ended when sound was added in America during his late 1920s European studies. As he put it conversationally for the *Hero's Journey* documentary on his life: "There was a wonderful art developing then of mime and all that. I come back and you have talkies. I never really caught on to the talkie as an interesting art. Too naturalistic, you know. Naturalism is the death of art" (181). Asked whether Hollywood filmmakers could be mythmakers in their own right, he responded: "They could be if they would make myths. All they do is put people into bed and take them out again" (182). His belief that films were uniformly obsessed with sexual eroticism was reflected early in the *Hero* when he accused married American women of styling themselves according to "our popular vanilla-frosted temples of the venereal goddess, under the makeup of the latest heroes of the screen" (12). One way to measure this boastful snobbery is to recall that Campbell had early taken an interest in the fate of Native Americans (*Power* 13-4, 75-9), yet knew nothing of revisionist Western films, exemplified by *Broken Arrow* (1950) and *Little Big Man* (1970).

Campbell likely had trouble restraining his flippant indifference at Skywalker Ranch, but he was gracious enough to return the flattery of Lucas's attention and invitation. He spoke with over-the-top generosity about the greatness of the *Star Wars* trilogy films he had just seen, fulsomely remarking, "You know I thought real art stopped with Picasso, Joyce, and Mann. Now I know it hasn't" (Larsen and Larsen 543). No Hesse, Faulkner, Solzhenitsyn, Miro?? Admittedly, Campbell at age 80 had earned the right to embalm his tastes in some remembered golden era or just to be grouchy. Yet he could also be the charming, polished guru in the context of a television production like *The Power of Myth*. But even in that setting, Campbell gave a reductive reading of the *Star Wars* trilogy by focusing on Darth Vader's failure to find his individuality: "When the mask of Darth Vader is removed, you see an unformed man, one who has not developed as a human individual" (144). For Campbell, the Vader tale was a parable about escaping the reach of bureaucratic systems, because the momentum of history has made them incorrigible:

> How do you relate to the system so that you are not compulsively serving it? It doesn't help to try to change it to accord with your system of thought. The momentum of history behind it is too great for anything really significant to evolve from that kind of action. The thing to do is learn to live in your period of history as a human being. (*Power* 144)

Almost all of *Star Wars* is omitted in such an account of its mythic significance. Where is the valorization of loyalty to the group? The appeal of torturing power over others? The importance of family recognition and reconciliation? The appeal of a Rebel Alliance that overthrows illegitimate power? The moral achievement in recognizing evil in oneself, as Luke does, and quelling vengeful anger? The interspecies respect? The prospect of friendly, humanized androids?

Perhaps Lucas, realizing how little Campbell found significant in what he had bled to create as a film artist, experienced a clarifying moment about the freedom of the franchise to go elsewhere. Lucas had paid his dues with a spiritually uplifting tale of inward-turning consciousness. If *Star Wars* was to march on into and through the twenty-first century, it would have to move beyond the artful shuffling of the archetypal tokens that Campbell had laid out. The dramatic logic demanded something else. As David S. DeWitt puts it so well, "The prequel trilogy is a downward dramatic spiral to the abyss, while the original trilogy is an upward, heroic spiral toward the heavens." In terms of character development, the new task was to show something unheroic: how the sweet little savior Anakin, the Chosen One, became a genocidal maniac before he found the redemption that enabled him to destroy the Emperor.

In addition to needing a way to extend the film canon, Lucas's management of the monomythic templates was getting into a slog with *Willow* (1988). An epic based on Lucas's sword and sorcery script and using the awesome effects of Lucas's Industrial Light and Magic, the film had a thudding impact. Roger Ebert spoke with cruel justice when he complained that:

> at the story level, "Willow" is turgid and relentlessly predictable. Not much really happens, and when it does, its pace is slowed by special effects set pieces that run on too long and seem to be recycled out of earlier movies. ("Review")

It was another epic of the little guy, with Willow (Warwick Davis, an Ewok from *ROTJ*) fighting the big guys—a recurrent theme for Lucas in life and in film fantasy. Almost every film-knowledgeable person noticed that General Kael (Pat Roach) was the bad guy, and it was seen as peevish retribution for Pauline Kael's criticisms of *Star Wars* in the *New Yorker* magazine.

The Republic and the Empire Become America

If we merely think of Joseph Campbell as George Lucas's lifetime Yoda, it will surprise us when—after Campbell's 1987 death—the *Star Wars* saga of the prequels began to look like an allegory of American politics and foreign policy. It did begin with the monomythic call to adventure for slave-born Anakin (Jake Lloyd) and his departure from home after Qui-Gon (Liam Neeson) counts the midi-chlorians and recognizes him as the Chosen One—a promise Anakin eventually fulfills after passing through possessive fears, retributive angers, and erotic passions that render him murderous in wielding the Force's dark side. Besides Anakin's furies, other failures explain the naïve disarray of the Republic. Obi-Wan (Ewan McGregor) bungles the mentorship of Anakin (Hayden Christensen) after the death of Qui-Gon and perpetually squabbles with him. The Jedi Council is drawn into spying on the emperor (*AOTC*), and the wise little Yoda is revealed as a general in the Grand Army of the Republic who wields a murderous lightsaber (AOTC). Not very spiritual, that. It is the failure of institutions that try to talk things over, agree on a course of action— and discover that they made the wrong decisions.

Working out the Republic's fall allowed Lucas's mythic imagination to wander into a political territory that would resonate for many adult viewers. Veering away from the Jungian archetypes, Lucas tailored an allegory that pinched the American situation uncomfortably in places. One could glimpse election fraud (TPM; America's 2000 presidential election?), the greed of the Nemoidian Trade Federation and the Intergalactic Banking Clan abetted by fraud (TPM and AOTC; the Enron scandal?), the bypass of the Jedi Council because of a military emergency (AOTC; the Patriot Act after 9/11?), Anakin Skywalker's slaughter of Tusken families on Tatooine and children at the Jedi Temple (AOTC and ROTS; Army Lieutenant William Calley at the My Lai massacre?), and the fomenting of war through deceitful representations to Congress (AOTC; the Bush administration taking the country and its campaign donor/defense contractors to war in Iraq?).[6] George Lucas himself seemed to make it explicit at the Cannes Festival in 2005 when he said, "The parallels between what we did in Vietnam and what we're doing in Iraq now are unbelievable" ("'Sith' Invites"). He had emphasized that many features of his story were about generic patterns of descent into dictatorship and aggressive war, but there it was. Lucas accepted the consequences in ROTS with the PG-13 rating that finally fell on one of his canonical films.

Stephen McVeigh's essay in this volume carefully argues that, in a time frame much longer than the interval between 9/11 and the final prequel films, Lucas was responding to the so-called Revolution in Military Affairs (RMA) that began with the U.S. Department of Defense's Office of Net Assessment created in 1973. Its purpose was to make the U.S. military forces overwhelmingly dominant through the application of technology that increasingly removed the American soldier from battlefield danger through the use of drones, smart bombs, cruise missiles, and other highly capitalized technologies. Like the Republic's duplicitous creation of the hidden clone army on Kamino, much of the Pentagon's weapons development and policy formation is secretive.

Lucas also had an apparent desire to help his audience look back at the initial trilogy and find contemporary cultural and political significance. For example, his director's commentary on ROTJ for the *Star Wars* trilogy remarks that the Ewoks of Endor were counterparts of the Vietcong guerillas— apparently meaning that the Imperial Stormtroopers with their glistening armor and high-tech weaponry would have to be ... a country rather well known in the United States.

Such allusive parallels, each steering us to controversial points in American politics, were hardly conceived in the spirit of Campbell's beyond-politics wisdom of the universal archetypes. Perhaps the encounters at Skywalker Ranch also revealed to Lucas the older man's squeamish diffidence about speaking as a public citizen. Campbell had always disciplined his career to exclude any mention of politics. As early as December 1940, he expressed resentful estrangement to the Sarah Lawrence College community when his idol Thomas Mann abandoned the idealized, "two-eyed" role of the artist who sees all and sunk into one-eyed advocacy of Churchill's England over Hitler's Germany (Larsen and Larsen 295-6).[7] That Mann's work was banned in Germany and Mann himself was formally expatriated in 1936 mattered not.

Indicating the temperament Campbell may have projected to Lucas during their friendship is a lecture "The Way of Art" he included in *The Inner Reaches of Outer Space*, the final publication of his life. Once again he continued to grouse about Mann's partisan stance against Germany in World War II (Campbell, *Inner Reaches* 146-7) and newly posed against it an "art for art's sake alone" position that he derived from the Stephen Dedalus character in Joyce's 1916 novel *Portrait of the Artist as a Young Man* (130-2). Campbell quotes with enthusiasm Dedalus's repetition of St. Thomas Aquinas's imperative for "wholeness, harmony, and radiance" as requirements for artistic beauty. Campbell ignores the ambiguous context for this lovely theory, which mimics the Scholastic philosophy taught by the priests at his school. Stephen's companion Lynch notices the simulation and laughs at him: "It amuses me vastly ... to hear you quoting him [St. Thomas] time after time like a jolly round friar. Are you laughing in your sleeve?" (Joyce 209). Campbell, eager for an aesthetic of social disengagement, did not laugh in his. He finds in Stephen's priestly repetitions a near scatological language for art that offends by moving us beyond a contemplative stasis; "improper art" is kinetic when it inspires any kind of "desire or loathing": "The arts which excite them, pornographical or didactic, are therefore improper arts" (Joyce 205). Stirred, improperly one must add, by Joyce's fantasy of a still, unmoved vantage point from which the beautiful is beheld, Campbell is willing to denounce anything else as perverted art (Campbell, *Inner Reaches* 123).[8] (It must have been puzzling for Lucas, who lived among the political leftists and liberals of Marin County and San Francisco.)

But given that vision of the artist as the withdrawn citizen who lures others into a quiet vision—and seeing himself in that role—Campbell could only act as a "twilight" political citizen in the spirit that German philosopher G. W. F. Hegel suggested in his famous maxim from *Philosophy of Right*: "The owl of Minerva spreads its wings only with the falling of the dusk." Hegel meant that a phase of history must end before it could be understood and this ignorance was a bar to intelligent action *within* that historical phase. Just as Hegel thought that philosophy lacked the wisdom to prescribe cultural rejuvenation,

Campbell had a clear vision of the distorting passions of his own turbulent times.

In his political thinking, the real basis for his irritation with Thomas Mann, one couldn't fairly oppose Hitler without also rejecting the self-righteous nationalisms projected both by Churchill and Roosevelt. As a person with an Irish lineage, Campbell knew that England could be cruelly imperialistic. He also understood the viciousness of America in the conquest of Native Americans and its intimacy with slavery's deliberate degradation of others. How could such countries proclaim their goodness as against Hitler's evil? In the eloquent "Permanent Human Values" address at Sarah Lawrence, he urged the academic community to see through the exaggerated claims of those who wished to go to war. He exhorted them to remember that

> every government, since governments began, has claimed to represent the special blessings of the heavenly realm, that every man (even an enemy) is human, and that no empire (not even a merchant empire), is founded on "kindly helpfulness." (Larsen and Larsen 288)

So pessimistic was Campbell—and so saturated with Oswald Spengler's vision of civilizational decline he had acquired early in his reading[9]—that even in the last decade of his life he identified three of Spengler's "Caesars" to Robert Bly. They were Hitler, Mussolini, and Franklin Delano Roosevelt: "Once the three Caesars have appeared, there's no sense in doing a political act, it makes no sense at all. Don't waste your time because everything is disintegrating" (Larsen and Larsen 509). Campbell, instead of risking the blinding commitment of a citizen who acted in the political present, preferred instead to work outside institutions as an artist/shaman—helping to renew individuals through an infusion of archaic mythic wisdom. He would denounce the times but in a generic way that restrained himself from publicly intimating accountability for deeds in his own country.

To the extent that Lucas had felt himself a Campbell disciple, any revelations of this sort that came through personal contact may have spurred Lucas to surpass the master by using myth as palette for painting contemporary issues more directly. Or perhaps Lucas developed a will to enrich the schematic myth of redemption with pointed references that gave them a sense of contemporary currency.

I admit that find no direct journalistic or biographical evidence to support this notion of a Lucas rebellion against his master of Jungian archetypes. But as Campbell would so often emphasize, deeper truths about the mythic life require symbolic interpretation rather than strict adherence to established fact. The truth about intent may lie far more in what Lucas did than in what anybody said. And the facts about the prequels do not permit us to flatly state that they merely extend Lucas's mythological debts to Campbell. Perhaps the symbolic son decides that he is now mature enough to displace the father—not in anger, but in cool disappointment, or perhaps merely in the spirit of desiring to grow. Campbell himself, in speaking about the father-tyrant/ogre-emperor said that "he is the representative of the set-fast, as the hero is the carrier of the changing.... the work of the hero is to slay the tenacious aspect of the father ... and release from its ban the vital energies that will feed the universe" (Campbell, *Hero* 352). In retrospect, we can see the result as a double trilogy with a plot thread connected by characters—but a radically disjunctive approach to issues of power and the political order. First *Star Wars* was monomythic, almost by recipe, and then it became a veiled commentary on American politics from which the thrilling, simplistic heroic archetypes recede.

To recognize all this is not to suggest strong democratic advocacy within the films. The victories of ANH (blowing up the Death Star) and ROTJ (tossing the Emperor/Satan into the power core/lake of burning fire) amount to redemption by violence—not the achievements of discussion or compromise. The conclusion of ROTS shows us the talking/conspiring Jedis in disarray. We never see an effective press or court system or legislature that is anything more than a patsy for the Caesars of the moment. It is a Campbell-like vision of corruption in the state, the consequence of "hard and unremitting competition for material supremacy and resources" (*Hero* 387) that Campbell saw as the essence of politics. Yet Campbell would not allow himself to speak that message with any particularity to his own contemporaries. Lucas did dare to speak to his own time, yet his new hope of redemptive violence by the Chosen One remains burdened by the same gloominess with which Spengler saw the *cul de sac* of European history:

> A power can be overthrown only by another power, not by a principle, and only one power that can confront money is left. Money is overthrown and abolished by blood. (414, author's italics)

A man with a hacked-off arm tosses a wizard down a shaft. That's salvation. It's mythic. It made us feel good. And one of the richest men in the world told us.

Notes for Chapter 2

1. Thanks for criticism and corrections are owed to David S. Dewitt, William G. Doty, Matthew Kapell, Marty Knepper, and Roger Kaufman.
2. In Campbell's video *Transformations of Myth through Time* (1987), Lucas remarks that he read *Hero* when he was a college student (Henderson 7).
3. Box office receipts for the separate titles in different countries are listed at the Internet Movie Database: <http://www.imdb.com>.

4. In the "Editor's Note" to Campbell's *The Power of Myth*, Bill Moyers indicates twenty-four hours of shooting with Campbell at Skywalker Ranch during the two years.

5. Campbell did participate in some public events with the Grateful Dead, who treated him as a sage (Larsen and Larsen 539–40).

6. Ann Lancashire ("*Attack of the Clones*") has listed some of the parallels mentioned here.

7. Campbell denounced Nazism and communism decades later when choices were no longer being formed about how the United States would respond.

8. Critics debate whether Joyce meant this to be his own final statement or an adolescent's sublimating diversion from the urgency of tormenting sexual desire. Umberto Eco, in his work *Aesthetics*, sees these Scholastic formulations "as a useful launching pad, a stimulating interpretive exercise whose sole purpose is to serve as the departure point for another solution" (26).

9. The Larsens' *Fire* biography reports that he was intoxicated by the book, reading it seven times in the German during a decade (177), and insisting that his fiancée Jean Erdman travel abroad with it so that they could discuss it in correspondence (243–6).

Works Cited

Campbell, Joseph. *The Hero with a Thousand Faces*. Princeton, NJ: Princeton UP, 1968.

——. *The Inner Reaches of Outer Space: Metaphor As Myth and As Religion*. New York: A. van der Marck Editions, 1985.

——. *Transformations of Myth through Time*. Video. Public Media Video, 1987. William Free, producer.

Campbell, Joseph, with Bill D. Moyers. *The Power of Myth*. New York: Doubleday, 1988.

Campbell, Joseph, Stuart L. Brown, and Phil Cousineau. *The Hero's Journey: The World of Joseph Campbell: Joseph Campbell on His Life and Work*. San Francisco: Harper, 1990.

DeWitt, David S. Letter to the author (email). 27 Sept 2005.

Ebert, Roger. Rev. of *Willow*, dir. Ron Howard. 20 May 1988. 25 Sept. 2005 <http://www.rogerebert.com>.

Eco, Umberto. *The Aesthetics of Chaosmos: The Middle Ages of James Joyce*. Tulsa, OK: U of Tulsa, 1982.

Hegel, Georg Wilhelm Friedrich. *Hegel's Philosophy of Right*. Trans. T. M. Knox. Oxford: Clarendon P, 1942.

Henderson, Mary. Star Wars: *The Magic of Myth*. New York: Bantam, 1997.

Joyce, James. *The Portrait of an Artist As a Young Man*. 1916. New York: Viking, 1965.

Lancashire, Ann. "*Attack of the Clones* and the Politics of *Star Wars*." *The Dalhousie Review* 82.2 (Summer 2002): 235–53.

Larsen, Stephen, and Robin Larsen. *A Fire in the Mind: The Life of Joseph Campbell*. New York: Doubleday, 1991.

"Of Myth and Men: A Conversation between Bill Moyers and George Lucas on the Meaning of the Force and the True Theology of *Star Wars*." *Time* 26 Apr. 1999: 90.

Schechter, Harold, and Jonna Gormely Semeiks. "Campbell and the 'Vanilla Frosted Temple': From Myth to Multiplex." *Uses of Comparative Mythology: Essays on the Work of Joseph Campbell*. Ed. Kenneth L. Golden. New York: Garland, 1992.

Seabrook, John. "Letter from Skywalker Ranch: Why is the Force Still with Us?" *George Lucas: Interviews*. Ed. Sally Kline. Jackson: UP of Mississippi, 1999. 190–215.

"'Sith' Invites Bush Comparisons." *CBS News* 16 May 2005. 8 Sept. 2005 <http://www.cbsnews.com/stories/2005/05/16/entertainment/cannes/printable695449.shtml>.

Spengler, Oswald. *The Decline of the West*. New York: Modern Library, 1965.

Zito, Stephen. "George Lucas Goes Far Out." *George Lucas: Interviews*. Ed. Sally Kline. Jackson: UP of Mississippi, 1999. 45–54.

CHAPTER 3

The Galactic Way of Warfare

Stephen P. McVeigh

Because [the prequel trilogy] is the back story (of the *Star Wars* saga) one of the main features of the back story was to tell how the Republic became the Empire. At the time I did that, it was during the Vietnam War and the Nixon era. The issue was: how does a democracy turn itself over to a dictator? Not how does a dictator take over but how does a democracy and senate give it away?... The parallels between what we did in Vietnam and what we are doing now in Iraq are unbelievable.

—George Lucas, at the Cannes Festival, 2005 (Kirkland)

This essay deconstructs the *Star Wars* trilogies as commentaries on the American experience and perceptions of war from the 1970s to the early years of the twenty-first century. The *Star Wars* phenomenon has received critical discussion from a range of perspectives. The saga has been presented to the public by no less than the U.S. government's Smithsonian Institution as a text dealing with the care and repair of the American mythological landscape (Henderson 6–7), and by others as vessels for spiritual and philosophical meaning among increasingly cynical and detached audiences,[1] as a series of movies that heralded the arrival and longevity of the special effects-dominated film—the summer blockbusters altering permanently the economic dimensions and possibilities of American cinema.[2]

Such perspectives are surely fruitful means of exploring the power and value of the *Star Wars* films. However, this essay takes a different approach to the six films in exploring the central trope, the engine that drives the narrative of the trilogies: war. Explaining the war dimension is by no means straightforward, given the rich layers of material executed during a twenty-eight-year period. This essay cuts into the saga's narrative heart, along three vectors. The first part considers the 1977–1983 trilogy within the historical context of the war in Vietnam and its cultural aftermath. The second part explores the 1999–2005 prequel trilogy from the perspective of the issues facing the U.S. military as it attempted to define its role in the post–Cold War global arena. The third part reviews the entire saga in relation to war and the motivation of its leaders. Examining these themes allows us to see *Star Wars* as a unique commentary on America's understandings of war over a thirty-year period. Within their historical moments the films cease to be simply "entertainment" and emerge as texts dealing with traumatic transitions and events. Such analysis reveals changing American perceptions of war, from the Cold War, post-Vietnam outlook of the first trilogy to the post–Cold War setting of *Episode I* to the post-9/11 production of *Episodes II* and *III*. Put simply, this analysis reveals the "wars" part of *Star Wars*: a singular set of connected commentaries on war and the United States.

One obstacle to situating the *Star Wars* films in this real world context is their overt, child-focused commercialism. The billion-dollar licensing of toys, clothes, and fast food leads some commentators to dismiss the films, especially the second trilogy, as little more than advertisements for *Star Wars* products. However, accepting their deeply commercial character, and acknowledging Lucas as a shrewd businessman, does not preclude the films from also being controversial and politically engaged. The films represent specific conflicts and wars from the earliest days of the (American) Republic to the most recent: asymmetric warfare with the attendant limitations of military technology when confronting rebel or guerrilla conflict; the Revolution in Military Affairs (RMA); the pivotal influence of leadership and the manipulation of crisis to furnish a hidden agenda.

A New Hope, The Empire Strikes Back, The Return of the Jedi, and the Shadow of Vietnam

In the beginning, there was *Star Wars: A New Hope*, released in 1977, when no one could anticipate that it would become the cinematic and cultural phenomenon it did. This means that *ANH* is unusual among the six films in that it is the only one with a traditionally complete narrative. Given that success was by no means guaranteed (and progress reports from the shooting set were largely negative, with cast and crew unsure of what exactly they were making[3]) and that the revolutionary licensing arrangement with Fox for the merchandising rights would not prove itself until much further down the line, it is interesting to explore the reasons behind Lucas's decision to make *ANH*.

Lucas commenced film school at University of Southern California in 1963 where he developed a reputation as an innovative filmmaker with flair. Indeed, one of his student films, *THX 1138 4EB: Electronic Labyrinth* (1967), won the drama category at the National Student Film Festival that year. This student effort became his first feature, retitled simply *THX 1138*, produced by Warner Bros. and released in 1971. Ostensibly science fiction, it is a film that illustrates a seriousness in artistic approach, with its minimalist sets, "fantasy-documentary" cinematography, haunting soundscape and provocative performances, especially from Robert Duvall as the hero who has his eyes opened to a dystopian Los Angeles as a cage without doors. The film's central theme—an individual against the system—is one that Lucas would replay in the *Star Wars* movies. Although a stunningly and innovatively realized vision of an Orwellian future, the film flopped at the box office, a circumstance that was pivotal in the position Lucas proceeded to create for himself as the individual against and outside of the Hollywood system.

Lucas bounced back and hit box office gold with a cheaply and quickly made semi-autobiographical comedy drama of his nights hot-rodding around his hometown of Modesto, California—*American Graffiti* (1973). The film is a valuable precursor to his engagement of war in the *Star Wars* saga, depicting as it does, with a heady nostalgia embodied in the constant rock and roll soundtrack, the innocence of the pre-Kennedy assassination, pre-Vietnam War United States, a mindset and landscape that *Star Wars* will go a long way toward recreating. After directing *American Graffiti*, Lucas returned to a project on which he and, screenwriter and director, John Milius had been working, *Apocalypse Now*. It was to be a film about the Vietnam War but one that would be entirely subversive. According to Lucas,

> It's the kind of film the government will probably run me out of the country for making. It's not about massacres or anything like that. It's about Americans. Like a super-John Wayne movie. It's the same argument as *The Wild Bunch*: an anti-violence film. Francis [Coppola] says the way to make an anti-violence film is to have no violence in it, but I feel there should be so much violence in it you're disgusted. (Baxter 140)

His intention was to make an antiviolence war film, not by cutting the violence out, as Coppola suggested, but by showing so much that the audience would be repulsed. His plan was to film this in almost documentary fashion, a style that he had used to striking effect in *THX 1138*. Presented in this way, the film would authenticate, make hyper-real, its images of war and suffering. Milius, the eventual screenwriter of *Apocalypse Now* (1979), offers some insight into how Lucas's version of the film might have looked:

> The idea was, we would have got the cooperation of the army, and filmed around the army. We'd shoot in 16 mm and get very gritty and real and look more like documentary ... we wanted to go to Vietnam and shoot the film while the war was on. This was cinema verite: getting close to real events, having film shot in and around the events. (Baxter 140-1)

The chances of such army cooperation diminished, however, as the cameras that were present in Southeast Asia fuelled the antiwar sentiment at home. Ultimately, Lucas dropped any idea of directing *Apocalypse Now*, but his stated reasons for doing so are telling: "After I finished *American Graffiti*, I came to realize that since the demise of the western, there hasn't been much in the mythological fantasy genre available to the film audience. So instead of making 'isn't-it-terrible-what's-happening-to-mankind' movies, which is how I began, I decided that I'd try to fill that gap" (Hellmann 209).

Star Wars then is a film that demands on several grounds to be seen in light of the war in Vietnam (even if the movie proceeds to comment upon various notions and instances of war). It is not surprising that George Lucas concerned himself with these themes in *Star Wars*. *Star Wars* reacts against the Vietnam era in the same way that *American Graffiti* did and in a very different way from what his *Apocalypse Now* would have been. Rather than detailing the horrors, he decided to offer a balm, to try and reinvigorate American mythic tropes, remap the mythic landscape that had been so badly traumatized by American involvement in the war in Southeast Asia. But he also took something else from the dalliance with *Apocalypse Now* that would significantly inform the *Star Wars* saga in its entirety: the representation of a technologically advanced military structure being challenged and ultimately defeated by primitive, untrained, under-equipped rebels, which is, to name it in the language of military theory, asymmetric warfare: "I was interested in the human side of war and the fact that here was a great nation, with all this technology which was losing a war to basically tribesmen" (Baxter 141). This is a point Lucas makes again in the director's commentary on *Return of the Jedi*: "The film was written during the Vietnam War where a small group of ill-equipped people were able to overcome a mighty power." (Lucas) Before analyzing the films themselves, it is essential to grasp the roots of the trauma that *Star Wars* would heal.

Critics tend to opt for a simplistic view of conflict in the *Star Wars* universe. This simplicity usually manifests itself in the suggestion that the Empire represents the communism of the Soviet Union or the Nazism of Hitler's Germany.[4] While there are some tropes that apply (faceless drones working purely for the military good, oppression, tyranny), the dark truth at the core of Lucas's evil Empire is that it presents a version of America itself. The opening crawl of the film places the narrative in a telling context: "It is a period of civil war." Necessarily then, the narrative that follows has strong roots within U.S. history and establishes *Star Wars* as more than simply representative of the maneuvering and posturing of the Cold War superpowers. Only by recognizing that the rebels and the Empire are one and the same side does Lucas's sustained mission come into relief. The American defeat in Vietnam was its most profound foreign policy setback to that point. Robert McNamara, secretary of defense under President Kennedy, wrote, thirty years after the event, of the reasons for American failure in Vietnam. He saw it as a series of misjudgments, underestimations, and failures. Lucas seems to have been intuitively drawn to one of these reasons, making it into the nucleus of his attempts to repair the damage done by the Vietnam War on the American psyche. McNamara writes, "we failed ... to recognize the limitations of modern, high-technology military equipment, forces and doctrine in confronting an unconventional, highly motivated people's movement" (McNamara 321-3). That Lucas should employ this one failure is fitting: It matches his intentions for *Apocalypse Now* and is fitting because it spoke to a specific set of American mythic constructions.

U.S. involvement in Vietnam had a corrosive effect on two competing myths that both stand as necessary, if contradictory, American metanarratives. A *metanarrative* is a story a culture creates that offers answers to questions such as "who are we?", "how did we get here?", "where do we go next?" In this way, a metanarrative links smaller stories together and creates a social and cultural unity. The first such metanarrative is the Myth of the Frontier, which embodies such values as democracy, independence, and freedom; within its frame, the individual, his innate abilities, and the innocence of his civilizing project receive privileged status. Many critics who talk of *Star Wars* as a Western in space (and as the earlier Lucas quote indicates, the Western was a point of origin[5]) are simply identifying these values in the narrative. In this vein, the film presents natural, pure, innocent heroes, the able underdogs in the face of overwhelming odds. It can be argued that this mythic narrative has its origins even further back than the frontier era, although it can also be seen to stem from the revolutionary period, the uprising of American national identity and sentiment and the breaking of colonial shackles.

The second metanarrative is the Cold War myth of superpower: huge military might that engenders the belief that the United States can shape the world to its own design. As noted, the defeat in Vietnam was the most significant setback in the history of American foreign policy, and it shattered the Cold War consensus at home. Antiwar demonstrations, the shootings at Kent State, and constant media reports of how badly the war was going, reports that emphasized the credibility gap between official accounts and the reality in the war zone, created a generation holding a "militant disbelief in the older axioms" (Allison 155). In this way, both of the core myths were damaged. It damaged the Frontier Myth of Americans as innocent civilizers of the world—how could Americans claim innocence after the atrocities of the My Lai kind committed in their name? After the rapid pardon of its leader, Lieutenant William Calley, by Richard Nixon? And it damaged the super power myth by showing, that for all its might, a collection of untrained, poorly equipped guerillas could stymie the vast resources of the American military machine. And it is in light of these diminished foundational ideals of America that any analysis of *ANH* must be undertaken. The 1977 film can be seen to reinstate these frontier values, to mend this mythic narrative at the expense of the super power myth. Essentially, *Star Wars* returned to the United States the frontier narrative, and it did this by, quite literally, making the military machine the bad guy. It is worth noting that this is in opposition to almost all other sci-fi films in the 1970s, most of which were representations of postapocalyptic earth, using this context as a means of exploring the furthest, demented reaches of American might.[6]

Lucas's strategy for such rejuvenation lay in referring back to pre-Vietnam, morally safe wars in which, crucially, the United States played a winning role. Tom Engelhardt offers insight into this function of the film:

> Star Wars denied the enemy a role "they" had monopolized for a decade—that of brave rebel. It was the first cultural product to ask of recent history, "Hey! How come *they* got all the fun?" And to respond, "Let's give them the burden of empire! Let's bog them down and be the plucky underdogs ourselves!" (Engelhardt 267)

This rejuvenation was in part achieved by using the cinematic motifs of World War II movies, most notably aerial dogfights. The Lucasfilm documentary *Empire of Dreams* (2004) demonstrates how integral such movies were in the creation of similar sequences for *ANH*, even down to the fact that they acted as an early version of animatics for the dogfight sequence that occurs as the Millennium Falcon escapes the Death Star. From the same historical period, although in a different context, Lucas employs a range of visual cues from Leni Riefenstahl's famous Nazi propaganda film, *The Triumph of the Will*.[7] Furthermore, the design of the ships, the costumes, and the weaponry of the *Star Wars* universe is modeled on examples from this war (Henderson 166-81).

However, in the film's opening moments, Lucas offered audiences a version of America's Revolutionary War. This conflict ideally suited Lucas's purpose, because it is perhaps the purest war in American history and a fitting antidote to the moral ambiguities and excessive violence of the contemporaneous war in Vietnam. All of this is established in the first scenes of *ANH*. The legendary opening shot of the small blockade runner being chased down by the massive Star Destroyer perfectly articulates all of these elements: asymmetric warfare, the context of America's Revolutionary War, the underdog versus the super power. It also provides the foundation for Engelhardt's persuasive reading of the film.

The sense of poorly equipped rebels versus a professional military force, created by the relative size of the two vessels, is further enhanced when the action comes aboard the smaller ship, *Tantive IV*. Once she has been captured and is about to be boarded, a small force of men await combat. However, these are not traditional soldiers; they are not young men at the peak of physical and psychological readiness. Rather, they are all older men, scared, a volunteer militia, and the coming combat, as John Hellmann suggests, resonates with the redcoats and the minutemen (213-4). The Empire's reliance upon technology is conveyed visually again once the army breaks through the door. The Imperial Storm Troopers, in their white armor, are identical, formidable, frightening. They also seem to be robotic, machine-like. Their leader, Darth Vader, in shiny black armor and with technologically assisted breathing, represents the reliance of the Empire upon technology. It emerges as something of a pattern across the films that the more an individual merges with the technology, the more ambivalent they become (consider Luke and Anakin's loss of their hands, for example). Given the visible superiority of the Empire here, it is telling that the original trilogy is the story of how this band of rebels defeats the might of the Empire.

This narrative arc illuminates Lucas's tendency to repair American mythology so that, even though the United States itself has become, if not evil, certainly an empire with a devastating military capability, the film positions the audience on the side of the rebels, the underdogs. He does this by articulating the simplicity of frontier and revolutionary narratives and the sense of innocence, purity, and heroism these stories contain. However, given his purpose, the Empire is no less a representation of an aspect of America than the rebel heroes. The nature of the separation between these versions of America emerges in the film through its representations of and the factions' interactions with technology.

Technology is everywhere in the *Star Wars* universe, and Lucas's concern with design in the preproduction stage is well documented in the various "art of" books that surround the films. The Empire has the "state of the art" technology—modern, devastating—while the rebels tend to use "used" technology that is inferior, simple, and sometimes unreliable. In general terms, this manifests itself in the conflict between military technological might and the Force that permeates both trilogies and which represents a spiritual, moral and very human might. This distinction speaks directly to Lucas's mission of transporting audiences to a space that is a long time ago and far, far away. This sense that technology is inherently bad or at least unnatural is depicted in several ways. The character of Darth Vader is described by Obi-Wan Kenobi as "more machine than man," a judgment that almost explains his evil disposition. Any torture (Leia on the Death Star in *ANH*, Han Solo in Bespin in *The Empire Strikes Back*) is delivered by droids and machines. The Empire's pride in the creation of the Death Star, the ultimate weapon of mass destruction (WMD), rests on its capacity to strike fear into the galaxy rather than provide security (and the destruction of Alderaan as a test firing and lesson to Leia is surely one of the most violent episodes in the history of American cinema).

Conversely, the primitivism of the rebels' technology, articulated through discussions of the Force, the use of the historic lightsaber, and an *ad hoc* fleet of ships some of which are temperamental, privilege the more primitive human in the equation. An interesting aside to this is Vader's comments in *ANH* when Admiral Motti is expounding the magnificence and invulnerability of the Death Star:

MOTTI. ... this station is now the ultimate power in the universe. I suggest we use it!

VADER. Don't be too proud of this technological terror you've constructed. The ability to destroy a planet is insignificant next to the power of the Force.

In this exchange, Vader privileges the natural power of the Force over technology, human over machine, an important example of the "good" that is left in him. And perhaps equally interesting in this regard is the fact that Luke has no qualms in destroying the Death Star, even though it will result in an enormous death toll (in terms of cloned Troopers and the clearly human officer class).

In a sense, the rebels' use of technology represents something of the mythic frontiersman's innate abilities. The depiction of such natural skills and innate ability as preferable to giving the self over to technology is precisely illustrated in the final trench run on the Death Star at *ANH*'s conclusion. After one computer-assisted attempt to shoot a torpedo into the exhaust shaft has failed, it is Luke's turn to make the run. Under pressure from Vader's TIE fighter, and with the immobilization of R2-D2, Luke begins to initialize his targeting computer. However, the ghost-like voice of Obi-Wan, somehow one with the Force since Vader struck him down, tells Luke to "let go." Luke switches off the targeting computer but nevertheless makes the crucial shot. With the assistance of the *Millennium Falcon* (and Han's cowboy Western yee-ha as he rides out of the sun) the return to a safer, innocent mythic space is complete. Ellen Goodman's 1977 review in the *Washington Post* speaks to some of these issues:

It's not just about bad guys and good guys, but about bad technology and good technology. The good guys are on the side of truth, beauty and the cosmic force, but they aren't opposed to machines.... The real battle is between one technological society that supports a Lone Rider and praises his instincts, and a technological society that overrules individuals and suppresses instinct.... *Star Wars* played out our own Good News and Bad News feelings about technology. We want a computer age with room for feelings. We want machines, but not the kind that run us. We want technology, but we want to be in charge of it.... [As Luke destroys the Death Star, the] audience applauds—for the man and his instinct, in the saddle, riding technology into the sunset. The good technocrats win the day.

So Vietnam acts as a point of origin for *ANH* and necessarily for the subsequent sequels. However, the two sequels present a differing, although never less than fascinating, series of war references and contexts. John Hellmann, in *American Myth and the Legacy of Vietnam* (1986), has offered perhaps the most coherent analysis of war in these films, and his points merit recapping. In his analysis of *ESB*, Hellmann sees a film deeply engaged with the ramifications of Vietnam on the American psyche. He sees in Luke's narrative a representation of American behavior and attitudes leading to the erroneous misstep into the quagmire of Vietnam. While on Dagobah, where Yoda is training Luke in the ways of the Jedi, he receives a sense that his friends are in danger. He abandons his training, against Yoda's wishes, and rushes into a situation for which he is entirely unprepared, taking with him only ideals and previous victories. What he finds is that, far from being able to help his comrades, he has endangered his own existence. The key moment in the film, the moment that unlocks Lucas's purpose, has Vader reveal the truth that he is Luke's father. In this moment, the true nature of the impact of Vietnam upon American myths and values is made apparent:

> Luke has been devastated by the discovery that [his] father, from whom he has derived both his natural traits and his mission, has actually been corrupted into the very principle of exploitative power that Luke thought he was opposing. This [overturns] the basis of both his self-concept and his quest. (Hellmann 216-7)

Lucas has, through this revelation, perfectly articulated the trauma suffered by the American self-concept as a result of the defeat in Vietnam. He compounds this with the symbolic severing of Luke's hand in the lightsaber duel, at once a physical image of trauma and a clear illustration of the limitations of Luke's power. All of this results in a film that remains one of the greatest examples of feel-bad American cinema; the heroes have been routed and are dispersed throughout the galaxy at the end of the movie, forcing audiences to feel a sense of their despair and hopelessness.

It is no mere coincidence then, or laziness on the part of Lucas, that *ROTJ* should replay many of the central motifs of the original *Star Wars*. Once the initial regrouping of characters has been achieved, the movie switches back to the various operations of the continuing civil war and rebellion against the Empire. It quickly brings us to focus on a guerilla operation against a shield generator whose destruction will allow an attack upon the second Death Star amidst a huge naval battle. Concurrently, Vader and Luke duel it out in front of the Emperor. This pattern of multileveled narrative conclusion establishes an architecture for the remaining films in the saga. A significant context in *ROTJ* and Lucas's interaction with the aftermath of Vietnam is the presidency of Ronald Reagan and, specifically, his attempts to recast the war into a "noble cause." Reagan set about to overcome the Vietnam syndrome, a reluctance amongst Americans to involve themselves in any future conflict attributed to the defeat in Vietnam. Reagan's presidency was informed by a spirit of regeneration, of healing the Vietnam and Watergate era. He set about this revisionist mission by suggesting that America's experience in Vietnam could be rationalized as aberrant and would not happen again. In an address delivered on Veteran's Day, 1988, at the Vietnam Veterans' Memorial, Reagan said:

Unlike the other wars of this century, of course, there were deep divisions about the wisdom and rightness of the Vietnam War. Both sides spoke with honesty and fervor. And what more can we ask in our democracy? And yet after more than a decade of desperate boat people, after the killing fields of Cambodia, after all that has happened in that unhappy part of the world, who can doubt that the cause for which our men fought was just? It was, after all, however imperfectly pursued, the cause of freedom; and they showed uncommon courage in its service. Perhaps at this late date we can all agree that we've learned one lesson: that young Americans must never again be sent to fight and die unless we are prepared to let them win.

A great deal of his rhetoric has the feel of wish fulfillment to it, and it allowed a kind of psychological comfort, while avoiding disturbing or problematic historical reality. *ROTJ* is generally reflective of this mission, reflective of the creation of a new consensus, healing rifts, overcoming the Vietnam syndrome. There are some specific episodes and themes worth highlighting. There is, for example, the highlighting of the rebels as primitive. One of the most hotly debated issues amongst dedicated *Star Wars* fans is how the Ewoks, the small, teddy bear-like, undeniably cute natives of Endor, could overcome the might of the Imperial forces.

Yet, placed in the context of Vietnam and its aftermath, the United States' own history holds the answer: This is Vietnam replayed, in microcosm, except now the United States allies itself with the guerillas to overcome the evil Empire. The destruction of the second Death Star is symbolic. Again, it works as a thematic reiteration in suggesting that the destruction of the first Death Star was no fluke and that the rebels stand on the right side of the moral equation. It demonstrates that the defeat felt at the end of *ESB* was aberrant. It represents Lucas's mission to create new myths from old ones. Here, it is not a white, male attack force but a multicultural mélange of races and technologies working together to bring down evil, led by the black Lando Calrissian. Such self-conscious imagery demonstrates the films' resonance with Reagan's mission to get over the Vietnam syndrome. Hellmann puts it this way: "The trilogy ... ends on a note of triumphant completion that includes a sense of terrible passage and renewed possibility" (219). The battle between Luke and Vader is also symbolic. The Emperor wants Luke to join him, to replace Vader. Luke, although tempted by the Dark Side as a means to save his friends, lays his lightsaber down and refuses to become a Sith. The Emperor, seeing Luke's resolve that he will not turn as his father did, begins to kill him. Fulfilling Luke's earlier observation that he senses some good in his loathsome father, Vader does save him by throwing the Emperor down a power generator shaft. This is the ultimate message for Lucas, and the conclusion of his attempt to redraw American mythological landscape post-Vietnam: "The main theme for the overall downfall of the Empire—it was basically overcome by humanity" (Lucas)

The Phantom Menace, Attack of the Clones, Revenge of the Sith,
and the Revolution in Military Affairs

The original trilogy was predicated on the reality, or more precisely, the aftermath of a specific war—Vietnam. The prequel trilogy has a different relationship to war (again with the first of the trilogy, *The Phantom Menace,* standing apart to an extent from the other two). The different relationship is predicated on the fact that, rather than looking back to deal with the anxieties caused by a past war, the prequels tap into the fears and concerns over the demands, shape, and nature of future wars.

Where the original trilogy created a mythic starscape against which the Vietnam War could be refought, the prequels have no such exact military or historical focal point. Indeed, the late 1990s represent a significantly quiet time for war in America. This post–Cold War period, devoid of any particular threat after the collapse of the Soviet Union, saw an American culture reaching out for the certainties of an enemy against which to test itself. In terms of cinema, natural disaster, aliens, millennialist angst, or a corrupt government provided the necessary villains for the good guys to overcome.[8] This trend was explicated elsewhere, for example, in the epochal work of social scientist Francis Fukuyama's *The End of History* in which he suggests that democracy, the rule of law, and the market economy have emerged victorious over every ideological rival, specifically communism.

When *TPM* appeared on cinema screens in 1999, the point of origin for this new set of *Star Wars* stories reflected some of this pattern. Ryan Gilbey, in his book *It Don't Worry Me* (2003), discusses his and the audience's reaction to the crawl at beginning:

> A few derisory chuckles ricocheted around the auditorium at the press screening of [*TPM*]—chuckles laced with dread.... The cause of amusement and apprehension could be traced to the film's prosaic opening credit crawl. It read: "Turmoil has engulfed the Galactic Republic. The taxation of trade routes to outlying star systems is in dispute."... Could there be a less enticing sentence with which to begin a movie? (29)

At the heart of Gilbey's criticism lies the wish to relive the perceived fantasy of the original trilogy that he felt as a boy. Concerns with real world issues, such as taxation, strip the *Star Wars* universe of its childhood magic. However, as already discussed, the original trilogy was as much a product of real world issues as the new trilogy would be, even if Gilbey, as a child, was not equipped to make the connection. That a trade dispute should be the occasion for the narrative fits well the tenor of late nineties American foreign policy and its concern with globalization. And it also immediately sets up a different relationship to the military, one that has moved away from certainties of the Cold War to one founded upon business interests, one that unfolds not from a simple binary conflict between the forces of good and evil but from complex politics. It is worth quoting the rest of the crawl to further place *TPM* in its proper context:

> Hoping to resolve the matter with a blockade of deadly battleships, the greedy Trade Federation has stopped all shipping to the small planet of Naboo.
>
> While the Congress of the Republic endlessly debates this alarming chain of events, the Supreme Chancellor has secretly dispatched two Jedi Knights, the guardians of peace and justice in the galaxy, to settle the conflict ...

The use of blockades, trade sanctions, political discussion, and, through the Jedi Knights, a United Nations–style organization charged with peacekeeping, negotiation, and observation, locates *TPM* in the historical context of the late twentieth century. However, as the title suggests, *TPM* fits the more traditional fears of U.S. culture: conspiracy and paranoia, concepts that took on new meaning in the wake of 9/11.

But before the attacks on the World Trade Center irrevocably altered the United States' view of war, the purpose of the military in a post–Cold War world was widely discussed. Philip Bobbitt, in his book *The Shield of Achilles* (2002), provides an interesting consideration of war's role and function in the post–Cold War world. His treatment illuminates the dynamic that seems to lie at the core of the prequel trilogy. Bobbitt argues that civilization has been defined by epochal periods of war and peace. The most recent, he suggests, is what he terms the "long war," which spans the First World War to the end of the Cold War, from 1914 to 1990. Looking at these historical moments, he argues that RMAs are fundamentally connected to revolutions in government. From this perspective, he offers in his book, as Lucas offers in his films, a means of "preparing for an uncertain future" (22).

The end of the "long war" meant that the nineties was the time of another RMA, a moment when the American military recognized that the nature of war had changed and sought to embrace new technology in the theatre of war, to bring about an evolution in military practice. And the narrative arc of the prequels, specifically *AOTC* and *ROTS*, shows Lucas engaging in some surprisingly direct ways with the implications of the RMA.

The notion of RMAs dates back to the seventeenth century and the creation of modern nation states organized around military power. Subsequent significant historical moments, such as the French, Haitian, and American Revolutions, the Industrial Revolution, the American Civil War, and the Great War, have powered the evolution of such a concept. At its core is the connection between technological change and the pursuit of military innovation, and this combination has changed the nature of war over the last three hundred years. That Lucas should produce narratives about war that also represent such evolution in military technology is no surprise. The level of detail in the shape, design, and practicality of the *Star Wars* universe is the subject of many fascinating coffee-table books. But the more uniquely American take on the RMA also has resonance with Lucas's saga. Andrew Marshall, director of the Office of Net Assessments, a think tank in the U.S. Department of Defense, describes RMA as "a major change in the nature of warfare brought about by the innovative application of new technologies which, combined with dramatic changes in military doctrine and operational and organizational concepts, fundamentally alters the character of military operations" ("Some Thoughts").

The Cold War offered a situation where the enemy was a known quantity, where there was a basic strategy for defending the United States and its interests, principally nuclear deterrence complemented by regional deterrence through the North Atlantic Treaty Organization (NATO), and other alliances and bases. In the post–Cold War situation, this simple enemy disappeared and in its place emerged new threats and challenges, and, with them, the necessity for new thinking in terms of American military strategy. The core aspiration of this 1990s RMA lies in mastery of electronic surveillance and information technologies and battlefield supremacy, or in military parlance, full spectrum dominance.

At the core of the prequels is the construction of new armies and new military technologies. The RMA, in the first instance, emerging as it did from the 1990–1991 Persian Gulf War, saw the U.S. military attempt to remove the human from the war zone. There was much rhetoric of war being fought between machines, with the human component controlling the action from far away. Certainly, the separatists' droid army fits this version of the RMA, in both the strengths of the vision as well as the weaknesses. That is, the human is removed from the equation, but the droids are fragile and stupid. This is evidenced most effectively in *TPM* where they are presented as dithering in general, easily dispatched by any weaponry, and totally useless once the droid control ship is destroyed by the young Anakin during the Battle of Naboo. The clone army is an interesting alternative, a middle ground between conventional human armies but with the expendability of droids. The Kaminoan Prime Minister, Lama Su, neatly sums up their virtues:

> Clones can think creatively. You'll find they are immensely superior to droids ... they are totally obedient, taking any order without question. We modified their genetic structure to make them less independent than the original host.

These qualities are chillingly demonstrated in *ROTS* when the Clone Troopers execute Palpatine's "Order Sixty-Six," a pre-programmed plan of rebellioin, which requires the Army of the Republic to eliminate their Jedi generals, without any qualms or hesitation.

TPM is a story about the machinations of a politician seeking to push the largely pacifist Republic toward war (something discussed in the next section).

There is a reluctance to engage in war, and, as Sio Bibble suggests in *AOTC*, "there hasn't been a full-fledged war since the creation of the Republic." In this arena, Lucas presents the military hardware as outdated and inadequate for the coming conflicts. *AOTC* becomes more directly concerned with war itself. And this more specific concern coincides with an American nation energized for war, albeit a new kind of war. The events of September 11, 2001, provided a new enemy for the United States but not one to be engaged conventionally in a single location. In a speech to Congress on September 20, 2001, just after the attacks on the World Trade Center, President George W. Bush detailed what this different war would entail:

> Americans are asking: How will we fight and win this war? We will direct every resource at our command—every means of diplomacy, every tool of intelligence, every instrument of law enforcement, every financial influence, and every necessary weapon of war—to the disruption and to the defeat of the global terror network. The war will not be like the war against Iraq a decade ago, with a decisive liberation of territory and a swift conclusion. It will not look like the air war above Kosovo two years ago, where no ground troops were used and not a single American was lost in combat. Our response involves far more than instant retaliation and isolated strikes. Americans should not expect one battle, but a lengthy campaign, unlike any other we have seen. It may include dramatic strikes, visible on TV, and covert operations, secret even in success. We will starve terrorists of funding, turn them one against another, drive them from place to place, until there is no refuge or no rest. And we will pursue nations that provide aid or safe haven to terrorism.

The implications of this can be seen in *AOTC*. One criticism leveled at the film was the planet-hopping nature of the narrative. Characters move around the galaxy, looking for answers, looking for the enemy. On the one hand, this creates a fragmented narrative. However, considered in the light of Bush's War on Terror and the intangibility of its enemy, this narrative structure is resonant. The two conflicts that have arisen thus far in the War on Terror, in Afghanistan and Iraq, have not been wars directed at the people of those countries but rather at the network of terrorists who have received shelter there. This narrative device continues in *ROTS* and is especially apparent in the action on the planet of Utapau. In the final analysis, echoing Bobbitt, the RMA became the engine that sustained a revolution in government.

Manipulating Menace: Leadership and War in the American and Galactic Republics

The impetus behind this galactic RMA is Palpatine, the "phantom menace" himself, and it is his will to power using the framework of constitutional democracy that allows perhaps the most complete analysis of America and war across the six films.

In the original trilogy, war was a given, a natural state against which the narrative unfolded. The prequel trilogy was conceived as a means of explicating the onset of the Civil War. Lucas, speaking at the world premiere of *ROTS* in Cannes in 2005, positioned the film and the two leading up to it as, in the words of a *Toronto Sun* reporter, "a wake-up call to Americans about the erosion of democratic freedoms under George W. Bush" (Kirkland). Unquestionably then, Lucas remains committed to an interrogation of war and its place in American culture and society. However, now he is not attempting to heal but to energize his audience, not attempting to offer a salve for the aftermath of a misguided military action but to prevent the conditions for the onset of a future one.

One thing becomes immediately apparent in Lucas's exploration of war. In each instance, in terms of contemporary historical reality and the construction of his own narratives, the focus, and the will, belongs to the leader, and Lucas focuses upon individuals—Nixon and Bush in history, Sidious/Palpatine and Vader in his own stories—who orchestrate and manipulate political contexts and electorates into granting them emergency powers against preexisting democratic institutions, which they subsequently use to further their own agendas. In the U.S. context, that such a situation should arise was a concern for the framers of the Constitution, and the concept of checks and balances between the three branches of government is aimed at preventing just this eventuality. Yet, in American politics, as in the Galactic Senate, such powers are seemingly readily granted. In American terms, this is because the founding fathers, while trying to prevent the focus of power in one branch of government, also recognized that democratic governance does not work well in times of crisis. In *Federalist*, No. 70, Alexander Hamilton proposed that the driving quality of the President is his "energy," which he considered to be "a leading element in the definition of good government." He continues:

> It is essential to the protection of the community against foreign attacks; it is no less essential to the steady administration of the laws; to the protection of property against those irregular and high-handed combinations, which sometimes interrupt the ordinary course of justice; to the security of liberty against the enterprises and assaults of ambition, of faction, and of anarchy. (Hamilton)

Although the Constitution does not define what should be done in an emergency or crisis, the Supreme Court in *Ex Parte Milligan*, a decision following the Civil War, makes clear that "the government, within the Constitution, has all the powers granted to it which are necessary to preserve its existence" (Commager 24).

This version of democracy, wherein the strong leader steers an anxious people through a crisis, has significant precedents that can be traced throughout American history. One example might be the trend of successful military leaders becoming president.[9] Another version of leadership in a time of crisis or emergency is apparent in the presidencies of Abraham Lincoln, Woodrow Wilson, and Franklin Roosevelt.

In each instance, the presidents extended and expanded the powers of the executive office to meet the emergencies they faced. Lincoln commenced the Civil War without the sanction of Congress (although congressional approval came later) following the secession of seven southern states and subsequently suspended habeas corpus. Wilson asked for and received almost dictatorial powers following continued attacks upon American ships by German U-boats in Atlantic waters and, in so doing, embroiled the United States in the First World War. Given America's severely limited capacity to wage war, Wilson received unprecedented authority to raise and equip an army to fight overseas while using the Alien and Sedition Acts of 1917 and the Palmer Raids of 1918–1919 to intimidate citizens domestically. Roosevelt is credited with establishing the modern presidency, of so transforming the structure of the office of the Chief Executive that "a modifier such as 'modern' is needed to characterize the post-1932 manifestations of the institution" (Greenstein 3). Interpreting his landslide victory as a mandate for change, Roosevelt's first hundred days focused on the immediate relief of the hardships of the Depression. In this period, he articulated a new foreign policy, took the country off the gold standard, and shepherded through Congress thirteen major pieces of legislation.

As John Gunther noted in 1950, "we are apt to forget nowadays the immense, unprecedented, overwhelming authority conferred on FDR by an enthusiastically willing Congress during the first hundred days of his administration. The Reichstag did not give Hitler much more" (139). In the wake of the attack on Pearl Harbor and the precipitation of American involvement in World War II, Roosevelt's administration, on February 19, 1942, signed Executive Order 9066, which provided for the internment of Japanese Americans. Later the same year, he reminded Congress that "the President has the power ... to take measures necessary to avert a disaster which would interfere with the winning of the war" (Roosevelt). This type of leadership, "a constitutional dictatorship" in the words of presidential scholar Clinton Rossiter, is representative of men acting undemocratically in order to protect democracy. That Lucas is interested in the implications of this aspect of American government comes across clearly in a passage from AOTC:

ANAKIN. I don't think the system works. We need a system where the politicians sit down and discuss the problem, agree to what's in the best interest of all the people, and then do it.

PADMÉ. That's exactly what we do. The problem is that people don't always agree.

ANAKIN. Then they should be made to.

PADMÉ. By whom? Who's going to make them?

ANAKIN. Someone ...

PADMÉ. You?

ANAKIN. No, not me.

PADMÉ. But someone?

ANAKIN. [*nods*] Someone wise.

PADMÉ. I don't know. Sounds an awful lot like a dictatorship to me.

ANAKIN. [*long pause*] Well, if it works ...

But this violate-democracy-to-save-it strand of American governance has a darker, more ambivalent resonance during the Cold War, specifically in relation to the war in Vietnam and the leadership of Lyndon Johnson and Richard Nixon, the very context from which the *Star Wars* universe was born.

An emergency that appears to require sanctioned action, often military, is a repeated pattern or trope in American history. This type of crisis, technically unconstitutional, remains a paradox of leadership in American democracy. Strong leaders secure extra powers in a time of crisis, foregoing Constitutional rules for the very purpose of protecting the document they ignore. Yet, arguably, such actions by the leader are a necessary feature of a strong democracy and are actively embraced by a fearful, anxious electorate. In his 1960 *Encounter* article, "On Heroic Leadership," Arthur Schlesinger Jr. argues an absolute need for strong individual leaders even within the framework of a mature constitutional democracy. This necessity arises, Schlesinger argues, at times of severe crisis, when democracy itself needs to be saved. This ability of the heroic leader to "exceed the norms or bounds of executive power for the public good" is predicated upon one fundamental limitation:

> [A strong democracy] can risk an interlude of crisis because the great preponderance of national values and institutions can be relied on to require reversion once the crisis is over. (Schlesinger 10)

The heroic leader knows when to take the reins and, crucially, when to relinquish them. Historian Richard Slotkin, in *Gunfighter Nation* (1992), offers a perceptive analysis of Schlesinger's article:

> In effect, Schlesinger finds that when a mature democracy is in crisis, "the people" are likely to become (for the moment at least) "weak" ... and for their good, and the good of the nation, the heroic President must control public authority with something like the willful rigor and extralegal authority of the Strong Man. (502)

The heroic leader then

> is not merely the instrument of popular or majority will. Rather, acting out of a higher and more perfect sense of the nation's mission and necessity than any popular majority could possess, he helps his race or nation to realize its latent destiny by leading it forward in directions it might not have chosen by or for itself. (Slotkin 502)

The heroic president so conceived knows what is best and has the character, the sheer will to enforce his beliefs. Historians point at such events as Pearl Harbor or, more directly relevant, the Gulf of Tonkin resolution, which effectively embodied a declaration for increasing American involvement in the war in Vietnam, as representing moments when leaders mobilize fear to secure extraordinary war powers and the concomitant restrictions of guaranteed democratic rights.

This is the pattern that Lucas uses to orchestrate Palpatine's rise from Machiavellian senator to Galactic Emperor. In *TPM*, Senator Palpatine is a mid-level politician, described as "a thin, kindly man" in the screenplay. However, Palpatine is one and the same as Darth Sidious, a Sith Lord who orchestrates the corrupt Trade Federation to blockade the peaceful planet of Naboo over taxation. The blockade escalates, under Palpatine/Sidious's manipulations, into a full-scale invasion. Through controlling the response of the Nabooans, by resisting the very military aggression he himself organized, Palpatine is able to engineer his rise to Supreme Chancellor of the Galactic Senate. *AOTC* begins a number of years later, where the conflict has widened and now threatens to destroy the millennia-old Republic. The Senate is debating the creation of an army of the Republic, and, in the opening sequence, an assassination attempt is made on Padmé Amidala, now senator for Naboo, because she opposes such a measure. Palpatine/Sidious continues to manipulate the crisis, all the while bringing new emergency powers to his office, passing antidemocratic legislation and escalating a massive military buildup. The battle on Geonosis that ends the film is another crisis, engineered by Sidious, the aim of which is to force the creation and use of the clone army (which already exists). Jar Jar demonstrates a loyal pliancy:

> JAR JAR. In response to the direct threat to the Republic, mesa propose that the Senate give immediately emergency powers to the Supreme Chancellor.
>
> PALPATINE. It is with great reluctance that I have agreed to this calling. I love democracy.... I love the Republic. But I am mild by nature, and I do not desire to see the destruction of democracy. The power you give me I will lay down when this crisis has abated, I promise you. And as my first act with this new authority, I will create a grand army of the Republic to counter the increasing threats of the separatists.

ROTS sees Sidious's plans come to fruition. The Jedi realize too late that the Clone Wars have been systematically orchestrated by the Sith to destroy the

Republic and eradicate the Jedi Order. The notion here is that, at every level, the institutions have implicated themselves in their own destruction. This is singly illustrated in that Anakin Skywalker, the Chosen One of the prophecy, is charged by Palpatine—now revealed as Sidious—to exterminate the Jedi and the leaders of the separatist movement, leaving all the enemies of the Sith dead or routed and the control of government in the Emperor's dictatorial grasp.

It is instructive to map this narrative arc onto Lucas's stated point of origin for the films: the war in Vietnam. Certainly, Johnson's manipulation of the incident in the Gulf of Tonkin, where it was reported that North Vietnamese torpedo boats had twice attacked American naval vessels, resonates. It emerged that the administration had not disclosed the full truth about the attacks (indeed, the publication of *The Pentagon Papers* in 1971 demonstrated that the affair had been almost entirely fabricated). However, his response, to order immediate retaliatory air raids against North Vietnam and then ask Congress for extra powers through a resolution that was overwhelmingly passed, is strikingly similar to Palpatine's machinations. Nixon's secret bombing of Cambodia, while publicly suggesting that his intentions were for peace, is also interestingly connected. Such links can also be made to the War on Terror. It can be no coincidence that dialogue between Anakin, now Darth Vader, and Obi-Wan rings with the rhetoric of the War on Terror:

OBI-WAN. You have allowed this Dark Lord to twist your mind until now ... you have become the very thing you swore to destroy.

ANAKIN. Don't lecture me, Obi-Wan. I see through the lies of the Jedi. I do not fear the dark side as you do. I have brought peace, justice, freedom, and security to my new Empire.

OBI-WAN. Your new Empire?

ANAKIN. Don't make me kill you.

OBI-WAN. Anakin, my allegiance is to the Republic ... to democracy.

ANAKIN. If you're not with me, you're my enemy.

This mirrors almost precisely President Bush's comments in his address to a Joint Session of Congress and the American people on September 20, 2001:

Every nation, in every region, now has a decision to make. Either you are with us, or you are with the terrorists. [*Applause*].

Given that, in the Obi-Wan/Anakin confrontation, Obi-Wan suggests that, in response to this form of binary thinking, "only Sith Lords deal in absolutes," Lucas's personal politics may come into perspective. Indeed, as can be discerned in the quote that opens this essay, Lucas is very much concerned with the American political landscape of the early twenty-first century. Clearly, he sees Bush engaged in the practice of extending the powers of his office. The extent of his concern is mirrored in the observation made by Padmé Amidala in the *ROTS* as Palpatine grants himself the ultimate in political and military power:

> PALPATINE. The war is over. [*Applause.*] The Separatists have been defeated, [*Applause*] and the Jedi rebellion has been foiled. We stand on the threshold of a new beginning.
>
> [*There is a period of long applause.*]
>
> PADMÉ. Well, this is the moment we discover if he intends to return the Republic to a democracy.
>
> PALPATINE. In order to ensure our security and continuing stability, the Republic will be reorganized into the first Galactic Empire, for a safe and secure society, which, I assure you, will last for ten thousand years ... [*Applause*] an Empire that will continue to be ruled by this august body, and a sovereign leader chosen for life... [*Applause*] an Empire ruled by the majority ... ruled by a new constitution ... [*Applause*]
>
> PADMÉ. So this is how liberty dies, with thunderous applause.

It is in such moments that the political perspective underpinning the original trilogy reverberates with the events of the twenty-first century and their presentation in the prequel trilogy.

Conclusion

The reasons for the phenomenal success of the *Star Wars* saga are legion. It is optimistic, keenly American, spiritual, and philosophical. And it is, in one sense, timeless, as mythologies tend to be, and, given Lucas's stated inspiration by such works as Joseph Campbell's *The Hero of a Thousand Faces* (1949), as John Shelton Lawrence examines in his essay in this volume, mythology is a key aspect in the understanding of the saga's origins. Yet it is also a sequence of far less mythical and more political stories that reflect and resonate with various moments in recent American history, stories that connect to become an account of the passage of American self-concept through the aftermath of Vietnam, the uncertainties of the post–Cold War years, and on into the War on Terror. It is this relevance, whether as a salve for a traumatized psyche or as a prescient discussion of contemporary American military affairs, that assures *Star Wars* its unique place within American popular culture.

Afterword: *Star Wars* in Great Britain

The *Star Wars* saga's phenomenal success has a global context. The themes, characters, and situations of the universe have been embraced around the world with the same fervor as the United States, and the British reception was similarly ecstatic. However, the historical and military contexts that this essay discusses are barely, if at all, relevant to a British audience. The defining influence of the war in Vietnam does not translate to the contemporary reality of the U.K. Indeed, the war in Southeast Asia, apart from some antiwar demonstrations outside the American Embassy, barely registered as an issue. Harold Wilson, Prime Minister from 1964 to 1970, for a variety of reasons, resisted British involvement. The question arises then, to what did U.K. audiences respond so positively? Why, in Britain in the late 1970s, was *Star Wars* so enthusiastically received?

British society in the 1970s was beset by economic problems: high inflation, spiraling unemployment, trade union conflict, a three-day working week that, in turn, led to power outages. Racial conflict escalated while the violence in Northern Ireland worsened. The winter of 1978–1979, "The Winter of Discontent" as it was labeled by Larry Lamb, editor of the popular British tabloid newspaper, the *Sun*, saw widespread strikes by workers demanding larger pay rises. The sight of rubbish collecting on streets and in public parks was an iconic illustration of the gloom and the pessimism of the decade in the same way in which the reports of bodies going unburied, because gravediggers were on strike, offers a sense of how a society was breaking down.

Into this context came ANH, released in the United Kingdom on December 27, 1977. It provided audiences with an escape, something cinema had always done, but this was an escape into a fairy tale, a universal mythology of heroes and villains, good and evil, a milieu where the good guys win. Lucas's fascination with world mythologies and his fascination with and conscious use of the work of Joseph Campbell, specifically *The Hero with a Thousand Faces* (1949), meant that the film transcended geographical or cultural boundaries. The "return to childhood" that Pauline Kael recognized in her *New Yorker* review of the movie was as appealing, accessible, and timely to a British audience as it was to an American one.

In this way then, although in relation to a different set of specific issues, Lucas's film provided for British audiences the same sense of optimism it had for Americans of the possibility of a new hope.

Notes for Chapter 3

1. See Decker, Star Wars *and Philosophy*; Porter, *The Tao of* Star Wars; Bortolin, *The Dharma of* Star Wars; and Staub, *Faith of the Jedi*.

2. See Biskind, *Easy Riders*.

3. The documentary, *Empire of Dreams*, meticulously illustrates the problems that surrounded the making of *Star Wars*: weather destroying sets in Tunisia, the inflexible union rules of the British crew in Ellstree, the slow development of the special effect shots by Industrial Light and Magic, and the general lack of faith directed toward Lucas.

4. See, as examples, Seed, *American Science Fiction and the Cold War*; Prince, *Visions of Empire*; and Decker, "By Any Means Necessary."

5. See also Slotkin, *Gunfighter Nation*, and Altman, *Film/Genre*.

6. See, as examples, *The Planet of the Apes* (1968), *The Omega Man* (1971), *Soylent Green* (1973), *Rollerball* (1975), *Logan's Run* (1976), *Alien* (1979), *Zardoz* (1973), and *Silent Running* (1971). *Star Trek*, which aired on U.S. television between 1966 and 1969, was a more optimistic version of the future and represented a science fiction that fully embraced American frontier mythology.

7. Visually and stylistically, a significant point of reference for Lucas and one that signals the breadth of war reference contained in *Star Wars* is the Nazi project. These references operate on a number of levels from the more obvious, including the Empire's army of Storm Troopers and the style of uniform worn by the Empire's officers, to borrowing shots from the Nazi propaganda film, *The Triumph of the Will*, directed by Leni Riefenstahl and released in 1936. The majesty and might of the Empire is exemplified in images resonant of the 1934 Nazi rally at Nuremberg, for example, the arrival of the Emperor into a shuttle bay with ranks of perfect Empire troops. The final sequence of Star Wars, where the heroes receive medals for the destruction of the Death Star, is also heavily influenced by shots from Riefenstahl's film. There exists another, more subtle connection to both the Nazis and Riefenstahl's film: the Nietzschean notion of the will to power, a philosophical underpinning of Nazi ideology. And it certainly speaks to the construction of the *Star Wars* saga: the few supermen operating at a level distinctly higher than the masses who are largely observers to the action. This Nietzschean connection is no accident. In very early drafts of the scripts, Lucas entitled the stories "The Journal of the Whills," immediately linking Nietzsche, the Nazis, and Riefenstahl in a single space. For more information, see Bouzereau, *Star Wars*.

8. See, for example, X-Files: The Movie (1998), Armageddon (1998), Godzilla (1998), Deep Impact (1998), Independence Day (1996), Mars Attacks! (1996), Volcano (1997), Dante's Peak (1997), End of Days (1999), and Strange Days (1995).

9. Ten presidents used successful military leadership as a foundation: Washington, Jackson, W. Harrison, Taylor, Pierce, Grant, Hayes, Garfield, B. Harrison, and Eisenhower.

Works Cited

Allison, Graham. "Cool It: The Foreign Policy of Young America." *Foreign Policy* (Winter 1970–1971): 144–60.

Altman, Rick. *Film/Genre*. London: BFI, 1999.

Baxter, John. *George Lucas: A Biography*. London: HarperCollins, 1999.

Biskind, Peter. *Easy Riders Raging Bulls*. London: Bloomsbury, 1998.

Bobbitt, Philip. *The Shield of Achilles: War, Peace and the Course of History*. London: Penguin, 2002.

Bortolin, Matthew. *The Dharma of* Star Wars. Somerville, MA: Wisdom Publications, 2005.

Bouzereau, Laurent. Star Wars: *The Annotated Screenplays*. London: Titan, 1998.

Bush, George W. "Address to a Joint Session of Congress and the American People." 20 Sept. 2001. 1 Oct. 2005 <http://www.whitehouse.gov/news/releases/2001/09/20010920-8.html>.

Commager, Henry Steele. *Documents of American History*. New York: Appleton, 1949.

Decker, Kevin. "By Any Means Necessary: Tyranny, Democracy, Republic and Empire." Star Wars *and Philosophy*. Ed. Kevin Decker and J. T. Eberl. Chicago, IL: Open Court, 2005.

Empire of Dreams: The Story of the Star Wars *Trilogy*. Dir. Edith Becker and Ken Burns. DVD (Bonus Material for the 4-Disc *Star Wars* Trilogy DVD). Twentieth Century Fox, 2004.

Engelhardt, Tom. *The End of Victory Culture: Cold War America and the Disillusioning of a Generation*. New York: Basic, 1995.

Fukuyama, Francis. *The End of History and the Last Man*. London: Penguin, 1992.

Gilbey, Ryan. *It Don't Worry Me*. London: Faber & Faber, 2003.

Goodman, Ellen. "A Star Wars Fantasy Fulfillment." *Washington Post* 30 July 1977.

Greenstein, Fred I. *Leadership in the Modern Presidency*. Cambridge, MA: Harvard UP, 1988.

Gunther, John. *Roosevelt in Retrospect: A Profile in History*. New York: Harper, 1950.

Hamilton, Alexander. "Federalist No. 70: The Executive Department Further Considered." The Constitution Society (online) Nov. 12, 2005: <http://www.constitution.org/fed/federa70.htm>.

Hellmann, John. *American Myth and the Legacy of Vietnam*. New York: Columbia UP, 1986.

Henderson, Mary. Star Wars: *The Magic of Myth*. New York: Bantam, 1997.

Kael, Pauline. "Contrasts." *New Yorker* 26 Sept. 1977.

Kirkland, Bruce. "George W. Vader." *Toronto Sun* 16 May 2005.

Kline, Sally. *George Lucas Interviews*. Jackson, MS: UP of Mississippi, 1999.

Lucas, George. Director's Commentary on *Return of the Jedi*. Star Wars: *Episode VI–Return of the Jedi*. Dir. Richard Marquand. Prod. Lucasfilm, Ltd. Distr. 20th Century Fox, 1983. Special Edition of 1997.

Marshall, Andrew W. "Some Thoughts on Military Revolutions: Second Version." Memorandum for the Record, Office of the Secretary of Defense. Washington, DC. 23 Aug. 1993.

McNamara, Robert S. *In Retrospect: The Tragedy and Lessons of Vietnam*. New York: Times Books, 1995.

Porter, John M. *The Tao of* Star Wars. Lake Worth, FL: Humanics, 2003.

Prince, Stephen. *Visions of Empire: Political Imagery in Contemporary American Film*. New York: Praeger, 1992.

Reagan, Ronald. "Veterans Day Ceremony Address at the Vietnam Veterans' Memorial." 11 Nov. 1988. 12 Sept. 2005 <http://americanrhetoric.com/speeches/ronaldreaganvietnammemorial.html>.

Roosevelt, Franklin D. "Message to Congress." 7 Sept. 1942. 17 Oct. 2005 <http://www.ibiblio.org/pha/policy/1942/420907a.html>.

Rossiter, Clinton. *Constitutional Dictatorship: Crisis Government in Modern Democracies*. Princeton, NJ: Princeton UP, 1948.

Schlesinger, Arthur, Jr. "On Heroic Leadership and the Dilemma of Strong Men and Weak Peoples." *Encounter* 15.6 (1960): 3–11.

Seed, David. *American Science Fiction and the Cold War: Literature and Film*. Edinburgh: Edinburgh UP, 1999.

Shone, Tom. *Blockbuster: How the Jaws and Jedi Generation Turned Hollywood into a Boom-town*. London: Scribner, 2005.

Slotkin, Richard. *Gunfighter Nation: The Myth of the Frontier in Twentieth Century America*. New York: Harper, 1992.

Staub, Dick. *Faith of the Jedi: Lost Wisdom of the Ancient Masters*. New York: Wiley, 2005.

CHAPTER 4

Pedagogy of (the) Force:
The Myth of Redemptive Violence

Michelle J. Kinnucan

Shortly after the release of *The Empire Strikes Back* (1980) writer-director-producer George Lucas said, "This is the kind of movie we need. There needs to be a kind of film that expresses the mythological realities of life—the deeper psychological movements of the way we conduct our lives" (O'Quinn 116). Then, in a 1983 interview, Lucas asserted,

> Film and [other] visual entertainment are a pervasively important part of our culture, an extremely significant influence on the way society operates ... for better or worse the influence of the church, which used to be all powerful, has been usurped by film. Films and television tell us the way we conduct our lives, what is right and wrong. (Harmetz 143)[1]

The success of the *Star Wars* films and related merchandise undoubtedly reflects a deep cultural resonance with its theme and narrative. Indeed, the mythological significance of *Star Wars* has become almost a commonplace in popular and scholarly work on the films. As with all cultural works, *Star Wars* is subject to multiple, if not equally persuasive, interpretations. My purpose here, though, is not to contest the validity of any previous interpretations of *Star Wars*; rather, I suggest another interpretation of the films.

I believe that the significance and the popularity of the *Star Wars* films lie in the most powerful, yet least acknowledged, mythological archetype in the saga. Theologian Walter Wink calls this archetype the "Myth of Redemptive Violence" (MRV), which also found expression in what mythologist Joseph Campbell—arguably, the best-known interpreter of *Star Wars*—termed the "mythologies of war." For reasons explored below, Campbell apparently never discussed these mythologies in the context of *Star Wars*. Finally, *Star Wars* is placed squarely within sociologist James W. Gibson's American "New War" that began in the 1970s and is still fought over issues of "power, sex, race, and alienation" (14).

The Origins of the Myth of Redemptive Violence

Wink has written extensively about the MRV. In his interpretation,

> It enshrines the belief that violence saves, that war brings peace, that might makes right. It is one of the oldest continuously repeated stories in the world.
>
> The belief that violence "saves" is so successful because it doesn't seem to be mythic in the least. Violence simply appears to be the nature of the things. It's what works. It seems inevitable, the last and often, the first resort in conflicts. (Wink, *Powers* 42)

Wink's notion of the normality of violence accords with sociologist and lexicologist Roland Barthes' assertion that myth depoliticizes "things ... it purifies them, it makes them innocent, it gives them a natural and eternal justification, it gives them a clarity which is not that of an explanation but that of a statement of fact" (Barthes 143). Myth "transforms history into nature," according to Barthes, and grants "natural" status to humanity's record of violence and war (129).

In Wink's reading, the MRV can be traced to the ancient *Enuma Elish* (circa 1250 BCE), which he summarizes thusly:

> In the beginning, according to the Babylonian myth, Apsu, the father god, and Tiamat, the mother god, give birth to the gods. But the frolicking of the younger gods makes so much noise that the elder gods resolve to kill them so they can sleep. The younger gods uncover the plot before the elder gods put it into action, and kill Apsu. His wife Tiamat, the Dragon of Chaos, pledges revenge.
>
> Terrified by Tiamat, the rebel gods turn for salvation to their youngest member, Marduk. He negotiates a steep price: if he succeeds, he must be given chief and undisputed power in the assembly of the gods. Having extorted this promise, he catches Tiamat in a net, drives an evil wind down her throat, shoots an arrow that bursts her distended belly and pierces her heart. He then splits her skull with a club and scatters her blood in out-of-the-way places. He stretches out her corpse full-length, and from it creates the cosmos. (*Powers* 45)

Creation is thus an act of violence; evil and violence are primordial facts of life. "As the French philosopher Paul Ricoeur observes, order is established by means of disorder. Chaos (symbolized by Tiamat) is prior to order (represented by Marduk, high god of Babylon). Evil precedes good" (Wink, *Powers* 45). Marduk's murder of Tiamat is not only a creative act, but it is also political; when he slays her, he establishes order in the world.

Later, Marduk kills an imprisoned god—he had sided with the elder gods—in order to create human beings as servants for other imprisoned gods. Humans—made from "the blood of an assassinated god"—are therefore "naturally incapable of peaceful coexistence" (Wink, *Engaging* 15), and, thus, "Life is combat" (16). In ancient Babylon, Wink argues, this myth bolstered "a highly centralized state in which the king rules as Marduk's representative on earth" and order was the highest social and religious value (15). Thus, any enemy of the divine order established by Marduk (and, therefore, an agent of Chaos) is "Evil and war is her punishment" (16). Wink claims that "The simplicity of [the *Enuma Elish's*] picture of reality commended it widely, and its basic mythic structure spread" far and wide into the mythologies of other cultures (14-5).

Even now, Wink argues, it is "the dominant myth in contemporary America" (*Powers* 48), where it is replete in the popular culture and mass media, including *Star Wars* (54). He locates the myth where, he claims, it has always been—at the heart of a "Domination System ... characterized by unjust economic relations, oppressive political relations, biased race relations, patriarchal gender relations, hierarchical power relations and the use of violence to maintain them all" (39). The myth "serves as the inner spirituality of the national security state" and "provides divine legitimation" for the Domination System (57).

The System is supported by a complex pecking order of latent and actual violence paralleling the other oppressive relations established within it. Because almost everyone, no matter how exploited, has someone below them in the pecking order, the System seems to give even the oppressed a stake in its continuation, lest they themselves be knocked down in rank (Wink, *Powers* 40-1). Yet, oppression breeds resistance, which, when violent, always strengthens the Domination System and reinforces the MRV, whether by its failure or putative success (127).

Anthropologist Claude Levi-Strauss argues that there is an "organic continuity apparent among mythology, legendary tradition, and what we must call politics" (2: 268; see also 1: 209). Barthes notes, "Myth is a system of communication ... it is a message" (109). What Wink identifies as the MRV is a core set of political ideas constituting the "message" of the *Enuma Elish*. The set includes the following ideas: Violence is necessary, right, and successful in addressing the threats to the highest cultural and social imperative—order; threats to order inevitably arise because of malevolent human nature; and *we* who wield violence in support of order are good, and our enemies are evil.

Levi-Strauss also observes that "the purpose of myth is to provide a logical model capable of overcoming a contradiction (an impossible achievement if, as it happens, the contradiction is real)" (1: 209). The central and impossible contradictions to be overcome by the *Enuma Elish*/MRV are obtaining lasting peace by means of violence, justice through injustice, and good out of evil.[2] The Domination System generates the "intellectual impulse" that produced and continually reproduces the myth in the never-ending task of overcoming its impossible contradictions (Levi-Strauss 1: 229).[3]

The Myth of Redemptive Violence in *Star Wars*

In what follows, I interpret *Star Wars* as a modern version of the *Enuma Elish* that effectively transmits the ancient myth's political message, the MRV. I do not try to show that *Star Wars* precisely reproduces the framework or code of the *Enuma Elish* nor do I offer a genealogy of the myth; however plausible, those efforts lie beyond my purposes.[4] It is the message of the *Enuma Elish*—the MRV—that interests me, because it has remained largely intact in *Star Wars* while maintaining its invisibility to an adoring culture. Lucas's aspirations to give audiences the "mythological realities of life" (O'Quinn 116) with a film that "tells us the way we conduct our lives, what is right and wrong" (Harmetz 143) are much older than he realized.

The theme of *Star Wars* is the battle of good versus evil fought out on both the cosmic and personal scale. The cosmic battle plays out around and through the hero's journey of Anakin Skywalker/Darth Vader.[5] Anakin (Jake Lloyd) is introduced to us in *The Phantom Menace* (1999). Two Jedi Knights, Obi-Wan Kenobi (Ewan McGregor) and Qui-Gon Jinn (Liam Neeson), are forced to land on the planet Tatooine for repairs after sustaining enemy-inflicted damage to the Nubian space ship in which they are traveling. On Tatooine, they encounter Anakin, a precocious nine-year-old slave living with his mother, Shmi (Pernilla August), also a slave.

In order to begin his hero's journey, Anakin must first be freed from his bondage (and his mother). Presumably, since Anakin is a child, Lucas chose not to set Anakin's liberation struggle in armed combat; rather, the device Lucas uses is sport-as-combat. Qui-Gon arranges the boy's entry into the Boonta Classic Podrace and wagers Anakin's freedom and the needed repair parts against the Nubian ship. The race is gladiatorial, and several competitors die. However, Anakin emerges victorious, his freedom gained in the violent contest with the wager enforced by the latent violence of both the 'gang' of Hutts who rule the planet (Lucas 38) and of Qui-Gon (80). Thus is justice obtained from injustice and good from evil.

Freed in this way, Anakin leaves his mother and Tatooine to join the Jedi, who initially reject him as, frankly, too old, and damaged goods. However, through a series of events, Anakin becomes Obi-Wan's protégé but is eventually turned to the Dark Side of the Force and takes the name Darth Vader. Vader's evil is presaged in *Attack of the Clones* (2002) when, in revenge for his mother's death, Anakin massacres the Tusken Raiders who abducted her, including the women and children of their families. Anakin's transformation into the evil Vader is complete by the end of *Revenge of the Sith* (2005).

The arch villain of *Star Wars* is Palpatine (Ian McDiarmid), also known as Darth Sidious, a secret master of the Force's Dark Side and a character—if, sometimes, a shadowy one—in all six films. By the end of *ROTS*, Palpatine's careful plots have enabled him to transform the Galactic Republic into an

Empire with him at its head. In neither trilogy do we learn what Palpatine's fundamental motivations are other than the quest for power through evil means. We do find out in *TPM* that he is motivated, at least in part, by revenge—for what real or imagined wrong we are not told. Palpatine is instrumental in Anakin's transformation and upon its completion becomes Darth Vader's master.

While Anakin is in the final stages of becoming Vader, unbeknownst to him, his wife, whom he thought dead, gives birth to his twin children: Leia and Luke.[6] Luke Skywalker (Mark Hamill) enters the series as an adult character at the beginning of *A New Hope* (1977). When a rebellion against Palpatine's empire begins to rage throughout the galaxy, Luke is a simple farm hand on his aunt and uncle's farm. Luke knows nothing of his sister and almost nothing about his father, but he soon encounters someone who does know about them.

While searching for a runaway android named R2-D2—who claims to belong to Obi-Wan Kenobi—Luke is attacked by Sandpeople. Obi-Wan rescues Luke and R2-D2 and takes them to his home where he tells Luke about his father and then plays the holographic summons of Princess Leia to Obi-Wan contained in R2-D2. Obi-Wan tries to talk Luke into joining him and the Rebel Alliance on Alderaan, but Luke refuses the "call to adventure" from a sense of duty to his aunt and uncle (Campbell, *Hero* 36). Luke later returns to the farm only to find his aunt and uncle dead after an attack. Thus, violently liberated from his familial responsibilities, Luke is free to pursue his destiny and begin his hero's journey. He does not mourn or bury his aunt and uncle.

Skipping to *Return of the Jedi* (1983), the last film in the series' narrative structure, Luke finally learns the full story of his father from the spirit of the now deceased Obi-Wan. He tells Luke, "Your father was seduced by the Dark Side of the Force. He ceased to be Anakin Skywalker and became Darth Vader. When that happened the good man who was your father was destroyed." Obi-Wan also tells him of his sister, Princess Leia, and charges him to defeat Vader. Luke responds, "I can't kill my own father."

Luke leaves Obi-Wan on the planet Dagobah to join his comrades battling against the Empire at the Endor moon. Hoping to turn him from the Dark Side of the Force, Luke determines to surrender and face Vader. When presented as a prisoner to him, he tells Vader, "Anakin Skywalker ... is the name of your true self." Vader responds, "It is too late for me, son. The Emperor will show you the true nature of the Force. He is your master now." Luke replies, "Then my father is truly dead."

Luke is then transported to the Death Star and brought to the Emperor, who provokes Luke to fight him. When Luke attacks, Vader protects Palpatine and begins a duel with Luke. During the course of the fight Vader senses from Luke that he has a twin sister, Leia, whom Vader then vows to turn to the

Dark Side of the Force. This infuriates Luke, and he finally defeats Vader, mortally wounding him. Palpatine encourages Luke to strike a deathblow and finish off Vader. Luke refuses and casts his lightsaber away. Outraged, Palpatine determines to destroy Luke, since he cannot turn him to the Dark Side; he attacks him with Force lightning.

Palpatine's deadly violence directed against his son finally arouses the latent goodness in Vader/Anakin. Luke's persistent love for and faith in the inherent goodness of the father he never knew are not enough to redeem Anakin Skywalker and turn him from the Dark Side. Only violence can redeem Anakin, and only violence can secure that redemption. Prompted by his witness of violence against Luke to committing his own violence, Vader/Anakin takes a key redemptive step by surprising Palpatine and throwing him to his death, thus saving Luke.

Luke recognizes the change in his father and goes to him. Anakin's redemption is completed with his unmasking and imminent death as Darth Vader. Knowing the Death Star will soon be destroyed, Luke attempts to help him to safety but Vader/Anakin is too seriously injured to survive. The final dialogue between Luke and his father, whom Luke himself has mortally wounded, is striking:

VADER/ANAKIN. [*now unmasked*] Leave me.

LUKE. I'll not leave you; I've got to save you.

VADER/ANAKIN. You already have. [*Vader/Anakin then dies, and Luke narrowly escapes.*]

We know Anakin has been fully redeemed, because, in the closing scenes of *ROTJ* at a victory celebration on Endor, Luke sees his smiling spirit (missing the scars and wounds of Darth Vader) together with the spirits of Obi-Wan and Yoda.

On the cosmic scale, the battle of good versus evil is resolved just after Vader's death with the destruction of the Death Star and the military defeat of the Empire. Unlike real life (and many other films), the collective and personal violence in *Star Wars* is tidy and uncannily bloodless. For example, during a lengthy battle scene in *AOTC* where Anakin has his arm severed at the elbow, we see not a drop of blood leave his body or pool on the ground.[7] Moreover, we are largely spared seeing the consequences for ordinary soldiers or citizens of large-scale warfare and the violent overthrow of galactic civil authority—there are no fields of dead and wounded soldiers, starving refugees, or homeless orphans in *Star Wars*.

In the first film released in the series, *ANH*, evil is presented to us full-blown in the form of the Galactic Empire, which is bent on crushing the good Rebel Alliance. The Empire is "a tyrannical regime, presided over by a shadowy and detached despot steeped in the Dark Side of the Force" ("Palpatine"). That despot is the ghoulish Emperor Palpatine. As noted by Mary Henderson, curator for the Smithsonian Institution's *Star Wars* "Magic of Myth" exhibition, "He is all ego with no spirit, locked within a fortress of hate and aggression" (Henderson 101). The imperial soldiers are human but dehumanized— "they are pawns who die in large numbers. Their inhumanity is clear from the fact that their faces, if they have any, are never visible" (Kuiper 78).

Thus, as in the Westerns Lucas sought to supersede with an inspiring new mythos, the viewer is presented with an unambiguous moral dualism—good versus evil—and given little or no context to understand the violent disposition of the evil enemy nor the reasons why most of his troops and other subjects follow him (Henderson 126).[8] As psychologist Lawrence LeShan observes, after the battle that climactically ends the saga, "The evil emperor is dead, his evil machines destroyed, his evil chief henchman ... *redeems* himself in death, and all the good people will clearly live happily ever after" (50; emphasis added). And Mary Henderson emphasizes the moral polarity: "There is no crossover between the two forces; when the Death Star is destroyed along with everyone on it, it is a clear-cut victory of good over irredeemable evil. There is no point in attempting to 'save' any of the Imperial troops" (117).

Thus, Lucas pits incomprehensible evil against manifest good in an inevitably violent—no other option is viable—although hygienic, conflict where good conquers evil. *Star Wars* fits the model of "reality construction used in wartime" that former U.S. Army clinical psychologist Lawrence LeShan and physicist-philosopher Henry Margenau term "the mythic mode" (LeShan 47–50). LeShan asserts that, in the mythic mode, (1) "we never question *why* evil exists; it simply is"; (2) the enemy is totally, inexplicably, and irredeemably evil; (3) we are good; (4) because the enemy are not really human like us, "there is no reason not to starve, torture or kill them"; (5) "the good people always emerge victorious"; and (6) force is ultimately the [only] answer" (47–51).

As the MRV dictates, over and over, violence redeems in *Star Wars*. Violence rescues young Anakin from slavery; it frees Luke from farm life and family obligations; it reclaims the older Anakin/Vader from the Force's Dark Side ; and, finally, it liberates the galaxy from Palpatine and his evil Empire.

Before moving on, a brief consideration of the Force is due. According to the character Obi-Wan Kenobi (Alec Guiness in *A New Hope*), the Force is "an energy field created by all living things. It surrounds us and penetrates us. It binds the galaxy together" (Henderson 44). It is telling that Lucas did not choose to call the ultimate reality for his universe the Energy, Strength, Field, Yield, Submit, Assent, Transcendent, etc. Instead, he chose a word whose meanings include: "to do violence to; *especially*: **RAPE** ... to press, drive, attain to, or effect against resistance or inertia ... to achieve or win by strength in struggle or violence ... to break open or through" ("Force"). Perhaps, the character of Darth Vader speaks more accurately than George Lucas knew or intended when Vader tells Luke at the conclusion of *Return of the Jedi* that the inexplicably and monstrously evil Sith Lord, Emperor Palpatine, "will show you the true nature of the Force." That is, violence and its endless repetition, whether perpetrated by the "good" Jedi or the complementary "bad" Sith, *is* the "true nature" of (the) Force.

Joseph Campbell and *Star Wars*

In 1985, at George Lucas's Skywalker Ranch, Bill Moyers interviewed mythologist Joseph Campbell for a documentary series entitled *Joseph Campbell: The Power of Myth* (1988). He spoke frequently about *Star Wars* in the series. In the companion book, Campbell is quoted as saying that Lucas "has put the newest and most powerful spin" to the classic story of the hero, which is "the message that technology is not going to save us.... We have to rely on our intuition, our true being" (*Power* xiv). In Campbell's view, the evil Empire represented the "state as a machine" (18), with the part-human, part-machine Darth Vader embodying the threat posed by modern society—"Is the system going to flatten you out and deny you your humanity, or are you going to be able to make use of the system to the attainment of human purposes?" (144).

Lucas cites Joseph Campbell's 1949 book, *The Hero with a Thousand Faces*, as a significant inspiration for *Star Wars* (Henderson 7). The premise of the book is the existence of a single mythological archetype or "monomyth" of the "hero" (Campbell, *Hero* 3–46). Campbell found expressions of this archetype manifest in the stories of myriad peoples, places, and times.

In *Hero*, Campbell does not discuss war and violence at any great length; they are largely taken for granted and backgrounded. For instance, in Campbell's view, the *Enuma Elish* illustrates

> the point that conflict in the created world is not what it seems. Tiamat, though slain .
> and dismembered, was not thereby undone. Had the battle been viewed from another
> angle, the chaos-monster would have been seen to shatter of her own accord, and her
> fragments move to their respective stations. Marduk and his whole generations of
> divinities were but particles of her substance. (287)

He proceeds to generalize mythologically: "From the perspective of the source [e.g. Tiamat in the *Enuma Elish*], the world is a majestic harmony of forms pouring into being, exploding, dissolving. But what the swiftly passing creatures experience is a terrible cacophony of battle cries and pain." Violence is thus not all that it seems to humans; it is creative and a normal part of the "cosmogonic cycle" (288).

Campbell elaborated upon the issues of war and violence in a 1967 lecture at Cooper Union College titled and reprinted as "Mythologies of War and

Peace." Campbell says it is "far easier to name examples of the mythologies of war rather than mythologies of peace," because

> conflict between groups [has] been normal to human experience, but there is also the cruel fact to be recognized that killing is the precondition of all living whatsoever: life lives on life, eats life, and would otherwise not exist. To some this terrible necessity is fundamentally unacceptable, and such people have, at times, brought forth mythologies of a way of perpetual peace. However, those have not been the people generally who have survived in what Darwin termed the universal struggle for existence. Rather, it has been those who have been reconciled to the nature of life on this earth. Plainly and simply: it has been the nations, tribes, and peoples bred to mythologies of war that have survived to communicate their life-supporting mythic lore to descendants. (169)[9]

Campbell notes that it is a "basic idea of practically every war mythology that the enemy is a monster and that in killing him one is protecting the only truly valuable order of human life ... one's own people" ("Mythologies" 171). Observing "in this literature" that "the enemy ... is handled ... pretty much as though he were subhuman," he quotes several lengthy passages from the Old Testament—one of the "two greatest works of war mythology in the West"— to "help us recognize that we have been bred to one of the most brutal war mythologies of all time" (174).[10]

Referring to the Israeli-Arab conflict, Campbell acknowledges that modern societies each have their "divinely authorized war mythology" ("Mythologies" 178) that "may yet explode our planet" (180). Despite the expression of such fear, in 1967, as the U.S. war in Vietnam escalated, Campbell lamented that "one of the great problems of" American society was the lack of psychological preparation for "youths" to become "warriors," leaving them "spiritually unprepared to play their required parts in this immemorial game of life and [unable] to bring their inappropriate moral feelings to support it" (172).

For Campbell, the mythologies of war are "affirmative" mythologies of "war as life, and life as war" ("Mythologies" 199), and, in them, the "monstrous precondition of all temporal life [i.e., killing] is affirmed with a will" (170). He is frankly contemptuous of the diametrically opposed "ascetic mythologies of peace" (198). Campbell derides the mythologies of peace—which he finds in strains of Christianity, Jainism, Buddhism, Taoism, and Confucianism—as being unnaturally ascetical in origin and life negating (186-92).

While Campbell would have disputed Wink"s ethical judgment, his work is nonetheless consistent with Wink's analysis; it can be fairly argued that Campbell's "mythologies of war" are all expressions of the single mythological archetype that Wink calls the MRV. Neither Campbell nor Lucas ever apparently discussed the mythologies of war with reference to *Star Wars*, although war figures prominently in both the story and the title. Given Campbell's scorn for the mythologies of peace and, most importantly, his bias that collective violence is part and parcel of both the natural, normal mythological and human conditions, it is unsurprising that he focused on the hero's journey in discussing *Star Wars*. Thus, as Wink predicts, "The myth [of redemptive violence] replays itself, without any awareness on the part of those who repeat it" or, one might add, those who watch it being played out in real life or on movie screens (*Powers* 51).

Conclusion: James William Gibson's "New War" and *Star Wars*

George Lucas began writing the script for *ANH* in January 1973, the same month the United States ceased offensive operations in Vietnam and announced its unilateral withdrawal (Gordon 74). Although not released until 1977, the film was produced in 1975, the year the last U.S. troops left Vietnam; the pro-U.S. South Vietnamese regime was completely defeated by April 30, 1975 (Collins 9).

In *Warrior Dreams: Violence and Manhood in Post-Vietnam America* (1994), sociologist James W. Gibson offers an analysis of post-Vietnam America that fits neatly with Wink's model.[11] Gibson asserts that America's "archetypal pattern [of] 'regeneration through violence' was broken with the defeat in Vietnam" (10). This loss undermined the *divine authority* of U.S. leadership and the warrior enterprise—igniting a cultural crisis. Concurrent with the loss of status for the warrior culture were the economic and social upheavals of the 1960s and 1970s, including the largely nonviolent civil rights, feminist, and antiwar movements (11–2). These struggles also represented a direct challenge to the Domination System and subverted the *divine legitimation* conferred by the MRV. As Smithsonian curator Mary Henderson writes of pre–*Star Wars* America, "Here was a culture that needed new stories to inspire and instruct it—stories that would speak to modern concerns and at the same time offer some timeless wisdom" (6).

From the psychic chaos of cultural crisis, Gibson claims, a refuge was created in "paramilitary culture and its New War fantasies" (12), that is, "a coherent mythical universe, formed by the repetition of key features in thousands of novels, magazines, films, and advertisements" (13). Gibson notes that the "fundamental narratives" of the New War "are often nothing but reinterpretations or reworking of archaic warrior myths" (12). He asserts:

> The vast proliferation of warrior fantasies represented an attempt to reaffirm the national identity. But it was also a larger volcanic upheaval of archaic myths, an outcropping whose entire structural formation plunges into deep historical, cultural, and psychological territories. These territories have kept us chained to war as a way of life; they have infused individual men, national political and military leaders, and society with a deep attraction to both imaginary and real violence. This terrain must be explored, mapped, and understood if it is ever to be transformed. (Gibson 14)

In Gibson's analysis, the *Star Wars* films constitute merely one, albeit prominent, element of the ongoing New War that began in the 1960s and is still being fought, sometimes with real bullets, over issues of "power, sex, race, and alienation" (14).

One telling anecdote he relates from the 1980s is that the men of an elite U.S. Navy, so-called counter-terrorism unit, SEAL Team 6—the apex of "the pyramid of warriors dedicated to maintaining [America's] cultural and national boundaries"—dubbed themselves the Jedi after the "spiritual fighters" in *Star Wars* (286; see also Meyer 99).

In conclusion, *Star Wars'* popular success is due in no small measure to its affirmation of widespread, profound assumptions about the supposed virtues and necessity of violence and war—Wink, Gibson, and, I think, even Campbell would all have agreed. Unlike stories rooted in the culturally dissonant mythologies of peace, *Star Wars* thus provides positive reinforcement about our place in the world and how society should and does function; that is, about our place in, and the functioning of, the Domination System. With their exceptional success, the *Star Wars* films are a good starting point to begin the exploration Gibson suggests. Once we begin to understand the insidious role of the MRV and war mythologies in our society, then, perhaps, we may reject them to reclaim ancient—and create new—mythologies of peace.

Notes for Chapter 4

1. See also Seabrook (205-6) for views expressed in 1997. Compare Lucas's remarks to those of Elmer Davis, WWII director of the Office of War Information: "The easiest way to inject propaganda ideas into most people's minds is to let it go in through the medium of an entertainment picture when they do not realize that they are being propagandized" (qtd. in Gibson 21).

2. It may be argued that World War II, for example, is *prima facie* evidence that these contradictions are, in fact, spurious. However, WWII (an outgrowth of the results of WWI—the "war to end all wars") set the stage not only for the violence and injustice that occurred during the war, including tens of millions of deaths; concentration camps; bombings of civilian population centers like London, Dresden, and Tokyo; and the use of nuclear weapons, but also for the Cold War. To follow just one Cold War thread, in 1979, the U.S. government funded militant Islamic fundamentalists in Afghanistan to purposely destabilize its comparatively moderate, pro-Soviet regime in order to provoke a Soviet invasion and hopefully give "to the USSR its Vietnam War," according to Zbigniew Brzezinski (qtd. in Blum 5). The USSR did invade Afghanistan and decades of war ensued, with the United States, in cooperation with Pakistan and Saudi Arabia, funding and arming *guerilla* fighters from around the world. Eventually, this led to the events of September 11, 2001, and all that has followed since.

3. Economic, political, and cultural elites promote the creation, propagation, and suppression of mainstream cultural texts according to their perceived interests; sometimes cynically. However, it is also true that they help reproduce the MRV, because they too believe it. For instance, several minutes of Frank Capra's Academy Award-winning film, *Lost Horizon*, were without apparent objection edited out of World War II versions of the film due to its pacifism. Dalton Trumbo's antiwar novel was also kept out of production during WWII with the complete agreement of Trumbo.

4. In discussing how "myths transform themselves," Levi-Strauss notes,

> These transformations—from one variant to another of the same myth, from one myth to another, from one society to another for the same myth or for different myths— bear sometimes on the framework, sometimes on the code, sometimes on *the message of the myth*, but without its ceasing to exist as such. Thus these transformations respect a sort of principle of conservation of mythical material, by which any myth could always come from another myth. (2: 256; emphasis added)

5. This is developed in both Campbell (*Power*) and in Henderson.

6. There are interesting parallels between the characters of Luke Skywalker and Marduk, the hero of the *Enuma Elish*. Marduk is the sun-god (Campbell, *Hero* 285). "*Luke*, as George Lucas himself must know, given his own surname, ... means 'Light,' the visual life nurturer of the cosmos," and the sun is a light that *walks* across the sky (Collins 2–3). Furthermore, as Marduk saves his father, Ea, from the wrath of Chaos (Tiamat), so Luke's father, Anakin (the product of a fatherless, if not a virgin, birth), is ultimately saved from the Dark Side of the Force by his son (Wink, *Engaging* 14; Wink, *Powers* 46; Lucas 61).

7. This is neither an argument for nor against realistic depictions of violence in film and television. While sanitized depictions of violence can make violence seem benign and convince individuals of an unfounded invulnerability, graphic depictions can also have a desensitizing effect that makes violence seem benign. On sanitized depictions of violence, see Gibson (22–5). On graphic depictions of violence, see Grossman (299–332).

8. The question of why ordinary people support despotic regimes is not as simple as it may seem. Philosopher David Hume observed, "that as Force is always on the side of the governed, the governors have nothing to support them but opinion. 'Tis therefore, on opinion only that government is founded; and this maxim extends to the most despotic and most military governments, as well as to the most free and most popular" (qtd. in Chomsky 352).

9. This short passage exemplifies the fallacious reasoning underlying Campbell's social Darwinism. Simply repeating the received cultural wisdom, Campbell offers scant justification for his assertion that "conflict between groups [has] been normal to human experience." Numerous scholars in a variety of disciplines have argued and offered evidence to the contrary; see, for example, LeShan's introduction, Kohn's chapter 2, and Grossman (1–39). Second, vegetarianism aside, the bare "cruel fact" of killing animals to eat simply has little explanatory power regarding the complex social phenomenon of human warfare. There are many species in which individual organisms survive by eating members of *other* species, but only a handful—mostly insects—can be said to engage in anything remotely resembling intraspecies war. On human biology, violence, and war, see the "Seville Statement on Violence" (also rpt. in Kohn Appendix). Third, as Campbell himself points out, Buddhism has at its core a mythology of peace. Nevertheless, it is one of the world's major religions and has been comparatively, if not entirely, successful in

transmitting a culture and practice of nonviolence. For recent critiques of evolutionary psychology see Rose, an excellent general treatment of social Darwinism is Lewontin.

10. Both Wink and Campbell argue that mainstream Christianity has largely rejected the mythology or gospel of peace exemplified and articulated by Jesus (Wink, *Powers*; Campbell, "Mythologies" 188-9).

11. Gibson makes no mention of Wink's work, and, thus, the use of Wink's terminology is solely mine.

Works Cited

Barthes, Roland. *Mythologies*. Selected and trans. Annette Lavers. New York: Noonday P, 1992.

Blum, William. *Rogue State: A Guide to the World's Only Superpower*. Monroe, ME: Common Courage P, 2000.

Campbell, Joseph. *The Hero with a Thousand Faces*. 2nd ed. Princeton: Princeton UP, 1968.

——. "Mythologies of War and Peace." *Myths to Live By*. New York: Arkana-Penguin, 1993. 169-200.

Campbell, Joseph, with Bill Moyers. *The Power of Myth*. Ed. Betty Sue Flowers. New York: Doubleday, 1988.

Chomsky, Noam. *Deterring Democracy*. New York: Verso, 1991.

Collins, Robert G. "*Star Wars*: The Pastiche of Myth and the Yearning for a Past Future." *Journal of Popular Culture* 11.1 (1977): 1-10.

"Force." *Merriam-Webster Online Dictionary*. 2005. 9 Oct. 2005 <http://www.m-w.com/cgi-bin/dictionary?book=Dictionary&va=force&x=0&y=0>.

Gibson, James William. *Warrior Dreams: Violence and Manhood in Post-Vietnam America*. New York: Hill & Wang, 1994.

Gordon, Andrew. "*Star Wars*: A Myth for Our Time," *Screening the Sacred: Religion, Myth, and Ideology in Popular American Film*, ed. Joel W. Martin and Conrad E. Ostwalt Jr. Boulder, Co.: Westview Press, 1995: 73-82.

Grossman, Lt. Col. Dave. *On Killing*. New York: Little, Brown, 1995.

Harmetz, Aljean. "Burden of Dreams." *George Lucas: Interviews*. Ed. Sally Kline. Jackson, MS: UP of Mississippi, 1999.135-144.

Henderson, Mary. Star Wars: *The Magic of Myth*. New York: Bantam, 1997.

Kohn, Alfie. *The Brighter Side of Human Nature*. New York: Basic Books, 1990.

Kuiper, Koenraad. "*Star Wars*: An Imperial Myth." *Journal of Popular Culture* 21.4 (1988): 77-86.

LeShan, Lawrence. *The Psychology of War*. Chicago: Noble P, 1992.

Levi-Strauss, Claude. *Structural Anthropology*. Trans. Claire Jacobson and Brook Grundfest Schoepf. Vol. 1. New York: Basic Books, 1963.

——. *Structural Anthropology*. 1963. Trans. Monique Layton. Vol. 2. New York: Basic Books, 1976.

Lewontin, R. C., Steven Rose, and Leon J. Kamin. *Not in Our Genes: Biology, Ideology, and Human Nature*. New York: Pantheon, 1984.

Lucas, George. *Star Wars: Episode I—The Phantom Menace: The Illustrated Screenplay.* New York: Ballantine, 1999.

"Palpatine." *Star Wars Databank.* 9 Oct. 2005 <http://www.starwars.com/databank/organization/theempire/>.

Meyer, David S. "Star Wars, *Star Wars,* and American Political Culture." *Journal of Popular Culture* 26.2 (1992): 99–115.

O'Quinn, Kerry. "The George Lucas Saga." *George Lucas: Interviews.* Ed. Sally Kline. Jackson, MS: UP of Mississippi, 1999. 98-134.

Rose, Hilary, and Steven Rose, eds. *Alas, Poor Darwin.* New York: Harmony, 2000.

Seabrook, John. "Letter From Skywalker Ranch: Why Is the Force Still With Us?" *George Lucas: Interviews.* Ed. Sally Kline. Jackson, MS: UP of Mississippi, 1999. 190-215.

"Seville Statement on Violence, Spain, 1986." *UNESCO (online).* 10 Oct. 2005 <http://www.unesco.org/cpp/uk/declarations/seville.pdf>.

Wink, Walter. *Engaging The Powers: Discernment and Resistance in a World of Domination.* Minneapolis: Fortress P, 1992.

——. *The Powers That Be: Theology for a New Millennium.* New York: Doubleday, 1998.

Religion

CHAPTER 5

"Hokey Religions and Ancient Weapons": The Force of Spirituality

Jonathan L. Bowen and Rachel Wagner

> Hokey religions and ancient weapons are no match for a blaster at your side, kid.
> —Han Solo, in A New Hope (1977)

The Star Wars films are well known for breathtaking special effects and aesthetic beauty, but there is also a spiritual reason behind their appeal. The films express the quest for meaning and purpose in a galaxy desperately needing balance. The quest for balance within the Force as the Jedi's singular most important goal is poignantly reflected in the story of Anakin Skywalker (Sebastian Shaw; Jake Lloyd; Hayden Christensen), Jedi Knight, father of Luke Skywalker (Mark Hamill), and known in his adulthood as the Sith Lord Darth Vader (David Prowse; James Earl Jones, voice). George Lucas has said that Anakin is the ultimate protagonist of the films, and, indeed, Anakin serves as a microcosm for the galaxy, so that his inner balance and spiritual well-being relate closely to that of the entire galaxy (Snider 1A–2A). Anakin is like Jesus in a Taoist world, a figure who falls from grace, unable to resist the Dark Side, but who ultimately fulfills the prophecy of bringing balance to the Force. The lessons that Anakin learns in the Star Wars galaxy "far, far away" are thematically similar to lessons articulated in more traditional philosophical and religious frameworks, such as Taoism, Buddhism, and Christianity, sharing some fundamental perspectives with these traditions and even functioning religiously for some viewers.

On Method

The question of religious influence on the *Star Wars* films is tricky, hardly helped by George Lucas's repeated insistence that any religious imagery is completely unintentional. The question taps into deep-seated academic debates about the relationship of a director's cultural, social, and experiential background to the film; about film as communication through image, text, and sound; about the viewers' role in creating meaning; and, indeed, about the complex relationships between culture and cultural artifact. As Graeme Turner has astutely observed, "film is not [just] one discrete system of signification" but is both "a cultural product" and a "social practice" (50). In short, it is difficult to say how much of any given film results from the director's own influence and how much should be attributed to the larger cultural systems that surround it.

Even given these qualifications, it would be a mistake to ignore the way that film *does* function religiously for some modern viewers, providing a sense of meaning and identity—and in our analysis—offering a vision of hoped-for balance in a chaotic, unbalanced world. John Lyden, who draws on Clifford Geertz's functional definition of religion, argues that film, like religion, can provide a set of symbols that mediate values, create motivations for behavior, provide a model of reality, and provide a narrative representing the way the world should be (45). Few films fit this definition better than the *Star Wars* series, which for decades has provided symbols, values, motivations, models, narratives, and hopes for millions of viewers, not to mention having produced a thriving community based upon these elements.

For Lyden, film can function as religion insofar as many viewers "desire alternate worlds because we find our own imperfect" (53). Film answers this need, showing us "how the world is as well as how it might be," offering an idealistic vision of a world in which things make sense, where justice and peace ultimately prevail (55). Jennifer E. Porter's observations (in chapter 6) rightly point out the difficulties of drawing the line between those who jokingly identify themselves as "Jedi Knights" and those with a "religious" conviction about this identity. Lyden cautions us that "questions about the 'truth' of religious beliefs must be bracketed by the religion scholar as they can never be definitively answered" (55). Perhaps the most we can say is that regardless of Lucas's intentions, the films *do* function religiously for some viewers. Providing analogues with other forms of religious experience is a helpful place to start to begin to understand this phenomenon.

Our analysis focuses on how the films offer viewers an articulation of the desire for balance, a theme that is important to many of the world's religious traditions and basic to Anakin's story. Our discussion focuses on thematic parallels between the films and select elements of Taoism, Buddhism, and Christianity, three religious traditions in which views about balance are clearly articulated, though, with more space, we could also have included elements of Hinduism, Jainism, Islam, and other traditions. With these cautions in mind, we provide a thematic analysis of the *Star Wars* films, pointing out how the films parallel other religious traditions in providing a model for viewing reality and crafting a picture of how the world should be. We especially focus on the notion that the *Star Wars* films, like traditional religious texts, describe a cosmos out of balance and in desperate need of healing, and we argue that, for some viewers, the films also nurture the development of values that motivate behavior. The question of whether or not the films' relationship to these religious traditions results from direct influence or reflects new synthetic cultural and religious processes in a modern multireligious age, we leave to the reader to decide

Taoism: The Balance of the Way

Taoism is rooted in the teachings of the sage Lao Tzu about the Tao (the Way) and the balance of yin (passive energy) and yang (active energy) within the Tao, although it is well known that Taoist teachings are much older than Taoism's great literary master. As John Blofield observes, "this [Taoist] perception of existence as a vast and timeless ocean of spotless purity upon which, through the interplay of dark and light, a myriad illusions play like ever-changing cloud formations or restless waves, is of such immense antiquity that none can say whence it first arose" (1). Many of the foundational tenets of Taoist philosophy still enjoy popularity, even though Taoist beliefs have largely been integrated into Confucian, Buddhist, and other Asian traditions such as *ch'i kung* (a modern Chinese program of self-exercise and therapy), not to mention the numerous schools of martial arts that are associated with Asian philosophies, such as *wu-shu* or *kung-fu*. As Liu Xiaogan quips, "The term Taoist may denote as much of an attitude as a person" (233).

The similarities between the Force and the Tao are instructive. As Xiaogan explains, early Taoism embraced several grounding principles: "that the Tao is the unique source of the universe and determines all things; that everything in the world is composed of positive and negative parts; that opposites always transform into each other; and that people should take no unnatural action (*wu-wei*) but follow the natural law" (232). Such a description sounds remarkably similar to the Force in *Star Wars*. The Tao and the Force are both nonmaterial in essence, infused within all things, and drive the movement of the world even though their existence cannot be directly perceived.[1]

In the *Star Wars* galaxy, the principle aim of the Jedi Knights is to understand and use the Force, which, as Obi-Wan Kenobi (Alec Guinness; Ewan McGregor) tells Luke, is "what gives the Jedi his power. It's an energy field created by all living things. It surrounds us and penetrates us. It binds the galaxy together" (*ANH*). In his teachings about the Force, Yoda (Frank Oz, voice) tells Luke that "life creates [the Force], makes it grow. Its energy surrounds us and binds us" (*The Empire Strikes Back*, 1980). The Force, like the Tao, is the energy that unites all of life together and directs it toward its appropriate end. The Force is light *and* dark; the Tao is yin *and* yang.

At first glance, the *Star Wars* worldview seems to partly defy the interconnectedness of dark and light supported in a Taoist perspective, instead presenting a rigidly dualistic division of light and dark: Anakin embraces the Dark Side but eventually returns to the Light Side; he is always completely devoted to either one or the other, and his moral value is easily determined based upon his allegiance. However, a closer reading reveals that Anakin, like other characters who inhabit the *Star Wars* world, contains within him constantly interacting opposites; his good choices are inextricably intertwined with other choices not so obviously benevolent, and his most redemptive act, saving Luke by destroying Palpatine (Ian McDiarmid), is itself undeniably violent and destructive. The palette of Taoist philosophy brings this interpretation into focus for film viewers, whether Lucas intended to import Taoist wisdom or not. Anakin's choices, far from being blanket choices for good or evil, reflect the complex amalgam of human experience and invite us as viewers to consider the difficulty of our own moral choices.

Such complexity is consistent with Taoist advice, as the *Tao Te Ching* explains: "The clearest Way seems obscure; / The Way ahead seems to lead backward" (chapter 41). Anakin indeed goes ahead in a way that seems "to lead backward." First he destroys the Jedi instead of the Sith, then later he destroys the Sith and paves the way for his son to reestablish the Jedi Order.[2] At the end of *Revenge of the Sith* (2005), Obi-Wan is disturbed by Anakin's choices, because he cannot yet see their larger implications. The Jedi Master says, "You were supposed to destroy the Sith, not join them! Bring balance to the Force, not leave it in darkness!" Anakin's actions suggest that perhaps the only way to restore balance in the galaxy is for him to join the Dark Side first, an experience that allows him to see both sides of the Force clearly, and to make choices that honor the complexity of the whole. Anakin's choice to embrace the Sith rather than simply destroy them may also hint at his persistent reluctance to see things in absolute dualisms, a perspective that allows him to fall but also allows for his ultimate redemption. Taoist wisdom teaches that in everything there lies the seed of its opposite, and such wisdom seems particularly applicable here.

The film also reflects features of one of the most widely emphasized teachings of Taoism, *wu-wei*, or nonaction and noncontention, the wisdom of which informs many schools of martial arts today. Those who understand *wu-wei* will act in a manner that flows naturally from the circumstances of the moment and accords with the Way. The *Tao Te Ching* explains that "[t]his is why sages abide in the business of non-action, and practice the teaching that is without words" (chapter 2). The Jedi are taught to value the strength of nonaction, so that every act flows naturally from the Force, based on the circumstances of the moment, as with a Jedi's ability to deflect laser blasts seemingly with little effort. Blofield describes Taoist wisdom of *wu-wei* as "avoiding action that is not spontaneous, acting fully and skillfully by all means but only in accordance with present need, being lively when required but never overstrenuous and certainly not strained, eschewing artfully calculated action and every activity stemming from profit motive" (10). Jedi Knights, too, are taught to pursue actions from a calm awareness of their surroundings with strength that "flows from the Force," as Obi-Wan tells Luke (*ANH*). In *Return of the Jedi* (1983), the ideal of *wu-wei* is reflected when Luke tells Han Solo (Harrison Ford) and Chewbacca (Peter Mayhew) to surrender their weapons to the Ewoks instead of trying to fight their way out. The violent response is most natural to Han, who prefers a "good blaster" to "hokey religions" based on beliefs about the Force, but Luke knows that nonaction and noncontention will eventually have more desirable effects. This insight is proven correct when they are able, as a result of nonviolence, to enlist the Ewoks' help in destroying the Imperial Forces guarding the shield generator on Endor. Luke's wisdom could have been drawn directly from the *Tao Te Ching*: "Sages enact non-action and everything becomes well ordered" (chapter 3).

The ideals of *wu-wei* are intricately related to the selflessness that is also a central goal of Taoism. Doing without doing enables one to let go of one's clinging to oneself and to flow more easily in accord with the Tao, letting its greater sense of the "way" become one's own. Anakin reflects this ideal in his childhood, as his mother Shmi (Pernilla August) relates: "He gives without any thought of reward. He knows nothing of greed" (*The Phantom Menace*). Taoist sages, also, "act with no expectation of reward" (*Tao Te Ching* chapter 2). By being selfless, the Taoist sage and the Jedi Master are capable of living very long lives, like Master Yoda, who lives 900 years. The Taoist teachings of sages like Ko Hung confirm that longevity is closely related to balance, spiritual perception, and meditation (Blofield 32–3).

Just as Taoists attempt to attain balance in a violent world, so also the Jedi Order seeks balance in a galaxy increasingly thrust into war and political unrest.[3] In *TPM*, when Qui-Gon Jinn (Liam Neeson) is fighting with Sith Lord Darth Maul (Ray Park), an energy field temporarily closes between the two in the middle of combat. While Maul paces back and forth like an animal awaiting his prey, Qui-Gon calmly kneels down and begins meditating, completely engaged in the moment and demonstrating the Taoist belief in *wu-wei* (Porter 31). In much the same way, Obi-Wan Kenobi allows Darth Vader to strike him down without even resisting, because he knows that noncontention will actually increase his power. He says to Vader, "You can strike me down but I will become more powerful than you can possibly imagine" (*ANH*). By letting go and becoming one with the Force through his very death, Obi-Wan increases his power by losing it, just as Taoist sages become immortal through the release of contingent, imperfect individual human existence when they become one with the Tao. Obi-Wan's refusal to fight affirms the wisdom of nonviolence achieved through an awareness of the interconnectedness of all things, dark and light.

Recognizing the value of non-action, both Taoists and Jedi Knights wish to avoid war and violence whenever possible.[4] The *Tao Te Ching* reads, "A military victory is not a thing of beauty" (chapter 31). Similarly, Yoda says to Luke, "Wars not make one great" (*ESB*). His words share the sentiments of a passage in the *Tao Te Ching*: "Those good at fighting are never warlike. / Those good at attack are never enraged" (chapter 68). Yoda embodies the wisdom of a Taoist sage in his attitude about war and violence, even though (and perhaps *because*) he is the most powerful Jedi in the galaxy.

When forced into combat, however, the Jedi willingly, if regretfully, use their powers to restore order and uphold justice. The recognition that violence is sometimes required in the overall balance of things is also acknowledged in the *Tao Te Ching*: "Those who are good at military action achieve their goal and then stop.... They achieve their goal but only because they have no choice" (chapter 30). The necessity of violence must be viewed within a pragmatic framework for Taoists, since its only justification is the eventual restoration of balance. As Yoda advises, "A Jedi uses the Force for knowledge and defense, never for attack" (*ESB*). This ideal is directly reflected in the films when Qui-Gon Jinn and Obi-Wan Kenobi venture to Naboo to negotiate with the Trade Federation Viceroy, Nute Gunray (Silas Carson) (*ROTS*). The wise Jedi, like the wise Taoist sage, will embrace *wu-wei* whenever possible as the most effective means of honoring the Tao and the Force.

Early in his life, Anakin seems to embody the values of *wu-wei* when he observes that "the Jedi are selfless ... they only care about others," whereas the Sith "think inward, only about themselves" (*ROTS*). However, as Anakin begins his journey toward the Dark Side, his actions accord less with the balance idealized within the Tao and the Force. In *Attack of the Clones* (2002), instead of being patient and following the ideals of *wu-wei*, Anakin impulsively rushes to his mother's aid on Tatooine, a choice that leads him to violence. When Anakin has joined the Dark Side to gain "the power to save Padmé" (Natalie Portman), as Palpatine promises him, she is no longer his to save.[5] As Anakin is increasingly motivated by his own desire for power and control, he is less able to view violence as a last resort. As Obi-Wan tells Anakin, his "lust for power" has lost him Padmé. Anakin's loss of balance culminates when he becomes a Sith Lord and leads the slaughter of the Jedi at the Temple. Anakin's own loss of insight is reflected in the larger loss of balance in the galaxy, which tips increasingly in the direction of darkness, gradually becoming engulfed by it. Put within Taoist terms, things have become imbalanced with too little yin and too much yang, as Anakin seeks greater and greater control over himself, over the galaxy, and over the Force.

Buddhism: Beyond Desire

The Buddhist doctrine of *upaya* supports the notion that the teachings of Buddhism should be disseminated according to the audience's spiritual, intellectual, and moral condition: "To the Hindu elite it presented its teachings in Sanskrit, to the Chinese in Chinese. In Tibet, where the pre-Buddhist religion of Bön contained magical features, it presented itself in a magical guise" (Abe 73). The earliest followers of the Buddha were eager to share the *dharma* (Buddhist wisdom) with "whoever was willing to accept it, in their own language, and in their own culture" (72). Therefore, if *Star Wars* indeed can be an effective means to learning the principles of nonattachment, it seems likely the Buddha would be all for it as a vehicle, regardless of authorial intent.[6]

Especially in its portrayal of the need for balance, the *Star Wars* films reflect marked thematic similarities with the ideals of Buddhist wisdom as taught by the great teacher Siddhartha Gautama and as developed by his numerous followers. The name of the films' greatest heroine, Padmé, seems to directly evoke the Buddhist mantra: "Om Mani Padme Hum," which means the "jewel in the lotus," the wisdom that can bloom even in the mud of life. Buddhism teaches about the interconnectedness of the entire world and embraces the Doctrine of the Middle Way, which eschews extreme solutions to the quest for enlightenment and urges moderation and balance in all things. The Buddha's first sermon, delivered at Deer Park, urges listeners to steer a careful course between "the two extremes of overindulgence and self-mortification," or between selfishness and self-destructiveness (Abe 108). As Walpola Rahula notes, Buddhism teaches that "all thoughts of selfish desire, ill-will, hatred and violence are the result of a lack of wisdom—in all spheres of life whether individual, social or political" (49). In the *Star Wars* films, the teachings of the Jedi Masters endorse a similar view of moderation and responsibility, urging students to recognize their relative place within the Force, to respect themselves and others, and to embrace nonviolence as the path of choice.

As the leading and oldest Jedi Master, Yoda functions as a wisdom teacher in the *Star Wars* galaxy, offering insights that, though not necessarily culled directly from Buddhist sources, certainly accord in certain respects with main principles of Buddhist teachings. Indeed, Yoda's great wisdom and desire to teach others may mark him as a sort of *bodhisattva*, one of the wisdom teachers of Mahayana Buddhism, who remains in the causal universe to raise others toward enlightenment. Just as Buddha attained enlightenment through medi-tation and deep thought, so too Yoda has reached an awareness of his rela-tionship to the Force and teaches his students about the Force as the unifying agent that permeates all things in the galaxy.

The Jedi Order expresses a particular affinity with Zen Buddhism, which combines a respect for martial arts and fencing with a strong emphasis on meditation and self-mastery (Star Wars: The Power of Myth). As Zen Buddhist priest Walter [Ritoku] Robinson has observed, in both Zen Buddhism and in the Jedi Order, there is an emphasis on the strong connection between mind and body. Combining aspects of Taoism, Buddhism, Asian fighting tech-niques, and teachings about the ch'i (inner spiritual force), Zen Buddhism rec-ognizes that action is as much a part of life as nonaction and acknowledges, like Taoist philosophy and the Jedi teachings, that there are times when one must use both body and mind to achieve balance (30).

Buddhism is grounded in the teachings of the Buddha, offering to adher-ents a basic guide to coping with the ubiquity of suffering in a material, causal world. As a spiritual master, Yoda also teaches about the origin of suffering and hints at a means for its elimination. As Yoda tells Anakin in TPM, "Fear leads to anger. Anger leads to hate. Hate leads to suffering." Anakin, however, struggles with the wisdom of moderation, expressed in the films as a respect for balance within the Force. When Anakin is afraid of losing his mother, he is unable to temper his emotions and rushes to Tatooine, where he becomes enraged at the Tusken Raiders who captured her and slays them in a fit of rage. As a mature Jedi, Anakin is expected to overcome attachments to people and to emotions, because, as Yoda warns Anakin, "Death is a natural part of life. Rejoice for those around you who transform into the Force. Mourn them, do not. Miss them, do not. Attachment leads to jealousy. The shadow of greed, that is" (ROTS). A Buddhist aims to extinguish the dichotomy between the self and the interconnected world, much as Jedi Master Yoda tries to feel the Force around him and within him, accepting death as natural within a changing, impermanent world.

The Four Noble Truths of Buddhism teach that one can overcome suffer-ing through overcoming desire, a teaching that the Jedi Masters teach the Jedi Knights, instructing them how desire can throw even Jedi Knights out of bal-ance. Such wisdom is echoed in the work of Thich Nhat Hanh, a modern Vietnamese Buddhist teacher: "Sometimes we are overwhelmed by the energy of hate, of anger, of despair. We forget that in us there are other kinds of en-ergy that can manifest also. If we know how to practice, we can bring back the energy of insight, of love, and of hope in order to embrace the energy of fear, of despair, and of anger" (191–2).

Relatively early in his career, Anakin tells Padmé that he wants to be "the most powerful Jedi ever" (AOTC). Once he has begun to acquire some power for himself, however, he again tells her, "I want more" (*ROTS*). The serenity of the Jedi way is not enough for Anakin. He continually lusts for more individual power, creating imbalance through his very quest for unexamined autonomy and through his inability to control his desires. As Edward Conze describes the Buddhist iteration of this problem, "The belief in a 'self' is considered by all Buddhists as an indispensable condition to the emergence of suffering. We conjure up such ideas as 'I' and 'mine,' and many most undesirable states result" (18).

Anakin's nightmare about his mother's fate and his ill-considered slaughter of the Tusken Raiders is followed by a nightmare about his own wife. His fierce attachment to Padmé and the consequent actions that follow from it are examples of why the Jedi Order forbids marriage or intimate relationships of any kind. Anakin is overwhelmed by desire and lusts for the power to prevent his nightmares from becoming real. He is out of balance, "always on the move," as Obi-Wan says of him (*ROTS*). He has fallen victim to the same sort of pain that the Buddha described in the Benares Sermon: "Truly, it is the thirst or craving, causing the renewal of existence, accompanied by sensual delight, seeking satisfaction now here, now there. That is to say, it is the craving for the gratification of the passions, or the craving for a future life, or the craving for success in this life. This, O monks, is the noble truth concerning the origin of suffering" (qtd. in Van Voorst 84). Anakin has abandoned the ideals of moderation, allowing sheer desire to rule him as he gives himself over to the quest for power and control.

The *Star Wars* films share with Buddhism a respect for meditation as a means to regain equilibrium in an unbalanced world. The principal aim of meditation is the elimination of dichotomous thinking to achieve (or recognize) balance, a perspective that fits neatly with teachings about nurturing balance in the Force through calm contemplation (Bortolin 158). When Luke asks Yoda how he is to know the good side from the bad, Yoda replies, "You will know when you are calm, at peace. Passive" (*ESB*). Through the calm of meditation, Yoda is able to connect with deceased Jedi Master Qui-Gon Jinn and, in so doing, embody the interconnectedness that is the fundamental nature of the Force (*ROTS*). By contrast, a lack of the ability to meditate quietly can have devastating consequences: Had Anakin properly meditated about his options while in the Jedi Temple waiting for Mace Windu (Samuel L. Jackson) to arrest Palpatine, he would have been able to let his desires pass through him and not cloud his judgment. Instead, Anakin is consumed by his desires and violates both Buddhist and Jedi teachings about balance and moderation.

Although the Jedi Order does not teach explicitly about rebirth, Jedi Knights are able to achieve unity with the Force upon death and transcend the material world of existence. Yoda tells Luke in *ESB*, "Luminous beings are we, not this crude matter." Such a teaching accords well with Buddhist teachings about enlightenment and the ability to transcend the limitations of mere causal reality. In support of this notion, Yoda tells Anakin that death is a part of life, not opposed to it (ROTS). In the Star Wars galaxy, enlightenment is possible only for a being strong in the Force who is able to transcend the material world and exist in spirit form after death, like Qui-Gon Jinn, Yoda, Obi-Wan Kenobi, and, ultimately, even Anakin Skywalker. Although not all forms of Buddhism teach about a transcendent plane of reality, many forms of Buddhism do adhere strongly to the notion that one must accept the impermanence of all things, and, in so doing, one can reach a higher realization about all being that allows one a sort of freedom from causality and enables one to live a life of balance in change. This recognition is sometimes described in terms of nonduality, so that "in Buddhism, the nonsubstantiality and emptiness of the notion of good and evil are clearly realized, and reification and substantialization of any sort are carefully rejected" (Abe 120). To be balanced is to desire *neither* good *nor* evil but to see beyond them both to something greater.

Anakin's loss of balance is reflected in his tendency to let his passions drive his choices, in his rage when crossed, in his unquenchable desire for power and control, and, ultimately, in the loss of his own identity when he is so eclipsed by darkness that he becomes Darth Vader and must encase his own body within a hard black shell. Clinging to embodiment in the crudest of forms, Anakin refuses the teachings of the Jedi Masters about letting go and becoming one with the Force, insisting on loyalty to either one side *or* the other. In so doing, Anakin rejects the possibility that he might view his own existence as shaped by the movement of something greater than himself. Not until Anakin finally realizes the emptiness of his selfish choices can he regain balance, loosening his grip on blind control, risking his own life to save his son, and symbolically removing his helmet to reveal his vulnerability.

Anakin's ultimate revelation can be expressed in light of Buddhist wisdom, when he realizes what modern Vietnamese Buddhist teacher Thich Nhat Hanh has expressed about human suffering and integration of the whole human: "In the case of Buddhism, we don't have to chase the evil spirit away; in fact we embrace the evil spirit, the energy of anger, the energy of despair, the energy of hate, the negative energies. Embraced by the energy of mindfulness, they are transformed. They don't need to be chased away" (191–2). According to this worldview, neither light *nor* dark exist as entities in and of themselves; instead, there are only ourselves, our choices, and our relationships. The Star Wars films show us in Anakin a profound example of the suffering that can result from ignorance and imbalance. Careening into a life dictated by violence and egoism, Anakin must take the hard road back to moderation, to peace, to balance, and to integration of the whole person.

Christianity: Good versus Evil

We end our discussion of religious thematic parallels with a discussion of Christianity, a religious tradition that, at least superficially, offers a markedly different approach from either Taoism or Buddhism to the relationship between light and dark. Given the ubiquity of Christian stories and ideas in American society, Christianity is also one of the most pertinent lenses to consider when attempting to assess what cultural influence Christian stories and beliefs may have played in the architecture of the film plots. Whether Lucas intended to, he has crafted a storyline with distinct thematic parallels to Christian stories about Jesus in the gospels.[7] However, with its stark dualism of light opposed to dark, of "us" opposed to "them," the films have the most in common with the gloomy, stylized apocalyptic dualism of John's *Revelation* on Patmos, in which forces of darkness battle with the forces of light in the end times. Despite the obvious thematic parallels with apocalypticism in the *Star Wars* films, Anakin's story ultimately undermines the rigid expectations of apocalyptic dualism, exhibiting for us a character who, in his own quest for balance, challenges such an obvious opposition of good and evil and invites us as viewers to see ourselves as capable of the same horror and the same final redemption.

The parallels between Anakin and the Jesus of the gospels are apparent. Jesus and Anakin both came into the world in desert environments in small communities. Anakin Skywalker begins life as the result, like Jesus, of an apparently virgin birth. As the young boy depicted in *TPM*, Anakin is identified as the "Chosen One" who is to "bring balance to the Force" according to an ancient prophecy. Shmi Skywalker, Anakin's mother, is a slave on Tatooine when Jedi Master Qui-Gon Jinn discovers the boy and remarks, "The Force is unusually strong with him, that much is clear." When asked who fathered the boy, Shmi responds, "There was no father. I carried him, I gave birth.... I can't explain what happened." Qui-Gon believes that Anakin could have been conceived by midi-chlorians, because a very high concentration of them appears in his blood.[8] This theory adds further weight to Qui-Gon's opinion that Anakin is the Chosen One who can bring balance to the Force, since such a high concentration of midi-chlorians bodes well for Anakin's ability to tap into the Force.

Just as Jesus could perform miracles, so Anakin performs miraculous feats, such as successfully racing pods on Tatooine, an act which Qui-Gon claims is impossible without Jedi reflexes. When Anakin is tested by the Jedi Council, he is able to discern what objects appear on a holographic reader without seeing them as the Jedi Masters await his answers. He also harnesses the Force to destroy the Droid Control Ship above Naboo, thus freeing the planet of Trade Federation oppression. Like Jesus, Anakin is expected to do more than perform miracles. Whereas many early Christians expected Jesus to save the Jews from the Romans, so the Jedi hope that Anakin will fulfill the prophecy of bringing balance to the Force by destroying the Sith. Similarly, as many Christians, following in the tradition of Paul, interpret Jesus' victory over death as the means by which he freed humanity from the power of sin and death, so Qui-Gon Jinn, Obi-Wan Kenobi, and others hope that Anakin will restore balance to the Force by defeating the growing power of the Dark Side.

Neither the gospel writers nor the *Star Wars* films have anything to say about Jesus's or Anakin's teenage years, but when the two appear again as adults, they exhibit markedly different characters. Jesus emerges as a respected leader with a loyal following of disciples who think he is the Son of God, whereas Anakin is less like the self-assured teacher and healer of Galilee and more like a Shakespearean protagonist, riddled by self-doubt and subject to fits of passion and rage. Whereas the gospels present Jesus as a leader who declines Satan's offer of earthly power (Luke 4: 1-13), in AOTC, Anakin is presented as rebellious, impatient and insolent, with an insatiable lust for power and control. The most obvious manifestation of this rage is Anakin's brutal slaughter of Tusken Raiders, including women and children, when he realizes that they have captured and killed his mother. Whereas Jesus of the gospels teaches a message grounded in prophetic demands for social justice, Anakin is increasingly driven by a desire for sheer selfish power at virtually any price.

Having forsaken earlier loyalties to the Light Side for the promise of power on the Dark Side, Anakin brutally defeats Count Dooku (Christopher Lee), cutting off both of his forearms (*ROTS*). In the midst of the battle, he grabs his opponent's lightsaber and holds his own blue lightsaber in one hand and Dooku's red lightsaber in the other. At that precise moment, Palpatine incites him to end Dooku's life: "Kill him. Kill him now." Anakin's handling of the two sabers simultaneously represents his own moral crossroads between good (blue) and evil (red). Thinking he must choose *either* one weapon *or* the other, he chooses to kill Dooku, a defenseless prisoner, a fateful decision that confirms Anakin's fall into the Dark Side and further reifies the categories of dark and light.

Palpatine is as close to the Devil in the *Star Wars* galaxy as anyone could get and comfortably plays the role of the tempter, the accuser, and the living emblem of darkness. Rising into galactic power like the beast of John's *Revelation*, a creature with malicious designs for undisputed rule, Palpatine has no redeeming qualities from a Christian viewpoint, though he earns reluctantly yielded admiration for his brilliance in battle and his flair for strategy.[9] Palpatine successfully serves as a metonym for undistilled evil, opposed to the Light Side absolutely. Indeed, the introduction of Palpatine alongside Anakin/Darth Vader calls viewers to carefully compare the two and hints at Anakin's more nuanced characterization as one who might challenge the reified categories of light and dark.

Palpatine reveals to Anakin that he knows the powers of the Dark Side, and he plays upon Anakin's affections by implying that he can help Anakin save Padmé by using the "unnatural" powers of the Dark Side to prevent her death. In his own metaphorical desert of temptation, Anakin cannot resist Palpatine's offer and agrees to serve him, a fateful decision that further reveals Anakin's contrast to Jesus: He has chosen what Jesus rejected and has been tempted by his fierce desire for control. Before long, Anakin has murdered younglings on holy ground inside the Jedi Temple, killed the Separatist leaders on Mustafar, and aggressively confronted his own master, mentor, and best friend, Obi-Wan Kenobi. Anakin's fall into darkness is portrayed through a poignant visual metaphor: Mustafar, a volcanic planet with lava flowing every-where and dark ash clouding the skies, looks much like the popular Christian vision of hell. After falling to the Dark Side, Anakin has descended onto a planet that outwardly mirrors his own internal spiritual and emotional imbal-ance. Anakin's choices are cemented when he watches Jedi Master Mace Windu locked in combat with Supreme Chancellor Palpatine. Anakin waits until Mace decides he must kill Palpatine and only then intervenes on Pal-patine's side, demonstrating his loyalty toward the Dark Side (ROTS).

When Palpatine is on the verge of killing Luke for the second time, Anakin finally intervenes and saves his son, hurling the emperor into a reactor shaft. This dramatic event thematically resembles the capture and destruction of the beast in John's Revelation, who is similarly "thrown alive into the lake of fire that burns with sulphure (Rev. 19:20). Palpatine's fate also resonates with the fate of the dragon defeated by Michael and thrown into the abyss, "so that he would deceive the nations no more" (Rev. 20). This event defines Anakin's rejection of his identity as Darth Vader and signifies a return to the Light Side, allowing Anakin, through analogy, to play the role of God's angel, defeating Satan and casting him away. Indeed, read in the light of John's Revelation, it is easy to laud Anakin's shift in loyalty and close the book (or film) confident that justice has been served and Anakin redeemed.

But is such a simple reading the richest one? Given the film's strong the-matic affinities with Taoism and Buddhism, two religio-philosophical tradi-tions that defy easy dualistic distinctions, should viewers not look a bit more closely at what the film may be saying about the true nature of the Force and, by extension, about balance between light and dark? In addition to the Taoist and Buddhist ideas contained in the Star Wars films' worldview, Anakin's final choice provides a crucial clue that a rigid dualistic reading of the films' presen-tation of the Dark Side and the Light Side is too simplistic. Anakin cannot be defined solely through his association with the Dark Side or with the Light Side, but only through a complex consideration of his entire life, which reso-nates with both. He is Anakin and Vader and remains both in the end, re-claiming his identity as Luke's father but unable to even breathe for long without his black shell. Through an act of loyalty and love to his son, Anakin enacts his own redemption, returning to the Light Side and embodying a personal return of the Jedi that reflects his shift from Sith Lord to Jedi Knight, a choice shaped and determined precisely by his fall into darkness.

Thus, Anakin's fulfillment of the prophecies is achieved, but not in the same way as followers of Jesus saw him fulfilling the prophecies about his messianic nature. Whereas the gospels depict a savior who saves through his own passive death, Anakin fulfills the prophecy in a much more complex fashion: He indeed restores balance to the Force, but only by first destroying Alderaan and all its inhabitants, throwing the entire galaxy into disarray, and defeating and killing Palpatine. This messianic figure resembles the Lamb portrayed in John's *Revelation* more than the Jesus of the gospels, since both the Lamb and Vader wreak horrible vengeance, and both save others only through violent annihilation of their enemies.[10] However, as we have shown, the *Star Wars* films resist a simplistic dualism of light versus dark, good versus evil. Anakin/Vader is a figure who saves, but in a very tumultuous, human fashion, and who defeats his enemies, but only by recognizing the enemy within himself, and who, even in his most glorious moment, is less than completely admirable, since he saves his son and the galaxy only after years of abhorrent behavior and only through murdering others. Balance, it seems, is not an idyllic fantasy of easy peace, but comes at a heavy price: Within each of us there lurks both a potential savior and a beast. Any enemy we kill was once a boy or girl, like young Anakin, trying his best to find love and a sense of belonging. Denying a reification of light and dark, good and evil, the *Star Wars* films portray the Force as encompassing both, inviting us instead to strive for balance, making the best choices we can.

"May the Force Be with You": *Star Wars* as Religion

The *Star Wars* films exhibit some intriguing thematic parallels with Taoism, Buddhism, and Christianity, sharing with them an emphasis on the importance of balance and a recognition of the complexity of human moral experience. However, in addition to providing some of the content of religious experience, one can also see that the films function as a religion for some viewers. Indeed, if we utilize John Lyden's definition of religion, then such a designation seems hard to avoid. We have shown already how the *Star Wars* films fulfill two of the items in Lyden's list: they provide a model of reality (the Force in relationship to the galaxy) and a narrative for how the world should be (Dark Side and Light Side in balance). By looking at the activities of the *Star Wars* fan community, we now show how the films also fulfill the remaining items in Lyden's taxonomy: providing for fans a set of symbols that mediate values and creating motivations for their behavior.

Star Wars fans examine the films and their symbolism in as much detail, and with as much dedication, as many devotees examine their own sacred texts. Every possible interpretation, contradiction, or implication is discussed endlessly among the fans at Internet forums, which have become in some ways the functional equivalent of Bible study groups. Although some of the discussion topics are fun and frivolous, focusing on such topics as the short life of R4-P17 in ROTS, many fans are also interested in seriously discussing the greater moral implications of the characters' actions and how the philosophy of the Jedi functions within the Star Wars galaxy, including how it can apply to life on earth, in our own Milky Way galaxy. Especially when viewed in light of thematic parallels with other religious traditions, the films' representation of the Force points toward an overall argument for balance, perhaps the strongest mediating value of the entire Star Wars mythology.

In addition to providing a moral framework, the films also offer a sense of group identity. Star Wars Webmasters serve what may be deemed a religious role in the fan community, providing fans with news about the greater Star Wars universe and of fan projects. Functioning in some ways very much like ministers, the Webmasters have a wide reach and can sway fans with their editorials and views. StarWars.com is like a virtual Catholic Church for Star Wars fans, offering a center for discussion and serving as the source of many important announcements. As with any religious group, not all fans agree about the way the Web site should be run. Most notably, in a postmodern quasi-Protestant move, when Lucasfilm revealed that fans would have to tithe for the all-access part of the site, Hyperspace, many fans felt their allegiance to the Official Site wane.

Followers of Star Wars are, like followers of other religious traditions, motivated to practice certain behaviors and rituals as part of their group identity. Fans have long referred to the first Star Wars trilogy affectionately as the "Holy Trilogy," departing from one another's company by saying, "May the Force be with you." The most devoted groups see their dedication to the films as a motivation to participate in charity or other community events. One of the most committed and well organized sects of Star Wars fandom is the 501st Legion, which is a group of more than 2,500 Star Wars fans worldwide spanning twenty-one countries ("501st Charter"). Members own various Imperial or Sith costumes and (ironically, given their costume choices) participate in charity and volunteer work. Some fans even create new virtual communities, as is the case with the 501st Legion. Best known for their Stormtrooper-costumed fans, the 501st is divided into garrisons, squads, outposts, and detachments throughout the world that form Star Wars fan communities that meet to watch the movies, help local charity events, attend conventions, or discuss costuming. The 501st even handled much of the security for Lucasfilm's officially authorized Star Wars Celebration III in Indianapolis, Indiana, before the premiere of *ROTS* in 2005. If religious groups can be defined by their sense of community identity in association with moral beliefs, rituals, and charitable acts, then the 501st surely should be defined in this way.

In the twenty-first century, thousands of *Star Wars'* devotees are fighting for official religious recognition. As Jennifer Porter explains in chapter 6, an e-mail campaign circulated in 2001 asking *Star Wars* fans in Australia and England to mark their religion as "Jedi Knight" on census reports. The grassroots effort forced the U.K. Census Bureau to take the movement seriously enough to provide a code for Jedi Knight on the census forms so that the results could be effectively tabulated. Given the resulting figures,[11] the Jedi "religion" would rank fourth in the United Kingdom among all religions if it were officially recognized. Even given the qualifications Porter rightly admits we must place on these results, they can hardly be ignored completely. Furthermore, when viewed in light of a functional definition of religion, such as the one embraced by Lyden and Clifford Geertz, the census figures encourage a serious reconsideration of what criteria are pertinent when determining what groups should be deemed worthy of societal recognition as members of a religion.

Conclusion

The idea that a film series could spur religious devotion may seem odd to some people, but there seems to be no logical reason why a book should be able to serve as the central element of religious teaching and not a film series, especially since proponents argue that *Star Wars* offers as relevant a guide for living as any other religious book. John Lyden has argued persuasively that film can function as religion for some people, claiming that "what we have always called 'religion' is identified by its function in society," and that "this function can be met even by cultural phenomena not normally called 'religions'"(3). The larger question of how one should understand new religious experience in popular culture is beyond the scope of this essay, but it is more than clear that the *Star Wars* films share some fundamental religious themes with some of the world's greatest religious traditions and, furthermore, that many *Star Wars* fans exhibit the same passion, devotion, and sense of community as followers of these traditional religions.

The intense devotion of *Star Wars* fans, when viewed in light of the films' expression of the crucial need for balance within the galaxy, strongly points toward our own societal feelings of imbalance in a world increasingly saturated with violence and mad quests for individual power at the expense of others. Furthermore, the willingness of some fans to dress up as Stormtroopers and even as Darth Vader suggests that there is something particularly compelling about this would-be villain turned savior and his compatriots. One might even go so far as to suggest that such a savior just may be more palatable than a wholly good savior, as we watch our own world crumble under the whims of men driven by impulse and desire and can only hope for their enlightenment. If the teachings of Taoism, Buddhism, Christianity, and the *Star Wars* films all call for awareness of our connectedness to one another and urge thoughtful consideration of the imbalance created by violent acts toward others, does it really matter if practitioners express their devotion through quiet contemplation in nature, through worship in a shrine or church, through meditation, through viewing movies, interacting with a Web site, or through donning costumes and attending community events? The Force, it seems, can take many different forms, and each of us, just like Anakin, must chart our courses in our own galaxy with the utmost care.

Notes for Chapter 5

1. The *Tao Te Ching* describes the Tao in a way that sounds very much like the Force: "Look for it and it cannot be seen / Listen for it and it cannot be heard / But use it and it will never run dry!" (chapter 35).

2. Anakin does accomplish this goal in future novels authorized by Lucasfilm, specifically the *Jedi Academy Trilogy* by Kevin J. Anderson. See also the *Star Wars: The New Jedi Order* series of books.

3. The background of violence and war in the *Star Wars* movies resembles the tumultuous sociopolitical environment of ancient China during the Warring States Period and the development of such religious and philosophical traditions as Confucianism and Taoism during this period.

4. When the Republic uses its newly created clone army to protect itself from the Separatist droid army, Yoda knows the Republic is in trouble. He says, "The shroud of the Dark Side has fallen. Begun, the Clone Wars have." Similarly, Lao Tzu writes: "Wherever an army resides, thorns and thistles grow" (chapter 30). Sure enough, the standing army of the Republic soon brings about the destruction of democracy in the galaxy.

5. The *Tao Te Ching* says of the Way, "Those who grab hold of it lose it," a statement also useful in describing power in the *Star Wars* galaxy (chapter 64).

6. Works such as Matthew Bortolin's *Dharma* support such a popular reading.

7. Of course, the films also have some intriguing parallels with material from Jewish tradition. Notably, the name "Anakin" is very close the Hebrew term "Anakim," which refers to an ancient pre-Canaanite tribe known for its warlike characteristics, eventually expelled by Joshua from the land (Num. 13:33). The Anakim were closely associated by tradition with the giants of the antediluvian period (Gen. 6:4) and, by some, with the Philistine giants of the David and Goliath stories (I Sam. 17–22). If Lucas did choose this name intentionally, the resonance of Darth Vader with the giants of antiquity is compelling and apt. Apart from the basic similarities between Christian apocalypticism and Jewish apocalypticism, a study of thematic parallels with Judaism in the films is beyond the scope of this chapter.

8. Midi-chlorians are essentially an intermediary between the Force and an individual, so the higher the concentration of the microscopic beings in one's blood, the greater the potential and ease for that person to tap into the Force.

9. Actor Ian McDiarmid quipped in a *BBC* interview that Palpatine's only redeeming quality is his patronage of the arts.

10. For a readable introduction to apocalyptic literature, see Collins, *Crisis and Catharsis.*

11. In Australia and New Zealand, 120,000 people marked "Jedi" as their official religion (Perrott). In the United Kingdom, 390,000 people declared themselves part of the Jedi faith, with up to 2.6 percent of respondents in some areas, like Brighton and Hove, allying themselves with the Force ("'Jedi'").

Works Cited

"501st Charter." *501st Legion Official Web Site.* 14 June 2005. <http://www.501st.com/documents/501stcharter.htm>.

Abe, Masao. "Buddhism." *Our Religions.* Ed. Arvind Sharma. San Francisco: Harper, 1993. 69–138.

Anderson, Kevin J. *Champions of The Force. Star Wars: The Jedi Academy Trilogy.* Vol. 3. New York: Spectra Publishing, 1994.

——. *The Dark Apprentice. Star Wars: The Jedi Academy Trilogy.* Vol. 2. New York: Spectra Publishing, 1994.

——. *Jedi Search. Star Wars: The Jedi Academy Trilogy.* Vol. 1. New York: Spectra Publishing, 1994.

Blofield, John. *Taoism: The Road to Immortality.* Boston: Shambhala, 2000.

Bortolin, Matthew. *The Dharma of Star Wars.* Boston: Wisdom, 2005.

Collins, Adela Yarbro. *Crisis and Catharsis: The Power of the Apocalypse.* Philadelphia: Westminster, 1984.

Conze, Edward. *Buddhism: Its Essence and Development.* New York: Harper, 1959.

Genesis, Book of. *The Holy Bible.* New Revised Standard Version. New York: American Bible Society, 1989.

Hanh, Thich Nhat. *Going Home: Jesus and Buddha as Brothers.* New York: Riverhead Books, 1999.

"'Jedi' Would Be 4th Faith if Permitted in Census." *Times Online* 13 Feb. 2003. 17 June 2005 <http://www.timesonline.co.uk/article/0,,1-576670,00.html>.

John, David, ed. Star Wars: *The Power of Myth.* New York: Dorling Kindersley, 1999.

Lucas, George. Interview with Bill Moyers. "Of Myth and Men." *Time* 26 Apr. 1999.

Luceno, James, et al. *Star Wars: The New Jedi Order.* Books 1–18. New York: Ballantine, 1999–2003.

Luke, Book of. *The Holy Bible.* New Revised Standard Version. New York: American Bible Society, 1989.

Lyden, John. *Film as Religion.* New York: New York UP, 2003

McDiarmid, Ian. Interview with Anwar Brett. "Ian McDiarmid, *Star Wars: Episode III.*" *BBC Web Site.* 12 June 2005. <http://www.bbc.co.uk/films/2005/05/18/ian_mcdiarmid_star_wars_episode_iii_interview.shtml>.

Perrott, Alan. "Jedi Order Lures 53,000 Disciples." *New Zealand Herald Online* 31 Aug. 2002. 17 June 2005 <http://www.nzherald.co.nz/index.cfm?ObjectID=2352142>.

Porter, John M. *The Tao of* Star Wars. Atlanta, GA: Humanics, 2003.

Rahula, Walpola. *What the Buddha Taught.* New York: Grove, 1959.

Revelation, Book of. *The Holy Bible.* New Revised Standard Version. New York: American Bible Society, 1989.

Robinson, Walter [Ritoku]. "The Far East of *Star Wars.*" Star Wars *and Philosophy: More Powerful Than You Can Possibly Imagine.* Ed. Kevin S. Decker and Jason T. Eberl. Chicago: Open Court Publishing, 2005. 29–38.

Samuel, Book of. *The Holy Bible.* New Revised Standard Version. New York: American Bible Society, 1989.

Snider, Mike. "*Star Wars* Universe Revolves around Vader." *USA Today* 22 Apr. 2005.

Tao Te Ching. Readings in Classical Chinese Philosophy. Trans. Philip J. Ivanhoe and Bryan W. Van Norden. 2nd ed. Indianapolis: Hackett Publishing Company, 2005. 157–201.

Turner, Graeme. *Film as Social Practice.* London: Routledge, 1988.

Van Voorst, Robert E. *Anthology of World Scriptures.* Belmont, CA: Wadsworth, 2003.

Xiaogan, Liu. "Taoism." *Our Religions.* Ed. Arvin Sharma. San Francisco: Harper, 1993. 229–290.

CHAPTER 6

"I Am a Jedi": *Star Wars* Fandom, Religious Belief, and the 2001 Census

Jennifer E. Porter

According to *Statistics New Zealand*, 53,715 New Zealanders listed "Jedi" as their religion in the 2001 census. More than four hundred thousand others throughout the United Kingdom, Australia and Canada joined them. Fans and skeptics alike agree that almost all of these half-million people were joking—but some of them were not. For some fans, *Star Wars* provides genuine spiritual inspiration. What does it mean, however, to suggest that some fans are spiritually inspired by *Star Wars*? According to sociologist of religion Wade Clark Roof, spirituality in contemporary society is "fluid, multilayered, and to a considerable extent personally achieved." Spiritual inspiration in this context is therefore about finding a connection to something transcendent, however personally defined, that connects the individual to something greater than the self; it is also about finding a source of values and meaning that resonates with one's own sense of inner awareness and the development of a sense of personal integration that helps make sense of the self and its place in the universe in the face of our fragmented, disenchanted, and commodified world (35).

Although *Star Wars* itself is a commodity successfully sold to millions worldwide, this essay suggests that it has also become the means by which some fans live, experience, and express their spiritual lives. Drawing upon participant-observation fieldwork, questionnaires, and online survey results, this paper suggests that the *Star Wars* saga has been extremely influential, both among those with traditional religious affiliations and those who self-identify as "Jedi." This paper also argues for the importance of taking the impact of *Star Wars* on religious belief seriously. To date, there are only a few scholarly works that explore in depth the influence of popular culture on people's religious lives.[1] Partly, this stems from the refusal of scholars and the general public to credit the idea that popular culture can *have* such a serious impact and the conviction on the part of some that popular culture ought not to impact people's spiritual lives in any meaningful way. The overwhelming media response to the Jedi census data, for example, and the response of almost everyone else to whom I spoke following the release of that data was incredulity and ridicule. In exploring the religious beliefs of *Star Wars* fans, this paper therefore serves to highlight the significant impact that popular culture can have on religiosity. Yes, *Star Wars* is a movie franchise; and yes, it has had a real, deep, and lasting impact on the lives of many fans.

The *Star Wars* Saga

As discussed elsewhere in this volume, the original *Star Wars* film as written and directed by George Lucas was released to theatres in 1977. It was initially followed by two sequels, making up the so-called holy trilogy, and then more recently by the films of the prequel trilogy. Numerous scholars have explored the mythic dimensions of the storylines in these films, among them Steven Galipeau (2001), Andrew Gordon (1995), and Michael J. Hanson and Max S. Kay (2001). The story lines involve classic mythic patterns: the hero's journey, the struggle between good and evil, and temptation, fall, and redemption. There is a mysterious Force that influences events and that can be tapped into by the Jedi, who are the guardians of peace in the galactic republic. Luke Skywalker (Mark Hamill), the hero of the original trilogy, learns the ways of the Force and becomes a Jedi, eventually toppling an evil empire and restoring peace and harmony to the galaxy. Anakin Skywalker, the hero of the prequel trilogy, surrenders to temptation and falls from grace, choosing to follow the Dark Side of the Force, and awaits the redemption that comes at the end of the original trilogy. According to George Lucas, he deliberately modeled his story in part on patterns drawn from world mythology, especially those identified by mythographer Joseph Campbell in his classic study *The Hero with a Thousand Faces* (1949). These patterns have been carefully mapped by Kristin Brennin (2004) and Muriel Verbeeck (2004), among others. The mythic dimensions of *Star Wars* have inspired and continue to inspire millions of fans worldwide.

The 2001 Census

The popularity and appeal of *Star Wars* for fans can be seen in the success of an email campaign launched one week before the March 2001 New Zealand census. At that time, a chain email letter began circulating encouraging people to list Jedi as their religion on their census forms. The email read, in part,

> if ... you believe in no one specific religion or just simply object to answering that particular question, then please consider the following alternative ... we are trying to

encourage people to tick the "other" box and then fill their religion in as "JEDI"—all *Star Wars* fans will understand, but the point of the exercise is two-fold ...

1. if 8000 people throughout New Zealand do this then JEDI will become an officially recognized religion which would be a laugh, and

2. it's a bit of an experiment in the power of email, as that has been our primary means of communication.... May the Force be with you ("The Original Email" 2001).

Phrased as a joke, a political protest against the religion question on the census, and as an experiment in the power of email, this campaign was clearly not intended to appeal solely to those who might genuinely have made *Star Wars* the central focus of their spiritual lives. It was aimed at anyone who wanted to poke fun at the government and who might also want to make a statement about his or her *Star Wars* fandom. The campaign was overwhelmingly successful. Despite threats from the governments of New Zealand and Australia to level fines of up to £1,000 against people providing false information on their census forms, 53,715 New Zealanders listed Jedi as their religion. The following month, the campaign spread to the United Kingdom, where 390,000 people listed Jedi on their census forms ("Jedi Would Be 4th"). In May 2001, 20,000 Canadians followed suit ("Some 20,000 Canadians").[2] They were joined in turn by 70,509 Australians in August 2001 (Perrott).

There is no real way to know for sure how many of these half a million people were serious in claiming Jedi as their religious faith. All we can assume is that most of them were joking or acting to obstruct the collection of religious information by the census office. According to the best estimate of Australian *Star Wars* Appreciation Society President Chris Brennan, for example, only about 5,000 out of the 70,000 Australians who claimed to be Jedis were probably serious, approximately 7.5 percent of the total (Perrott). The basis for his estimate, however, is unknown. In my own survey results of *Star Wars* fans, 75 percent (9/12) of those who actually wrote Jedi on their census forms identified themselves as genuine followers of the Jedi path, seeing themselves as representatives of the faith and practice epitomized by the fictional Jedi of Lucas's *Star Wars* saga. The other 25 percent of the census-declared Jedis who participated in my survey identified the Jedi path as a genuine religion (2/12) or philosophy (1/12) but did not admit to following it themselves. Those in the survey who self-identified as Jedi but who either did not participate in the 2001 census or who did participate but did not write Jedi on their census forms ranged from 7.9 percent (3/38) of respondents to a questionnaire distributed at a *Star Wars* Weekend at Walt Disney World Resort to 12.8 percent (21/164) of respondents to an online survey posted on my Web site.

Now, indulging for a moment in sheer speculation and fantasy, if we halved the smallest figure of 7.9 percent mentioned above, for caution's sake, and applied the remaining 3.95 percent to the 534,224 self-declared Jedis in the 2001 census, we would have over 21,000 Jedi believers throughout Canada, the United Kingdom, Australia, and New Zealand. If we wanted to be even more cautious and took a simple 1 percent of the total number, we would still have over 5,000 Jedi believers. Becoming even more cautious, we could take a simple 0.001 percent of the total number, leaving us with a mere 534 genuine Jedi believers in four countries. And yet, this number is still significantly larger than the membership of some new religious movements that have received serious scholarly attention. Furthermore, this figure does not touch on the number of Jedis who might live in the United States (a country whose census does not ask questions about religion). Nor does it touch on those who do not self-identify as Jedi but who nonetheless have been strongly influenced by Star Wars in their religious beliefs.

The Impact of Star Wars on the Spiritual Lives of Fans

So what do fans mean when they claim to be Jedis? What impact has Star Wars had for those who do not claim to be Jedis, but nonetheless acknowledge that Star Wars has influenced their religious beliefs? In May of 2003, I attended a Star Wars Weekend event at Walt Disney World Resort in Orlando, Florida, and handed out questionnaires to fans waiting in line to get autographs from Star Wars actors.[3] Based upon the results of this preliminary study, I designed a more detailed questionnaire, which I subsequently put on my Web site in July 2003. I then posted the URL address to the discussion forum affiliated with the Official Star Wars Web Site (<http://www.starwars.com>). Thirty-eight people filled out the survey at Walt Disney World. One hundred and sixty-four fans filled out the online survey.

Although this is an admittedly small sample, based upon these responses, it is possible to identify three broad categories of influence on the spiritual lives of Star Wars fans. First, there are those who identified no influence whatsoever or who identified nonspiritual influences, such as choice of career, love of films or science fiction, or more abstract influences, such as love of justice, equality, and tolerance.[4] Second, there are those who identified clear spiritual influences, while simultaneously affirming a commitment to another spiritual path. Third, there are those who were so influenced by the themes in Star Wars that it has led them to adopt what they call the Jedi path. With reference to the first category, 41.5 percent (68/164) of online respondents chose either not to comment on any influences Star Wars may have had on their lives, to deny any influence, or to identify influences nonspiritual in nature. In the second category, 40.2 percent (66/164) of the total respondents identified some spiritual or philosophical influence of Star Wars on their lives. And, in the final category, 18.3 percent (30/164) of the total respondents were so influenced by Star Wars that they made the Jedi path the central focus of their spiritual lives.

Jedis for Jesus

The overwhelming majority of respondents who claimed to have been influenced in their spiritual lives by *Star Wars* identified themselves as Christian of one denomination or another. For virtually all of the Christian respondents who identified *Star Wars* as a source of spiritual influence, the fictional Jedi in the films are seen as role models for how to live a good Christian life. According to communications studies scholar Will Brooker, "the mix-and-match mythology of *Star Wars* can persuasively be mapped onto Christianity" (8). Jonathan Bowen and Rachel Wagner in this volume identify numerous parallels between the characters of Anakin and Jesus and identify a number of Christian themes that can be found within the *Star Wars* saga. It is therefore not surprising that a number of Christian ministries and individuals have attempted to draw upon *Star Wars* to spread the Christian message. One of the earliest attempts to map *Star Wars* onto Christianity was a book released in the late 1970s titled *The Force of* Star Wars: *Unlocking the Mystery of the Force* by Frank Allnutt (1999). According to a recent adaptation at his Web site, Allnut proclaims, "*Star Wars* says to the moviegoer: Listen! There's something better in life than wallowing in the mud of pornography, dope, materialism, and vain philosophies. You have a higher calling—a calling to be someone, to do something. You have a date with destiny. You have potential in you that you haven't begun to develop" ("Unlocking").

Allnutt also suggests that the way to become a real Jedi (JEsus DIsciple) is to become a Christian: "To become real Jedi, we must believe in Jesus Christ and receive Him as our Personal Savior, Lord, and Life" ("How to Become"). Various other Christian ministries have also promoted this message. In Ventura, California, youth minister Tom Kiskin meets his congregation at a skate park and urges them to be Jedis for Jesus. A church in Seattle holds a "Jedi Sunday" service and promises that, if you attend the service, you can learn to be a real Jedi in a single day and, as an added bonus, get a free ticket to *Revenge of the Sith* just for doing so (Apple(b)logue).[5] For most of the Christian respondents to the online survey, however, being a Jedi for Jesus is a much less public affair. Instead of calling themselves Jedis for Jesus, they simply identify themselves as Christians who have found in the fictional Jedi a role model for how they would like to act as Christians in the world. As role models, the Jedis in the *Star Wars* films are seen as guardians of peace, defenders of the republic, calm, cool, wise warriors whose goal is to serve others and to maintain peace and harmony in society. For many Christian respondents, the idealization and emulation of these characteristics form the central core of how *Star Wars* has influenced their spiritual lives. According to one respondent to my online "*Star Wars* Fan Questionnaire," for example,

> I'm a Christian and find that living my life as a good Christian is essentially very similar to living as a Jedi. The Force, to me, is simply a metaphorical name given to faith and personal accomplishment. Spirituality, to me, means doing things the right way as much as possible, using my God given gifts in the way he wants me to use them. I've found added benefit to doing things the right way- emulating my heroes from the Trilogies is a very positive addition to my life. (Porter)

According to another,

> According to John Wesley, all truth is God's truth. Therefore it follows that anything that is true can be useful in aligning one's life to the God of truth. Many of the philosophical concepts of "Jediism," such as defending the defenseless while not being aggressive, are useful philosophies applied to the Christian life; in much the same way that Eastern religious traditions, such as Taoism or Buddhism, offer truths useful to the Christian. (Porter)

A third Christian respondent claimed:

> The philosophies of the Jedi Knights in the movies, such as fighting for the good of mankind, working towards peace and understanding, and restraint, are things that can be applied to everyday life to make one a better person. Star Wars has made me a person who is more open to the thoughts and views of others. The many races of Lucas's galaxy have shown me that even though skin color and languages may differ, you must treat everyone as an individual and unique person: no one is above another. (Porter)

That Christian fans have found in the fictional Jedi role models for personal and spiritual behavior is not surprising. According to Dick Straub, author of *Christian Wisdom of the Jedi Masters*, the *Star Wars* saga is filled with imagery borrowed from, or at least appropriate to, the Christian message. As Jonathan Bowen and Rachel Wagner in this volume point out, the figures of Anakin and Luke Skywalker easily fit the messiah role, and the stories of Anakin's fall from grace and the power of Luke's redeeming faith and love resonate easily with the Christian message. Although not identical to Christian theological teachings, themes within the *Star Wars* saga can therefore fit easily into a mythological dimension for fans. According to religious studies scholar Mircea Eliade, a primary role of myth in traditional cultures is to provide narratives that teach community members how to live (8). Wendy Donniger adds that it is this dimension of myth that transforms it from static storytelling to larger-than-life "really real" narrative (31–2). Although mythic heroes are rarely without flaws, their experiences and their reactions to those experiences teach us how to live in an imperfect, dangerous world. For many fans, the Jedi Knights of the films fill this role, giving a clear mythic dimension to the fan response to the *Star Wars* saga.

The Force of Godhood

Christian fans are not the only ones who have found spiritual inspiration in the *Star Wars* saga. As demonstrated by Bowen and Wagner elsewhere in this volume, *Star Wars* can be persuasively mapped onto many religious faiths, containing as it does examples of spiritual teachings drawn from many of the world's religions. According to Bowen and Wagner, the *Star Wars* saga resonates clearly with teachings drawn from Taoism and Buddhism, as well as Christianity. Among the respondents to my online survey, there were those who practiced both Taoism and Buddhism. Other faiths represented among respondents included Judaism, Hinduism, and varieties of neo-paganism. Like the Christian respondents discussed above, several of these respondents also identified the fictional Jedi as spiritual role models. The theme that emerges most strongly in the comments of these respondents, however, is that of the Force as a metaphor for godhood that resonates with and inspires within them a deeper commitment to the godhood recognized within their own traditional faiths.[6] Identifying both of these themes, one Jewish respondent wrote,

> *Star Wars* hasn't so much influenced the way I view the world and live my life as put a name to what I already believed and was already seeking. When I first saw *Empire Strikes Back* when I was 12 years old, something about that universal connection through the Force really grabbed something within me. That and the concept of the Jedi respecting and protecting all life and developing mind, body, and soul reflected my own path in life. From that point, I made it my personal journey to become a Jedi. I wasn't counting on being able to move objects with my mind and the thought of creating a true functioning lightsaber didn't even cross my mind, but I did seek to control my emotions, to be more aware of the consequences of my actions, to honor and respect all life in both people and creatures, and to find peace and serenity and beauty in everything around me. (Porter)

The Force, in *Star Wars*, is depicted as an impersonal energy field that binds and penetrates all things and that is generated and sustained by life itself. According to George Lucas, he deliberately included the idea of the Force in the films so as to add a spiritual dimension. He stated,

> I put the Force into the movie to try to reawaken a certain kind of spirituality in young people. I see *Star Wars* as taking all the issues that religion represents, and trying to distil them down into a more modern and easily accessible construct. (qtd. in B. Johnson 16).

For some religious fans, this distilled image of an all-pervasive Force helped clarify their own religiously held notions of godhood. For example, one fan wrote,

> As a Hindu I believe that all paths lead to the Ultimate Reality, the Brahman. In essence, it is like saying that God's house has many doors that people can enter from. There are definitely parts of the "Jedi" and *Star Wars* that I can see and interpret from

my religious understanding, as I think many people can. *Star Wars* is a doorway that God opened for fans in order to bring them closer. The Force is a great representation of Brahman, Ultimate Reality, Supreme Being, God, or whatever term you wish to use: that which is eternal and always exists and creates the universe and that which is connected through every aspect of the universe. (Porter)

And according to one Wiccan respondent,

As a Wiccan, I believe that there is a Divine Power but that that Divine Power resides in everything. Unlike other religions in which the Divine Power resides in a God, I believe that it is present in all things living and I call that the Force. To me, the Force is like the God and Goddess. It is the energy held within each Deity. To me, then, the Force is within the God and Goddess and that which is upon the Earth, and I combine it with my religious practices.... When I meditate and draw on the Force, I do so to find answers to my struggles, solutions to problems, energy to face tasks, and calmness and serenity. By doing so, I bring balance to my life. When I have missed meditation, I have noticed that things just do not go quite as well as when I manage to meditate on a regular basis. I soundly feel that it is because I have become used to having the Force to balance my life. Thus, to me, I see the Force as being a very large part of my religion. (Porter)

Although all of the above fans self-identify with religious traditions other than Jedi, they clearly have found enough significance within the concept of the Force to integrate it with their own spiritual paths. The Force as found in the *Star Wars* films is clearly fictional, and yet it also serves as a powerful metaphor for the spiritual convictions and experiences of fans.

It is not that these fans are unaware that the Force in the *Star Wars* films is a created construct used for plot purposes in a fictional narrative. It is simply that this construct matches their preexisting notions of the divine and helps them articulate elements of their own spiritual lives that resonate with this particular construct. Believing as they do that "the Force is with them" within their own spiritual lives and on their more traditional spiritual paths adds a dimension to their faith that enriches their religious lives, even though they have not chosen to make the Jedi path the central focus of those lives.

The Jedi Path

Almost 82 percent of the respondents to my online survey and 89 percent of the respondents to my in-person survey at Walt Disney World did not consider themselves to be Jedis. Clearly, most fans of *Star Wars*, even those deeply affected by the spiritual dimensions of *Star Wars*, do not go so far as to make the Jedi path the center of their religious lives. But some do. Within the ranks of contemporary Jedi believers, there are two main camps. The first of these camps is known as Jedi Realism, and the second is known as Jediism.[7] At this time, both groups are primarily online communities, although the latter group has a much smaller Web profile than it did even a year ago. Although some respondents identified themselves as solitary Jedi, not affiliated with any online community, the majority of Jedi respondents participated in one or more online Jedi discussion forums.

Jedi Realism

The online Jedi Realist community has changed rapidly over the last few years. Web sites that were central to the community only a few years ago have now disappeared, and new sites are emerging regularly. Like any other Internet community, the online Jedi Realist community is also somewhat factionalized, with differences of opinion leading to the demise of some Web sites and the emergence of others. The earliest Jedi Web site, known as the Jedi Academy, was founded in 1996. It was followed by several others, including an influential site known as the Jedi Creed, founded in August of 1999. The Jedi Creed's URL address was published in several media stories covering the 2001 Jedi census campaign, and, according to one source, partly as a result of this negative media attention, the Jedi Creed closed in April 2001 ("JEDI Web Site"). There are, as of this writing, currently three well-supported Jedi Realist Web sites that are central to the online Realist community. These sites are the Jedi Knights of Canada, founded in 1998; the Force Academy, founded in 1999; and JEDI, founded in 2001. Other sites, such as the Jedi Consortium, the Jedi Mythos, the United Jedi Order, the Jedi Realist Academy, the Jedi Temple, the Unified Jedi Academy, Contemplari Eruditio, and numerous others also provide discussion forums and lectures on the way of the Jedi Realist.[8] These latter groups, however, tend to have fewer registered members and are cited less often as groups to which respondents were affiliated.

The three central Jedi Realist Web sites all cite the Jedi Code as the starting point for Jedi Realist beliefs. The Code reads,

> There is no emotion; there is peace.
>
> There is no ignorance; there is knowledge.
>
> There is no passion; there is serenity.
>
> There is no death; there is the Force.[9]

JEDI offers an exegesis of the Code that reads,

> First line: There is no Emotion; there is Peace. A Jedi must not have anger, fear, and aggression in mind; these are the ways of the Dark Side. Without these, a Jedi's connection to the Force is stronger and clearer. A Jedi must not let emotions cloud his judgment. A Jedi must be at Peace at all times, there is no room for unwanted emotions.

Second line: There is no Ignorance; there is Knowledge. A Jedi does not seek knowledge for his own personal gain, but for the good of others. A Jedi shows no ignorance, or his training and growth in the Force will be stunted. You seek knowledge through the Force so that you and others may understand better the teachings of the Jedi.

Third line: There is no Passion; there is Serenity. A Jedi does not desire money and power. In Yoda's words: "Adventure. Ha! Excitement. Ha! A Jedi craves not these things!" You must find Serenity within yourself, and use what you have to its fullest extent.

And, finally, the last line:

There is no Death; there is the Force. If a Jedi is true to the Force and has a righteous spirit, mind, and heart, then he need not fear Death. For the true Jedi, there is no Death; there is only oneness with the Force. Obi-Wan Kenobi, Yoda, and Anakin Skywalker all became one with the Force upon their Death. Follow the Code and its teaching, and you too will be granted such gifts.

Now, after reading this lesson, you may think you have finished studying the Code. This is not true. We Jedi study, observe, and act it every day in our lives. You must not simply memorize the words and the lectures; you must actually act them out in your lives. Try to find Peace, seek Knowledge, give up your Passions, and feel the Force. ("The Code")

Based upon the Jedi Code, Jedi Realists argue that the Jedi path is not a religion but a way of life. As one respondent put this,

I do follow the Jedi ways as my way of Life. But I do so as for example a Samurai would have followed Bushido. It is how one lives. It is not what one prays to. The Force for me, while true and real and existing, is simply energy. It is what we do with it that matters.

Another Jedi Realist reinforced this point. She wrote,

I don't believe that being a Jedi is a religious faith—as so many would have us think, but it is more a way of life—it is not something you merely follow or worship, but something that is part of you through every minute of every day. Your entire mindset is altered by the training we all participate in. As a Jedi Realist, I prefer to think that while some, like the Jediists, consider the Jedi path to be a point of faith, we tend to allow for other religious beliefs as well—Christian Jedi, Islamic Jedi, and so on are all common denominations. What unifies us is our belief in the Force and our association and loyalty to one another. We need no religious structure to put those into place and maintain them.

But a different Jedi Realist respondent did acknowledge the spiritual dimensions of this commitment to the path of the Jedi as a way of life. He wrote,

We, the Online Jedi Community, tend to think of the Force as a spiritual belief, not a religion ... the Online Jedi Community has expanded the very essence of the term Force and have debated and discussed for years on end about the spiritual nature of the Force and how it relates to life and our very lives ... [the Force is] simply a spiritual belief in which anyone may choose to uphold and take with them on their journey in life...many of the members of the Online Jedi Community do not even like *Star Wars*, yet they believe in the spirituality of the Force and our drive, as Jedi Realists, to apply that spirituality to our very lives, welcoming and accepting any religion into the Jedi Order, any faith, any belief, and attempting to find the unifying characteristics of them all and celebrating our unity as much as our diversity.

Within this conception of the Jedi way as a spiritual life path rather than a religion, the Force is conceived of as impersonal spiritual energy, rather than god. As one respondent explained, within Jedi Realism

The Force is basically a form of Life Energy—a different expression of both Western and Eastern Vitalist theories, following other concepts like those of Chi, Prana, Elan Vital, and so on. According to *Star Wars*, it is inherent in everything in the Universe, and is capable of affecting both living and inorganic materials. [10]

For most of the Jedi Realists respondents, as well as Jedi Realist Web sites, *religion* appears to be something associated with doctrines, churches, and exclusionary practices. They therefore reject the religion label, even though many of them clearly recognize the element of faith and the spiritual dimensions inherent in their practices and beliefs.

Jediism

Members of the Jedi Realist camp claim that there are approximately five times more Jedi Realists than Jediists. In my own survey results, 36.7 percent (11/30) of those who self-identified as Jedi were practitioners of Jediism: The remaining 63.3 percent (19/30) were Jedi Realists. However, in the past year, the two main Jedi religion Web sites (Jediism and the Jedi Religion) have gone offline, leaving Jediists with few places on the Internet to come together to discuss their religion. [11] Given the importance of online discussion forums for fostering a sense of community among Jedi, the loss of these sites may diminish the number of Jedis who see their Jedi path as a religious one.

The central difference between Jedi Realism and Jediism is that followers of Jediism do consider their path to be religious, while Jedi Realists do not. According to the Jediism Web site (which is no longer found on the Web), for example,

Jediism is not the same as that which is portrayed within the *Star Wars* saga by George Lucas and Lucasfilm LTD. George Lucas's Jedi are fictional characters that exist within a literary and cinematic universe.... The Jedi™ discussed within this Web site refer to factual people within this world that live or lived their lives according to Jediism, of which we recognize and work together as a community to both cultivate and celebrate. We embrace Jediism as a real living, breathing way of life, and sincerely strive to seek out and emulate real life examples of Jediism in the long rich history of mankind. Jediism bases less of its focus on myth and fiction, and more upon those real life examples of Jediism found in the hearts of heroes and within the actions of such. The history of the path of Jediism traverses thought based on age-old principles that have held fast through the ages. It shares many themes embraced in Hinduism, Confucianism, Buddhism, Gnosticism, Stoicism, Catholicism, Taoism, Shinto, Modern Mysticism, the Way of the Shaolin Monks, the Knight's Code of Chivalry, and the Samurai Warriors.... [Jediism is] a theology that embraces what we consider to be the golden thread of universal truth that runs through every major religion and theology. [It is a] means to promote inner and world peace. A path that can lead to the Light ... which can take the Jedi much higher into the world of spirit and embrace much higher truths than any that were ever conjured up from the science fiction series. ("Mission Statement")

Jediism.org provides twenty-one maxims gleaned from world religions and the fictional Jedi that constitute an extended version of the Jedi Code (referred to on the Jediism Web site as the Jediism Code, but known to most Jediists as the Twenty-One Maxims). Although too lengthy to cite here in full, in point form, these Maxims are

I. Prowess. II. Justice. III. Loyalty. IV. Defense. V. Courage. VI. Faith. VII. Humility. VIII. Fearlessness. IX. Nobility. X. Franchise. XI. Pure Motive. XII. Discipline. XIII. Focus. XIV. Discretion. XV. Meditation. XVI. Training. XVII. Integrity. XVIII. Morality. XIX. Engaging in Conflict. XX. Intervention. XXI. Harmonizing. ("Official Code")

Several respondents referred to the central place that the Jediism Code or the Twenty-One Maxims held for them in guiding their spiritual path. One respondent recommended the Jediism Code as the main tool for separating true Jediists from simple *Star Wars* fans. He wrote,

If you get a chance in your study, ma'am, read the Code. Read the Code. It will help you separate the true Jedi from the little trekkie movie fans who have no Code.

Jediist followers of the Jedi Code and the Twenty-One Maxims conceptualize the Jedi path and the Force in explicitly religious ways. According to one Jediist respondent, for example,

As a Jedi, I see the Force as a Divine Power that is present in everything much like another sees God as a Deity and that which is on the Earth as His creation. I practice meditation on a daily basis. I have a Code, much like the Ten Commandments, that I follow as well as Maxims and such. And I put these into practice every day. I gauge my actions against these Jedi beliefs much like a Christian would gauge their actions against their religion. Since I practice "Jediism" in my daily life and see the Force as a Divine Power, I definitely do feel that Jediism is a religion. Jedis are the image of goodness, compassion, tolerance, control, honesty, temperance, courage, prowess, harmony, discipline, and so on. These things are often found in many other religions. The difference is that Jedis are asked to not think of themselves but to think of others, to put others first. That is the most important aspect of Jediism. All actions should lead to doing good for other people. In order for that to occur, it is necessary for the Jedi to practice their beliefs as a religion.

This willingness to see Jediism as a religion leads Jediists to speak frequently in terms of the Force as divine and often to speak of prayer to the Force, gratitude to the Force, and so on. For example, according to one respondent,

> The Force is what some people view as god, the entity that surrounds us, protects us; it is what we pray to. To me, it isn't sentient, but it is the power that fuels us all. It is everywhere, in everyone, and we are kept alive in it, we are made of it.

Another wrote:

> The Force to me is God, the life source of all living things, or to me God the Lord of all living beings. Because the Force is made of midichlorians, in a sense the midichlorians are the Force and the Force is God.

The issue of whether the Jedi path constitutes a religious path is a divisive one among Jedis. Despite this, both Jedi Realists and Jediists argue that the Jedi path is inspired by, but not governed by, *Star Wars*. Both groups argue that the true inspiration for the Jedi path is not so much the films as it is the spiritual traditions of the world, drawn upon by Lucas and presented in the films in distilled form. And members of both groups see themselves as genuinely spiritual, in pursuit of a connection to something that is greater than us all and that unites us all into a unified human Force.

Conclusions

There is no shortage of critics of *noncreedal* spirituality, a spirituality divorced from churches or tradition. When this noncreedal or distilled form of spirituality is packaged in a popular culture format, the critics multiply tenfold. One Presbyterian respondent to the online survey, for example, wrote,

> I think that [the Jedi path] is being used by many young people who have become detached or alienated from their traditional religious backgrounds as a surrogate religion. It is easier to believe in a religion one only sees in film. I suspect that all or most of these so-called Jedi are not really practicing the faith they profess to believe in anyway. They just want cool light sabres. Would any of these people give up all strong emotion? Would they meditate? No: they are just looking for all the side-benefits without the sacrifices of any faith system: real or otherwise.

On a more academic front, Jesuit priest and film studies scholar Marc Gervais suggests that *Star Wars* gives "an impression of spirituality...but there's a whole other side that makes me uneasy...this is kiddie pop culture as the terrorizer of everything" (qtd. in B. Johnson 16). Mary Jo Leddy, theology professor at the University of Toronto, argues that "what is now being marketed is a cheap grace. You can get a spiritual high that's instantaneous. What is astonishing to me is the number of people who know the *Star Wars* script by heart, as opposed to any form of the scriptures" (qtd. in B. Johnson 17).

What these critics fail to acknowledge is that, for many fans, the spiritual conviction of impersonal divine immanence, the interconnectedness of all things, and the moral responsibility of those who can to help others less fortunate preexisted the metaphors and terminology that *Star Wars* provided. For virtually all of my Jedi respondents, and many of the respondents who followed more mainstream religious paths and yet had found their spiritual lives influenced by *Star Wars*, Jedi and *the Force* are words, and images, that resonate with a spiritual impulse already present. Furthermore, in the contemporary context, for many fans, traditional religious affiliations fail to provide the sense of interconnectedness that such a hugely popular film as *Star Wars* provides. *Star Wars'* popularity transcends the boundaries of class, race, ethnicity, culture, and religion, and this universal appeal provides a concrete manifestation of the spiritual conviction that we are all interconnected through a Force that binds the universe together.

Sociologist Emile Durkheim argues that, in a modern, pluralistic, secular age, only those spiritual elements that tie us all together as human beings in search of the sacred will remain as the basis of religion. As a hugely popular film franchise, the *Star Wars* saga provides fans with a source of symbols to unite those in search of the sacred in our profane world. *Star Wars* teaches fans what it means to be a good person in a universe caught in the struggle between good and evil. Although fans are aware that Han Solo, Luke Skywalker, and Yoda are fictional characters, they nonetheless see in them a message about what makes us truly human. And as Durkheim observed over one hundred years ago, the qualities that make us truly human are what spirituality in a postindustrial, pluralistic, and secular world is all about.

Sociologist Peter Berger (49–56) argues something similar when he suggests that elements of human experience that "signal" the transcendent might become the basis for a new, universal spirituality in a world where traditional religious affiliation is declining. Many of the Jedi respondents testified to a heartfelt experience of the Force in their own lives, seeing in their personal experiences signals of a transcendent reality that had been missing in other contexts. This transcendent reality, in which a spiritual and scientific Force binds everything in the universe together, draws upon, for fans, both the creative ideas of George Lucas and also the spiritual inspirations of the world's religious traditions. For Berger, play is one way that humans touch the transcendent and come to know that there is something more to reality than the mundane world of everyday life. *Star Wars* fans know how to play and have fun with their favorite movie franchise, but, in doing so, they touch something beyond themselves and find access to a spirituality that resonates with truth in our pluralistic and postindustrial world.

This emphasis on play, or creativity, is further echoed by sociologist Robert Bellah (20–53). Bellah argues that religion in the contemporary context is multivocal, recognizing both the created and creative aspects of religion, while simultaneously allowing people to tap into a sense of transcendence. In *Star Wars*, many fans have found in the Force a universal, transcendent power drawn from many of the world's religions, a Force that can blend seamlessly with other spiritual paths, while simultaneously acknowledging the creative and created nature of the fictional Force of the *Star Wars* saga. In acknowledging the fictional nature of the Force from *Star Wars*, yet finding in it nonetheless some transcendent truths about reality and our place within it, those on the Jedi path and other fans who have been influenced by the spirituality of *Star Wars* reflect a growing trend, a trend in which religious doctrine is seen as simply creative metaphor for the transcendent truths that lie beyond.

Sociologist Adam Possamai calls the construction of a created, creative, and popular culture–inspired form of spirituality a "hyper-consumer religion" (49-52) According to Possamai (21), popular culture in our commodified world is "a medium for the autodetermination of social actors, and more specifically...spiritual self-determination" (20). He suggests that the corporate nature of popular culture, and the consumerist packaging of it, is secondary to the uses to which popular culture is put by individuals constructing their own sense of spiritual identity. As Possamai notes,

> even if popular culture is part of global capitalism managed by multinational corporations, even if it provides a form of escapism from our "anxious" and/or "hidden" reality at the same level as window shopping, it is also a platform for our own biography. We live through and with it. We create our lives and view ourselves through popular culture. (20)

Possamai cites "Jedi Knightism" as an example of hyper-real religion, because practitioners identify themselves with, emulate, and are inspired by fictional rather than real events or persons. Hyper-real religions reflect an easiness with consumer culture and blur the boundaries between real and imaginary, thus becoming hyper-real. Those on the Jedi path, and other fans who have found spiritual inspiration from *Star Wars*, are clearly participants in a consumer culture that elevates popular culture to the same status as more traditional sources of spiritual inspiration. They acknowledge the created and marketed nature of their source of inspiration, while simultaneously affirming the legitimacy of the spiritual impact that *Star Wars* has made in their lives. Although hyper-real in the sense that the *Star Wars* saga is a fictional narrative and the Jedi are fictional role models, those on the Jedi path and others spiritually inspired by *Star Wars* dwell in the real world—a world that now must take into account the influential role popular culture can have on people's religious lives.

Star Wars is clearly a film franchise. It is also the beginning of spiritual inspiration for thousands of fans. As a scholar of religion, I believe it is time we begin to give genuine credence to the idea that people's spiritual paths can be and often are influenced by popular culture. In our modern pluralistic world, it is often the narratives of popular culture rather than traditional religious narratives that cross the lines of gender, race, ethnicity, class, and culture to inspire those who hear them. In the case of the Star Wars saga, the narratives resonate with mythic themes and powerful metaphors for the divine that have affected millions of people, many of them in spiritual ways. It is time we begin to treat the spiritualities influenced and inspired by popular culture as seriously as we treat other religious traditions. Although the Jedi census campaign was shaped as a joke and a political protest, it pointed to a truth about the spiritual lives of some Star Wars fans. The Jedi are not, as Moff Tarkin in A New Hope would have it, extinct. Their religion is alive and well in the hearts of many fans and is likely to remain so for some time to come.

Notes for Chapter 6

1. See A. Frykholm and Possamai.

2. In Canada, the Jedi census campaign was apparently orchestrated by B.C. native Dennis Dion, again as an attempt to protest the census religion question and as an attempt to see how many people would respond to the campaign. See "Some 20,000 Canadians."

3. The patrons at Disney World's Star Wars Weekend were a diverse group of people, many of them simply patrons of Walt Disney World who happened to have arrived for their vacation that weekend to discover that Star Wars-related events were scheduled at Disney/MGM studios and who took advantage of that fact because they were fans. Others had traveled to attend the event precisely because they were Star Wars fans and wanted the chance to obtain autographs, ride the Star Tours ride, and hang out with other fans.

4. For examples of this kind of testimony, see <http:\www.thankyougeorge.com> (defunct at this writing).

5. See the "Jesus was Jedi" service advertising poster at apple(b)logue, <http://www.appleogue. net/2005/05/jesus-was-jedi-improbable.html>.

6. This emphasis was occasionally present in the responses of Christians also. For example, one Christian respondent wrote, "I'm a member of the Community of Christ. For me, Star Wars reinforced the idea of the spirit within us all. It was a new way to describe that kind of experience and therefore beneficial. It made a connection in me to something that was already part of my life."

7. One graduate student and member of the online community, nicknamed Hellflower, identifies a third camp, called Jedi Metaphorism, but the Web sites associated with this

camp appear to have been subsumed under the Jedi Realist umbrella. See Hellflower (pseudonymous Jedi name), *Luminous Beings and Crude Matter: Ethos and Elective Centre in the Online Jedi Community.*

8. The URLs of these sites are the following:

the Jedi Knights of Canada, <http://www.angelfire.com/ca4/jediknightsofcanada>; the Force Academy, <http://www.forceacademy.com>; JEDI, <http://www.jedi.ws/>; the Jedi Consortium, <http://www.angelfire.com/ab6/jediconsortium>; the Jedi Mythos, <http://p214.ezboard.com/bthejedimythos>; the Jedi Realist Academy, <http://b13.ezboard.com/bjedirealistacademy>; the Jedi Temple, <http://www.jeditemple.freehosting.net/home.html>; the Unified Jedi Academy, <http://www.unifiedjedi.com>; and Contemplari Eruditio, <http://www.contemplarieruditio.com>. Such Web sites sometimes change their host locations or disappear entirely.

9. The Jedi code is taken from the official "Expanded Universe" lore of the Jedi. It can be found in its canonical form in the "Databank" at <http://www.starwars.com>.

10. Almost belying her earlier insistence that Jedi Realism was not a faith-based religion, she adds, "According to modern Jedi Realism, the Force is mainly a concept best explained in spiritual and philosophical terms—after all, it is a belief we hold to be dear, but not one we can necessarily prove. While we have evidence for the existence of the Force, associating it with many of our primary human instincts, intuitions and various behavioral forms, we can't say for certain that the Force truly does exist—it is a matter of faith."

11. Both Jediism (<http://www.jediism.org>) and the Jedi Religion (<http://www.jedireligion.org>) have disappeared from the Internet in the last year. Many Jedi Realist sites, in contrast, are still active.

Works Cited

Allnutt, Frank. "How to Become a Real Jedi." *Frank Allnut Page.* 18 July 2005. <http://www.frankallnutt.com/How_to_become_a_real_Jedi.htm>.

———. *Unlocking the Mystery of the Force.* 5th ed. Denver, CO: Allnut Publishing Company, 1999.

———."Unlocking the Mystery of the Force." *Frank Allnutt Page* 18 July 2005. <http://www.frankallnutt.com/Force_Returns.htm>.

Apple(b)logue. *apple(b)logue.* 18 July 2005 <http://www.appleogue.net/2005/05/jesus-was-jedi-improbable.html>.

Bellah, Robert. *Beyond Belief: Essays on Religion in a Post-Traditional World.* Berkeley: U of California P, 1991.

Berger, Peter. *A Rumor of Angels.* Garden City, NY: Doubleday/Anchor, 1970.

Brennin, Kristen. "Joseph Campbell." *Jitterbug Fantasia Webzine.* 20 May 2004. 2005 <http://www.jitterbug.com/origins/myth.html>.

Brooker, Will. *Using the Force: Creativity, Community and Star Wars Fans.* New York/London: Continuum, 2002.

"The Code." *JEDI.* 12 July 2005. 2005 <http://www.thejedi.org/lectures/code>.

Donniger, Wendy. *Other People's Myths: The Cave of Echoes.* New York: MacMillan, 1988.

Durkheim, Emile. "Individualism and the Intellectuals." 1898. Trans. S. Lukes. *Political Studies* 17 (1969): 14–30.

Eliade, Mircea. *Myth and Reality*. New York: Harper & Row, 1975.

Frykholm, Amy Johnson. *Rapture Culture: Left Behind in Evangelical America*. Oxford/Toronto: Oxford UP, 2004.

Galipeau, Steven A. *The Journey of Luke Skywalker: An Analysis of Modern Myth and Symbol*. Chicago: Open Court, 2001.

Gordon, Andrew. "*Star Wars*: A Myth for Our Time." *Screening the Sacred: Religion, Myth, and Ideology in Popular American Film*. Ed. Joel W. Martin and Conrad E. Ostwalt, Jr. Boulder, CO: Westview, 1995. 73–82.

Hanson, Michael J., and Max S. Kay. *Star Wars: The New Myth*. Philadelphia: Xlibris, 2001.

Hellflower. *Luminous Beings and Crude Matter: Ethos and Elective Centre in the Online Jedi Community*. Master's Thesis, Goldsmiths College, University of London, 1999.

"JEDI Web Site History." *JEDI.*. 25 June 2005. 2005 <http://www.thejedi.org/website/history>.

"Jedi Would Be 4th Faith if Permitted in the Census." *Times Online*. 13 Feb. 2003. 19 May 2004 <http://www.timesonline.co.uk/article/0,,1-576670,00.html>.

Johnson, Brian D. "The Second Coming: As the Newest *Star Wars* Film Illustrates, Pop Culture Has Become a New Religion." *Maclean's* 24 May 1999: 14–18.

Kiskin, Tom. "Skateboards n' Surfing Get through to the Hard-To-Reach." *San Angelo Standard-Times* 7 Aug. 1999. 18 July 2005 <http://web.gosanangelo.com/archive/99/august/7/9.htm>.

"Mission Statement." *Jediism: The Jedi Religion*. 19 May 2004. <http://www.thejedi.org/website/mission>.

"The Official Code of Jediism." *Jediism: The Jedi Religion*. 19 May 2004. No longer hosted at the original but re-posted at a Yahoo Group. 23 Jan 2006 <http://groups.yahoo.com/group/Jedi_Knight_Movement/message/33>.

"The Original Email." *Gonmad*. 2001. 28 July 2005 <http://www.gonmad.co.uk/jedicensus/>.

Perrott, Alan. "Jedi Order Lures 53,000 Disciples." *New Zealand Herald* 31 Aug. 2002. 19 May 2004 <http://www.nzherald.co.nz/storydisplay.cfm?storyID=2352142>.

Porter, Jennifer E. *Star Wars* Fan Questionnaire (ongoing). Host site <http://www.mun.ca/rels/jporter/index.html>.

Possamai, Adam. *Religion and Popular Culture: A Hyper-Real Testament*. Brussels: P.I.E.–Peter Lang, 2005.

Roof, Wade Clark. *Spiritual Marketplace: Baby Boomers and the Remaking of American Religion*. Princeton: Princeton UP, 1999.

"Some 20,000 Canadians Worship at the Altar of Yoda." *Canada.com*. 13 May 2003. May 19 2004 <http://www.canada.com>.

Straub, Dick. *Christian Wisdom of the Jedi Masters*. Hoboken, NJ: John Wiley and Sons, 2005.

Verbeeck, Muriel. "Campbell, Star Wars and the Myth." 20 May 2004 <http://ibelgiquie.ifrance.com/sw-anthropo/txt/camptexteanglais.html>.

Sexuality
and
Gender

CHAPTER 7

Thawing the Ice Princess

Philip L. Simpson

The *Star Wars* franchise films in many ways seem constructed almost exclusively for adolescent male audiences. The films' mythic elements resonate with audiences reacting to the quests and tribulations of males. A virtuous son redeems his corrupt and fallen father. Boy pupils rebel against older male mentors but ultimately learn the wisdom of the paternal restrictions placed upon them. Lonely farm boys become culture heroes and saviors. Male mystics achieve transcendent powers through occult knowledge. Men engage in epic struggles for galactic control. And so forth. However, there are two primary female characters in the series of films as well: Queen Padmé Amidala of *Episodes I* through *III* and Princess Leia of *Episodes IV* through *VI*. Within a fictional cosmos predominantly gendered as male, how do these two females function within the narratives?

At first glance, Amidala and Leia seem as straightforwardly heroic as male protagonists Qui-Gon Jinn, Obi-wan Kenobi, Anakin Skywalker (before his fall from grace), Luke Skywalker, and Han Solo (following his conversion from self-centered smuggler to Rebellion leader). Both women satisfy the basic prerequisites for screen heroism: They are dedicated to higher ideals, physically courageous, skilled in combat, athletic, and so forth. Additionally, they occupy positions of royal authority traditionally designated for males and are charged with heavy leadership responsibilities in a Byzantine political system that spans a galaxy. Generally speaking, men do not question this female leadership. Han Solo, as the one prominent male to challenge brashly the individual decisions of Leia, is quickly converted to her cause by her dedication. As wielders of institutional power, Amidala and Leia are self-assured and assertive. It is ironic, then, that a narrative that features two such strong female characters then works so hard to contain and even break down their power, first by coding their exercise of autonomy as *frigidity* and then placing both women in relationships that demand not just *thawing* but melting of their icy feminine royalty.[1] These women must suffer sexual abjection to an extent that subverts whatever power they otherwise manifest.

In one sense, in a series of films that do not deal overtly with sexual situations, it seems odd or even nonsensical to argue that sex occupies a center stage in the narrative trajectory.[2] Yet critics have long noted that the superficial comic book action of the films encodes sexuality or conspicuously evokes sex. Probably the most extended analysis of the sexual undertones of the original trilogy is found in an essay by Andrew Gordon, wherein he argues persuasively that "the *Star Wars* movies are as far from being chaste beneath the surface as they appear to be on the surface" ("Power" 196). Citing specific instances of sexual imagery in the films, Martin Miller and Robert Sprich rather bluntly state that Luke's bodily surrender to the Force and the subsequent destruction of the Death Star in *Episode IV* is an orgasmic act: "Luke is required to take aim and travel through a narrow tunnel to shoot a missile into a small opening where it will explode. There can be no doubt that this is a symbolic act of sexual intercourse" (212). Yet once such sexual images are invoked, the films then deny mature expression of sexuality within their signification structures. Jim Holte, for one, argues that "sexuality [in *Star Wars*] is present in a very traditional way" (188) but that the central triumvirate of characters in *Episodes IV* through *VI* (Luke, Leia, and Han) becomes sexless because their "quest is too important to risk letting sexuality interfere" (189). The fact that Anakin's unleashed sexuality in *Episodes II* and *III*, though sublimated in the language and rituals of courtly love, leads to disaster would seem to strengthen Holte's contention that the *Star Wars* galaxy is constructed in puritanical ideological terms.

Certainly, sexual temptation and its corresponding metaphysical connotations of self-absorption and worldly pleasure for the puritanical are considered to be part of the Dark Side of the Force—companions on the "quick and easy path" that Yoda warns of in *The Empire Strikes Back*. In the sense that the *Star Wars* mythos consistently places its characters in situations involving temptation and/or exile, it is not surprising that Amidala and Leia face their own desires to abdicate the public burden of leadership and withdraw into isolation and the singular pleasures of romantic and carnal love. Put another way, these females embody what John Rieder identifies as one of the primary nostalgic conceits of the *Star Wars* films: "yearning ... for private, bodily freedom from the over-administered, bureaucratic world of management" (34). But one suspects that, as women in a patriarchal fairy tale, Amidala and Leia are subject to additional burdens and narrative punishments not demanded of the male characters who wish for the same individual freedoms—that the individual expression of their female sexuality is acceptable only if it produces heirs who can wield the Force for a greater good.[3]

By virtue of their sex, Amidala and Leia carry a heavy mythic burden.[4] They are the maternal progenitors of the resurrected Jedi Knights—for all intents and purposes, earth goddesses in function if not origin—and as such ensure the galaxy's future. Amidala survives the tragic events of *Revenge of the Sith* just long enough to bear Anakin's children. As one of those children carrying the midi-chlorian–laden Skywalker bloodline, Leia grows up to become (so the resolution of *Episode VI* implies and subsequent authorized literary additions to the *Star Wars* mythos have confirmed) mother of future Jedi Knights like her mother before her. However, both women are depicted as not only devoted to duty but also so virginal, unattainable, uptight, and/or sexually repressed that they must be overwhelmed by the romantic passion of strong males in order for the women's true maternal destinies to be fulfilled. In other words, for the narrative arc to play out, Amidala and Leia, otherwise capable and independent women fiercely dedicated to social justice and reform, must be seduced from their positions of responsibility by Anakin and Han, respectively. Complete fulfillment of these two women's heroic functions depends on their sexuality and fertility taking precedence, at least temporarily, over their allegiance to politics. The epic narrative insists that Amidala and Leia must surrender their principles as well as their bodies. These character arcs are signaled by a literal stripping away of royal costume, outer marker of authority, to reveal the sexualized female body beneath. *ROTS* carries the theme one step further: rendering Padmé subject to death because of her female biology.

When *Star Wars* premiered in 1977, audiences were quick to notice that Princess Leia as a lead female character was a paradox. She was that most hackneyed of character types—the damsel in distress waiting to be rescued for heroic men. At the same time, she was a warrior princess befitting the at least marginally feminist social climate of the 1970s. As Star Wars: *The Visual Dictionary* has it, "Trained in military discipline, techniques, and strategy, Leia is an excellent tactician and an expert shot with a blaster. She virtually never misses" (Reynolds 13). Certainly, she can handle a blaster at least as well as the space pirate who helps rescue her and certainly better than the callow youth who leads the charge to her cell. Not only is she a courageous fighter, but she is a powerful political figure in a traditionally male environment, located, furthermore, at the center of galactic intrigue involving an evil, off-stage Emperor and the various governmental minions representing him. Perhaps by virtue of her social and political status, she is verbally aggressive as well, leading one critic to call her "a tough-talking cowgirl. It's a wonder she doesn't smoke cigars" (Horstman 53). Yet for all this assertiveness and social importance, she seems little more than an innocent girl. Clad in virginal white and literally never letting her severely confined hair down, she seems at times repressed, even sexless.

At other times in *A New Hope*, Leia's mature sexuality is deliberately fore-grounded. At these moments, the symbolic weight of Leia's last name, Organa, becomes evident. If the Force is an energy field generated by living things that binds the galaxy together, Leia represents the organic feminine in all of its glo-rious potentiality. She can be held prisoner by evil bureaucratic males tempo-rarily, but, as a fluid organic force, she will inevitably escape containment and boundary, with just a little help from the heroic males. These sexualized scenes occur later in the film, after Luke and Han arrive in physical proximity to Leia and presumably stir her libido. The first such scene is when Luke Skywalker first sees her in person as she reposes languidly in her prison cell—all rounded thigh and breasts in lush contrast to the angular lines of the technology that confines her.

Revealing a calculated sensuality that has by no means been evident before this point, Leia stretches her body in an unmistakably suggestive gesture and playfully disparages the masculinity of what she assumes to be another anony-mous Imperial: "Aren't you a little short for a stormtrooper?" The scenes that immediately follow propel an aggressively dominant Leia down a sexually sug-gestive narrow tunnel that she herself has opened for her two potential lovers to follow—an act of penetration that foreshadows Luke's orgasmic penetration and destruction of the Death Star—into a foul-smelling ("What an incredible smell you've discovered," Han growls sarcastically to Leia) garbage dump in-habited by a predatory monster that represents, for Peter Lev, "the threat of bodily functions and unknown organic antagonists" (35) and, for Freudian critics Miller and Sprich, the unconscious mind of primal urges.[5] She plunges into filthy water that stains her white gown, rendering this symbolic vestment of purity corrupt, and makes her breasts even more noticeable as the wet fabric clings to them. Finally, this late narrative tendency to sexualize Leia concludes in the triumphal march where Leia's ceremonial gown (her second costume change of the film) daringly reveals her décolletage to Luke and Han at the head of an admiring crowd of males.

As the film's final award ceremony makes visually explicit, at least one of her character functions in the narrative is to serve as the pivot point in a sub-plot involving a growing rivalry between Luke Skywalker and Han Solo for her love.[6] As David Wilkinson summarizes the Leia character paradox, "Some-times [Leia] fulfills the role of hero ... while at other times she seems to have slipped back into the stereotype of the love interest who stands wringing her hands while the men go out to do battle" (103). Miller and Sprich maintain that, because of this ambiguity or open-endedness of characterization, Leia has a type of "Rorschach quality" and in "trying to be all things to all people—the madonna, the coquette, the liberated woman—she becomes a rather two-dimensional figure."[7] The authors conclude that the "attempt to portray her as a modern, phallic, competitive woman is overdone" (218). True enough, in the sense that all of the central characters in the films are melodramatically over-done as heroic figures. In Leia's case, her heroism cannot be separated from her status as a feminine, organic force that inspires the male heroes to rally to the political cause she embodies. In this stage of the epic narrative, Leia looms large over the men, who are literally at her feet in thrall to her power. She has not been broken yet.

In the *ESB*, the narrative agenda to sexualize Leia and, in the process, di-minish her autonomy becomes overt. She is placed in a subservient romantic relationship with the rogue Han Solo, who represents the *animus* of the Force to Leia's *anima*. Leia loses control of herself sexually, which in some contexts might be read as liberation but in this mythos means subjugation to a stronger will. Clearly, sex is much more evident in this installment.[8] Sexual innuendos are obviously present for the first time in the film's dialogue, which David Wyatt speculates is perhaps a contribution of screenwriter Leigh Brackett, a veteran of Howard Hawks' comedies (610). A seemingly trivial comic exchange early in the film between the droids C-3PO and R2-D2 is one example.

Right after a sexually charged scene between Han Solo and Princess Leia in the corridor of the rebel base on the ice planet of Hoth, C-3PO and R2-D2 argue about R2-D2 having turned on a thermal heater in Leia's living quarters. C-3PO complains to R2-D2, "I merely commented that it was freez-ing in the princess' chamber. But it's supposed to be freezing. How are we go-ing to dry out all of her clothes?" Superficially yet another example of the ongoing amusing banter between C-3PO and R2-D2, C-3PO's statement and its placement in the film suggests through environmental metaphor that Leia, thus far configured as a rigidly repressed and virginal girl, is beginning to awaken to the sexual possibility represented by the worldly and hyper-masculine Han Solo. In other words, the Ice Princess, as Reynolds deems her in Star Wars: *The Visual Dictionary* (13), on an ice planet is beginning to thaw.

The remainder of Princess Leia's character arc in the middle film of the middle trilogy is devoted to chronicling this thawing process through her love affair with Han Solo. In the few quiet spaces between their flight from Darth Vader's Imperial fleet, Han takes the initiative to tease and push an extremely resistant Leia toward an acknowledgement of her feelings for him.[9] He does so with a combination of barely checked physical force (rendered acceptable in narrative context because Leia is so clearly in need of release) and dialogue that is clearly sexual in intent. It is significant to note that Leia's true awakening to sexuality takes place deep within what the characters assume to be a cave in an asteroid but turns out to be a monster's gullet, a setting that is a symbol of be-ing consumed by primal biology.[10] Han seizes the opportunity to hold Leia momentarily captive when she is thrown into his hands by a seismic shift in the cavern floor. She demands to be released from his grip, whereupon Han petulantly does so and tells her "Don't get excited." Leia's retort—"Captain, being held by you isn't quite enough to get me excited"—is met with Han's most devilish grin and his departing line, "I don't have time for anything else."

However, what appears to be a hindrance to romance—the imminent threat of the Imperial pursuit and the necessity of repairing Han's ailing ship— is precisely what gives Han his best chance at seducing the duty-conscious Leia. Without time for her to dwell upon her feelings and therefore a chance to retreat into her signature reserve, Leia, by working in close proximity to Han, who ever has one eye on wooing her even as he tries to effect repairs to his ship, is relentlessly shoved toward a cathartic explosion of passion by Han's dominating masculinity.[11] Han corners her in a narrow cranny of the *Millennium Falcon* and ignores her feeble protestations of disinterest by literally blocking her in. Given very little choice in the matter and yielding momentarily to her feelings, Leia kisses Han briefly until this coupling is interrupted by C-3PO.

Such frustrated encounters prove to be the leitmotif of the courtship of Han and Leia. In fact, it is possible to read the middle part of *ESB*, at least in the scenes between Han and Leia, as a metaphoric exploration of the tension of sexual frustration. Significantly during these scenes, the well-worn *Millennium Falcon*, as an extension of Han's body and the background of much of Han and Leia's courtship, is unable to achieve light-speed—a canonic moment of audience ecstasy established in *ANH* that is consistently denied in *ESB* until the film's climax.[12] The impotence of Han's ship forces the couple to sneak away from the Imperial fleet, fittingly enough, in the Freudian terms dictated by *ANH*, amidst a covering field of garbage dumped into space by the Star Destroyers before they effortlessly jump to light-speed. Han and Leia must seek refuge at the nearby Cloud City, whose administrator, Lando Calrissian, happens to be a so-called old friend of Han's. Lando almost immediately begins his own courtly wooing of Leia right in front of Han, posing yet another threat to Han's besieged sense of masculinity. Shortly thereafter, Lando's betrayal of Han to Darth Vader and the bounty hunter Boba Fett compounds Han's helplessness. Tortured and delivered over for freezing (a persistent theme in this chilling installment of the series), Han is ultimately denied the relationship both he and Leia have been cultivating.

But even as Han is frozen in the carbon-freezing chamber of Cloud City, Leia is fully vitalized, or unfrozen, through her climactic verbal confession of love to Han in front of a decidedly bizarre wedding party presided over by her Dark father, Vader. Yet if her utterance is triumphant and liberating in the context of admitting an emotion she has denied, this scene is also the moment at which Leia surrenders her independent identity as leader of the Rebellion and instead becomes a passively suffering woman in a romantic tragedy—a much more traditional female narrative position.

Leia's public declaration, an expressive act that is supremely difficult for this most repressed of characters, is devalued in that Han does not return the oath but rather defaults to the egocentric retort, "I know." Han's line (reportedly ad-libbed on the set by actor Harrison Ford as much preferable to the script's line "I love you too") often generated enthusiastic audience applause in first showings of the film in 1980 and fully highlights the degree to which the success of the storyline depends on Leia's deference to the type of masculinity represented by Han even in his most helpless, feminized moment.

In *Return of the Jedi*, the first film after Leia has declared her love to Han in personally less-than-satisfying terms, Leia's status as abject sexual object is signaled to the audience by the sight of her fully sexualized body on display as a nearly nude prisoner of the gangster Jabba—a stark contrast to her first white-veiled appearance in the series as a feisty but repressed freedom fighter.[13] Tellingly, Leia's entry in the *Guide to the Star Wars Universe*, which textually goes to great pains to emphasize her diplomatic and military skills, is illustrated with a line drawing of her in her revealing slave-girl costume (Slavicsek 273), thus in some ways subordinating the verbal description of her abilities to her visual sexual appeal.

Now she completes her sexual surrender, not just to Han but to the disreputable world of gangsters from which he originates, in that she has momentarily abandoned the Rebellion to pursue this highly individual rescue mission. Later in *ROTJ*, she redons her mission clothing and reembarks on her traditionally heroic career as rebel warrior and culture hero, but the point has been made. She is now a fully realized, but somehow violated, sexual being who, in her dual role as rebel hero and Skywalker heir, carries the future of the Jedi Knights in her womb.

Thus, the three films that feature Leia as the central female character empower her to assume traditionally masculine heroic roles—leader of men and courageous warrior—but also predicate this heroism on her gradually revealed sexual desirability and reproductive utility. She cannot achieve her true apotheosis as mythic hero without thawing and becoming receptive to the sexual heat generated by forceful male presence. If *Episodes IV* through *VI* are said to be the patriarchal story of the salvation of Anakin Skywalker through his son Luke, it can also be fairly said that the middle episodes are the story of the future restoration of the Jedi Knights through the empowerment (and corresponding abasement) of Leia Skywalker as sexual being.

Much the same character arc for another main female character is replicated twenty years later in the first three episodes in the Star Wars mythos, *The Phantom Menace, Attack of the Clones*, and *ROTS*. Princess Leia is recast this time in the form of her mother, the Queen of the planet Naboo and key figure in a trade conflict instigated by the Sith Lord, Darth Sidious, that will eventually unravel the Republic and help give rise to the mature Empire of the middle episodes. Queen Padmé Amidala, the future wife of Anakin and mother of Leia and Luke, is also introduced as a formidable female character in a traditional male leadership role. Like Leia, she too is first defined by her social role and not her sexual identity. In *TPM*, the transition from royal figure to sexual object is complicated in that Padmé is significantly older than the ten-year-old Anakin who will one day be her husband, so any conventional romantic storyline such as the one between Leia and Han has to be deferred until the second episode. Thus, Padmé as female character is initially thawed by disguising herself as her own handmaiden to escape danger and, in this more accessible identity, subsequently forming a friendship with thus-far innocent Anakin. Yet, in the puritanical universe constructed by Lucas, Anakin's boyish innocence, even more innocent than that of naïve but sexually developed Luke in *ANH*, is a prerequisite for the tale of a sexual fall from grace that Lucas will begin in *AOTC*.[14]

In *AOTC*, as a sexually mature Anakin (of roughly the same age as Luke in *ANH*) proclaims his love and underlying sexual desire for Padmé, the process of thawing or stripping down Padmé into a sexually provocative being can proceed without further delay. In the couple's brief romantic exile to Naboo that forms the middle part of *AOTC*'s narrative, Padmé dresses ever more revealingly, showing more skin even as she resists Anakin's roughly earnest supplications for her sexual favors. Just as Leia will later push away and then succumb to her ardent suitor Han, Padmé rebuffs Anakin's entreaties until a climactic sacrificial moment. Liberated from her confining royal robes and handmaiden's disguises and dressed in a tight white tunic that accentuates her feminine form, Padmé finally proclaims her love for Anakin as they are carried as helpless prisoners toward the gladiatorial arena on Geonosis. Through a plot contrivance that frees the prisoners, Padmé then proceeds to demonstrate her prowess in combat as well as her sexual suitability for the warrior Anakin when her midriff (and, by implication, her womb) is bared throughout the melee between gladiatorial beasts, Jedi, Geonosians, bounty-hunting Fetts, and Dooku. Only then can she be married at the end of *Episode II*. The pairing of Anakin and Padmé is ambiguous, of course, in that the forbidden marriage is a rebellion against duty and tradition—a transgression that will not only destroy the couple's lives but also contribute to massive suffering and the downfall of an entire Republic—but is also the one act that will restore that destroyed tradition through the couple's offspring.

ROTS completes the abjection of Padmé in a dramatically overdetermined fashion—through Padmé's death in childbirth. Indeed, after all the years of speculation by *Star Wars* fans as to what exactly precipitated Anakin's embrace of evil, fueled by persistent rumors of a love triangle involving Obi-Wan and Padmé,[15] Anakin's turn to the Dark Side is revealed to be primarily a function of his desperate desire to save his wife from an agonizing death brought on by what he assumes, in his limited prophetic vision of the future, to be the rigors of childbirth. (Ironically, what Anakin does not see in his fragmentary vision is that Padmé dies essentially by losing her will to live following the heartbreak of witnessing Anakin's fall from grace.)

Of all the possible plot developments that writer/director George Lucas could have selected to provide motivation for Anakin to succumb to the temptations of the Dark Side, the death of Padmé during labor is particularly telling in the series' tendency to reduce initially powerful central female characters to hapless prisoners of their biology and sexuality.[16] While it cannot be denied that the series' male characters suffer various forms of disempowerment, as gruesomely literalized in the numerous amputations of limbs that serve as metaphoric castrations and that are given fullest catastrophic expression in Anakin's mutilation and immolation by lightsaber and lava, it is arguably Padmé who undergoes the severest and ultimately fatal declension of personal dignity in *ROTS* and one specifically configured as female.

The formidable Queen of *Episode I* and the strong-willed Senator of *Episode II*—a woman who at least for a time convinces the love struck and strong-willed Anakin to curtail his romantic passion in deference to the reality of his status as a celibate Jedi—is first introduced in *Episode III* as a woman who hides in the shadows behind a pillar.[17] She beckons her heroically triumphant husband, returning from a key battle of the Clone Wars, away from his male circle of companionship to tell him in private that she is pregnant. She reveals the depth of her helplessness by asking Anakin: "What are we going to do?" Anakin tries hard to pretend he is happy about this news, but both know that the pregnancy will likely end Padmé's political career and perhaps expose Anakin to expulsion from the Jedi order. This introductory scene, illustrating the depth of Padmé's secrecy and isolation, as well as a secondary character in the drama of Anakin's temptation and fall, sets the tone for the remainder of her appearances in *Episode III*.

The next scene in which Padmé appears is set in Anakin and Padmé's penthouse apartment on Coruscant. A briefly romantic interlude, in which Padmé plans for their baby's future on her home planet of Naboo and Anakin and Padmé cloyingly try to outdo one another in their affirmations of love, is followed by Anakin waking up from a nightmare in which he sees Padmé die in childbirth. Characteristically, Anakin refuses to tell a concerned Padmé what his nightmare was. Padmé protests: "How long is it going to take for us to be honest with each other?" Thus chastened, Anakin admits his dream to her.

Throughout this scene, Padmé demonstrates a nearly complete turning away from her social and political responsibilities to her troubled marriage with a stubbornly secretive man. Even when Padmé discusses larger obligations with Anakin, she typically returns to the theme of idyllic isolation from society, as evidenced in the next scene between Anakin and Padmé in their apartment. In response to Anakin's petulance about his shabby treatment by the Jedi Council, Padmé asks him, "Have you ever considered that we may be on the wrong side?... What if the democracy we thought we were serving no longer exists? And the Republic has become the very evil we've been fighting to destroy?" She asks Anakin to use his influence with Chancellor Palpatine to stop the fighting. Anakin becomes visibly angry with her, telling her she sounds like a Separatist and that she needs to make such a request on the floor of the Senate, through proper channels. Padmé retreats from her brief political stand and makes an appeal to pastoral nostalgia to mollify Anakin: "Don't do this. Don't shut me out. Let me help you. Hold me, like you did by the lake on Naboo, so long ago when there was nothing but our love. No politics, no plotting, no war." Basically, throughout these two key scenes in Anakin and Padmé's apartment, Padmé renounces her political power and reestablishes herself solely as Anakin's conscience but therefore subordinate to his prideful temper tantrums, childish plotting, and self-destructive desires.

In the remainder of her scenes in this most tragic of *Star Wars* episodes, Padmé can only stand by helplessly and watch her husband distance himself from her. Of course, the truth is even worse than she knows. As Anakin betrays the Jedi and swears allegiance to his new Sith master, Padmé watches from her lofty citadel the turmoil in the capital city far beneath her, unable to comprehend or influence any of the political events she once helped direct as queen and senator. Returning from his slaughter of Jedi at the Temple, Anakin lies to her about what he calls the Jedi rebellion against the Chancellor, and her only response is "Anakin, I'm afraid." She is defined personally by her subservience to Anakin's moods and politically by her inability to effect any kind of change in the inevitability of Chancellor Palpatine's ascendancy to Emperor status. She only makes one comment in private to the spectacle of Palpatine declaring before the Senate the dissolution of the Republic and the formation of the First Galactic Empire: "So this is how liberty dies. With thunderous applause." Once an active political figure, Padmé is reduced to a passive role as an ineffectual figurehead of a senator and a weeping, heartbroken wife who pleads with her increasingly deceptive and ultimately physically abusive husband for some modicum of honesty.

Padmé's climactic scenes in *Episode III* involve her learning from Obi-Wan the truth about Anakin's fall and rushing to confront her husband. Refusing to believe Obi-Wan or to tell him where Anakin is, Padmé nevertheless is troubled enough by what she has heard and seen to fly to Mustafar to find Anakin so that she can hear him deny what Obi-Wan told her. Slowly realizing the truth about Anakin in their final discussion, even to the extent that she recognizes Anakin indeed killed Jedi younglings in the same fashion as he slaughtered Tusken Raider children years before, she still tries to get him to leave the Jedi and run away with her. In a reversal of the relationship dynamic of the previous film, Padmé has at this point rejected the bulk of her moral principles in favor of an attempt to save a doomed yet passionate relationship.

In yet another temptation scene in a film full of such moments, Anakin, with a suitably hellish backdrop of lava and fire to add mood to the scene, offers Padmé the galaxy as a gift for her loyalty to him. He offers to make her a co-ruler once he has overthrown the Emperor. In what will prove to be her final words to Anakin, she rejects him: "I don't believe what I'm hearing. Obi-Wan was right. You've changed.... I don't know you anymore. Anakin, you're breaking my heart. You're going down a path I can't follow." Enraged by her rejection and Obi-Wan's sudden appearance on the ramp of Padmé's ship, Anakin telekinetically begins to strangle Padmé. Perhaps the most telling imagery of the entire film's treatment of Padmé shows her next sprawled unconscious on the landing platform at Mustafar as Anakin and Obi-Wan circle her supine form, absorbed only with one another in the high drama of male-on-male confrontation and heedless of her plight.

Padmé's final scenes in the film serve to highlight her utter subordination to the demands of biology and patriarchy. Padmé never recovers from the shock of her betrayal by Anakin. She seems literally drained of life, and it is not too fanciful to say she dies of heartbreak, perhaps aggravated by Anakin's telekinetic strangling of her. Yet she speaks only of Anakin to Obi-Wan, asking what has happened to her husband. Obi-Wan, though motivated by kindness, denies her knowledge of her husband's ultimate fate (dismembered, burned, and apparently dead), further rendering her a passive victim of others' manipulations.

To compound her defeat by the type of brutal masculinity represented by Anakin unleashed, her weakened body enters labor. She eventually dies in painful misery, openly exposed and vulnerable to a coldly medical procedure attended only by droids and defeated male Jedi and politicians. The birthing of her children provides little comfort to the dying Padmé; the scene serves as little more than a necessary step in the eventual redemption of the father, whose simultaneous birth as the black-clad Darth Vader is the true focus of the narrative's interest. Padmé's secondary function in the scene is underscored by her last words, which are of the disgraced Anakin that brought her to ruin and foreshadow her son Luke's words to her daughter Leia twenty-some years hence: "There's good in him. I know. I know this." The last we see of Padmé Amidala, former Queen of Naboo and Senator of the Republic, is her body being taken to its final repose during a funeral procession on Naboo. In her hand, she still clutches the small wooden carving given to her long ago by a still-innocent Anakin. Even in death, she cannot let him go.

Now that the *Star Wars* trilogies are completed, at least for the time being, it is startling in retrospect to see how consistent the theme of female sexual abjection to masculine prerogative and privilege has been across six movies that were shaped by literally hundreds of creative collaborators in addition to George Lucas's controlling vision. This lopsided gender dynamic is prominently displayed in a series that supposedly eschews overt sexuality in favor of a preadolescent fairy-tale sensibility. If, in the larger picture, the *Star Wars* movies are about awakenings to adult responsibility, the dawning of sexual desire is depicted as fraught with danger, especially for the central female characters. Padmé and Leia, the mother/daughter "Ice Princesses," pay a heavy price for their thawing.

Notes for Chapter 7

1. Koenraad Kuiper succinctly states the problem of women's roles in the *Star Wars* films: "Ultimately women are vulnerable even if they belong to political elites" (80).

2. Peter Lev states flatly that "In *Star Wars* there simply is no sex" (34). To some extent, George Lucas deliberately attempted to keep his characters free of adult sexuality, most famously in his ordering Carrie Fisher's breasts bound with tape underneath her white gown to reduce the "jiggle" factor. As Dale Pollock puts it, "Lucas simply didn't want sexuality in his fairy tale—no mushy stuff" (165).

3. If the original trilogy strives to keep Luke "always guilt-free and sexually innocent even as he acts out aggressive and sexual impulses against various parent figures" (Gordon, "Power" 199), then Leia takes on the burden of narrative guilt through the various indignities that expose her femininity to voyeuristic public inspection and implied sexual exploitation, most famously in her tenure as Jabba's concubine. Likewise, Leia's mother, Padmé, suffers one of the heaviest prices for Anakin's Satanic fall in *Episode III*.

4. Of Leia, Andrew Gordon writes that her mythic role in the narrative (as constructed by Lucas on the template provided by Joseph Campbell in *The Hero with a Thousand Faces*) is to fulfill the requirement that Luke, the archetypal male hero, must engage in a "Meeting with the Goddess" ("*Star Wars*: A Myth" 80).

5. David Wyatt catalogues what he calls "the ubiquity of garbage" in the films (R2-D2 dumped into the Jawas' sandcrawler, the Death Star garbage masher, the escape from the Star Destroyer in *Episode V*) and links it to an ecological theme—that through these images of broken technology "we are being buried by what once promised to save us" (611). One could also make the case, as does Marguerite Waller, that garbage represents what is messy and disorderly and unacceptable to the Imperial technocrats but, in some ways, is the logical environment of the nonconformists who will save the galaxy from evil. Waller elaborates: "The Empire, which must insist on the fundamental fixity of its categories in order to sustain its single and singular significance, hides its garbage, the evidence that even Imperialists are subject to processes they cannot control, deep inside the Death Star, next to the cell block" (65).

6. For David Wyatt, writing before the release of *Return of the Jedi*, this romantic triangle "will seem merely obligatory until the film comes up with some comfortable beds—this is a world

of hard surfaces—and receptive women" (609). Wyatt, intuitively skeptical that the trilogy will come to any kind of adult reckoning with the complexities of passion, thus anticipates the original trilogy's nearly complete erasure of the Luke/Han/Leia triangle in its third installment. While Lucas claims to have always had in mind that Luke and Leia were brother and sister, the textual evidence of *Episodes IV* and *V* suggests otherwise. Han's brief jealousy about Luke's closeness to Leia in *Return of the Jedi* is the last vestige of this formerly prominent love triangle. Any discomfort on Luke's part that he has been in the past unmistakably attracted to a woman who turned out to be his sister is steadfastly and disingenuously denied by the narrative.

7. Of course, the flatness of the *Star Wars* main characters irrespective of their genders has been the subject of an ongoing critical debate, with those who maintain that the shallowness of characterization betrays an artistic deficit or even soullessness on the part of George Lucas and with others who advocate that what makes the films so overwhelmingly popular is precisely this type of sketchily drawn character who can be all things to all people. For example, Robert Horton writes that "The simple, clean lines of *Star Wars* are exactly what makes the films evocative. We can project our own colors into its many blank spaces" (4).

8. Garry Jenkins observes that "The *Empire* storyline raised the sexual stakes between Solo and Leia. Gone was the asexual dialogue of *Star Wars*" (204).

9. An enthusiastic Andrew Lewis Conn exults that the "sparring" between Han and Leia "brings to mind the best Cary Grant/Rosalind Russell/Tracy/Hepburn screwball comedies" (8). Perhaps, but the key confrontation between Han and Leia, wherein Han tells Leia she likes him because he's a scoundrel and there aren't enough scoundrels in her life, is more reminiscent of the antagonistic sexuality between Rhett Butler and Scarlett O'Hara in *Gone with the Wind*. Indeed, one of the advertising posters for the *Empire Strikes Back* shows a pose between Han and Leia, with Han dominant and Leia supine, that is very similar to the famous iconography of Rhett and Scarlett on the *Gone with the Wind* posters. Interestingly, Garry Jenkins writes that George Lucas, in creating the love triangle of Han/Luke/Leia, intended the trilogy to be "an intergalactic *Gone with the Wind*" (78). Lucas's biographer Dale Pollock concurs: "Lucas wanted the sexual rivalry between Han and Luke over Leia to duplicate the classic screen jealousy of Clark Gable and Leslie Howard over Vivian Leigh in *Gone with the Wind*" (144).

10. Steven A. Galipeau elaborates: "The space slug represents for these characters the threat of being 'devoured' by their undifferentiated, unconscious emotions" (121).

11. On the evidence of this scene, Steven A. Galipeau sees Han as a teacher—someone who can instruct Leia in what it means to be alive and passionate: "As Yoda will do for Luke, Han begins educating Leia about herself" (111).

12. In reference to *Episode V's* continually deferred jump to light-speed, David Wyatt calls the bulk of the film "foreplay" (611) to the rather anticlimactic moment when the stars finally streak past the *Millennium Falcon's* cockpit and the heroes escape Darth Vader. Given the frustratingly interrupted courtship of Han and Leia, the scene feels anticlimactic, perhaps because Han is disconcertingly absent at the moment that symbolizes the type of orgasmic release that ended *Episode IV*.

13. Andrew Gordon says of this scene: "From one extreme, the tough, mannish woman, [Leia] is reduced to the other extreme, a shapely sex slave" ("Power" 201). Tom Carson goes one

step further, claiming that the scene reveals Lucas's fascination with the theme of miscegenation: "When Princess Leia is in captivity, it's unmistakably the outer-space version of that classic darkest-Africa pulp fantasy: the white girl about to be despoiled by slobbering savages. Revealingly, the sequence is also the only time our heroine gets to exhibit any erotic allure—who'd have guessed that, under that bland pie-face, Carrie Fisher was pure hubba-hubba below the neck?" (169).

14. In his personal reflection on the meaning of the two trilogies, Todd Hanson describes the memory of his own boyhood reaction to seeing Leia on-screen and then equates it to what Anakin feels about Padmé: "Princess Leia was one of my first crushes ... and it's strange to remember that presexual version of desire, when you were awed by and drawn to physical beauty, aching for the unapproachable object of your affections from the impossible distance of being too young, but you didn't fantasize about sex, you just wanted to marry them.... And it is that exact feeling of childhood longing that's evoked by Anakin's little-boy crush on Padmé, the handmaiden that he is not yet aware is not only a queen, but also the future mother of his son and daughter" (196).

15. See, for example, this passage in Pollock's biography of Lucas: "There will also be a torrid love triangle among the grown-up Queen (who will give birth to twins, Luke and Leia), Annakin Skywalker, and Ben Kenobi. The consequences of this love triangle are one of the great betrayals layered throughout the three prequels that have enormous impact on all of the major characters in the story" (287). Some hint of this love triangle remains in the completed film, notably in a scene in Anakin and Padmé's apartment where Anakin reacts with suspicion to the knowledge that Obi-Wan was there earlier in Anakin's absence and again at the film's fiery climax when Anakin believes Padmé has brought Obi-Wan to Mustafar to kill him.

16. George Lucas is quoted as joking that Anakin's turn is precipitated by Padmé's nagging: "Small talk turns to what exactly will push Anakin to the dark side. 'It'll be Padmé,' George says. 'She'll get so angry at him for not picking up his socks'" (Rinzler 18). While Lucas's comment is obviously tongue-in-cheek, the joke is indicative of the trilogies' focus on adolescent male fear of female criticism and a corresponding need to disempower those women, often by stripping them of clothing or otherwise making them look absurd (Byzantine hairdos, etc.). Along these lines, Jeff Bond, writing before the release of *Episode III* and obviously without foreknowledge of Padmé's fate, jokes that "Hottie Amidala's with child(ren) in this one, so no CG monsters will be conveniently ripping her clothes off." Again, a comment like this illustrates a tendency of some segments of *Star Wars* fandom to respond favorably to the series' misogynistic reductiveness of its own heroines.

17. Olly Richards describes the change in the characterization of Padmé between *Episodes II* and *III* in rather flippant but nonetheless accurate terms: "In *Episode II*, you may remember, Queen-turned-Senator Padmé Amidala let down her bizarrely coiffed hair and exhibited a gung-ho spirit unusual in a royal. But thanks to some furtive nookie with the future Most Evil Man In The Universe, she now finds herself consigned to 'little country getaways,' resting her swollen ankles, flicking through baby-name books (Larry? Liam? Luke!), and waiting for her one true love to get back from a hard day's murdering" (102).

Works Cited

Bond, Jeff. "Sith Happens: The 10 Things to Watch for in *Revenge of the Sith*." *Cinefantastique* 37.3 (June 2005): 39.

Carson, Tom. "Jedi Uber Alles." *A Galaxy Not So Far Away: Writers and Artists on Twenty-Five Years of* Star Wars. Ed. Glenn Kenny. New York: Henry Holt and Company, 2002. 160-71.

Conn, Andrew Lewis. "*Star Wars*: Always." *Film Comment* 33.3 (May/June 1997): 2, 7-8.

Galipeau, Steven A. *The Journey of Luke Skywalker: An Analysis of Modern Myth and Symbol.* Chicago: Open Court, 2001.

Gordon, Andrew. "The Power of the Force: Sex in the *Star Wars* Trilogy." *Eros in the Mind's Eye: Sexuality and the Fantastic in Art and Film.* Ed. Donald Palumbo. New York: Greenwood P, 1986. 193-207.

———. "*Star Wars*: A Myth for Our Time." *Literature/Film Quarterly* 6.4 (Fall 1978): 314-26. *Screening the Sacred: Religion, Myth, and Ideology in Popular American Film.* Eds. Joel W. Martin and Conrad E. Ostwalt, Jr. Boulder, CO: Westview P, 1995. 73-82.

Hanson, Todd. "A Big Dumb Movie about Space Wizards: Struggling to Cope with *The Phantom Menace*." *A Galaxy Not So Far Away: Writers and Artists on Twenty-Five Years of* Star Wars. Ed. Glenn Kenny. New York: Henry Holt and Company, 2002. 172-202.

Holte, Jim. "Pilgrims in Space: Puritan Ideology and the American Science Fiction Film." *Eros in the Mind's Eye: Sexuality and the Fantastic in Art and Film.* Ed. Donald Palumbo. New York: Greenwood P, 1986. 181-92.

Horstman, Joey Earl. "Twenty Years Ago, in a Galaxy Not So Far Away ... *Star Wars*." *Other Side* 33.2 (Mar./Apr. 1997): 52-4.

Horton, Robert. "*Star Wars*: Enough A'ready." *Film Comment* 33.3 (May/June 1997): 3-4.

Jenkins, Garry. *Empire Building: The Remarkable Real Life Story of* Star Wars. Secaucus, NJ: Citadel P, 1999.

Kuiper, Koenraad. "*Star Wars*: An Imperial Myth." *Journal of Popular Culture* 21.4 (Spring 1988): 77-86.

Lev, Peter. "Whose Future? *Star Wars, Alien,* and *Blade Runner*." *Literature/Film Quarterly* 26.1 (1998): 30-7.

Miller, Martin, and Robert Sprich. "The Appeal of *Star Wars*: An Archetypal-Psychoanalytic View." *American Imago* 38.2 (Summer 1981): 203-20.

Pollock, Dale. *Skywalking: The Life and Films of George Lucas, Updated Edition.* New York: Da Capo P, 1999.

Reynolds, David West. Star Wars: *The Visual Dictionary.* New York: DK Publishing, 1998.

Richards, Olly. "The Senator: Natalie Portman." *Empire* (June 2005): 102-4.

Rieder, John. "Embracing the Alien: Science Fiction in Mass Culture." *Science Fiction Studies* 9.1 (March 1982): 26-37.

Rinzler, J.W. *The Making of* Star Wars: Revenge of the Sith. New York: Del Rey, 2005.

Slavicsek, Bill. *A Guide to the* Star Wars *Universe.* London: Boxtree, 1995.

Waller, Marguerite. "Poetic Influence in Hollywood: *Rebel without a Cause* and *Star Wars*." *Diacritics* 10.3 (Fall 1980): 57-66.

Wilkinson, David. *The Power of the Force: The Spirituality of the* Star Wars *Films*. Oxford: Lion Publishing, 2000.

Wyatt, David. "*Star Wars* and the Productions of Time." *Virginia Quarterly Review* 58.4 (Autumn 1982): 600–15.

CHAPTER 8

How the *Star Wars* Saga Evokes the Creative Promise of Homosexual Love: A Gay-Centered Psychological Perspective

Roger Kaufman

On the surface, it appears that few of the main characters in the six-film *Star Wars* space opera have any sexual romantic love in their lives. Only two heterosexual romances are featured in the movie saga, and the first of these, the fateful courtship of Padmé Naberrie (Natalie Portman) and Anakin Skywalker (Hayden Christensen), is portrayed as horribly destructive for the individuals involved and for their entire civilization. The second relationship, a fitful flirtation between Han Solo (Harrison Ford) and Princess Leia (Carrie Fisher), is distinctly secondary to the primary plot.

Yet, when the *Star Wars* film narrative is viewed from a gay-centered psychological perspective, a vibrant galaxy imbued with the propulsive, creative "intelligence" of archetypal homosexual love is revealed. It's not clear to what extent George Lucas knowingly intended these themes of gay love to be a primary aspect of *Star Wars* symbolic meaning, but I will suggest that, whether the filmmaker is conscious of it or not, the distinctive allure of homosexual romance is so potent, inspiring, politically relevant, and potentially curative that it has found its way from the depths of his mind to the scripts and screen. At the same time, I will highlight what I suspect are homophobic aspects of Lucas's approach, which muffles and sometimes twists the depiction of same-sex love and its archetypal significance in the *Star Wars* universe.

This analysis focuses primarily on the six feature-length *Star Wars* films produced, written, and/or directed by Lucas and does not address story aspects portrayed in some ancillary novels, games, or other materials.

Laying the Groundwork: The Theory of Gay-Centered Psychology

My exploration of homosexual themes in the *Star Wars* films is informed by the gay-centered psychoanalytic point of view pioneered by contemporary psychologist Mitch Walker, who has explicated a penetrating archetypal understanding of gay subjectivity and homosexual love through a synthesis of the concepts of Freudian psychoanalysis and Jungian psychology with the homocentric thought of numerous generations of gay liberation thinkers, many of whom based their work on the foundational ideas seminally expressed by the Greek philosopher Plato. Writing almost 2,400 years ago, the ancient sage described "celestial" homosexual love in his *Symposium* as uniquely capable of birthing immortal "children" of the mind in the form of wisdom, poetry, and art (53). Significantly inspired by Plato, the German activist Karl Heinrich Ulrichs (1825–1895) became the first Western person since the days of antiquity to publicly come out as a homosexual, followed by the writer Edward Carpenter (1844–1929), who was the first English-speaking person to discourse openly about the distinctive qualities of homosexual individuals. In 1950, the political activist Harry Hay (1914–2002) cofounded the first gay rights organization in the United States, the Mattachine Society. He helped to inspire the modern gay liberation movement by describing homosexuals as "a separate people whose time has come" with distinctive social, creative, and spiritual qualities (Hay 279).

In order to develop and deepen the revolutionary ideas of these homosexual visionaries, Walker has grounded his gay-centered theory in the work of the psychologist C. G. Jung, who articulated an unparalleled appreciation for the unconscious human psyche as a vast, subjectively "real" inner world structured by *archetypes*, or root feeling-laden images, that shape and inspire people's experiences and actions when they manifest as *complexes* or semi-autonomous "persons" within the mind that interact with each other in a constant internal drama. Jung suggested that this dynamic interior world is driven by the *libido*, which he understood as the vital "energy" of the mind, featuring its own symbolic intelligence and "intentionality," encompassing but not limited to the central sexual instinct first articulated by Sigmund Freud (Jung 137). Moving beyond Jung and Freud in his 1991 article, "Jung and Homophobia," Walker proposed the concept of *homosexual libido*, which describes the distinctive archetypal configuration of purposive psychic energy that can be seen to provide the impetus for same-sex romantic love, modern gay identity, and homosexual self-realization (60).

Prior to his clarification of homosexual libido, Walker introduced another archetypal concept that is fundamental to understanding homosexual romance and its psychological meaning, as well as virtually all same-sex relationships. In his 1976 article, "The Double: An Archetypal Configuration," Walker elucidated the archetype of the *double* as a distinct same-sex figure in the psyche of each individual, understood as a metaphoric foundation for congruent ego identity and also as the basis for "brotherly" and "sisterly" love when projected onto other persons of the same sex (165). It is frequently symbolized by the image of twins, such as the zodiacal Gemini or the inseparable Dioscouri of Greek myth, as well as myriad other similar images of same-sex partners throughout art, literature, and mythology.

Walker further described how the double archetype, when it is infused by homosexual libido in the psyche of an individual, functions as what Jung called the *soul-figure*. This autonomous complex of singular erotic romantic charge within the mind of each individual must be related to consciously in a most important way as a central personification of the psyche in order for a person to fully *individuate* and achieve integrated *psychological wholeness*. According to Jung, it is when this inner complex is projected onto another person that romantic love occurs. In his homophobia and heterosexism, Jung thought that the soul-figure always manifested in the image of the sexually alluring opposite sex, known as the *anima* in men and the *animus* in women, but Walker has shown how the double archetype, when charged by homosexual libido, provides just such a soul-figure relationship—in this case same-sex—for an individual's ego identity ("Jung and Homophobia" 62). As Walker describes it for gay men, this is the experience of "having a special, erotic, twin 'brother' who is felt to be the 'source of inspiration'" inside the psyche (62). Such a homosexual dynamic is naturally most prominent in the psychology of gay-identified individuals, but I would suggest that the visceral experience of watching the *Star Wars* films combined with their symbolic evocation of homosexual love may help people of *all* sexualities in their journey of individuation. In this understanding, affection inspired by the double has a distinctive quality of *libidinal twinship mutuality* that can be developed inside the mind of both gay and non-gay people, leading toward a homosexually romantic relationship between the conscious ego and the unconscious psyche that can birth a more spirited, profound, and politically alive experience of autonomous individuality, vital new creativity, and personal moral centeredness.

This deep view of human subjectivity is intentionally introverted, focusing primary attention on the libidinal *inner world* of the psyche, and could be described as essentialist, in contradistinction to the academically popular theories of social constructionism or postmodernism as exemplified by French theorist Michel Foucault in such works as *The History of Sexuality, Vol. 1*. While certain superficial aspects of personal identity and cultural style may indeed be influenced by the insidious power dynamics that Foucault and his followers highlight, the central libidinal urge of a positive attraction for the same sex, in my view, cannot be determinatively so constructed by external factors. I argue that homosexual libido aboriginally arises from the deepest center of the unconscious, where the social forces and discourses of any particular historical period have minimal influence. This essentialist perspective is grounded in my own felt experience of my homosexual libido as indigenous and numinous, a term Jung used to highlight the hypnotically compelling and fascinating quality of psychic contents when they rise into consciousness. This soulful, gay-centered point of view is further supported by recent historical research conducted by, for example, Louis Crompton in his *Homosexuality and Civilization*. He has documented how countless individuals have experienced romantic same-sex love and even a kind of stable homosexual personhood since at least the earliest days of recorded history—often in the face of condemnation or even the threat of death—long before there were modern terms such as *homosexuality* or *gay identity*.

My theoretical approach also departs from the standard Jungian literature, which, with the notable exception of Mitch Walker's work and that of a handful of other writers, has almost completely ignored homosexual archetypes. A typical example of this homophobic lacuna appears in the classical Jungian analysis of *Episodes IV through VI* entitled, *The Journey of Luke Skywalker*, by psychotherapist Steven Galipeau. Galipeau otherwise provides a reasonable assessment of *Star Wars* symbolism while completely disregarding any possible homosexual themes in the trilogy, and he thereby seriously limits the depth and import of his discussion.

While Jung himself was unable to fully appreciate the significance of homosexual archetypes, I agree with him that "the psyche is the greatest of all cosmic wonders" (qtd. in *Matter of Heart*), and the *Star Wars* epic, for all its imperfections, provides a richly condensed, symbolic representation of the grandly numinous, evolving unconscious psyche. Many of the other essays in this anthology that highlight such limitations in the *Star Wars* films as sexism, racism, violence, and fascism do have their merits, just as my own analysis identifies homophobia in the saga. Yet these largely extroverted concerns, often making highly literal interpretations of details in the films, are not able to uncover the kind of meaning revealed when a more introverted and symbolic—though no less politically aware—perspective is embraced instead, as I will endeavor to demonstrate below.

Romance by Any Other Name: Same-Sex Partnerships in *Star Wars*

The *Star Wars* galaxy is notable for the prominence of the many abiding same-sex partnerships depicted, with at least twenty-eight different pairs of twin relationships featured in the six films, as listed in the following table. All these same-sex bonds evoke the archetype of the double, and many can also be seen as meaningfully inspired by homosexual libido, since, viewed in their fullest depth, these companionships strongly resemble the typical patterns of same-sex

Table 1. Archetype of the Double: Significant Same-Sex Twinship Pairs in the Six-Film *Star Wars* Saga

Qui-Gon Jinn & Obi-Wan Kenobi M, P, E, L, TF, TM, TS

Qui-Gon Jinn & Anakin Skywalker M, P, L, TF, TM

Qui-Gon Jinn & Yoda   M, E, TF, TM, TS

Qui-Gon Jinn & Jar Jar Binks M, L, TF

Obi-Wan Kenobi & Anakin Skywalker   M, P, E, L, TF, TM, TS, C, FS

Obi-Wan Kenobi & Yoda   M, E, L, TF, TM, TS

Anakin Skywalker & Yoda   M, L, TF, TM, TS

Anakin Skywalker & Watto   EX, FS

Darth Sidious & Darth Vader EX, P, L, TF, TM, FS, F

Darth Sidious & Darth Tyranus   EX, P, TF, TM

Darth Sidious & Darth Maul EX, P, TF, TM

Luke Skywalker & Obi-Wan Kenobi   M, P, E, L, TF, TM, TS

Luke Skywalker & Han Solo   C, M, E, L, TF

Luke Skywalker & Yoda M, P, E, L, TF, TM, TS

Luke Skywalker & Darth Vader   C, P, L, TF, TS, FS, R

Padmé & Queen Amidala   M, P, E, L

Padmé Naberrie & Cordé   M, L

Padmé Naberrie & Dormé   M, L

R2-D2 & C-3PO   M, P, E, L, TF, TS

R2-D2 & Anakin Skywalker   M, L

R2-D2 & Luke Skywalker   M, E, L

C-3PO & Anakin Skywalker   M, L, TF, F

Han Solo & Lando Calrissian C, M, E, L

Chewbacca & Han Solo M, P, E, L

Chewbacca & C-3PO   M, L

Boba & Jango Fett M, P, E, L, TF, FS

Nute Gunray & Rune Haako M, P, E

Two-Headed Troig: Fode & Beed   M, P, E

Luke Skywalker & Princess Leia   E, L, TF, O

KEY

M = mutual; P = primary; E = enduring; L = lifesaving;

TF = transformative; TM = transmissive; TS = transcendent;

EX = exploitive; C = competitive; R = redemptive;

F = Frankenstein motif; FS = father-son motif;

O = opposite-sex biological twins

romantic love even though there is no sexual contact shown or implied on the screen. To explore this hypothesis, I have identified seven qualities that are conspicuous in many of the same-sex partnerships portrayed in the *Star Wars* narrative. They describe relationships that are (1) *mutual*, (2) *primary*, (3) *enduring*, (4) *lifesaving*, (5) *transformative*, (6) *transmissive*, and (7) *transcendent*. Each of these facets will now be described and illustrated with pertinent examples from the films.

1. Mutual Relationships

In a caring bond between two people of the same sex, there is often a distinct, twin-like mirroring quality achieved that, as Walker writes, "creates an atmosphere ... of profound equality and deep familiarity, a mysterious joyful sharing of feelings and needs, a dynamic, intuitive understanding" ("Double" 169). Mutual regard of this sort is a most notable feature in many *Star Wars* relationships where commensurate worth of personhood is present, even though the participants are often not of the same rank or age. Walker has described a particular manifestation of the double archetype termed the *youth-adult*, where "an older person [is] guiding a younger one into adulthood, while in return the younger person inspires new strength in the principles or the particular quest of the older" ("Double" 171). This is perhaps the most common type of twinship in the *Star Wars* galaxy, especially as it is the foundation for the eons-old training method of the Jedi Knights, who, as Padawan learners, are each linked in a close one-on-one relationship with their masters. A prominent example of this tradition is shown by the kind fellowship between Jedi Knight Qui-Gon Jinn (Liam Neeson) and his apprentice Obi-Wan Kenobi (Ewan McGregor). Lucas emphasizes the mutual, twin-like aspect of this mentor relationship by first showing the two Knights enter in *The Phantom Menace* (1999) wearing matching hooded robes, identical except for the shade of brown used. Through the course of the film, we see Obi-Wan and Qui-Gon experience some disagreements, but, overall, they operate together as highly synchronized partners who can respond intuitively to one another's cues. We watch their reciprocal regard and respect steadily grow until, when Qui-Gon is impaled by Darth Maul (Ray Park), Obi-Wan cries out an extended, painful, "NOOOOO!" of agony, thereby revealing the depth of his affection. After he succeeds in destroying Darth Maul, Obi-Wan rushes to his fallen master, who fondly strokes Obi-Wan's cheek with his finger just before dying. Overwhelmed by grief, Obi-Wan rests his face on Qui-Gon's. Only death is able to interrupt the intimate mutuality of their steadfast bond.

Another prominent example of twinship mutuality can be seen in the relationship between Obi-Wan and Anakin Skywalker. At the opening of *Attack of* the Clones (2002), there is substantial father-son friction between the two characters, but a more brotherly dynamic of their friendship develops to the point where, in the opening sequence of Revenge of the Sith (2005), we see two identical Jedi fighter spacecraft swirling and twirling together in a beautiful duet through a breathtaking space battle, the occupants of which are soon revealed as Obi-Wan and a newly mature Anakin. When Obi-Wan's craft is inundated by buzz droids, Anakin disobeys his order to abandon him, saying, "I'm not leaving without you, Master." Obi-Wan may officially hold the senior position, but the relationship has been equalized by his Padawan learner's growing prowess. The immensely close bond that develops between Obi-Wan and Anakin is strikingly evoked in the authorized novel version of Revenge of the Sith by Matthew Stover, who writes, "Blade-to-blade, they were identical. After thousands of hours in lightsaber sparring, they knew each other better than brothers, more intimately than lovers; they were complementary halves of a single warrior" (397).

An additional example of abiding mutual regard can be seen in the odd-couple partnership of R2-D2 (Kenny Baker) and C-3PO (Anthony Daniels). These two droids may not look at all like each other, and have distinctly different personalities, but their unique, mirroring kinship is obvious through many trials and tribulations over the course of the film saga. Indeed, C-3PO sometimes refers to R2-D2 as his "counterpart," which Webster's Dictionary defines as "a person or thing closely resembling another, esp. in function...a copy or duplicate ... one of two parts that fit, complete or complement one another," which is an ideal description of mutuality, effectively echoing the novelized description of Obi-Wan and Anakin cited above as "complementary halves of a single warrior."

Double imagery that provides supportive visual and thematic echoes of mutuality, equality, and mirroring appears virtually everywhere in the Star Wars galaxy. There's the intimate affiliation of Queen Amidala and her loyal bodyguard Padmé shown in The Phantom Menace, where both characters are played by the same actress, Natalie Portman. In Attack of the Clones, bounty hunter Jango Fett (Temuera Morrison) is raising an identical cloned copy of himself as his son, Boba (Daniel Logan). There's also the resilient alliance of Viceroy Nute Gunray (Silas Carson) and his attaché, Rune Haako (Jerome Blake), lasting through Episodes I through III until they are murdered together at the end of Revenge of the Sith. Even the planet of Tatooine, childhood home of both Anakin and Luke Skywalker (Mark Hamill), features twin suns. And although it is between members of the opposite sex, the biological brother-sister twinship of Luke and Princess Leia provides an echoing variation on the more ubiquitous theme of same-sex twinships throughout the narrative.

As Walker puts it, "Double fuses the fate of two into one" ("Double" 169). This ultimate unity of the twins can be seen imaginatively depicted in The

Phantom Menace by the enthusiastic, bilingual, two-headed, four-armed celebrity announcer for the dramatic pod race on Tatooine, a Troig named Fode and Beed, two male personalities in one body who speak and even sway together in mutual harmony.

2. Primary Relationships

As can be seen in the above example of the two-headed Troig, mutual twin partnerships in *Star Wars* are often also the *primary* relationship in the characters' lives, superceding all others in intensity, quality, significance, and sheer amount of time spent together. For example, Obi-Wan successively shares primary bonds with both Qui-Gon and Anakin. In each case, the partners are virtually inseparable during their time together, traveling everywhere throughout the galaxy as a team, with the physical and emotional closeness that such space-faring logistics require. As noted above, this pattern of same-sex primary relationship is the *standard* mode of operation for the Jedi Order, which has operated as guardian of the Republic's basic values for thousands of years. It's also relevant to note that with the single exception of Anakin, none of the male Jedi Knights are ever shown in the films to be married or have any sort of romantic liaisons with women. In fact, it is explained in *Attack of the Clones* that such attachments are forbidden in the Order.

Primary same-sex partnerships are also the standard mode of relationship on the dark side of the Force, which features principal affiliations between Darth Sidious, also known as Chancellor Palpatine and the Emperor (Ian McDiarmid), and his successive apprentices, including Darth Maul, Darth Tyranus (Christopher Lee), and Darth Vader (Hayden Christensen/David Prowse/voice by James Earl Jones). In all these cases, the apprentice's life is utterly devoted to his master's wishes. In *Return of the Jedi* (1983), the Dark Sith Lord even proposes such a relationship to Luke Skywalker when he says, "Fulfill your destiny and take your father's place at my side!"

Luke is strong enough to refuse the offer partly because of the nurturing he has gained from his more fruitful primary relationship with "Ben" Obi-Wan Kenobi (Alec Guinness), as first shown in *A New Hope* (1977). Although the time span of the relationship while both are alive is relatively short, there is no question of their prime importance to each other. A similar statement could be made about Luke's relationship with Darth Vader, as will be discussed below. One more example of note is the "counterpart" bond between R2-D2 and C-3PO, who are clearly the primary person in one another's lives. They each have meaningful relationships with other characters, but always, without fail, return to one another's company after any separation. As R2-D2 heads off into the climactic space battle shown in *A New Hope*, C-3PO cries out, "Hang on R2, you've got to come back. You wouldn't want my life to get boring, would you?"

3. Enduring Relationships

The resilient affection between many characters of the same sex in the *Star Wars* films lasts throughout their lifetimes, sometimes shaken but never fully broken by the tensions within the relationship or by external threats. Obi-Wan and Qui-Gon clearly have an indissoluble kinship, suspended only when Qui-Gon is slain by Darth Maul. Another prominent example is the affiliation between Obi-Wan and Yoda (Frank Oz), who are not often the primary figures in one another's lives, but who appear to have a fecund and steadfast lifelong connection. Luke Skywalker's bonds with Obi-Wan and Yoda do not last long in life but do have an abiding quality once the bond is made. And all of these relationships just named eventually continue past death, as will be discussed below. One more example is the reliable pair of R2-D2 and C-3PO, whose enduring partnership survives multiple separations, dismantlings, and even C-3PO's mind-wipe at the end of *Revenge of the Sith*.

4. Lifesaving Acts in Relationships

The stakes are often extraordinarily high in same-sex partnerships throughout the saga. In *Revenge of the Sith*, Anakin must carry an unconscious Obi-Wan on his back through a burning spaceship in order to keep him alive. Afterward, the partners playfully argue about whether Anakin has saved Obi-Wan's life nine times or ten. As they are constantly in life-or-death situations together, it's safe to say that in almost all of the master-Padawan relationships, there are multiple opportunities for each to save the other's life. On the Dark Side of the Force, it is Darth Sidious who saves what's left of Anakin's life after Obi-Wan has left him amputated and on fire beside the lava flows of Mustafar. In *A New Hope*, Obi-Wan saves Luke from the vicious sand people and even uses a little Jedi power to bring him back to consciousness. As Walker has written, "The double is a powerful helper, full of magic to aid in an individual's struggles" ("Double" 168). Later in the same film, Obi-Wan sacrifices his own life, instantly transforming into a still-helpful spirit, so that Luke, Han, Leia, R2-D2, and C-3PO can escape from the clutches of Darth Vader.

5. Transformative Relationships

One of the most symbolically meaningful aspects of same-sex pairs in *Star Wars* is their life-changing, transformative nature. Anakin could never have become a powerful Jedi Knight if it wasn't for his fast bond with Qui-Gon, who managed to free him from slavery and whose offer of Jedi training was strong enough to separate the prepubescent boy from his mother. Along these lines, it seems reasonable to state that the very *purpose* of the relationships between Jedi Masters and their Padawan learners is to transform the younger person into a full-fledged Jedi Knight who is capable of effectively manipulating the Force, while the intensity of the relationship often ends up transforming the master, too. Clearly, the course of Obi-Wan's life is set in motion by his meeting and partnership with Anakin, even as his influential training of Anakin spurs the Chosen One toward many fateful choices that utterly transform *his* life, including a gruesome, Frankenstein-like metamorphosis into Darth Vader by Darth Sidious. Additional examples of life-changing relationships are seen in Luke Skywalker's journey, which is defined by mutually transformative encounters with Obi-Wan, Yoda, and Darth Vader.

6.   Transmissive Dynamics in Relationships

Transformative relationships in the *Star Wars* films most often also have what I am naming here as a *transmissive* nature, which means that mystical knowledge and powers are experientially transferred from the mind and body of the master to his apprentice. This concept is derived from, for example, Buddhist meditative traditions in which a true enlightenment experience cannot be merely described but must be impelled to occur in the monk by his or her spiritual teacher through various techniques and exercises over many years of dedicated practice in close proximity.

It may be helpful to imagine an embodied sense of what these *Star Wars* relationships *feel* like for the characters involved, particularly as they revolve around intimate training in the perception and manipulation of the Force. To appreciate this more viscerally, consider the experience as a Padawan of being taught by your master how to move the Force with and through your body. As one aspect of this experience, perhaps your master would give you a felt experience of the Force by propelling it through your anatomy for you. As Obi-Wan says about the Force to Luke in *A New Hope*, "It surrounds us, it penetrates us, it binds the galaxy together." Learning the special penetrative properties of the Force is not something a Padawan can do merely by reading some sort of high-tech Jedi textbook. As depicted in the *Star Wars* films, the manipulation of this fundamental life energy with magical properties must be taught through an intimate, transmissive, same-sex partnership extending over many years. A similar dynamic can just as easily be imagined in the relationship between Darth Sidious and his apprentices, as he transmits to each of them what he claims to be the even more powerful magic of the Dark Side of the Force.

7. Transcendent Relationships

Perhaps the most remarkable aspect of certain same-sex twinships in *Star Wars* is that their enduring quality continues past the death of one or both of the partners. This ultimate achievement is first articulated at the end of *Revenge of the Sith* when Yoda explains to Obi-Wan that his former beloved master, Qui-Gon, has transcended death and achieved immortality. "How to commune with him, I will teach you," Yoda says to a very surprised and heartened Obi-Wan. A once-durable relationship that had seemingly ended in the tragic slaying of Qui-Gon at the end of *The Phantom Menace* is finally revealed to be stronger than death. And perhaps now it's easier to imagine how Obi-Wan spends his time while living alone during the nineteen years of exile in his Tatooine hideout.

Using the skills he has presumably learned from Qui-Gon during that period, Obi-Wan is able to keep his own spirit intact beyond the sacrifice of his bodily life at the stroke of Darth Vader's lightsaber, as shown in *A New Hope* and *The Empire Strikes Back* (1980). Now, as a sentient ghost, he continues his mentorship of Luke throughout the young man's heroic journey. Obi-Wan's spirit is joined at the very end of the saga by those of Yoda and the pre-Vader Anakin, once he has been redeemed by Luke. Amongst the still-living characters, the younger male Jedi is the only one who has the ability to commune with the ghosts of his father and male mentors. It also seems particularly relevant that these three older male Jedi are shown together in the afterlife, no spirits of the opposite sex anywhere in sight, their bonds now apparently eternal.

Section Summary: The Symbolic Meaning of Same-Sex Relationships in *Star Wars*

Most of the prominent same-sex partnerships in *Star Wars* feature several, if not all, of the fundamental relationship qualities described above. As an initial summarizing example, emblematic of the Jedi Order tradition, the warm companionship between Obi-Wan and Qui-Gon can now be seen as mutual, primary, enduring, lifesaving, transformative, transmissive, and ultimately transcendent of death, possibly lasting into eternity. What could be a better description of romantic love, in this case between members of the same sex? That we are never shown the two Jedi sexually relating seems like an insignificant detail when these aggregate qualities are considered together. Along these same lines, it can be seen that Luke Skywalker has mutual, primary, enduring, lifesaving, transformative, transmissive, and transcendent relationships with both Obi-Wan and Yoda. A much more complicated but similarly libidinal relationship also occurs between Luke and Darth Vader, as will be discussed below. One more prominent example is the lifelong dynamic between Obi-Wan and Anakin. This passionate alliance includes a horrible descent for both men into antagonistic destructiveness, and, yet, when viewed from its ultimately immortal perspective, the overall pattern can be seen to have all seven qualities of intimate bonds as delineated above.

Many of these facets of relationships are especially prominent in—if not exclusive to—romantic same-sex love. In particular, I wish to highlight the distinct mutuality that is a central feature of the mirroring that occurs when members of the same sex love each other, which can be contrasted with the typical dynamics of heterosexual romance in virtually all human cultures where there are blatant, problematic power imbalances between women and men.

Along these lines, I would suggest that it's not accidental that many of the ardent same-sex relationships in *Star Wars* and in our own world that feature twinship mutuality are also transformative, transmissive, and transcendent. Just as Plato suggested that homosexual love has its own "mentally pregnant" nonbiological creativity (52), so it can be additionally seen, as Walker has described, that same-sex romance is a particularly rich catalyst for shamanic endeavors moving toward self-realization and enlightenment ("Double" 170; "Jung" 64). Support for this concept can be found in Will Roscoe's *Jesus and the Shamanic Tradition of Same-Sex Love*, which describes the central importance of transmissive, same-sex rituals that were an integral part of many mystical sects in the Middle East during the time of Jesus, including possibly how this central figure in Western civilization may have related to his own disciples and other followers (12). It was in particular the reciprocal, equal, and mirroring aspects of same-sex intimacy that provided the "charge" for these often-naked rituals, Roscoe explains, and he bolsters his thesis with examples of homosexual shamanic traditions that have appeared in cultures throughout human history, ranging from the spiritual "soft man" of Siberian indigenous peoples (119) to the Native American "two-spirit" *berdaches*, who often crossed gender lines and lived homosexually with other men as "married" while they descended into the unseen mystical underworld in order to bring new consciousness and healing to their people (139). Similarly, a Jedi Master is a kind of shaman in a same-sex primary relationship that transmits his knowledge of the invisible Force underlying the visible world to his Padawan learner.

Here, I'd like to suggest that, as it inspires both the Jedi and Sith, the Force functions in the same way that homosexual libido can be seen to spur the spiritual traditions described above, as well as same-sex romantic love itself. In other words, the Force can be understood as a vivid conceptualization of homosexual libido, especially as it becomes the focus of Jedi and Sith relationships.

Objections might be raised that I am describing same-sex relationships as *romantic* and inspired by *homosexual libido* that are at best *homoerotic* or *homosocial*. In my view, these two latter terms are homophobic euphemisms intended to avoid what may actually be the psychologically meaningful libidinal roots of such partnerships. An honest exploration of what really drives passionate same-sex relationships in *Star Wars* and in our own world must consider the role that homosexual libido may play in their fundamental dynamics.

Homosexual Samurai Love as Inspiration for the Jedi Partnerships

At this juncture, another useful historical reference may help to further flesh out the possibly romantic nature of same-sex relationships in *Star Wars*. On the DVD commentary of *A New Hope*, George Lucas describes how his original concept for the Jedi Knights and their lightsaber weapons was inspired in part by the Samurai ethic of Japan, which offered "a more humane way of being a warrior." In a previous article for *The Gay & Lesbian Review*, "High Camp in a Galaxy Far Away," I have described how this Samurai tradition actually revolved around the homosexual partnership pattern known as *shudo*—the "way of the youth"—where a young man would learn his spiritual warrior's path through a loving sexual relationship with an older male Samurai, closely paralleled in *Star Wars* by the Padawan learner's committed relationship with his Jedi Master (35). In their book, *The Love of the Samurai: A Thousand Years of Japanese Homosexuality*, Tsuneo Watanabe and Jun'ichi Iwata cite the essayist Ijiri Chusuke, who wrote in 1492 that

> In the world of the nobles and warriors, [male] lovers would swear perfect and eternal love, relying on no more than their mutual goodwill ... [and] they were greatly moved by the spirit of this way ... [which] must be truly respected and ... must never be permitted to disappear. (109)

The "mutual" and transcendent nature of "eternal love" is effectively revealed in these words, while the transformative and transmissive nature of such homosexual relationships is captured in a text from 1653:

> If you learn the teachings of the Buddha and expect to achieve Awakening, you will surely practice *shudo*. For this way is really like that of the true Awakening, in that we may give ourselves wholly to it. (qtd. in Watanabe and Iwata 113)

By devoting themselves "wholly" to homosexual love, the Samurai warriors were able to experience psychological and spiritual enlightenment. The fifteenth century Zen monk Ikkyu, who also practiced *shudo*, expressed it this way: "Its pleasures are like an endless circle; men shout with pleasure when they attain entrance" (qtd. in Crompton 414). Likewise, the Padawan learners in *Star Wars* can be seen to experience their own kind of "awakening" in the Force through close, transmissive partnerships with their Jedi Masters.

In certain cases, as discussed above, this magical relationship in *Star Wars* continues transcendentally beyond the death of the master. The vivid images of the spirits of Obi-Wan, Yoda, and Anakin as they aid and support Luke poetically evoke the idea of the same-sex soul-figure, which Walker has described as the "wraith-buddy" or "ghost-twin" of the gay man's psyche, functioning as an internal guide into greater consciousness ("Uranian Coniunctio" 145). Just as the Samurai and Jedi could be said to have found connection with their enlightening soul-figures through love between warrior and youth, likewise viewers of the *Star Wars* films can foster their own psychological self-realization by utilizing *Star Wars* imagery to spur their imagination for relating to the double soul-figure within their own minds.

The Love That *Still* Dare Not Speak Its Name

Many particular qualities of relationships, some of them specific to homosexual romance, have been identified above in the *Star Wars* twinships, and I have discussed how Lucas's original idea for the Jedi Knights was inspired by the homosexual Samurai tradition, but it's also true that this kind of romance in the *Star Wars* films is still mostly "the love that dare not speak its name," as Oscar Wilde famously described it. For the most part, Lucas assiduously avoids showing the Jedi as overtly affectionate with each other, only allowing love to be expressed in the darkest moments of their relationships. As noted above, Obi-Wan and Anakin are described as "complementary halves of a single warrior" (Stover 397) in the authorized novel version of *Revenge of the Sith*, but this potent two-in-one image of the Jedi pair only comes in the midst of their ultimate fight *against* one other on the primeval volcanic planet of Mustafar. Through many tensions and competing influences, their fond partnership has collapsed. When Anakin attempts to attack him, Obi-Wan slices off Anakin's legs and remaining arm, as shown in the film version. Reduced to a helpless, limbless trunk on the ground, Anakin screams out in excruciating pain, *"I hate you,"* and only then at the most gruesome moment of the entire saga can Obi-Wan cry out in despair, *"You were my brother, Anakin; I loved you,"* at which point Anakin's dismembered body bursts into flames. Thus, the only blatant statement of love between Jedi Knights throughout the six-film narrative occurs at the grotesque conclusion of an almost-lethal battle between two of them.

Conflicting forces within the filmmaker's psyche may be revealed by this scene. On the one hand, the director has created a dazzling climax overflowing with primeval libidinal energy as the two men fervently wield the Force in their battle amidst surging red-hot lava, but Lucas also seems to struggle with homophobic influences, as he chooses only this moment, when the Jedi are combating each other, to reveal the depth of passion and love between them.

As I am imagining it here, this conflict between creative homosexual libido and destructive homophobia within the filmmaker's psyche plays out in many other places throughout the chronicle as male-male affection is consistently muted, in contrast with the two heterosexual romances portrayed, where the erotic charge between characters is shown explicitly.

But it's not only the filmmaker's homophobia that's at issue here. When Lucas has fleshed out particular male characters with more obviously queer characteristics, he has been lambasted by many critics and fans. As Richard Goldstein described in his June 9, 1999, *Village Voice* cover story, "The Nelly Menace," Jar Jar Binks (Ahmed Best) has been so meanly hated and attacked by journalists and filmgoers mostly because he has been perceived as gay. Here is an uninhibited, organically libidinal creature, who freely exclaims, "Oh mooee, mooee, I wuv you," after Qui-Gon rescues him from a fast-approaching military hovercraft. Just one of many possible ways to appreciate Jar Jar's archetypal significance is to recognize his arrival in the midst of the partnership of Obi-Wan and Qui-Gon, thereby functioning perhaps in his whimsical vitality as a symbol of otherwise-hidden, vigorous homosexual libido growing stronger between the two Jedi.

Another overtly queer character in the films, C-3PO, has managed to avoid the level of hatred that Jar Jar has suffered. Yet, in a venomous review of *Revenge of the Sith* in the *New Yorker* (May 23, 2005), Anthony Lane writes, "I still fail to understand why I should be expected to waste twenty-five years of my life following the progress of a beeping trash can and a gay, gold-plated Jeeves." In answer to this dismissive statement, I would suggest that the loyal, lifesaving, resilient bond between R2-D2 and C-3PO, as discussed above, demonstrates a humanity superior to the behavior of many actual humans and clearly demonstrates in a symbolic way the life-giving qualities of libidinal twinship mutuality possible in the archetypal double relationship. Although he often complains to R2-D2, C-3PO always shows his true love when the stakes are high. Just one of many examples throughout the narrative occurs at the end of *A New Hope* when R2-D2 returns from battle badly damaged, and C-3PO exclaims, "You must repair him. If any of my circuits are useful, I'll gladly donate them." It could even be suggested that R2-D2 and C-3PO experience a particular kind of transcendence in their relationship, in the sense that they grow beyond their metallic construction to feel and love as conscious living beings.

Just as Jar Jar can be seen to represent the veiled libidinal energy between Qui-Gon and Obi-Wan, so C-3PO can be seen as a symbol of Anakin Skywalker's homosexual libido. As a boy, Anakin builds C-3PO and first brings the gay protocol droid with six million forms of communication to life, thereby evoking and foreshadowing the *Frankenstein* motif that will be more darkly activated when Anakin himself is transformed into Darth Vader. As

Mitch Walker has discussed, the Frankenstein monster can be understood as the personification of the libidinal same-sex soul-figure made ugly by the creator's projection of his own homophobic shadow ("Problem of Frankenstein" 12). The fact that C-3PO is not really monstrous at all as Anakin's childhood creation suggests the secretly homosexual, possibly redemptive treasure buried in this dark theme.

As discussed in the film documentary of *The Celluloid Closet* (1995), homosexual characters could only be portrayed in Hollywood films during much of the twentieth century if they were comic sissies, evil villains, or both. In this context, Jar Jar and C-3PO as significant characters seem like a partial redemption by Lucas of the sissy stock character, especially as they are both eventually given a certain dignity, Jar Jar as a mature senator in his elegant floor-length robes and C-3PO as a golden god for the Ewoks. But in the character of the treacherous Darth Sidious, Lucas has echoed the all-too-familiar stereotype of the queeny villain. Aspects of this characterization can be seen, especially during *Revenge of the Sith*, in the Sith Lord's effete tone of voice, smarmy smile, big puffy sleeves—and most of all in his seductive attitude toward Anakin, where homosexual libido manifests more blatantly than in the Jedi bonds or perhaps anywhere else in the saga. The salient point here is not that there is anything wrong *per se* with an effeminate male nemesis. Rather, it's the gross imbalance caused by the fact that the heroes in Hollywood films are to this day almost *never* shown as openly gay, even in *Star Wars*. That said, accepting that a villain *could* be homosexual or at least queeny, it's important to illuminate the dynamics of the portentous relationship between these two main characters, as will be explored in the next section.

Consumed by the Shadow: The Terrible Descent of Anakin Skywalker

To more deeply understand possible homosexual symbolism in the *Star Wars* epic, it's necessary to explore the odyssey of the central character who links all six films, Anakin Skywalker, grappling initially with his highly problematic and unique venture into love with a woman.

Homophobia as an influence in Lucas's psyche may have spurred him to dampen and mask the depiction of same-sex love in the *Star Wars* films, but the filmmaker appears to be downright negative about the prospects of heterosexual romance, at least as he portrays it in the painful, fateful relationship and marriage of Anakin and Padmé. Here is the *only* opposite-sex courtship amongst main characters shown to be fully consummated in the whole six-movie chronicle—Han Solo and Princess Leia never go beyond a couple of kisses in the films—yet the manifestly romantic scenes between Anakin and Padmé are shown in a strange manner that is vividly operatic on the surface while feeling flat at its heart. Lucas has explained on the DVD commentary for

The Phantom Menace and *Attack of the Clones* that the dialogue of the films is *intended* to reflect the stilted style of 1930s Saturday matinee film serials such as *Flash Gordon's Trip to Mars* (1938) and *Flash Gordon Conquers the Universe* (1940). This homage gives these scenes in particular what can best be described as a subtle camp quality, as I have discussed in my earlier article, suggesting an ironic intent on the part of the filmmaker ("High Camp" 33).

In the relationship between Anakin and Padmé, romantic heterosexual love is shown primarily as bitter suffering. In an especially dramatic moment, Anakin says to Padmé, "Now that I'm with you again, I'm in agony. The closer I get to you, the worse it gets.... I can't breathe.... What can I do? I will do anything you ask." Anakin's obsession with Padmé throws him off balance, making him unable to partner his anger and fear, thereby triggering a violent descent for both individuals. His original excuse for going over to the dark side, in order to save Padmé's life, is soon enough replaced by his quest for ever-greater power, as shown at the climax of *Revenge of the Sith*. Anakin reveals how tortured he has become when he exclaims, "Love won't save you, Padmé. Only my new powers can do that."

When viewed from the perspective of the full character arc, Anakin's psychology appears to be bisexually influenced alternately by both heterosexual and homosexual libido. It seems that homosexual libido is strongly activated in both loving and competitive ways with Obi-Wan but then gradually shifts to Darth Sidious, while his heterosexual libido once directed toward Padmé greatly subsides as his relationship with the Sith Lord becomes primary. Evidence of this shift is revealed when Anakin uses almost the same words to pledge allegiance to his new master that he once spoke to her. "I will do whatever you ask," he says, kneeling in front of the Dark Lord who appears deeply satiated for having won over the handsome young Jedi. Proclaims the greatly aroused, triumphant Sidious, his voice reverberating through the depths of the Dark Side, "the Force is strong with you!"

The great Sith Lord can be understood here as a vivid embodiment of the Dark Side of the double archetype. In Jungian psychology, *every* archetype is understood to have a negative side. In an ideal situation, when the double is charged by homosexual libido and functions as the soul-figure, leading the individual into deeper relationship with the archetypal inner world, then it can be seen that the light and dark aspects of the complex work together in a balanced, dialectical manner to spur a person's individuation. As Walker has written, "the negative archetype always contains the force of the positive, including the drive toward individuation" ("Double" 174). Echoing this idea in his own dark way, Chancellor Palpatine says to Anakin in *Episode III*, "The Sith and the Jedi are similar in almost every way, including their quest for greater power." But in Anakin's case, there appears to be an imbalance in the constellation of the archetype, where its Dark Side is able to almost completely dominate him.

Yet it is not merely the negative aspect of the double archetype that an individual must contend with. As Jung described, every person has a distinct *shadow complex* in the psyche, understood here as the most shamefully violent and painful aspects of the personality resulting in large part from the aftereffects of early childhood trauma. In our own world, Judeo-Christian society has demonized this dark side of the psyche for more than two millennia, encouraging individuals to become over-identified with the light, which spurs them to project the dark out onto others, thereby making it extremely difficult for anyone to take full, personal, moral responsibility for their own aggressive and controlling urges. In *Star Wars*, Anakin does not have sufficient support from Obi-Wan—who could be understood in this context to represent the light side of the double archetype—in order to effectively work through this complex in a psychological manner. Obi-Wan admits his own imperfections as a mentor when he says in despair to Anakin during the climax of *Revenge of the Sith*, "I have failed you." Soon after, he leaves Anakin amputated and on fire to die by a river of lava, and, in a painful irony where light and dark trade places, it is Darth Sidious who saves Anakin's life.

In a distinct echo of the Frankenstein story, the older Sith Lord now transforms what's left of Anakin into the great dark phallus of Darth Vader, who could be viewed as a stark symbol of the cruel exploitation of homosexual love's promise twisted and mechanized for nefarious purposes by evil. As Darth Vader, Anakin becomes grossly over-identified with his shadow complex rather than partnering and integrating this black half of his psyche, thereby halting almost forever his humane individuation.

Homosexual Oedipal Dynamics: Luke Skywalker's Redemption of Darth Vader

In contrast with his father, Anakin, who as discussed above becomes almost completely consumed by the Dark Side after giving over to his disorienting lust for a woman, Luke Skywalker merely flirts with a princess who turns out to be his *sister* and instead finds his own creative potency through intense same-sex bonds with Obi-Wan Kenobi, Han Solo, Yoda, and, ultimately, his father.

In his analysis of *Episodes IV* through *VI*, Steven Galipeau appropriately suggests that Princess Leia represents Luke's anima, or the feminine, receptive side of his personality (23), but the author fails to adequately explain why Luke is not actually romantically involved with Leia, a dynamic which is a key aspect of the complex's libidinal coalescence in the psychology of heterosexual men. This is because Galipeau does not recognize the possibility of a *homosexual* relationship to the anima, which takes on a more sisterly, less sexual tone than in heterosexual psychology. In a gay-centered understanding, it is through his relationship with his anima that a man can become receptive to penetrative love from another man—as well as the forcefully inspiring imagery of the libidinal psyche itself—while still maintaining his deeply felt phallic masculinity sourced in the erotically charged double soul-figure that is central in that psychic imagery. Luke begins to learn about this particular kind of masculine receptivity in *The Empire Strikes Back*, when he begins his training with Yoda, who encourages him to be passive as a Jedi, instead of merely aggressive.

Not yet aware that Darth Vader is his father, Luke first faces his nemesis in a magical sequence where an imaginary Vader is revealed to have Luke's own face—to be Luke's own shadow, but also foreshadowing the redemptive, twinship aspects of their relationship. At the end of *The Empire Strikes Back*, Luke confronts the actual Darth Vader for the first time. Vader symbolically castrates Luke by slicing off his hand with a lightsaber in an attempt to dominate him, then reveals his true identity as Luke's father, and passionately invites him to the Dark Side: "Luke, join me and together we can rule the galaxy as father and son!"

A consideration of oedipal dynamics between gay boys and their fathers can possibly shed light on this devastatingly climactic scene, as well as the ones that follow between Darth Vader and Luke. In a reversal of Freud's oedipal complex, young gay boys at about the age of four or five can be seen to fall into romantic love with their fathers instead of their mothers in a crucial developmental initiation usually played out unconsciously. In most cases, especially in our homophobic society, the father will cruelly reject the son, rather than gently, lovingly frustrate his desire to physically act out the incest (Isay 29; Sadownick 68; Walker, "Uranian Complex" 46).

I would suggest that the fateful encounters between Darth Vader and Luke get much of their great pathos and impact from the intensity of homosexual libido incestuously activated between father and son. In contrast with how the situation usually plays out between gay sons and their fathers in our culture, Darth Vader is initially the one actively seducing his son, albeit for dark purposes, using the persuasively libidinal method that Darth Sidious originally used on him. At this point, Luke says "I will never join you!" Yet, after this scene, Luke and his father are newly connected through the libidinal Force, able to sense one another's presence as well as intuit each other's thoughts and feelings. The incestuous romantic yearning between father and son has been awakened for both of them and ultimately demands resolution.

In their final battle at the climax of *Return of the Jedi*, it appears that Luke may kill Darth Vader as Obi-Wan has encouraged him to do. He does indeed aggressively castrate his father by slicing off his mechanical hand. This can be seen as retaliation for his father's earlier metaphoric castration of him and also as an act to separate out his ego identity from that of his father, but this only reveals their twin nature, because Luke himself has a mechanical hand result-ing from his father's earlier attack, as he recognizes in this pivotal moment. Fi-nally, Luke realizes that some key ethical action other than aggression is required here. He tosses away his lightsaber, rejecting its aggressive phallic qualities, refusing to kill his father, fight the Emperor, or even defend himself. In this instant, as I see it, Luke has learned how to *partner* his own shadow complex, in the form of vengeful hostility, and contain it rather than act it out any further. This allows him to recollect the projection of his own darkness that he had placed on Darth Vader, see "the good" deep within his father, and then become so phallically secure in his newly whole sense of self that he can make himself completely receptive to his father's love, potentially reborn. Now masterfully in touch with his own homosexual libido as symbolized by the Force, no longer needing a weapon as a violent substitute for genuinely indi-viduated masculinity, Luke has an inner sense that his father's capacity to love will prevail over the Emperor's unredeemable evil.

Only in this psychological and, I would say, homosexual way, is Luke Sky-walker able to "bring balance to the Force" for the galaxy, his father, and him-self. Darth Vader's sincere love for his son, as opposed to his earlier exploitive seduction, is reactivated by his son's homosexual receptivity, and he is finally able to reclaim his humanity and save Luke from the Emperor, who seems hell-bent on annihilating the young Jedi. After Darth Vader destroys the Em-peror by throwing him down an open shaft into the nuclear core of the battle station, a great blue surge of what could be seen as homosexual libido is re-leased from its exploited entrapment in the Emperor, now newly available to propel a profound father-son reunion. Luke removes the shadow-phallic metal-lic helmet and mask to reveal the loving-phallic, bald crown of his true father, finally redeemed just before dying. Soon after, Luke is reunited once again with his father who is now in spirit form along with the ghosts of Obi-Wan and Yoda, symbolically suggesting the soul-figure as eternally present in Luke and also potentially present in the psyche of the individuals watching the film. Through the creativity that was cooked in him through his twinship bonds with Obi-Wan and Yoda, Luke finally has grown beyond them both. He has begun to realize the true creative promise of homosexual love: By being openly receptive at the same time that he is phallically strong, a man can gain a uniquely rich experience of the meaningful wholeness of the psyche in both its light and dark aspects. He can then birth from the tension of the two a new, nonaggressive, truly humane awareness and action.

Watching *Star Wars*: Getting Off by Being Receptive to Penetrative Imagination

Now this integrative *phallic receptivity* can be further seen in how many enthusiastic audience members actually experience the *Star Wars* films. In the May 20, 2005, issue of *Entertainment Weekly*, reflecting on the memory of initially seeing the first *Star Wars* in 1977 with its groundbreaking special effects and mythic grandeur, Steven Spielberg said, "We all lost our virginity, in a sense. We joined the Force. All of us" (26). Never before had people been stimulated in that particular way by a motion picture. Since that time, each successive *Star Wars* film has grown more and more imaginatively stunning, culminating in *Revenge of the Sith*, with its overwhelming visual-aural depth, texture, and grandeur, allowing viewers to be, I would suggest, penetrated by their own unconscious psyches as those inner worlds are projected onto the film's imagery and drama, in what can be described as a homosexual experience for male members of the audience in particular.

Twinship Themes and Visual Spectacle in Other Fantasy Films

This phenomenon of impactful creativity combined with what I understand as abundant homosexual symbolism is not unique to the *Star Wars* space opera and can be seen in many of the most imaginative fantasy and science fiction films of the past four decades. Perhaps the most pertinent example of this theme is found in Steven Spielberg's *E.T.: The Extra-Terrestrial* (1982), originally released between *The Empire Strikes Back* (1980) and *Return of the Jedi* (1983). This uniquely heartfelt film could be seen as a highly emotive brother to the *Star Wars* films, inspired in part by them, even sharing the same composer, John Williams, who, in the liner notes for the Twentieth Anniversary soundtrack of *E.T.*, freely describes the film as a "love story."

Here is the journey of a modern human boy, Elliott (Henry Thomas), who has already seen the first two *Star Wars* movies—as evidenced by his excitement over his Lando Calrissian and Boba Fett action figures—and who now develops his own real-life relationship with a whimsical, magical alien creature. (Lucas later returned Spielberg's homage by placing a group of E.T.s in one of the Senate "pods" in *The Phantom Menace*.) Together, Elliott and E.T. achieve an unabashedly affectionate bond that becomes mutual, primary, lifesaving, transformative, transmissive, and transcendent, referencing the relationship categories described above. The human boy and male alien learn to communicate by mirroring each other's gestures and then quickly become emotionally, telepathically linked. When E.T. is drinking beer, for example, Elliott gets drunk. And when E.T. feels frightened or homesick, Elliott experiences similar emotions. As the film progresses, the boy and the alien become ever more attached, to the point at which, at the climax of the narrative, one of the doctors tending to them together says, "EEG analysis shows complete coherence and synchronization of brain wave activity between both subjects." When E.T. dies, Elliott offers a poignant speech culminating in the vow, "I'll believe in you all my life, every day. E.T., I love you." The film ends when the resurrected E.T. explains that he "will be right here" in Elliott's mind in a love that will last forever. This final gesture can be understood as E.T. letting Elliott know that he will continue to exist transcendentally as an internal same-sex soul-figure in the boy's psyche.

Experiencing the double soul-figure complex and the vast psyche as subjectively "real" is the central theme of Wolfgang Petersen's *The NeverEnding Story* (1984), where a human boy named Bastian (Barret Oliver) reads in a magical book about an imaginal hero-boy Atreyu (Noah Hathaway) who is embarking on a great heroic quest. The developing plot of the story requires that these two boys must find a way to connect with each other across the divide between reality and imagination in order to save the colorful dreamworld of Fantasia.

More recently, Peter Jackson has brought J. R. R. Tolkien's novel, *The Lord of the Rings* to the big screen, where, in a series of three visually dynamic films—*The Fellowship of the Ring* (2001), *The Two Towers* (2002), and *The Return of the King* (2003)—enduring, loving, same-sex partnerships are the primary focus of the narrative, as I have discussed in my previous article, "*Lord of the Ring* Taps a Gay Archetype." In this moving chronicle, the fate of Middle Earth completely hinges on the resilient bond between hobbits Frodo (Elijah Wood) and Sam (Sean Astin)—a companionship that can be meaningfully described as mutual, primary, enduring, lifesaving, transformative, and transcendent. The steadfast affection of this heroic twosome is beautifully echoed in the warm closeness found in many other same-sex partnerships, including the fond fellowship of hobbits Merry (Dominic Monaghan) and Pippin (Billy Boyd), as well as the odd couple pairing of Legolas the elf (Orlando Bloom) and Gimli the dwarf (John Rhys-Davies).

It's no accident that vivid depictions of transformative same-sex love come hand in hand with the pictorial and auditory virtuosity that is the hallmark of these prominent fantasy films. Although they may publicly (and personally?) identify as heterosexuals, I would argue that archetypal homosexual libido is a central factor in the filmmakers' creativity, as richly evidenced by the plentiful imagery in their movies that can be implicatively, reasonably understood as homosexual. In this gayly seen way, these imaginative films can be appreciated as contemporary versions of the children of the mind that Plato suggested were birthed out of homosexual love, because "the offspring [art, poetry, etc.] of this [kind of] relationship are particularly attractive and are closer to immortality than ordinary children. We'd all prefer to have children of this sort rather than the human kind" (52–3).

Figures 3 a-c: Some Male Erotic Bonds in *Star Wars*

a: The enthusiastic pod race announcer, a Troig named Fode and Beed, provides a vivid symbol of libidinal twinship mutuality as two harmonious male personalities in one body. *The Phantom Menace* (1999).

b: Jedi Knights Obi-Wan Kenobi (Ewan McGregor) and Qui-Gon Jinn (Liam Neeson) share an affectionate bond so deep it ultimately transcends death. *The Phantom Menace* (1999).

c: Luke Skywalker (Mark Hamill) gazes upon his loving father, Anakin Skywalker (Sebastian Shaw), for the first time. *Return of the Jedi* (1983).

Conclusion: *Our* New Hope

In this essay, I have fleshed out a vision of transformative, same-sex relationships in the *Star Wars* films as romantic, patterned by the archetype of the double and charged by galvanic homosexual libido. I have also described how the phallic receptivity actualized by homosexual love's libidinal twinship mutuality offers a new, potent attitude for relations with the unconscious, where individuals of all sexualities can potentially become receptively open to loving penetration and subsequent enlightenment by the archetypal richness of the living psyche.

Such a gay-centered psychological perspective reclaims the films, first of all, for gay men seeking archetypal imagery supportively reflective of their distinct psychology, offering in particular many quickening soul-figure images as portrayed by the heroic *Star Wars* characters and their transformations. Lesbians, too, with some necessary gender translating, can possibly resonate with the plethora of twinship imagery that spurs a particular kind of homosexual creativity. For non-gay people, cultivating the spirit of libidinal twinship mutuality in their minds has the potential to radically enhance their experience of their own particular archetypal dynamics, beneficially leading toward a newly romantic relationship with their own psychology. This may be particularly challenging and important for many non-gay men in our culture, whose oppressive strictures against the expression of same-sex love has, it seems to me, made it especially difficult for them to be sufficiently receptive to a meaningful relationship with the fullness of their own unconscious psyches.

The *Star Wars* narrative as analyzed here shows why the symbolic birth of homosexual children of the mind in the form of creative revolutionary ideas is so desperately needed in our own contemporary world, where, it seems to me, the extroverted, worn-out platitudes of both left and right political positions hold no legitimate promise for humanity's viable survival. Especially in *Attack of the Clones* and *Revenge of the Sith*, the epic depicts an obscenely overgrown civilization disquietingly all too much like ours that, through an ultimately catastrophic lack of psychological awareness, tragically descends into utter disaster. Even the Jedi, supposedly so full of wisdom, are unable to anticipate the coming devastation that consequently befalls them and are almost completely, murderously wiped out.

In his depiction of the nascent coalescence of a titanic, galaxy-dominating Empire, it appears that Lucas is offering a clear warning about the dark side of our own current American Empire, which can perhaps not so unrealistically be seen as a pseudodemocracy much like the one in *Star Wars*. Dominated by unjust political power that is forcefully maintained through the massive manipulation of ubiquitous unconscious group-mindedness, this oppressive organization of societies all too well enables the intensifying destructive juggernaut of militaristic state violence and regimenting control, as well as, in the case of our present world, soul-killing consumerism and severe environmental degradation.

True emancipation for all human beings will come, in my view, only when primary value is placed on the introverted, psychological project of deepening human subjectivity, with the clear intent of ideologically supporting the empowered development of authentically self-determined individuality and personal moral authority that can stand in autonomous political opposition to the destructive group-mind dynamics of corrupt contemporary civilization. The primary culminating themes of the *Star Wars* film saga suggest just such a hopeful development in human self-awareness. By beginning to experience what I have described as a nonaggressive phallic receptivity birthed out of romantic, transformative same-sex relationships, the character of Luke Skywalker laudably represents in his portrayed psychological growth an inspiring movement toward the kind of homosexually creative and conscientiously individuated personhood so ethically and politically necessary for humanity's future.

Works Cited

Crompton, Louis. *Homosexuality and Civilization*. Cambridge: Harvard UP, 2003.

Foucault, Michel. *The History of Sexuality–Volume I: An Introduction*. New York: Vintage Books, 1978.

Galipeau, Steven. *The Journey of Luke Skywalker: An Analysis of Modern Myth and Symbol*. Chicago: Open Court, 2001.

Goldstein, Richard. "The Nelly Menace." *Village Voice* 9 June 1999 <http://www.villagevoice.com>.

Hay, Harry. "A Separate People Whose Time Has Come." *Gay Spirit*. Ed. Mark Thompson. New York: St. Martin's, 1987.

Isay, Richard A. *Being Homosexual : Gay Men and Their Development*. New York : Farrar, Straus, Giroux, 1989.

Jensen, Jeff. "What a Long Strange Trip It's Been." *Entertainment Weekly* 20 May 2005: 22–30.

Jung, C. G. *Symbols of Transformation*. Princeton: Princeton UP, 1956.

Kaufman, Roger. "High Camp in a Galaxy Far Away." *Gay & Lesbian Review Worldwide* 9.5 (2002): 33–5.

——. "*Lord of the Ring* Taps a Gay Archetype." *Gay & Lesbian Review Worldwide* 10.4 (2003): 31–3.

Lane, Anthony. "Space Case." *New Yorker* 23 May 2005: 94.

Plato. *Symposium*. Trans. Robin Waterfield. New York: Oxford UP, 1994.

Random House Webster's Unabridged Dictionary. 2nd ed. New York: Random House Reference, 2001.

Roscoe, Will. *Jesus and the Shamanic Tradition of Same-Sex Love*. San Francisco: Suspect Thoughts P, 2004.

Sadownick, Douglas. "My Father, My Self." *The Man I Might Become*. Ed. Bruce Shenitz. New York: Marlow & Company, 2002.

Stover, Matthew. *Star Wars: Episode III–Revenge of the Sith*. New York: Del Rey, 2005.

Walker, Mitch. "The Double: An Archetypal Configuration." *Spring–A Journal of Archetypal Psychology* (1976): 165–75.

——. "The Problem of Frankenstein." Unpublished essay, 1977.

——. "Jung and Homophobia." *Spring–A Journal of Archetypal Psychology* (1991): 55–70.

——. "The Uranian Complex: Father-Son Incest and the Oedipal Stage in Gay Men." *The Uranian Soul: Studies in Gay-Centered Jungian Psychology for a New Era of Gay Liberation*. Unpublished manuscript, 1997.

——. "The Uranian Coniunctio: A Study of Gay Identity Formation and the Individuation Model of C. G. Jung." *The Uranian Soul: Studies in Gay-Centered Jungian Psychology for a New Era of Gay Liberation*. Unpublished manuscript, 1997.

Watanabe, Tsuneo, and Jun'ichi Iwata. *The Love of the Samurai: A Thousand Years of Japanese Homosexuality*. London: GMP, 1989.

Williams, John. Interview with Laurent Bouzereau. *E.T.: The Extra-Terrestrial: The 20th Anniversary*. Liner notes for the soundtrack CD. MCA, 2002.

Other Films Cited

The Celluloid Closet. Dir. Rob Epstein and Jeffrey Friedman. Brillstein-Grey, Channel 4 Films/HBO, 1995.

E.T.: The Extra-Terrestrial. Dir. Stephen Spielberg. Amblin Entertainment/Universal Pictures, 1982.

Flash Gordon Conquers the Universe. Dir. Ford Beebe and Ray Taylor. Universal Pictures, 1940.

Flash Gordon's Trip to Mars. Dir. Ford Beebe and Robert F. Hill. Universal Pictures, 1938.

The Lord of the Rings: The Fellowship of the Ring. Dir. Peter Jackson. New Line Cinema/Wing Nut Films/Saul Zaentz, 2001.

The Lord of the Rings: The Return of the King. Dir. Peter Jackson. New Line Cinema/Wing Nut Films/Lord Dritte, 2003.

The Lord of the Rings: The Two Towers. Dir. Peter Jackson. New Line Cinema/Wing Nut Films/Lord Zweite, 2002.

A Matter of Heart. Dir. Mark Whitney. Production: Horizon Films/Kino International, 1985.

The NeverEnding Story. Dir. Wolfgang Petersen. Production: Bavaria Studios/Neue Constantin Film, 1984.

Genetics, Social Order,
and
Domination

CHAPTER 9

Eugenics, Racism, and the Jedi Gene Pool

Matthew Wilhelm Kapell

"Different races, like different individuals, vary considerably in their natural instincts."

—Francis Galton, 1905

"There is a natural aristocracy among men. The grounds of this are virtue and talents ... the moral and physical qualities of man, whether good or evil, are transmissible in a certain degree from father to son."

—Thomas Jefferson, 1813

"The Force is strong in my family. My father has it ... I have it ... and my sister has it."

—Luke to Leia, *Return of the Jedi*

The six-film *Star Wars* series tells of an empire's rise and fall, a republic's restoration, and a fallen hero's redemption. In the saga's frame, the villainous elite are overcome by a farm boy, Luke Skywalker (Mark Hamill), who also saves his father. This is not, however, so clearly a tale of impulse transformed into character by virtuous effort. In the films, as in the many *Expanded Universe* novels and games, abilities and behavioral traits of individuals are consistently traced to their inheritance. Whether it is the Force-mastering abilities of the Skywalker family, the creation of an army of clones from the template of a hard-fighting bounty hunter, or the suspiciously racist representation of aliens in overtly stereotypical fashion, understanding the *Star Wars* franchise requires us to consider Western traditions of eugenics, racism, and pseudoscientific justifications for discrimination here on Earth. As for the larger plot of rebellion, the heroes and villains of the series manage to overthrow one elitist system in favor of another. Their powers to dominate as oppressors or liberators are rooted in their own elite biology. This thorough re-importation of aristocratic and biological justifications of individual worth confounds the often-ascribed message of rebellion against tyranny. In the end, we are simply left with a deeply conservative ideology of hereditary rule.

It all begins in *A New Hope* (1977). Obi-Wan Kenobi (Alec Guinness) tells Luke Skywalker about the Force. He says, "the Force is what gives a Jedi his power. It's an energy field created by all living things. It surrounds us and penetrates us. It binds the galaxy together." We later hear about this force in *Return of the Jedi* when Luke says, "the Force is strong in my family. My father has it ... I have it ... and my sister has it." He does not invoke any science to explain this fact, but the mere fact of tracing such power through biological inheritance makes inevitable the eventual creation of a microscopic symbiote—a biological reason—to explain that power. The fulfillment of this tendency to explain conduct through some preexisting essence occurs in *The Phantom Menace* (1999), when Qui-Gon Jinn (Liam Neeson) tells young Anakin Skywalker (Jake Lloyd) about the Force. He does this through a brief discussion of "midichlorians," microscopic organisms that make all life possible and without which "we would have no knowledge of the Force." Rather than presenting itself to mystical and ephemeral moments of awareness, the Force now renders itself observable and quantifiable. Qui-Gon simply takes a sample of young Anakin's blood, assays his level of midi-chlorians, and estimates his potential to use the Force.

Thematically, we encounter many of these narrative moments that turn either on the prescientific or the *Star Wars*–scientific version of our essential biological destiny. Luke Skywalker's abilities are determined by his lineage, and Anakin's abilities are determined by his status as a "vergence in the Force," which, it is strongly hinted, was determined at his very conception by the presence of midi-chlorians in his genetic makeup. Rather than centering the narrative on effective prime ministers and legislatures, Lucas offers queens and a princess. Rather than tracing Luke's powers as a Jedi to his training and education by Yoda (Frank Oz), the story links them directly to his parentage: a queen for a mother and "the Chosen One" as father. It will be the strong lineage of the Skywalker family that ultimately saves the day and provides the heroes of the Rebellion. It is the elected official of Palpatine (Ian McDiarmid), very strong in the Force, who will be revealed as the ultimate evil in the galaxy and the prime minister of the "cloners" on the planet Kamino who will be complicit in the creation of an army that topples the Republic. And it will be rebels, by virtue of their biological inheritance, who destroy the Emperor's Sith

Empire and found a New Republic, in which their leadership qualities will be, ironically, determined not by an equality suggested by the name *republic*. *Star Wars* is an aristocratic fable about having the best stuff in your genes—and the prequel trilogy articulates what that stuff is in a peculiar scientific sense. Those films reflect "the way in which an elite justifies and maintains its position over less powerful sections of society" (Emslie).[1] It really takes us back to the dawn of biological understandings of inheritance and the earliest crude attempts to sort out the relations of social dominance and submission.

Eugenics, "Race," and History

Western society's tradition of explaining an individual's abilities through appeals to scientific biology is relatively new. However, the practice of suggesting that certain people have a right to a higher or better position in society is not. A century before the initial publication of Charles Darwin's *On the Origin of Species* (1859), an individual's place in society may not have been justified wholly through biology, but a rationalization for that station still existed. Each individual knew their position and status in society, be it nobility, clergy, or the peasantry. A person's place was both "known" by all and "foreordained in heaven" (Manchester 55). Darwin's theory, the main ideas of which were already in place at the time he presented it, merely allowed for "science and history" to "come together to present the ideas of the whole of nature advancing slowly but relentlessly to some high goal" (Butterfield 236). Evolution was immediately taken up within the broader culture as a method for organizing society in a hierarchy of worth for each individual. The justification through science was new; the idea itself was not. This kind of hierarchy is also strikingly obvious in the original *Star Wars* trilogy. Fans and more casual viewers might have objected to midi-chlorians as justification for power in the Force in the prequel films, but the original trilogy had already provided a rationalization for each character's position in the hierarchy of the *Star Wars* universe. Rather than being explained by midi-chlorian levels, Luke's power is "foreordained by the Force" through his parentage. The result is the same—only the explanation is different.

The original trilogy harkens back to previous conceptions of class- and race-based systems in Western culture, while the prequels reflect more contemporary views of such predictors of status, but both proclaim that there are immutable reasons for an individual's position. Prior to the Darwinian revolution, that status was more ephemeral—as ephemeral as the Force in the original trilogy of films. But a clear demarcation of status still remains inherent in those films, just as it did in pre-Darwinian Western Europe and North America. Class status—the status of the nobility versus the peasantry, for example—was understood by that nobility as the result of "God's plan." Prior to Darwin, if a person's status was truly different, any suggestion of a biological basis for that fact likely revolved around a concept of divine destiny. The pre-Darwinian justifications of racism were explained through the idea that each group or "race" was the result of a "unique creation" by God—a concept known as polygenesis. Polygenesists argued that the different "races" of humanity were, in fact, "separate biological species, the descendants of different Adams" (Gould 39). From the perspective of the twenty-first century, such an idea may seem strange, but it is certainly recapitulated in the strange virgin parentage of Anakin Skywalker. His creation, as well as his status as "the Chosen One" who eventually destroys the Sith Order and "brings balance to the Force," is explained in the *Star Wars* narrative by his own "unique creation."

Darwin did use phrases like "the races of man" in his two most famous works, *On the Origin of Species* and *The Descent of Man* (1871). However, he never suggested quantifiable differences within races other than in his use of the common terminology of his time.[2] Yet, his system of thought would lead to new justifications of discrimination based on the perception of biological differences. Where Darwin described a model by which biological traits could develop within a population, many took the merest ideas of Darwinian thought and applied them to human society. Indeed, Darwin would argue that such mental faculties as emotions were, like biological traits, subject to the laws of evolution—even publishing an entire book on the subject. He did not, however, suggest that more obviously cultural traits were, by necessity, subject to natural selection. For that idea, Darwin left the origination of such theories to others, and "it wasn't long before leading thinkers were distilling" Darwin's ideas "into a new concept" (Black 12). The ideology of social Darwinism, most closely associated with the social scientists Herbert Spencer and William Graham Sumner, argued that the lower classes in European society of the period were of that status due to their individual evolutionary failures.[3] Social Darwinists would take Darwin's principles and apply them not to biology—as Darwin had—but to society.

It was Darwin's cousin, Francis Galton, who would take Darwinian theory, as applied to culture by the social Darwinists, and suggest that selective breeding within human populations would help increase the fitness of the species. Galton coined the term "eugenics" to describe this process. In the preface to the 1882 edition of his most famous work, *Hereditary Genius*, he put the idea this way: "The improvement of the natural gifts of future generations of the human race is largely, though indirectly, under our control" (3). Comparing human breeding to that of dogs and horses, where humanity had bred those species for speed or other traits, he argued, "it is quite practicable to produce a highly-gifted race of men by judicious marriages during several consecutive generations" (5).

Of course, Galton's underlying conception—that some people are "better" than others by some measure—is not a new one. Plato, in his *Republic*, had argued the same thing almost 2,500 years before Galton. Plato argued for the division of people into different classes based on their talents, which he named "gold," "silver," "brass," and "lead." Like later eugenicists, Plato worried that, should these classes of people interbreed, the result would be "dissimilarity and inequality and irregularity" (224). His solution was specialized training for each class he described, so that the best—the "gold"—could be trained to lead, while the other groups could be educated for less important and less intellectually challenging positions in Greek society. As will become apparent, Plato's use of metals as metaphors will remain a useful bit of rhetoric for those who advocated eugenics throughout the nineteenth and twentieth centuries.

Social scientists that still argue those differences in abilities, intelligence, or general evolutionary fitness are primarily due to heredity or genes no longer appreciate being associated with social Darwinism or eugenics. However, their positions remain largely unchanged from the ideologies of nineteenth century scientists who did use those terms or, indeed, from the original positions of Plato, for that matter. These contemporary social scientists are more reticent to argue that human populations should be bred, or that certain groups should, at the very least, be discouraged from breeding. Rather, they concentrate, much like Plato did, on the formulation of educational systems to provide proper training and make the most out of inherent, or biological, talents.

IQ and the "g" Factor: Genetic and Midi-Chlorian Determinism

Since the advent of the so-called intelligence quotient (IQ) tests in the early twentieth century, social scientists have attempted to both evaluate individuals based on a single, easily testable variable and organize those individuals into groups. Not surprisingly, the IQ test quickly became proof for many that the inequalities seen in societies were reasonable. The confluence of ideas among social Darwinists and psychologists testing intelligence allowed a quick leap to the conclusion that tested differences in intelligence were the result of biological factors. The inequality seen in society was now "the inevitable consequence of biological inequality" (Tucker 239).

The initial hopes for the IQ test were simple: Educators would be able to simply test for the inherent abilities of their students and thus provide a learning experience that would match with those abilities. Like Qui-Gon testing young Anakin's midi-chlorians to determine his potential abilities within the Force, educators would be able to test a student's intelligence and determine their ability to learn. Quickly, however, this "byproduct of education...became a determinant of education as well as of social action" (Montagu 191–2). Instead of a test to aid in the education of students, the IQ test became, instead, a test to show that, for some individuals, educational resources would simply be wasted. Many social scientists argued that such testing would help create a better democracy, separating from the masses those intelligent enough to be suited to leadership. The ardent eugenicist Charles Spearman argued exactly this in 1927, arguing that ranking social classes through testing would eradicate "class hatred" and allow for "perfect justice" to be combined with "maximum efficiency" in society (8). Of course, others realized quickly something that George Lucas seems to have missed entirely: that the separation of the betters through a test is fundamentally anathema to democracy. For Lucas, it is the Jedi, separated by similar testing, who are to protect the democratic Republic. As two critics of such testing, the psychologists Harold Stevenson and James Stigler, succinctly describe the problem, the "emphasis on innate abilities is harmful and is undermining the pursuit of public education—indeed, of democracy itself" (95).

Table 2: Fictional Midi-chlorian Count compared with the Estimated IQ of famous people

Name	Midi-chlorians	Name	Est. I.Q.
Anakin Skywalker	27,700	John Stuart Mill	190
Palpatine	20,500	George Sand	150
Yoda	17,700	Lord Byron	150
Luke Skywalker	14,500	Mozart	150
Princess Leia	14,500	Thomas Jefferson	145
Count Dooku	13,500	Galileo	145
Obi-Wan Kenobi	13,400	Charles Darwin	135
Mace Windu	12,000	Isaac Newton	130
Darth Maul	12,000	George Washington	125
General Grievous	11,900	Abraham Lincoln	125
Qui-Gon Jinn	10,000	Bach	125
Average Jedi	10,000	Martin Luther	115
Lando Calrissian	3,300	Rembrandt	110
Boba & Jango Fett	1,500	Copernicus	105
Han Solo	1,500	**Average Person**	100

"Midi-chlorian Count" is taken from Supershadow.com and other locations on the Web. IQs are derived from Catharine M. Cox's famous 1926 Genetic Studies of Genius whose childhood scores (AI IQs) were selectively reproduced in Wallechinsky and Wallace's Book of Lists and often posted at Web sites. Comparing the rankings of the fictional Star Wars characters with the equally fictional historical estimates of IQ highlights the cultural desire to reduce ability to a single number within a hierarchy.

This argument is still being fought among scholars. One side suggests that such tests are fair, objective, and a measure some real aspect of intelligence, while their opposites maintain that the tests "involve a string of assumptions, each of which can be shown to be highly improbable, if not completely spurious" (Cohen 221). These rarified academic arguments have not kept such testing and hierarchical rankings from surfacing, however. The use of the IQ test or, later, of Charles Spearman's "g" factor has continued to allow scholars to suggest that certain individuals, because of their inherent genetic superiority, are simply better suited to leadership roles in society. Whether true, useful, and accurate or not, such rankings continue to have cultural currency. As the table 2 shows, those rankings also provide justifications for nonacademics to allege the superiority of some individuals over others.

The historian Robert Bannister, calling such rankings a "smashing success" in "dramatizing outcomes in a world without social conscience" (xiii), suggests that the reason for their continued popularity is their continued "dependence on [the] social myth" of easily testable group differences (251). This is why certain psychologists continue to base their careers on such measurements and why the ranking of both historical geniuses and fictional Jedi can be found throughout popular culture. It is also why George Lucas can imply such rankings in his narrative with only limited criticism.

The best known psychologist still arguing for genetic differences in ability is Arthur Jensen.[4] His lifetime research, summarized in his 1998 book *The g Factor*, argues that a single number can be attributed to individuals to represent their "general intelligence." Jensen then uses this concept to argue that the subjects' levels of "general intelligence" could be used to rank the various *groups* (he really meant "*races*") of humanity. Jensen's former teacher, the British psychologist Hans J. Eysenck, both defended Jensen's work and used it to advocate educational proposals strikingly similar to those of Plato, and to the Jedi. Accepting the notion that the majority of "general intelligence" was a trait that was inherited from one's parents, Eysenck argued that educational systems should be organized to recognize those of differing abilities and organize their education appropriately. In his suggestively titled *The Inequality of Man* (1973), Eysenck proposed that educators, and society as a whole, should "scrutinize each child to see what metal had gone into his making, then allocate or promote him accordingly" (266-7). Using Plato's own metaphor for individual worth—that of "metal"—caused at least one reviewer to comment: "How revealing is the rhetoric" (Lewontin 24). Indeed, while the psychological jargon was new, the idea most certainly was not.

On the surface, the idea that educators should identify the abilities of children and teach to those strengths is appealing. Where the social Darwinists, eugenicists, and contemporary psychologists like Jensen and Eysenck differ is the suggestion that such abilities are largely, if not wholly, inherent in the genetics of the individual child.

For those who carefully watch the films of the *Star Wars* franchise, it is not surprising that Eysenck's notions of inborn superiority match precisely the Jedi selections of their Padawan learners. When Qui-Gon learns of young Anakin's high midi-chlorian count in *TPM*, he discusses the ramifications with Anakin's mother, Shmi (Pernilla August). Shmi pleads with Qui-Gon, saying, "is there nothing you can do for him?" In his reply, Qui-Gon, Jedi Master, arbiter of peace and justice, offers a statement that would sound natural coming from Eysenck or any other eugenicist: "Had he been born in the Republic, we would have identified him early, and he would have become Jedi, no doubt ... he has the way. But it's too late for him now." Failure to identify the biologically gifted, those with the correct microscopic organelles, and weed them from the degenerate as early as possible, for eugenicists like Eysenck, as well as the Jedi, means that the child is beyond help. Those without the biology for success are already lost.

It may be helpful as an explanatory analogy to refer to the "*endosymbiotic theory*," the idea that Earth organelles are symbiotic that was first proposed in the early twentieth century but revived and popularized by the biologist Lynn Margulis in the early 1980s. It is now widely accepted. In many secondary school biology classes, mitochondria and chloroplasts are famously called "the powerhouse of the cell," since it is the energy they provide that makes complex cellular life possible. It is also appropriate to call the midi-chlorians of *Star Wars* the "powerhouse of the Force." As Qui-Gon tells Anakin, "without the midi-chlorians, life could not exist, and we would have no knowledge of the Force." However, the Earth organelles provide energy for individual cells, while midi-chlorians provide power in the Force for the entire organism. Furthermore, since an individual's midi-chlorian count is determined by his or her own biological makeup, speaking of a person's ability with the Force is simply another way of talking about what he or she inherits from his or her parents.

This is made particularly relevant by the description of Anakin's abilities in *TPM*. Anakin is the only human ever known who can race pods, the "very fast, very dangerous" vehicles of the sporting event that will be the central action scene of the first half of that film.

Anakin's incredibly fast reflexes allow him to race pods. He tells his mother that their owner, the blue-skinned junk-trader Watto, has said that no human has ever raced pods. Qui-Gon replies, "You must have Jedi reflexes if you race Pods." But it is not merely Anakin's "Jedi reflexes" that allow him to Podrace. Qui-Gon will later explain to Anakin's mother that, "he can see things before they happen. That's why he appears to have such quick reflexes. It is a Jedi trait."

It is the combination of Anakin's abilities in seeing the near future, the appearance of very fast reflexes, and his high midi-chlorian count that reduces his—and any individual's—ability to use the Force to a mere biological trait.

In *TPM*, and the entire prequel trilogy of films, the idea of midi-chlorians is new, of course. But they merely reinscribe Force traits that are also present in the original trilogy. In *The Empire Strikes Back*, Luke's own ability to manipulate the Force is traced to his parentage even before the viewer knows exactly who his father might be. The Emperor worries to Darth Vader that Luke could destroy them both. Rather than suggesting that Luke's training might offer him an advantage, as would be the case if ability with the Force were primarily learned, the Emperor declares, "The Force is strong with him. The son of Skywalker must not become a Jedi."

Later in the same film, Luke rushes away from his Jedi training with Yoda to help his friends who are being held in the Cloud City of the planet Bespin, where Darth Vader is torturing them. As Luke prepares to leave, Obi-Wan Kenobi (Alec Guinness) declares that Luke is their "last hope" to destroy the Emperor and Vader. "No," Yoda replies, "There is another." It will not be until the *ROTJ* that viewers will discover who is that person: Luke's sister, Leia (Carrie Fisher).

The narratives of *ESB* and *ROTJ* could have easily presented events that established the ability to use the Force as primarily learned, essentially a product of training, or the result of the right cultural traditions, or a combination of the two. Instead, the two films work hard to establish that Darth Vader, née Anakin Skywalker, has produced two offspring who, because they too are Skywalkers, are also powerful in the Force.

What little room for the training a Jedi will receive as a Padawan learner is useless if the individual does not carry the right level of midi-chlorians in his or her body. Where Jensen would advocate a "g" factor in assessing a person's worth, it would appear that the Jedi have an "f" factor for assessing a potential for their Force abilities. Michael Reaves and Steve Perry, in their *Expanded Universe* novel *Medstar II* (2004), establish that the training each Jedi receives is of great importance in developing their Force talents. Yet, in the end, the authors present the idea that any potential is circumscribed by their midi-chlorian count: Jedi or Sith training is important, but only if there are already enough midi-chlorians.

Not surprisingly then, fan discussion about the importance of midi-chlorians abounds. Perhaps most telling is the popular Supershadow.com Web page that not only posits the biological necessity of a high count but also provides quantitative data!

Jar Jar Biology: Meesa Drivin' Missa Padmé

A major critique of TPM revolved around the character of Jar Jar Binks (Ahmed Best). In addition to being very annoying for many critics and fans, Jar Jar looked like a racist stereotype for African Americans. Others suggested that Jar Jar represented a stereotypical Jamaican. Entire Web pages were created to decry the character. Critics looked for examples of racism in other TPM characters.[5] Writing in the culturally liberal newsmagazine, the *Nation*, Patricia Williams, a professor of law at Columbia University, attacked TPM at all levels for its racism:

> The Phantom Menace is filled with the hierarchies of accent and class status. The Jedi knights speak in full paragraphs, resonant baritones and crisp British accents. White slaves (like Anakin Skywalker and his mother) and the graceful conquered women of the Naboo speak with the brusque, determined innocence of middle-class Americans. The "status-obsessed," hive-dwelling Neimoidians, on the other hand—who are "known for their exceptional Organizing abilities," and who lead "a labyrinthine organization of bureaucrats and trade officials from many worlds that has insinuated itself throughout the galaxy"—speak like Charlie Chan. (9)

Such popular critiques also transcended linguistic boundaries. One viewer reported that seeing TPM for the first time in a dubbed version in Spain had led him to the conclusion that the Neimoidians were not Asian in stereotype, but actually Italian. Their voices, dubbed into Spanish, had profound Italian accents. After watching the film in a number of different languages, that reviewer decided that each dubbed version used whatever local accent was most easily vilified in racist terms (Bogin). Viewers found these racist stereotypes so obvious that John Leo, a far more conservative essayist than most, wrote in *US News and World Report* that TPM "is packed with awful stereotypes." Reviewing many of the same details as William's *Nation* essay, he concluded, "It is a teaching instrument and a powerful, non-verbal argument saying that racial equality is a hopeless cause" (14).

While these popular critiques of the obvious racism in TPM are significant, they were somewhat surprising to many academic critics. Science fiction, both written and filmed, has traditionally been a genre about *the other*. Those who have been others in such fiction, be they robots, aliens, or different kinds of human beings, have always been convenient stand-ins for those socially discriminated against (Kilgore). Different alien "races" have frequently been simple representations of the various genders, nationalities, and "races" of Earth.[6] The issue for science fiction consumers has been the use to which images of "race" are directed. For the socially critical, "race" can be beneficially employed in such fictions to "subvert those structures and relations ... of subordination" (Wolmark 27). Or they can be used in the manner seen in the *Star Wars* franchise: to reinforce ideas of difference and to reinforce discriminatory practices.

The explosive and rapid response to *TPM*, from the political left and right, decrying the perceptions of racism is not the entire point. Such apparent stereotypes merely serve to emphasize the larger underlying fact that *Star Wars* reduces the behavior of both aliens and humans to their biology. Yes, the various aliens draw upon racist stereotypes, but so do the humans. Heredity explains ability, be it the imaginary biology of aliens or the somewhat less fantastical biology of the human characters.

The Emperor's New Clones

Perhaps no other part of the *Star Wars* narrative more fully establishes the biological determinism of the franchise than the very existence of clones and the Clone Wars. Obi-Wan Kenobi (Ewan McGregor) discovers a clone army on the planet Kamino, where the prime minister of the planet, Lama Su (Anthony Phelan), explains that the clones' genetic structure has been altered from their original host—the bounty hunter Jango Fett (Temuera Morrison). And Jango's status as a bounty hunter reminds us again that *Star Wars* is promoting the idea that genetics equal personality and behavioral achievement. Jango Fett is a talented fighter and able to attack and even kill the vaunted Jedi Knights. He can operate outside the legal parameters of the Republic's governmental system. If these abilities were related primarily to his personal background—childhood experiences and previous military or law enforcement training, for example—then there would be no point in cloning this specific individual for an army of warrior clones.

Yet, Prime Minister Lama Su tells Obi-Wan Kenobi that not only was Jango Fett used as the template, but that the genetic structure was also altered somewhat. "You'll find they are totally obedient, taking any order without question," Kenobi is told. "We modified their genetic structure to make them less independent than the original host." Thus, *Attack of the Clones* not only provides a significant clue to the *Star Wars* narrative as an example of mere genetic determinism, but also provides the possibility that behavioral traits—independence and violent abilities—are not merely genetic but so biologically based that they can be modified.

When the Republic gets its Grand Army,[7] it is one in which the very biological makeup of the individual soldiers has been specifically altered to assure competent soldiering ability. This genetic alteration also suggests why "Order sixty-six" was so easily executed in *Revenge of the Sith*. As Emperor Palpatine calls individual clone troopers on various planets to execute his commands, viewers see those clones instantly and apparently without remorse turning against, attacking, and killing their Jedi generals. If the *Star Wars* narrative had suggested other than biological possibilities for tracing individual behavior, one might view the clone soldiers as psychologically prepared for the implementation of Order sixty-six. Yet it is already firmly established that the clone army has been altered genetically so that there is a single deterministic explanation: Because of their genetic manipulation, they were thus prepared for instant action when the order was given.

Conclusion: "Luke ... It Is Your [Biological] Destiny!"

Darth Vader tells his son, as they battle in the bowels of Cloud City in *ESB*, that Luke "can destroy the Emperor. He [the Emperor] has foreseen this." Yet Luke's destiny, like that of his father before him, is biologically determined. The Emperor knows that the Skywalkers can destroy him because they bear high levels of midi-chlorians within their bodies. This quantifiable reality means that Luke has at his disposal the ability to use the Force at lethal levels to the Emperor. The fact that the eventual destruction of the Emperor and the Empire itself results from Luke's plea for aid from his father in no way changes this equation. Vader, like his son, was destined to "bring balance to the Force." From the Skywalker family's abilities in the Force to the racist representations of the Neimoidians of the Trade Federation or the slave owner Watto, all are reducible to their biology.

As *ROTS* moves to its end, Yoda and Obi-Wan discuss the fate of the newly born twins Luke and Leia. "Strong the Force runs, in the Skywalker line," Yoda tells Kenobi as they plan to hide the infants. Luke, destined to be "a new hope," overthrow his father and the Emperor, and finally aid Darth Vader/Anakin in bringing balance to the Force, is defined as that hope because of his parentage. Measured against democratic notions of individual responsibility, a problematic message of the entire *Star Wars* saga is that rebellion against tyranny is less about choice and more about your genetic makeup. It is the message that choosing to rebel is about having inherited abilities that make a successful rebellion possible. Your destiny, like that of the Skywalker family, is a destiny determined by your lineage, by your midi-chlorians or genes. It is immensely entertaining, but it is not about merit or the insights that we ordinary people can attain. By importing traditions of racism, social Darwinism, and even eugenics, whether intentionally or not, Lucas has provided a narrative that undermines its own story. Instead of championing the victory of nonelites over the vile Empire, too much of *Star Wars* remains merely the replacement of one elite by another. The rebellious young Skywalkers, the return of the Jedi, and the destruction of the Emperor are all made possible by having the right biological inheritance. The aliens and humans that aid in the rebellion are also equally defined by their biology. Perhaps with the end of the *Star Wars* films, the next sprawling and popular epic story can present a new message. A story that, for a change, the hero's journey—and the journey implied for the viewers—will not equate destiny with biology.

Notes for Chapter 9

John Shelton Lawrence and William G. Doty provided continued readings on multiple drafts of this essay. Josh Bogin provided insights into *TPM* as it was dubbed into various European languages. Stephanie J. Wilhelm also read multiple drafts and suggested restructuring the essay in ways that made it more readable.

1. Emslie's essay primarily deals with *TPM*, and, while much briefer, it covers some of the same ground as does the present essay. The author did not discover Emslie's writing until near the end of writing work, but it should be noted that Emslie's brief essay mirrors this work in many useful and insightful ways, including especially an analysis of social Darwinism in Western culture.

2. Though Darwin did not use his theories to suggest differences between human groups, he corresponded with many who did, often encouraging their own use of his ideas of natural and sexual selection. Thus, Darwin is not innocent in this process.

3. Herbert Spencer created the term "survival of the fittest." Initially intending the term to apply only to economics, Spencer would later apply it to biology after the publication of Darwin's *On the Origin of Species*. Shipman and Bannister, the source of many ideas in this essay, each provide an excellent analysis of this development,.

4. The contemporary psychologists discussed here do *not* represent mainstream thought within the discipline.

5. The number of Web pages devoted to decrying racism in *TPM* specifically is too large to list here. The anonymous *Death to Jar Jar* citation is likely the most famous and contains multiple links useful in discovering more Internet sources on the topic.

6. "Race" is such a common and continuing trope in speculative fiction that any set of references to the issue is seriously incomplete. However, Scholes and Rabkin (187-9) provide a useful definition. Bernardi makes many of the general points on the topic that he then specifically directs to the *Star Trek* franchise. Slusser and Rabkin's edited volume provides multiple essays of aliens and *the other* in ways that resonate with the *Star Wars* franchise. More recently, Leonard has edited a useful volume on the topic specifically for post-structuralist academics. Molnar provides an anthropological perspective on the idea of biological difference that underlies the perspective presented here.

7. The clone army is known as the "Grand Army of the Republic." The surprising irony, though, is the name's direct reference to the American Civil War, in which the North's army carried the same name and fought for, among many other reasons, an end to the very kind of biological and "racial" determinism that *Star Wars* symbolically promotes.

Works Cited

Anderson, K. J., et al. *Star Wars: Young Jedi Knights*. Ser. New York: Boulevard, 1995.

Bannister, Robert C. *Social Darwinism: Science and Myth in Anglo-American Thought*. Philadelphia: Temple UP, 1979.

Bernardi, Daniel Leonard. *Star Trek and History: Race-ing toward a White Future*. New Brunswick,

NJ: Rutgers UP, 1998.

Black, Edwin. *War against the Weak: Eugenics and America's Campaign to Create a Master Race.* New York: Four Walls, Eight Windows, 2003.

Bogin, Josh. Letter to the author. 11 Apr. 2000.

Butterfield, Herbert. *The Origins of Modern Science.* 1957. 2nd ed. New York: The Free Press, 1965.

Cohen, Mark Nathan. "An Anthropologist Looks at 'Race' and IQ Testing." *Race and Intelligence: Separating Science from Myth.* Ed. Jefferson Fish. Mahwah, NJ: Lawrence Erlbaum, 2001. 201-223.

Cox, Catharine Morris. *The Early Mental Traits of Three Hundred Geniuses. Genetic Studies of Genius.* Vol. II. Ed. L. M. Terman. Stanford, CA: Stanford UP, 1926.

Darwin, Charles. *The Descent of Man, and Selection in Relation to Sex.* London: John Murray, 1871.

——. *On the Origin of Species by Means of Natural Selection, or the Preservation of Favored Races in the Struggle for Life.* London: John Murray, 1859.

Death to Jar Jar Binks Home Page. 28 Oct. 2005 <http://www.mindspring.com/~ernestm/jarjar/deathtojarjar.html>.

Emslie, Carol. "The 'Gene' for Jedi Knights? The 'New Genetics' and Social Stratification." *Radical Statistics* 14 Nov. 2005. <http://www.radstats.org.uk/no072/article5.htm>.

Eysenck, Hans J. *The Inequality of Man.* London: Temple Smith, 1973.

Galton, Francis. *Hereditary Genius: An Inquiry into Its Laws and Consequences.* 1869. London: Macmillan, 1892.

Gould, Stephen Jay. *The Mismeasure of Man.* New York: Norton, 1981.

——. "Studies in Eugenics." *American Journal of Sociology* 11.1 (1905): 11-25.

Jefferson, Thomas. "Letter to John Adams, October 28, 1813." *The Portable Thomas Jefferson.* Ed. M. D. Peterson. New York: Penguin Books, 1975. 533-9.

Jensen, Arthur R. *The g Factor: The Science of Mental Ability.* Westport, CT: Praeger, 1998.

Kilgore, DeWitt Douglas. *Astrofuturism: Science, Race, and Visions of Utopia in Space.* Philadelphia: U Pennsylvania P, 2003.

Leo, John. "Fu Manchu on Naboo." *US News and World Report* 7 Apr. 1999: 14.

Leonard, Elizabeth Anne. *Into Darkness Peering: Race and Color in the Fantastic.* Westport, CT: Greenwood, 1997.

Lewontin, Richard C. "Further Remarks on Race and the Genetics of Intelligence." *Bulletin of Atomic Scientists* 24 (1970): 24, 53-65.

Manchester, William. *A World Lit Only by Fire.* New York: Little, Brown, 1992.

Margulis, Lynn. *Symbiosis in Cell Evolution: Microbial Communities in the Archean and Proterozoic Eons.* New York: W. H. Freeman, 1992.

Marks, Jonathan. "Folk Heredity." *Race and Intelligence: Separating Science from Myth.* Ed. Jefferson Fish. Mahwah, NJ: Lawrence Erlbaum, 2001. 95-112.

"Midi-chlorian Count List for the Major Star Wars Characters." *SuperShadow Web Site.* 28 Oct. 2005 <http://www.supershadow.com/starwars/midi.html>.

Molnar, Stephen. *Human Variation: Races, Types and Ethnic Groups.* 5th ed. Englewood Cliffs, NJ: Prentice-Hall, 2002.

Montagu, Ashley. "The I.Q. Mythology." *Race and I.Q.* Expanded ed. Ed. Ashley Montagu. New

York: Oxford UP, 1999. 29–45.

Plato. *The Republic*. Trans. Allan Bloom. New York: Basic, 1968.

Reaves, Michael, and Steve Perry. *Medstar II: Jedi Healer*. New York: Del Rey, 2004.

Salvatore, R. A., et al. *Star Wars: The New Jedi Order*. Ser. Books 1–19. New York: Del Rey, 1999.

Scholes, Robert, and Eric S. Rabkin. *Science Fiction: History, Science, Vision*. New York: Oxford UP, 1977.

Shipman, Pat. *The Evolution of Racism: Human Differences and the Abuse of Science*. New York: Simon and Schuster, 1994.

Slusser, George E., and Eric S. Rabkin, ed. *Aliens: The Anthropology of Science Fiction*. Carbondale: Southern Illinois UP, 1987.

Spearman, Charles. *The Abilities of Man*. New York: Macmillan, 1927.

Spencer, Herbert. *Social Statics, or, the Conditions Essential to Happiness Specified, and the First of Them Developed*. London: John Chapman, 1851.

Stevenson, Harold W., and James W. Stigler. *The Learning Gap: Why Our Schools Are Failing and What We Can Learn from Japanese and Chinese Education*. New York: Summit, 1992.

Tucker, William H. *The Science and Politics of Racial Research*. Urbana, IL: U of Illinois P, 1994.

Wallechinsky, David, and Amy Wallace. *The Book of Lists: The Original Compendium of Useless Information*. New York: William Morrow, 1977.

Williams, Patricia J. "Racial Ventriloquism." *Nation* 5 July 1999: 9.

Wolmark, Jenny. *Aliens and Others: Science Fiction, Feminism and Postmodernism*. Iowa City: U of Iowa P, 1994.

Wolverton, Dave. *The Courtship of Princess Leia*. New York: Bantam, 1994.

CHAPTER 10

Imperial Plastic, Republican Fiber: Speculating on the Post-Colonial Other[1]

Stephanie J. Wilhelm

Introduction

The cinematic historical epic, from its inception in the early twentieth century to the present, has been consumed with the telling and retelling of human history. From D.W. Griffith's *Birth of a Nation* (1915) to Cecil B. Demille's *The Ten Commandments* (1923) and *King of Kings* (1927) to William Wyler's *Ben-Hur* (1959) through to present day blockbusters such as *Troy* (2004), there are recognized thematic constancies. Hollywood History via spectacle has always been portrayed as a series of events created for and narrated by Caucasian (white) males and their engagement with the rise, decline, and fall of the nation-state's empire status. Included in this super spectacle is a reliance on the best technology and special effects of the era to visually represent binary oppositions between good and evil, darkness and light, totalitarianism and democracy, slavery and citizenship. Set architecture is massive, the costumes are extravagant, there are scores of both human and, in *Star Wars*, digitally created extras (as Andrew Plemmons Pratt notes in his essay), and all are packaged within fast-paced action plots from start to finish.

George Lucas's bifurcated universe of good and evil in *Star Wars*, where the strong and more technologically advanced seek to oppress the weak, especially embodies a pervasive and wholly static understanding of historical events. The struggle of the virtuous to triumph over imperial hegemony borrows heavily from the conventions of Roman epics. And yet Lucas's universe is clearly fantasy—replete with its own history, chronological continuities, and future possibilities—and decidedly without contextualized historical referents. However, when Hollywood stars such as Harrison Ford, Carrie Fisher, Mark Hamill, Natalie Portman, Hayden Christensen, et al. are given the task to interpret Lucas's fantastical vision, a mediated bridge is created between human history and fictional history. One of the greatest dangers in this representation, as Vivian Sobchack observes in her essay "'Surge and Splendor': A Phenomenology of the Hollywood Historical Epic," is that

> [S]tars both dramatize and construct Hollywood's particular idea of History—lending the past a present stature, attributing its production to select individuals, and providing the literal 'embodiment' of Hollywood's faith that historical events give rise to the occasion of exceptional human romance. (281)

Audiences can therefore conflate, when viewing the *Star Wars* films, visual spectacle and narrative form with humankind's perceived shared or common pasts, presents, and possible futures. This representation, however inclusive as it may seem, neglects the individual's struggle to achieve autonomy against history as the triumph of hegemony; that is, history that empathizes with the victors of war rather than those who are conquered. Reflecting on this tendency to display civilization as the triumph of the powerful over the weak, Walter Benjamin notes the dangers of displaying such neatly written histories for unquestioning mass consumption: "[T]here is no document of civilization which is not at the same time a document of barbarism... [A]nd just as such a document is not free of barbarism, barbarism taints also the manner in which it was transmitted from one owner to another" (256). Thus, when we view movies depicting epic warfare and timeless romance, we are really viewing documents of cultural history and recycled narratives of human progress.

This chapter explores this display of an apparently seamless continuity of fictional historical narrative in the *Star Wars* films and is especially concerned with the consequences of a democratic republic's ascension to empire status, a plot emphasized in *Attack of the Clones* (2002) and *Revenge of the Sith* (2005). Through this analysis one can see that defining the colonizers necessitates a definition of the colonized, the "others" who have been viewed as having no agency or voice in their historical representation. By clarifying the status of the colonizers and their "Others," we can thus determine who is represented as *in* history and who is left *outside* of history, whose stories are told and whose stories are left untold.

Post-Colonial Theory Goes to the Movies

The perspectives of "post-colonialism" and "post-colonial theory" are illuminating in the analysis of the *Star Wars* films. The terms, at first, can be misleading. The "post" seems to signify an after-effect of an empire's colonization process, such as a former colony's post-emancipation status, as when India gained its independence from Great Britain. However, Bill Ashcroft, Gareth Griffiths and Helen Tiffin, "use the term 'post-colonial' to represent the continuing process of imperial suppressions and exchanges throughout this diverse range of societies, in their institutions and their discursive practices" (3). Post-colonialism and post-colonial theory, therefore, emerge at the point of contact between the peripheral indigenous society and the metropole of, for the most part, a European-style hegemonic force. It serves not only as a mode of historical explanation but also as a means of creating a dialectic between the oppressed and the oppressors.

Post-colonial theory as a field of academic inquiry stems from the work of Edward Said. His seminal text, *Orientalism* (1978), laid the foundations for examining how literary and historical representations of a given people descriptively encode a method of negotiating difference and dominating of "the other." From the works of Edward Gibbon to Daniel Defoe to Jane Austen, this narrativization of "othering" as Said calls it,

> [C]an be discussed and analyzed as the corporate institution for dealing with the Orient—dealing with it by making statements about it, authorizing views of it, describing it, teaching it, settling it: in short, Orientalism as a Western style for dominating, restructuring, and having authority over the Orient. (3)

The positive and negative connotations associated with geographical locus demonstrate how facile it was for explorers to justify exploiting the populations of Africa, India, New Zealand, Australia and the early Americas for their natural resources and their labor. For countries such as England, the process of building an empire required a national identity affixed firmly to notions of civility and barbarism, mastery and subservience, literacy and illiteracy, progress and stagnation. This ideological framework was further legitimized by a profound belief in God's providence to guide explorers in their mission to turn heathens into proper Christians.

Since the publication of *Orientalism* many scholars have emerged as important readers in the field of post-colonial studies. The writings of scholars such as Ranajit Guha, Gayatri Spivak, and Homi K. Bhabha have become the authoritative guides to understanding and exposing colonialism as a heterogeneous—that is, multi-voiced—experience. The popularity of Salman Rushdie's article "The Empire Writes Back with a Vengeance" (1982) underscores the importance of indigenous literature, from countries such as India, as a response to the empire's representation of colonial subjects as a single entity with a homogenous identity. Rushdie's playful allusion to *The Empire Strikes Back* (1980) can be seen as a broader attempt to highlight cinema's own visual and cognitive replication of the triumph of conquest while virtually ignoring the effects of such struggles: disease, poverty, humiliation, suffering and the systematic institutionalization of such practices.

The Peripheral Planet as Anachronistic Space

A primary tenet of Anne McClintock's *Imperial Leather: Race, Gender and Sexuality in the Colonial Contest* (1995) is that the invention of anachronistic space appeared in the nineteenth century as a means to control and regulate subjects, slaves, and colonized people of the British Empire. This space, administratively formulated by the British government to support colonial ideology, became part of the larger "civilizing" mission included within the rubric of imperial gain. "Within this trope," McClintock states, "the agency of women, the colonized and the industrial working class are disavowed and projected onto anachronistic space: prehistoric, atavistic and irrational, inherently out of place in the *historical* time of modernity" (40). Of course any discussion involving space—whether as a locus of time or of geography—also requires a discussion of movement, a departure as well as a return. According to McClintock, it was thought that the farther one travels away from the metropolis, the farther away one moves from civilization and "[B]y extension, the return journey to Europe is seen as rehearsing the evolutionary logic of historical progress, forward and upward to the apogee of the Enlightenment in the European metropolis" (ibid.).

The importance of the city as center is not lost on Lucas. The metropolis of Coruscant is so crucial to the *Star Wars* galaxy that it spans an entire planet and becomes the place of departure and return for wayward Jedis and Senators alike. Visually and culturally speaking, Coruscant evokes some of Western history's best-known cities. Its architecture and penchant for holding magnificent parades are reminiscent of ancient Rome, and its place as the heart of the Republic's political process reminds one of the parliament in London. The robust economy—complete with flashy billboards advertising consumer products—can be seen as a replication of New York City's Times Square. Coruscant is visually represented as fast-paced, intellectually enlightened and as a bastion of Republican ideals. The political body that governs the rest of the galaxy convenes within the Senate's chambers on Coruscant and the Jedi Temple also resides at the center of this metropolis. In the spatial scheme of *Star Wars*, the farther geographically removed a planet in the *Star Wars* galaxy is from the watchful gaze of Coruscant, the more it is portrayed on screen as being inferior and susceptible to coercion, fear, and violence. Mapping one's course and the use of maps as guides have been central tools in dominating new lands and acquiring new wealth. Explorers in the New World, such as Christopher Columbus and Bernal Diaz, painstakingly charted their courses across the oceans so that later explorers could follow in their footsteps. The same holds true for fans, or explorers if you will, of the *Star Wars* Galaxy. As Lucas reached further out in to his fictional universe, fans created their own maps to pinpoint the exact locations of the various rims and star systems. These maps, which can be found on various unofficial Web sites and fan blogs, ensure easy access for those who wish to understand how a planet's geographical position affects its relationship to other planets and to the empire itself.[2]

Take, for example, the planet Naboo. Introduced in *The Phantom Menace* (1999). Its position on the Middle Rim makes it the closest featured planet to Coruscant, and as such, it is closest in comparison to their way of life. Its fertile land and constitutional monarchy are reminiscent of India or Jamaica (especially if we consider the water-based inhabitants, or Gungans, as racist stereotypes (suggested by Kapell in chapter 9) under the control of Britain. The people of Naboo enjoy a peaceable existence in their practices of mercantilism with the Republic until the Trade Federation grows dissatisfied with the terms of their agreement. The increasingly evil Republic uses its powers to tax trade routes, and through the "phantom menace" of Palpatine and the Trade Federation, blockades and invades Naboo in order to assert power and enforce economic policy on its subjects. The ensuing battle between the Gungans and the droids of the Trade Federation are a cinematic replication of such indigenous uprisings as the Sepoy Rebellion (1857) in India and the Morant Bay Uprising (1865) in Jamaica, displaying armed conflict between the native peoples and imperial-minded forces. The sepoys, or native soldiers of Bengal, revolted against British rule when they suspected that the British were trying to convert them to Christianity. The uprising at Morant Bay centered on the ruthless exploitation of British rulers over the native Jamaican population.

In both of these historic instances and in Lucas's veiled representation of such uprisings, the military industrial complex mercilessly squashes the initial rebellions to colonial rule. Indeed, the uprising in *TPM* is not even the central point but is merely a distraction to the reverse coup plotted by Queen Amidala. However, as the Martinique-born psychiatrist Frantz Fanon pointed out in his discussion of the anti-colonial activities of the 1950s, the message of such military actions remains clear: "[T]he armed struggle mobilizes the people, i.e., it pitches them in a single direction, from which there is no turning back... [W]hen it is achieved during a war of liberation the mobilization of the masses introduces the notion of common cause, national destiny, and collective history into every consciousness" (50–51). Self-determination is essential to revolution and eventual freedom; war is linked to colonialism and empire expansion.

The desert planet of Tatooine, located on the Outer Rim, is far removed from Coruscant in climate, geography, and social structure and its visual depiction relies upon familiar stereotypes of "the absolute and systematic difference between the West, which is rational, developed, humane, superior, and the Orient, which is aberrant, undeveloped, inferior" (Said 300). Tatooine's inferiority is displayed prominently by its primary method of commerce: the buying and selling of beings (both human and "other") as chattel property. Note, however, that it is not the act of owning or selling slaves that deems Tatooine inferior, it is that the slaves exist in the center and not the peripheries of Tatooine society.

If we examine the history of slavery and abolition in both Britain and the United States, slavery is first banned in their largest and industrialized cities—London, New York, Boston, etc.—and abolished much later in their colonies. The first anti-slavery arguments were centered on the "peculiar institution's" threat to capitalism and the rights of the rising working class. It wasn't until the late eighteenth century, aided by the emergence of print culture, that moral arguments surfaced to admonish the inhuman cruelty of slavery. In *The Phantom Menace* Padmé expresses shock that slavery still existed in the galaxy. It had, after all, been banned in the metropole many years earlier. Similarly, Anakin's pod race in *AOTC*, homage to the chariot race in William Wyler's *Ben-Hur* (1959), recalls the system of slavery in ancient Rome and the gladiatorial blood sport as an opportunity for entertainment for the masses and potential freedom for the slaves. While Anakin secures his own freedom through cunning and skill, he is still unable to free his mother. This separation, a frequent occurrence in slavery, proves to be a pivotal moment in young Anakin's life and, according to Lucas's narrative in *AOTC*, signifies his alignment with "the dark side of the force." Anakin makes a conscious decision after being traumatized by the barbarity of his mother's captors that he would rather inflict such pain than be victim to it.

In *AOTC* Obi-Wan Kenobi (Ewan McGregor) finds himself looking for a planet on the Outer Rim called Kamino. Obi-Wan finds himself at a loss, for the planet cannot be located in the Jedi's massive archival system. Obi-Wan's search indicates, once again, the importance of map-making in determining what information is deemed valuable by the establishment and what information is ancillary. He addresses the issue with Jocasta Nu, the chief archivist, to which she replies "[I]f an item does not appear in our records, then it does not exist." Her dismissive and cryptic response gives the discerning audience pause; both Obi-Wan and the audience know that Kamino must exist because Dax had supplied such information earlier in the film. However, Nu's insistence on privileging written (or electronically stored) information as the basis of knowledge, rather than the orality of experience, reinforces what Karl Marx called a "history of the successive intruders who founded their empires on the passive basis of that unresisting and unchanging society" (Qtd. in Hardt and Negri 120). Though Marx, himself, was referring to why Indian society retained no "known" history, we can easily see how his concept of an immutable foreign culture transfers to Nu's preconceived notions of Kamino. Because she cannot imagine another planet's history taking place or being recorded outside the realm of the Jedi's archives, just as Marx could not see India's history evolving apart from European history, she cannot value the existence of Kamino as a physical place, inhabited by nonhuman "cloners" with both a culture and a history. Thus, it is not surprising that this archival material was so easily erased, in effect silenced, from the archives for the purposes of building an intergalactic empire.

It is significant, however, that though planets such as Naboo and Tatooine are considered marginal to Coruscant, the centrally located metropolis, they are also home to the most dynamic rebel leaders. Further, they are also places of exile for the vanquished heroes as the empire rises to power at the end of *Revenge of the Sith*. Luke, like his father Anakin, must negotiate the deserts of Tatooine. He is raised there, departs for Jedi training, and returns to rescue a loved one (Han Solo) from certain death. Leia, like her mother, is encouraged to be politically active from a very young age and is raised on a planet, Alderaan, very similar to the landscape of Naboo.

The dual nature of the peripheral planets as both a point of departure and return, as well as their climatic extremities, reinforces the extreme dissimilarities between the natural worlds inhabited by the rebels and the vacuous nothingness of outer space inhabited by the empire.[3] Whether in the vast deserts of Tatooine, the frozen planet Hoth, the lush landscapes of Naboo, the murkiness of Dagobah, or the hustle and bustle of the metropolis Coruscant, Lucas reminds audiences that each of his characters has an origin rooted in the traditions of their home planets; the most important of traditions is clear: the ability to evade, adapt, and survive the machinations of the empire's evil forces.

Imperial Plastic, Republican Fiber

The fluidity of movement becomes essential for the rebels' survival. Nowhere do we see in the films a more stark contrast between good and evil, natural and unnatural than in Lucas's costume choices for the heroes and villains of *Star Wars*. The long brown robes worn by Kenobi and the other Jedi are similar to the kimonos worn by traditional samurai. The color and fiber of the Jedi costumes are of the natural world and indicate a harmonious relationship with their surroundings. This harmonious relationship is further emphasized by the Jedi Order's willingness to aid and be aided by ethnically diverse peoples. In the prequel trilogy there are at least ten different ethnicities represented on the Jedi High Counsel alone, and the alliance of the Jedis with the Wookies and the Ewoks in the original trilogy proves to be essential in combating the Empire's Storm Troopers. Lucas's use of make-up and hair as costumes for the rebels, rather than the plastic body armor donned by the agents of the Empire, denotes their status as the "Other," as colonials existing in their natural world resisting the chains of homogenized imperial oppression.

The expanse of Darth Vader's costume, however, denotes a drastic distinction between the forces of good and the forces of evil. Hayden Christensen points out, when donning Vader's cloak "[A]s each piece comes on, layer by layer, you feel the essence of Darth Vader overcoming you" (48). The claustrophobic layers of plastic and leather to which Christensen refers symbolize the visage of a once-man now turned machine, a victim of the state and its synthetic powers of reproduction.

They Cannot Represent Themselves, They Must Be Represented

How seriously can the audience take Lucas's representation of a democratic republic turned evil empire? If we consider the status of America on the world political stage at the time of A New Hope's release in 1977, the answer invariably becomes serious. The relatively young country had had its share of military and political debacles centered on the rising threat of communism to democracy. The conflict in Vietnam (1965–1973) and President Richard M. Nixon's subsequent impeachment and resignation in 1974 led to a very weary and wary nation. As disillusionment with their government's actions grew, and America became burdened with accusations of imperial expansion on the international stage, the very fiber of American republicanism in the late 1970s became exposed to an array of social critiques.

Enter Lucas and a cinematic phenomenon that has lasted almost three decades. The technological feats of Industrial Light and Magic and their impact on the way movies would subsequently look and feel are not to be undervalued. However, we can not minimize the importance of Lucas's most palpable theme: an evil senator's quest for and eventual rise to power that leaves countless dead and, as Senator Amidala puts it, the death of democracy "to thunderous applause" (ROTS). Lucas knows his history and he knows the fragile fabric used to weave its tales. After all, it had been written before.

Notes for Chapter 10

1. A very early draft of this essay was read and critiqued by Kirsten Thompson, who has my
   thanks. The editors were generous with their feedback and deadline extensions and I thank

them as well. Thanks also to Fyodor Wilhelm for his willingness to listen to the ideas in draft and offer comments.

2. Multiple "maps" of the *Star Wars* galaxy exist. For the purposes of this essay I draw on the map at <http://www.supershadow.com/starwars/map.html>, which is useful in that it corresponds to many other, similar maps, includes planetary systems of the prequel trilogy, and is popular.

3. This suggests what Mircea Eliade says in his study of world religions called the *Myth of the Eternal Return*. He found the existence of a so-called "Seth-type" (Sith, perhaps in our case?) of simultaneous time in which repetition of an exemplary pattern produces a timeless stasis to the event, thus giving rise to an "archetype," or "archetypal" situation.

Works Cited

Ashcroft, Bill, Gareth Griffiths, and Helen Tiffin, eds. *The Post-Colonial Studies Reader.* London and New York: Routledge, 2002.

——. *The Empire Writes Back: Theory and Practice in Post-Colonial Literatures.* London: Routledge, 1989.

Benjamin, Walter. "Theses on the Philosophy of History." *Illuminations.* Tr. Harry Zohn. Ed. Hannah Arendt. New York: Schocken Books, 1978.

Christensen, Hayden with Gavin Edwards. "The Many Faces of Vader: The Actors who Brought Evil to Life Look Back." *Rolling Stone* 975 (June 2005): 48.

Eliade, Marcea. *The Myth of the Eternal Return or, Cosmos and History.* Tr. Willard R. Trask. New York: Pantheon, 1954.

Fanon, Frantz. *The Wretched of the Earth.* Tr. Richard Philcox. New York: Grove Press, 1963.

"*Star Wars* Galaxy Map, The." Web site dedicated to the "expanded universe" of *Star Wars.* 14 August 2005 <http://www.supershadow.com/starwars/map.html.>

Hardt, Michael, and Antonio Negri. *Empire.* Cambridge: Harvard U P, 2000.

Marx, Karl. *The 18th Brumaire of Louis Bonaparte.* New York: International Publishers, 1869 (reprinted in 1998).

McClintock, Anne. *Imperial Leather: Race, Gender and Sexuality in the Colonial Contest.* New York: Routledge, 1995.

Rushdie, Salman. "The Empire Writes Back with a Vengeance." *The Times* (London) 3 July 1982: 8.

Said, Edward. *Orientalism.* New York: Vintage, 1978.

Sobchack, Vivian. "'Surge and Splendor': A Phenomenonology of the Hollywood Historical Epic." *Film Genre Reader II.* Ed. Grant, Barry Keith. Austin: U of Texas P, 1995. 280–307.

Playtoys
and
Collecting

CHAPTER 11

Growing Up in a Galaxy Far, Far Away

Jess C. Horsley

Growing up, I wanted to be Luke Skywalker. Like Luke, I was a blonde-haired farm boy living in the middle of nowhere. And though I had the misfortune of being born in 1979—two years after *Star Wars: A New Hope* found itself atop the box office—I remember watching the films in 1982 at the tender age of three.

Though neither of my parents, who had lived in Iowa all of their lives, were major sci-fi fans, both had seen *Star Wars* in the theater years before I was born. My father, a fan of action movies, enjoyed the adventure of a space rebellion, the Rebel Alliance fighting against the evil Empire. However, it wasn't so much the way the story was told as it was the story itself that impressed my mother. A religious woman, my mother found the *Star Wars* films a perfect vessel for an amazing lesson on life.

And so, at the age of three, after seeing the films numerous times and walking through the massive toy aisle of the local department store, I told my mother that I really needed *Star Wars* action figures. At the time, they represented little more than playthings. But later, much later, these first figures became reverend objects representing not only the *Star Wars* characters, but also the memories and lessons of *Star Wars* and days gone by.

My mother, recognizing the need for a four-year-old boy to have an action figure based on his favorite film character, finally surrendered and allowed me to pick one. And so, after scanning the rows and rows of toys, I chose my very first action figure—Jedi Knight Luke Skywalker.

Dressed completely in black, Jedi Luke was the epitome of cool. Unlike many of the *Star Wars* figures, Jedi Luke included not one, not two, but three accessories: a removable brown cloth cloak, a laser gun, and a green lightsaber. What more could a kid ask for?

Luke's lightsaber made quick work of any "bad guys" brave enough or stupid enough to challenge a trained Jedi Knight. Be they the brave 12" G.I. Joes or the heroic 10" Mego figures lying around our house, my Jedi Luke would fight and defeat evil in any toy form. Heck, even the 99-cent vinyl dinosaurs ran for the toy box when Jedi Luke came out.

Every time we'd stop at the store, I'd beg my mother to buy me another *Star Wars* toy, and, though I didn't always get my way, often enough I would. She understood the need for positive role models, and, though Luke did kiss his sister on the lips in *The Empire Strikes Back* (1980), there were few better ways to reach a generation of children than through the *Star Wars* mythos. Watching the good Rebel alliance, despite trial and tribulation, overcome incredible odds and eventually defeat the ruthless and tyrannical Empire gave us hope. Hope for a better future, hope for a better life, and hope for more toys. My mother understood the need for these different types of hope, and my collection grew.

My *need* for other *Star Wars* toys combined with the toy licensing boom of the mid-1980s quickly emptied my parents' pocketbooks. Though there were fewer than one hundred basic *Star Wars* figures made between 1977 and 1985, I had them all (see fig. 4). And so, I grew up in "a galaxy far, far away," playing with Luke, Leia, Han, Chewbacca, and Darth Vader.

By the time I was seven years old, however, *Star Wars* action figures were no longer the "cool" toys on the playground, and newer figures replaced the once inspirational Jedi Knight Luke. The *Masters of the Universe* cartoon became a hit in 1984, and He-Man suddenly became the go-to good guy when evil invaded the sandbox. Optimus Prime, the leader of the *Transformers*, took to the living room carpet battlefield and linoleum superhighways of our home, both as a robot and as a semi truck. Eventually Lion-O, fearless leader of the *ThunderCats*, along with his teammates quietly pushed Han Solo, Boba Fett, Darth Vader, and even Jedi Luke to the deepest parts of my toy boxes. My *Star Wars* toys were all but forgotten.

Then, in 1995, ten years after the last *Star Wars* action figure had been released; Hasbro announced a new series of 3 3/4" *Star Wars* figures. I was 15 years old, and, like me, other young men and women who had grown up with *Star Wars* realized they again *needed* their favorite childhood toys. Thus, Hasbro created *Star Wars: The Power of the Force 2* series of figures and inspired not only older fans, but also a new generation who had yet to experience *Star Wars*—except for the Saturday afternoon reruns on television and the miscellaneous hand-me-down toys.

Fans, both young and old, showed the power of a single epic film trilogy by turning out in droves to purchase the new and improved 3 3/4" *Star Wars* figures. Hasbro, understanding a need to capture not only the children's market but also the collector's market, released figures of not only well-known characters like Luke and Leia, but also lesser-known characters like Momaw Nadon (Hammerhead) and Saelt-Marae (Yakface), two aliens that only collectors would recognize. Sales of *Star Wars* toys again soared, along with Hasbro's and fans' hopes that the line would continue.

Since 1995, ten series of basic *Star Wars* action figures have been released, each capturing a different and specific part of the *Star Wars* mythology. When new and important characters—like the Jedi Council members from the prequel films—appeared onscreen, fans demanded action figures. And Hasbro responded in kind.

I often blame my current situation on my parents allowing me to watch *Star Wars* at such a young age. It was, after all, my love of *Star Wars* that first made me *need* action figures, and it's now a love of action figures that all but rules my life. Not only do I appreciate the artistic talent and skill required to design these so-called children's toys, but I also, even now at the age of twenty-six, enjoy playing with them. As an editor for an online action figure Web site, I have what many my age would consider a dream job—playing with toys. And now, twenty years after I originally played with Luke, Leia, Han, and Chewy, I again find myself surrounded by my favorite figures.

By today's standards, the *Star Wars* action figures from twenty-five years ago were crudely made and designed. But, to a child of six in 1985 with a creative imagination and the majority of George Lucas's epic film trilogy memorized, those toys were gold. I'd spend hours in the sand box or on the living room carpet playing "Jedi Knights" or "Stormtroopers" with my younger brother, and we'd fight over who was Luke or Han, Chewie or Leia. Every so often, we'd even want to be Darth Vader.

Children today don't fully understand what it was like growing up in the early 1980s. Or maybe they do. Now, more than twenty years later, I'm reminded of my childhood when I walk through my local toy aisle and see Superman, Spiderman, and Batman on one side; G.I. Joes, Transformers, and He-Man on the other. And there, right smack-dab in the middle, is a massive section of *Star Wars* toys. Like the young child's father standing next to me, I check my wallet, frown, and grab a cart. Then, like the young child eyes wide with excitement, I smile, fill the cart, and feel a *need* to once again play in "a galaxy far, far away."

Figure 4: Author Jess Horsley with his collection of *Star Wars* action figures of his early youth. As he relates, the toys satisfied his need for more adventure in rural Iowa. But they eventually led to the Marines and to his editorial role at Figures.com. Photography: Jess C. Horsley.

CHAPTER 12

Two Generations of Boys and Their *Star Wars* Toys

John Panton

A Long Time Ago...

The bitter Hoth wind cuts a swath across the bleak, desolate landscape. Han and Luke, in the trench with the other Rebel fighters, ready themselves for the imminent onslaught. C3-PO is keeping lookout. He panics. On the horizon, he spots the first of many AT-ATs (All Terrain-Armored Transports), the huge four-legged mechanical walkers slowly lumbering towards the Rebel base. The smaller two-legged AT-STs (All Terrain-Scout Transports) swiftly appear, charging toward the trench. "They've got to be stopped!" shouts Luke over the deafening pounding of the oncoming machines. "Follow me!" screams Han. They run to a nearby snowspeeder, climb in, take off, and rush toward the nearest AT-AT. Han's at the controls, dodging the stream of laser fire aimed at them. Some of the stray laser fire hits the trench, blowing C3-PO to pieces. Han shouts to Luke, "Use the harpoon!" and flies toward the legs of the AT-AT. Luke releases the harpoon, as they circle dangerously close around the legs. The AT-AT slowly succumbs to its inevitable demise, hitting the icy ground as the speeder flies on to its next victim ...

Except the icy ground is not actually icy ground, but a bedspread (naturally, with a *Star Wars* image). And the AT-AT is a stuffed elephant toy (my parents couldn't afford the real thing, so I improvised), and the snowspeeder is actually a landspeeder (which I had "borrowed" from my brother). But none of that really mattered. That was me, at age eight, playing in and expanding on a "narrative frame" created by George Lucas. Han always took the lead because he was "cooler" than Luke, and C3-PO lost his limbs because he was a C3-PO *Empire Strikes Back* (1980) figure that came apart to fit into Chewie's backpack.

Admittedly, it is not quite how George Lucas intended the Hoth battle sequence to be portrayed, but it does illustrate both the freedoms and restrictions of play within the *Star Wars* universe.

As a child of the 1970s, my peers and family were caught up, to a greater or lesser extent, in the *Star Wars* phenomenon. This essay compares my generation with those whose childhoods coincided with the prequels of 1999 through 2005, describing styles of play common in the late 1970s and early 1980s, the type and level of interaction with the original film texts, and how this differs from the new generation of fans. Developing technology's impact on play will be addressed, as well as the negative aspects associated with boys' play techniques. The analysis focuses mainly on boys' engagement with *Star Wars* play, drawing on my own personal experience and two case studies. The first case study summarizes personal interviews conducted with ten male participants between twenty-nine years and thirty-eight years of age from England. This group will be compared to two classes of thirty pupils from a small rural school, consisting of five- and six-year-olds and ten- and eleven-year-olds who engaged in written work and permitted recorded conversations.[1]

What Developmental Functions Are Accomplished by Play?

Play is a crucial element of childhood development, permitting children to create their own fictional space for escape and, by doing so, lay the foundation for adolescent and adult social interaction. Styles of play depend on age and gender, and the play experience fulfills several needs. Think of the myriad of ways one can play within the *Star Wars* universe—from playing alone with a few figures, to group role play in which friends act out scenarios based on the films, to an online multiplayer game, in which you play cooperatively in a team of players from across the world.

Play is integral to everyday life, and, as early childhood education writer and researcher Olivia Saracho acknowledges, researchers "have attempted to define it, explain it, understand it, create criteria for it, and relate it to other human activities" (87). Because of its often open-ended and free-form nature, play is difficult to quantify and analyze; however, *Star Wars* play can offer an insight into the complexities of this process. As former teacher and now researcher Vivian Paley suggests in *The Boy Who Would Be a Helicopter* (1990), children quickly expand on their ingrained skills:

> Without instruction, these skills flourish. No one is taught to walk—or to act out a fantasy.... The fact that all children share this view of play makes play, along with its alter ego, storytelling and acting, the universal learning medium. Children, at all ages, expect fantasy to generate—indeed they cannot stop it from doing so—an ongoing dialogue to which they bring a broad range of intellectual and emotional knowledge at a very early age. (9)

Paley, along with many of the other sources referencing play in this essay, demonstrates the continued attempt by Western-centric academics and researchers to clarify the role and importance of play. As far back as the late nineteenth century, Karl Groos (1861–1946) was stressing the importance of play to child development, identifying it as a process of gaining life skills and as a natural way of expending excess energy. Sigmund Freud (1856–1939) emphasized the cathartic aspects of play, suggesting that the ability to control play helped children to deal with traumatic experiences in the real world. The most frequently cited academics with regards to play are Jean Piaget (1896–1980) and Lev Vygotsky (1896–1934). Piaget, a cognitive theorist, saw play as a facilitative learning process that allowed children to engage with new experiences and scenarios, developing both physical and mental skills. Vygotsky, a sociocultural theorist, believed play to be the route to abstract thinking skills that enabled control of children's real-life behavior. More recently, anthropologist Laurence Goldman has tried to redress this Western-centric approach by objectively studying the play patterns of the Huli society of Papua New Guinea, contextualizing play in a more "universal" paradigm. He sees play as utilizing "pretence as the passageway between mimesis and mythos" (260), stressing the universal themes of fantasy, simulation, and improvisation in play. This is the tip of the iceberg in terms of research into play, but each of these theories presents valid ways through which *Star Wars* play can be analyzed.

The Function of *Star Wars* Toys

As part of his deal with Twentieth Century Fox, George Lucas held on to the merchandising rights for *A New Hope* (1977) and, in doing so, helped to kickstart a revolution in movie tie-in products, building on the success of Spielberg's *Jaws* in 1975. Film companies realized, after the success of Lucas's licensing deals, that a profitable sideline was open to them. It is easy to be somewhat cynical about the commercialized approach now taken for granted in the industry and among its consumers, but this process was a key element in extending and defining the *Star Wars* universe and, importantly, in inspiring styles of play for its fans. However, in the longer view, this commercial approach is nothing new. Nineteenth century children's books were sometimes accompanied by a small figure that "allowed the child creatively to extend the possibilities of the written story" (Hilton, "Children's Literacy", 20). Children desire to creatively play in and around the narratives they associate with toys, and *Star Wars* figures can serve that desire. Through play, children recreate a similar sense of wonder, excitement, and friendship found through the films, as well as the easily definable moral dynamic of good versus evil that arises out of fantasy war.

Toys themselves are more than mere physical objects. Stephen Kline, expert on children's play and the effects of advertising, looks at how toys can inspire play and, in particular, how character toys are "fantasies condensed into objects" and "afford the child a chance to express attitudes and practice behaviors in the protected realm of play that usually remain incommunicable" (347).

Some adult fans of the original trilogy have noted with disdain the even higher levels of commercial enterprise centered on the prequels. Simon Pegg, writer and star of *Shaun of the Dead* (2004) and cult British sitcom *Spaced* (which is laced with a barrage of *Star Wars* in-jokes), is a passionate fan but had a negative critical reaction to the prequels. He was interviewed in Will Brooker's book, *Using the Force* (2002), and highlights the gulf between his early experiences of *Star Wars* and his reaction to *The Phantom Menace* (1999):

> *Star Wars* was extremely important in my development as a child. It stimulated my imagination, increased my vocabulary, informed my notion of morality. My friendships were, to an extent, influenced by it at an early age. I mixed with other *Star Wars* fans. Played "it" in the playgrounds of my junior school. It was a social touchstone, an ice breaker, a common ground, shared by so many. (82)

And here are Pegg's views on George Lucas after watching *TPM*:

> He did not make *The Phantom Menace* for himself, he made it for an assumed consumer ideal. When he made *Star Wars*, he was Luke, when he made *TPM* he was Jabba. Go figure. (Brooker 83)

However easy it may be to dismiss *Star Wars* toys as a one-dimensional consumerist by-product, it still does not detract from the importance of toys in play. Toys are important, they tell us that a complex and important process is going on in the minds of those who play with them. Saracho sees toys as tools—tools that can trigger the following three benefits:

> (1) assist the children in assuming various roles or in dramatizing adult experiences, (2) supply young children with information and meaning, and (3) help children understand the social life surrounding them by allowing them to assume a variety of roles and access others' thoughts and feelings. (97)

These are indeed lofty and worthy traits of toys, which may jar with a cynical interpretation of *Star Wars* toys as purely promotional merchandise. In whatever form play takes, it is still important, as it is an obvious process of learning, and *Star Wars* toys do not hinder these learning processes any more than other toy forms. In their most basic form, toys can be viewed as props that encourage pretence in play, and, as Goldman recognizes, "pretence is recognized as the loquacious courier of childhood cognition" (9).

Why Are *Star Wars* and Play So Compatible?

Because of licensed novels and comics, fan fiction, clubs, and extensive licenses for *Star Wars*-themed merchandise, the franchise has considerably extended interaction with its audience. Looking at *Star Wars* play helps us understand the types and level of this interaction and some effects that *Star Wars* has had on society. George Lucas has created a universe that is appealing due to its sense of history—carrying with it a sense of depth. I believe this can imbue the toys with a greater significance, the tantalizing mystery of a seemingly limitless fictional universe that allows for greater imaginings, unrestricted by tighter narrative frames commonplace in mainstream film. The sheer size and scope of the fictional *Star Wars* universe, incorporating the six films, their television spin-offs, multiple planets, races, and characters, stimulates imagination and, therefore, play itself. As with the *Star Trek* franchise, the longevity and popularity have been sustained foremost by the fans, who made it very clear that there was still a huge market for Lucas's own brand of fiction. The perception of internal narrative history present in the films as highlighted through the "used universe" design ethic hints of previous conflict, and starting the series with *A New Hope*, "... a long time ago," reflects Lucas's overt attempt to apply his understandings of Eastern and Western myths in a filmic context. The deployment of a broad array of mythological characters and narrative arcs offers children numerous starting points for play, as Kline states regarding Lucas:

> His ambitious undertaking was to infuse character narrative with cosmological pretensions and moral underpinnings. Indeed, if by myth we simply mean a system of signs that makes reference to other myths, then, following Lucas's work, all the elements of mythology are present in the newly minted pantheon of demigods for children, often in a seemingly kaleidoscopic potpourri. (297)

Consider the range of characters that *Star Wars* offers. For example, using the theories of structuralist scholar Vladimir Propp (1895–1970), who studied fairy-tale and folktale narratives, Kline identified key characters integral to the narrative. In *A New Hope*, Luke Skywalker (Mark Hamill) exhibits the characteristics of the "hero" role, Han Solo is the "helper," Darth Vader is the "villain," and, rather obviously, Princess Leia (Carrie Fisher) is the "princess." (This parallels the mapping of *Star Wars* with the Joseph Campbell archetypes.) Each of these characters invites a variety of fan identifications.

The Original Players: Then

Using *Star Wars* play as the starting point, one can see that it does not differ from other forms of popular culture-inspired play. Naima Browne, early childhood development researcher and writer, suggests that "it is necessary to acknowledge that what children watch on videos and television offers potential dramatic playscripts" (107). In the late 1970s and early 1980s, my own generation, before the boom of home video, was inspired by the experience of attending cinema by itself. In the case study interview situations with peers from my generation, it was obvious that certain scenes from Star Wars inspired play more than others. My personal memories of the Hoth battle sequence were not unique; almost all individuals interviewed for this essay referenced this as a key starting point for play, regardless of what age they were when they saw The Empire Strikes Back. It is certainly considered one of the key sequences of the film and is often critically seen as the best of the entire film series. The scene's excitement is generated by the build up, the expectant atmosphere. When the scale of the attack on the rebel base by the AT-ATs is revealed, the epic battle that ensues is a thrilling piece of action spectacle cinema, utilizing all manner of special effects to convince the audience that they are eye witnesses to the action.

In her study of early years' children and the effect of televised narratives, early years' expert Helen Bromley observed that children can be inspired into play after watching films. One particular incident after watching a film is noted: "They were not, however, re-enacting the film but rewriting it with many original ideas," allowing the children to "reflect on prior knowledge, speculate on possible outcomes and use both of these actions to support the task in hand. This serves as a powerful reminder of the importance of narrative" (77). The creation of narrative in play drives the scenario forward, offering the child different avenues to explore, propelling skill in imaginative and creative processes. Vivian Paley's observations of play in the early 1980s (in this case, a kindergarten class) frequently encountered references to Star Wars, and many incidents highlighted children's improvisational techniques. The following example of role-play from Boys and Girls: Superheroes in the Doll Corner (1984), shows a typical adaptation of items and space in the classroom environment:

"This is the computer terminal," he declares.

"Put it over here," says Paul. He picks up the fallen chairs and sets them in two straight rows. The oven is now covered by the shoe rack. Andrew turns two shoes back and forth and speaks into a silver slipper:

"Pilot to the crew, pilot to the crew, ready for landing. Snow planet down below."

"Watch out! It exploded!"

"Darth Vader is coming!"

"Millennium Falcon, where are you?" (Paley 8)

Seeing how children identify with a character or themes presented by the *Star Wars* movies helps to focus our understanding of the heartfelt impact on play amongst its fans, both children and adults. For example, Luke Skywalker's quest is an obvious parallel for the difficulties in growing up, establishing your personal identity, and discovering the consequences of adulthood. These traits may only be interpreted subconsciously in childhood, but, in adulthood, these parallels become more obvious. Alternatively, Han Solo's (Harrison Ford) "devil-may-care" attitude is appealing due to his self-confidence (fans in the case study often wanted to "be him"), illustrating perhaps a lack of confidence in the real world. Kline also points out that what he calls "socio-dramatic play" serves a higher purpose. Rather than merely improvising construction of a narrative (which in itself is a skill),

> Socio-dramatic play with fictional characters engages far more profound psychological processes than theories of behavioral modeling and imitation admit. Identification is itself a mental process which implies both an emotional investment (cathexis) with the toy and some internalization of traits, motivations and attitudes exhibited by the character into the child's sense of self. (325)

Because each of the *Star Wars* films dominated popular culture during the time of their release, play based on the narrative prompts of the films was obviously going to be widespread. Due to its popularity, interaction with peers demanded certain knowledge of the *Star Wars* universe. Another scenario Vivian Paley described in *Boys and Girls* highlights a certain amount of pressure that this exerts on childhood behavior:

> Jonathan has not seen *Star Wars* and is always eager to increase his knowledge. "This is Boss's spaceship," he says, pointing to a drawing he has just made on his lunch place mat.
>
> "Boss don't have no spaceship," Franklin tells him.
>
> "Well, anyway, who's he the boss of?" Jonathan asks.
>
> "Snaggletooth. And Snaggletooth, he not anybody's boss."
>
> The brochure that accompanied Andrew's latest *Star Wars* doll shows "Boss" to be a bounty hunter named Bossk. Whether he is really Snaggletooth's boss is not important in these conversations. The appearance of knowing is as good as the truth itself. Certainty is valued over accuracy. (21)

This mild form of peer pressure is important to acknowledge in a classroom situation, as it highlights classroom dynamics. It emphasizes the need to engage socially with one's peers to establish a social structure. This peer pressure (and, it could be argued, consumerist societal pressure) can also increase and probably will be unnoticed by teachers in a school environment, often due to a lack of awareness of the subtleties and complexities of popular culture movements.

I recall the bitterness I felt when some of my peers discussed the intricacies of playing with their AT-ATs and I did not feel skilled enough to join fully their conversation. In reaction, I launched a diatribe against the speed and agility of the AT-ATs, commenting that the AT-ST was far superior—as though I were proving my knowledge was worthwhile even though I did not own the toy. Of course this seems trivial now, in adulthood, but, out of any cultural objects given to children, toys "are the most culturally salient because they provide a flexible and engaging tool of socialization" (Kline 15), and that situation denied me a moment to engage fully with my social group. Indeed, knowledge of *Star Wars* could be crucial to a child during social development. Jackie Marsh's classroom research and observations on Batman and Batwoman highlighted that "the role play area provided a chance to contribute their 'cultural capital' ... to the unfolding culture of shared interests and understandings that was occurring in the classroom" (Marsh, "Batman and Batwoman" 126).

The interviews I carried out revealed the very clear delineation between the school play environment and the home play environment. Obviously, the school environment allowed for much role-play (toys are often restricted in their use—teachers often seem to regard the popular culture artifacts as harmful in some way), and the home environment with friends or family allowed for more detailed and creative interaction with toys. It is interesting how filmmaking techniques themselves influenced style of play. Consider the following two examples from my older group of interview subjects. The first, now thirty-five years of age, married and with four children, recalls a frequent style of play from his childhood:

> I would set out all the figures I had at the time on the dining room table or the carpet, and all the ships, monsters and vehicles. Then when I was playing, I would have the *Star Wars* music playing in the background ... it gave it authenticity. (Moreby)

The second recollection is from a thirty-year-old single male:

> Every Saturday during one summer holiday, my friend and I set up and recreated the Battle of Hoth using a white bed sheet sprawled across the table, crumpled up, covering pillows and cushions to simulate mountains. We used his Dad's huge VHS camera to make films of what we were playing. (Crane)

As with my personal example at the beginning of the essay, the play was obviously more than a mere recreation of the film. These two examples also illustrate a longing for a more "real" experience, as well as attention to planning how the play session would be structured. Kline recognizes the multiple skills that can be developed through this style of play:

The linguistic and cognitive skills involved in constructing narrative in play are precisely those that children need to understand television and to transfer its tales to their play. In one sense, there is evidence of a potential new complexity in play: the child is the playwright devising a script, a director staging the dramatic event, and the actor making appropriate voices, gestures and noises—all at the same time. (339)

It is not ludicrous to suggest that most *Star Wars* fans are regular consumers of television and film media. The interplay between these forms of media and play continues the tradition of play being inspired by a text. For example, instead of play being influenced by books, modern Western play is increasingly dependent on contemporary media texts as a starting point for play.

The Original Players: Now

The subjects I interviewed for this chapter all revealed a strong present-day attachment to *Star Wars*, even if their style of interaction has modified from traditional toy play and role-play. Nostalgia seems to be the key element in accounting for this bond, as though interacting with the *Star Wars* of their youth helped them to remember the freedom and excitement of their childhood experiences. This escapism (whether positive or negative in psychological terms, an issue with which this essay is not concerned) is the driving force in play, even though the players have now developed an objectivity that recognizes the technical flaws of the films and related merchandise. Marsh comments in her essay "But I Want To Fly Too!" on the transition that children experience as they mature:

Children appear to have a need to explore the world in terms of its opposed extremes: good/evil, male/female, right/wrong.... as they grow older they begin to deconstruct these oppositional discourses and reveal a world in which layers of meaning are woven into and around each other and nothing is as concrete or absolute as it first appears. (211)

The original trilogy could be viewed as a metaphor for this process of complication. The first film is an easily identifiable story, with clear-cut character types and themes, but *The Empire Strikes Back* introduces darker themes, with the revelation of Luke's father (Darth Vader) at the end of the film and Luke's training with Yoda highlighting his weaknesses and capacity for evil.

The polarized good-versus-evil discourse presented by the original *Star Wars* could have imprinted on the psyche of its childhood fans. Certainly, both case studies revealed that young children do see the characters as one-dimensional signifiers (i.e., "Goodies" and "Baddies") without being drawn into the complicated political plot points or the character arcs that blur the definitions of what constitutes a "good" or "bad" role. *Star Wars* characters help to define both play criteria and also *initially* offer a safe and simplistic way of viewing the fans' own society. Obviously, this narrow vision could not be easily sustained. It could be argued, however, that this one-dimensional way of looking at the world, due to its uncomplicated surface narrative, fuels a nostalgia and a longing for another era's less problematical perception of the world. As Kline suggests, "The toy is therefore an effective symbol of a simpler form of gratification steeped in pleasure alone and not in the rational adjudication of a product's attributes, benefits and construction" (59).

This presents an interesting duality. In terms of childhood development, play is seen as part of the process of developing and maturing, yet perhaps adults can also play in a regressive way, in which the play is no longer about learning, just a purely escapist pastime.

Among the adult case study pool, specific toys and figures are fondly remembered, and, in some cases, collections are still cherished. Boba Fett still remains popular, as do figures that were considered rare at the time, such as *Empire Strikes Back* bounty hunters IG-88 and 4-LOM or the FX-7 medical droid. Children can create an emotional bond with toys, and, in adulthood, that attachment can still be significant. "Children's most cherished objects invoked a strong emotional response or attachment associated with their inner world of reference" (Kline 15), and children "take pride in a complete set or the possession of a prized or faddish toy. The toys, when used, are exercises in remembering and imagining" (336). The significance of collecting cannot be denied. A large collection of *Star Wars* toys during childhood certainly added to a child's material cultural capital, and I recall a personal satisfaction gained from the collection process. Was this in itself a process of identification, cementing one's own self-image as defined by one's understanding, control, and owning of *Star Wars* toys?

One interviewee explicitly acknowledges the nostalgic elements of his continued interaction with *Star Wars*. As a child, he played with Lego building blocks, and he is now able to combine two sources of childhood interest by collecting and constructing the entire range of *Star Wars* Lego toys. In his own words,

> In some respects I think I am reliving my childhood. Now, being 31, I enjoy the building of the models as much as I do the finished article. It is a combination of my two favorite inventions that appeal to me, and surprisingly, visitors to my house are equally interested. Everyone seems to know the names of the ships and their pilots, and which film they debuted in. (Muller)

In what seems a very postmodern development, a *Lego Star Wars* (Eidos Interactive) video game has been produced, ironically transferring a clearly identifiable icon of the toy world (building blocks) into a form compatible with what could be argued as, increasingly, the main play space—the virtual construct of the video game. The Lego gaming experience is a stereotypical battle/war play style, removing most of the traits that define Lego in its nonvirtual construct. The first case study group of adult *Star Wars* fans who physically played with toys in childhood has witnessed the furious pace of technological change, and, in most cases, due to their love of the *Star Wars* franchise, they have kept up-to-date with these innovations and now participate within the *Star Wars* universe through these electronic means.

From creating physical reconstructions of the Hoth battle with toys, these fans have been able to pursue their desire to immerse themselves within a fictional universe—emphasizing the desire to 'live' and participate and escape into it. Playing the Hoth scenario level on Nintendo's N64 game, *Star Wars: Shadows of the Empire* (LucasArts), in 1998 was a revelation to me. In 3-D, I was able to actually fly a snowspeeder towards an AT-AT, and let loose a tow cable. Memories of childhood excitement flashed back, and my most favored playable scene was catapulted into the hyper-real by the then-astonishing technology.

It could be argued that a desire to interact more fully within a fictional universe has actually resulted in a more restrictive play dynamic, yet some new technological developments could be seen to echo some of the key themes in the films—working together, being comrades, and creating bonds of friendship. Perhaps the successes of the online multiplayer games, such as *Star Wars Battlefront* (Pandemic Studios), allow the players to more successfully interact with the fictional universe, by working together as a team, replicating the desire instilled by the film that cooperative work (and, indeed, play) was exhilarating and positive and could be read as mirroring childhood play in which cooperative play was commonplace in the playground or between neighborhood friends.

In terms of lifelong educative skills, video games have many positives, obviously including hand-to-eye coordination but also constructive use of reasoning and logic. But, realistically, gaming technology still remains incapable of providing a truly interactive and gaming experience, as trends still veer toward the predictable, highly structured visions as laid down by the programmers. The ability to truly improvise is hampered as soon as an understanding of the object of play is achieved. Children may indeed want to interact with the fictional world of *Star Wars*, but are their imaginations limited due to their increasingly passive involvement with a fictional universe that is mapped out for them by Lucasfilm? Film and television itself might ultimately "narrow the framework of play because the possibilities for pretending are confined to the actions and situations associated with particular toys" (Kline 327). This makes it "difficult for children playing with character toys to change the perceived structure laid down by the toy's universe" (334).

Six of ten interviewees are now parents themselves. This allows them the chance to compare their recollections of their own play with the differing style of their children. Obviously, technological developments have made an impact, with most of the parents indicating that their children tend to spend more time using role-play (assuming various characters and acting out scenarios based on the film) and video game technology. Interestingly, there was usually a time limit placed on video game use, as though the parents (who themselves played the video games) perceived such play as a negative if indulged in long-term use:

> My kids tend to prefer role play rather than actually playing the toys—even though they always seem to demand them! I find this sad, because they don't seem to have the patience to play imaginatively with their toys, and seem to rely more on the computer games for stimulation. (Moreby)

Two parents actively encouraged their children to engage with traditional toy play, often by participating themselves in their play and allowing their children to use their own collection saved from childhood (albeit with a great amount of care and respect for the antique toys!). They set up scenarios and guided their children through what they considered to be apt play techniques, reflecting the ways in which they once played with *Star Wars* figures and toys.

Their obvious enthusiasm for this reengagement with the *Star Wars* universe seems to inspire their children to participate more often and in greater depth. One parent encourages his children (one girl, two years of age, and one boy, four years of age) to play with *Star Wars*, even though he considers them too young to watch the films yet. The following scenario gives a wonderful example of a cross-pollination of play styles, popular culture effects, and gender boundaries:

> Today we were playing with Darth Vader in Tally's dollhouse. He was upstairs stamping his feet to annoy C3PO who was living downstairs. C3PO eventually moved out. Boba Fett popped in to see Darth, who offered him a cup of tea made from mud. Boba declined and went to visit C3PO instead, who gave him a proper cup of tea. Meanwhile, Buzz Lightyear came to sort out Darth Vader, but soon gave up and went to Woody's birthday party instead. Darth then tried to con Obi-Wan and Han into getting out of the Millennium Falcon, but they were clever and could see he was trying to trick them. The Gamorrean Guards (the kids call them "Baddie Pigs") gave up being bad and went to Woody's party, etc., etc. This was over the course of about forty-five minutes. I was in charge of Darth and the kids were very happy to go along with my silly ideas and introduced many of their own. (Paxton)

The narrative freedom here is nothing short of dazzling.

Playing with the Prequels—The New Generation of Fans

How do the developing technology and the overt gender boundaries that exist in society affect childhood play? On the surface, *Star Wars* appeals proportionally more to boys, with, in this case study, only two girls who shared a knowledge of *Star Wars* that was as or more extensive than their male counterparts. What was also made clear was that the new films were less pervasive within popular culture than were the originals. The keen *Star Wars* fans still used their knowledge and toys/games as a form of cultural capital, but this was contained within smaller subgroups within the class. Both classes contained thirty students, with a core subgroup of about six or seven dedicated *Star Wars* fans in each class. When expressing their knowledge of *Star Wars*, the same patterns were highlighted as those in Paley's research. The confident assertion of knowledge remained key, even though, in most cases, information presented was incorrect in many of the fundamental narrative details. For example, one six-year-old child in the research group named his favorite film as "*Return of the Sith* because it is funny and they got fed into a giant plant," using a wrongly remembered image of the Sarlacc Pit of *Return of the Jedi* to join in conversation.

Interestingly, the most favored character from any of the films is the young version of Obi-Wan, played by Ewan McGregor. He was praised for his ability as a good fighter and his ability to take on Darth Maul and other characters, contrasting with the original generation's fondness for the lovably headlong heroic styling of Han Solo or the mystery and menace imbued in the character of the bounty hunter Boba Fett. The boys often role-played fight scenarios, revolving around the use of the still popular lightsaber; girls, on the whole, did not want to engage in that style of play, preferring a more low-key play style that was not so dependant on physical exertion. Overall, the number of toys used in play was markedly less than the number of those used by earlier generations. But the desire to collect these toys remains prevalent among the overt fans. Perhaps this suggests a consumerist social trait that indicates a need for material possessions adding to their cultural capital. Thus, a more complete collection results in a child's more secure position within his or her social group.

As Mary Hilton highlights, there are "cultural messages embodied in plastic figures" (44). Is a General Grievous figure more appealing to a young boy than a figure of Senator Amidala? If boys have both, are they playing with them in scenarios that reflect traditionally stereotyped Western gender roles? Do boys only want to play in battle scenarios, and, if so, is this type of play too one-dimensional to truly benefit the child? Toy advertising for children is tailored to be very gender specific. Does this reliance on stereotypes suggest that society needs more awareness and willingness to combat these narrow margins of gendered play? Anne Dyson, literacy-in-education researcher and writer, states,

> Muscles, machines, and magic are the secret of keeping catastrophe at bay—and of marketing associated action toys to small boys.... Commercial marketing strategies emphasize physical action and technological dazzle when targeting boys, unlike the physical beauty and soft feelings usually emphasized when targeting girls. (15)

Recent research suggests that boys and girls do indeed naturally play in different ways. But to be limited by an acceptance of these stereotypes, children would then be restricted in their play participation, affecting their learning processes. Marsh argues in her essay "But I Want To Fly Too!" that parents and educators need to intervene in "superhero" play:[2]

> Girls need to feel safe and be given the permission and space in which to explore these roles. Intervention in such play is also needed if boys are to be challenged into experimenting with alternative versions of masculinity.... Unless we try to shape the discourse in this way, girls and boys will continue to use superhero play to carve out gendered identities which cast in stone the stereotypes that are an integral part of children's popular culture. (2000)

Recalling my opening reminiscence, the description of my own youthful play could indeed be seen as a narrow play construct that purely reflects a stereotyped gender role that I was already fulfilling at an early age. I may have been acting out what Ellen Jordan calls "the 'warrior' discourse, a discourse that informs epic narratives stretching from Hercules and Beowulf to Superman and Dirty Harry and that depicts the male as a warrior, the knight errant, the superhero" (76). However, the perceived stereotypically male traits of battle and warfare in play must not be viewed as the entire scope and depth of male play. Isobel Urquhart's play research recognizes that "deploring fighting fantasies as social 'conditioning' into a masculinity that celebrates violence might similarly miss the complexity of boys' involvements with these popular fictions" (159). As Paley observes in *Boys and Girls*, while watching role-play taking place,

> Yet these dramas, I am suddenly aware, include many tender scenes. Jonathan watches Andrew die and then revives him. Andrew gives himself a maternal role, with Jonathan as the newborn robot who can never be broken. And of course, they continually rescue each other. (73)

Again, new technology could be seen as having an impact on the level of developmental richness. Most of the children's households contained a computer or video game console, or both. The avid *Star Wars* fans either had access to *Star Wars* video games or greatly desired them. Children (and adults) increasingly transfer their "play space" into cyberspace. Depending on parental control, children will often exhibit a stronger will to engage with a video game rather than the more traditional role of toy play. Ironically, the apparent immersive freedom available to video game players could possibly have negative ramifications. As the amount of time children spend playing video games increase, children engage less and less with free-form play, in which they can creatively improvise among peers or alone.

The dawn of the home video recorder/player has allowed for a stronger bond with film texts, in much the same way as revisiting a book time and time again creates a higher process of interaction and personal interpretation. It is possible then that the increased use and popularity of this technology in the home has intensified the attachment with the *Star Wars* texts, and this allows for play to develop and be inspired in greater depth than previously. Browne looks at this changing process. In particular, she examines the elements of the source text that can induce feelings of fear and how play can resolve those issues:

> Adopting a role and playing it out enables the child to take control of it and, in so doing, work towards a resolution in terms of the fear or anxiety induced by the character or the situation or the video or television program. As the story and characters become more familiar the children's play may gradually diversify in order to explore further possibilities. Playing out a story or assuming a role in order to explore a character has an important part to play helping a child develop a deeper understanding of the plot or motivations of the characters. (110)

Technology has impacted on the way children play, and the study of *Star Wars* play helps to highlight these changes. Urquhart's observations in school reveal another key factor that technology can have on style of play:

> I found it interesting that Liam and Dean both said they preferred computer games to TV and reading because "you've got more control." Perhaps the interactive nature of playing the computer game itself is incorporated into the fantasy of competence. (161)

This longing for control may indeed stifle creativity and improvisational skills, yet it is a valid and understandable sentiment. However, a truly free-form approach to play is a desirable trait in children, as "children are 'free' from the constraints of concrete objects, real actions, and, indeed, from their own voices. They infuse their own intentions—their own meanings—into those objects and actions" (Dyson 13). Kline sums up the worthy and complex factors that make free-form play such an important asset in child development:

> Pretend play can be a complex and sophisticated mental process consolidating social and perceptual schema and demanding anticipatory planning and negotiation. Dolls and action toys in particular can encourage complex linguistic structures (as the child shifts between the perspectives of character, player, narrator and self).... Even children playing alone with their toys at imaginary scenarios confront the task of thinking about motivations, enacting multiple points of view, co-ordinating multiple actions and ultimately solving problems of conflicts in social relations. (338)

There needs to be a balanced awareness from those in both educative and parental roles, making sure that children can still develop improvisational and creative play skills while allowing children to progress through the skills that video gaming can allow. Teachers often worry about the negative effects of popular culture-based play and "do not wish to endorse the exploitation of young children by the entertainment industry, a view based on the premise that young children are passive, powerless consumers of what is offered on television" (Browne 165). But as Paley in *Boys and Girls* concedes, "*Star Wars*, despite its commercial hokum, comes close to being a perfect vehicle for small boys' play" (24). And, it has to be said, a worthwhile indulgence for adults too.

Notes for Chapter 12

1. Research carried out at St. John's Catholic Primary School, Melbourne Street, Tiverton, Devon, England. EX16 5LA. Head/Principal: Mrs. D. Carr. Many thanks to Matthew Jones and Clare Farion.

2. Marsh's chapter looks at superhero play involving Batman and others. These characters exhibit many of the same qualities as Jedi, and the term can be used metaphorically.

Works Cited

Bromley, Helen. "Video Narratives in the Early Years." *Potent Fictions: Children's Literacy and the Challenge of Popular Culture*. Ed. Mary Hilton. London: Routledge, 1996.

Brooker, Will. *Using the Force: Creativity, Community and* Star Wars *Fans*. New York: Continuum, 2002.

Browne, Naima. *Young Children's Literacy Development and the Role of Televisual Texts*. London: Falmer P, 1999.

Crane, Alan. Personal interview. 12 May 2005.

Dyson, Anne. *Writing Superheroes: Contemporary Childhood, Popular Culture, and Classroom Literacy*. New York: Teachers College P, 1997.

Goldman, L. R. *Child's Play: Myth Mimesis and Make-Believe*. New York: Berg, 1998.

Hilton, Mary, ed. *Children's Literacy and the Challenge of Popular Culture*. London: Routledge, 1996.

——. "Manufacturing Make-Believe." *Potent Fictions: Children's Literacy and the Challenge of Popular Culture*. Ed. Mary Hilton. London: Routledge, 1996.

Jordan, Ellen. "Fighting Boys and Fantasy Play: The Construction of Masculinity in the Early Years of School." *Gender and Education* 7.1 (1995): 69–86.

Kline, Stephen. *Out of the Garden: Toys and Children's Culture in the Age of TV Marketing*. London: Verso, 1993.

Lego Star Wars. LucasArts Entertainment, 2005.

Marsh, Jackie. "Batman and Batwoman Go To School: Popular Culture in the Literacy Curriculum." *International Journal of Early Years Education* 7.2 (1999): 117–31.

——. "'But I Want To Fly Too!': Girls and Superhero Play in the Infant Classroom." *Gender and Education* 12.2 (2000): 209–20.

Moreby, Christopher. Personal interview. 15 May 2005.

Muller, Neil. Personal interview. 23 May 2005.

Paley, Vivian. *Boys and Girls: Superheroes in the Doll Corner*. Chicago: U of Chicago P, 1984.

——. *The Boy Who Would Be a Helicopter*. Cambridge, MA: Harvard UP, 1990.

Paxton, James. Personal interview. 28 May 2005.

Saracho, Olivia. "The Role of Play in the Early Childhood Curriculum." *Issues in Early Childhood Curriculum*. Ed. Bernard Spodek and Olivia Saracho. New York: Teachers College Press, 1991.

Star Wars Battlefront. LucasArts Entertainment, 2004.

Star Wars: Shadows of the Empire. LucasArts Entertainment, 1997.

Urquhart, Isobel. "Popular Culture and How Boys Become Men." *Potent Fictions: Children's Literacy and the Challenge of Popular Culture*. Ed. Mary Hilton. London: Routledge, 1996.

Other Films and Television Programs Cited

Jaws. Dir. Steven Spielberg. Universal, 1975.

Shaun of the Dead. Dir. Edgar Wright. Big Talk/Studio Canal, 2004.

Spaced. TV Ser. Dir. Edgar Wright. London Weekend Television/Paramount Comedy. Channel Four. 1999–2001.

CHAPTER 13

Aging Toys and Players: Fan Identity and Cultural Capital

Lincoln Geraghty

> Luckily for me *Star Wars* has not only led me to have a room full of colorful plastic toys, but it has also provided me with a multitude of highly educated, knowledgeable, and articulate friends and colleagues.
> —Jeremy Beckett, author of *The Official Price Guide to* Star Wars™ *Memorabilia* (2005)

This chapter examines the cultural and social importance of one aspect of the *Star Wars* franchise: the toys. The action figures bought, sold, and collected around the world are an intrinsic part of the *Star Wars* franchise universe. The commercial success of the 3 3/4" action figures is well known. A more difficult question lies in determining to what extent the popularity of the toys resulted from the political and social climate. I contend that the production and collecting of *Star Wars* toys from the first trilogy of films represented a return to the tradition of war "play" in American youth culture. This is in response to America's own lack of self-security after defeat in Vietnam and the effects of the "end of victory culture" as described by Tom Engelhardt (1995). Those children who watched the films and then played with the action figures were participating in a fictional world created by adults (the toy company, the government, and the parents who bought the toys) that represented a redressed and revised form of reality in which the psychic wounds of Vietnam could be healed.

As the original films passed into Hollywood legend and the prequels moved to the forefront of Lucas's mind, *Star Wars* fandom continued to thrive, and toy collection became an integral part of belonging to and participating in adult fan groups, just as it still remained part of traditional child play. As the children who once played with Luke and Leia were growing up and learning the fiscal advantages of having kept some of their toys sealed in their original packaging, notions of "war play" were changing due to the reactionary nature of contemporary American foreign policy. I want to point out that adults who used to play with the original action figures may not have necessarily understood them to represent the American national consciousness; however, it is important to remember that, as America recovered from Vietnam and set its sights on other military crusades around the world, *Star Wars* and its fans were becoming more global, therefore distancing themselves from a specifically American identity. As new toys were released to coincide with the three new prequels, issues over fan collecting become far more significant than the experience of playing at war.

Perhaps one could argue that, as video technology developed and war games became popular with both children and adults, the childlike bipolarity popular in American politics instead influenced the video game narratives rather than the toys. I would argue that the production and collection of toys in the late 1990s and early 2000s represent a new form of cultural capital, where fans collect the actions figures as part of their "self-identity," as Anthony Giddens (1991) would define it, while claiming some form of personal ownership over the *Star Wars* movies and texts. Therefore, my main thrust is that *Star Wars* toy collecting is no longer part of American national identity, as outlined in "The Politics of War Play" section of this chapter; instead, as suggested in the "Toying with Identity" section, collecting has become a process of self-making a fan identity of fans through the products of what is now a global media franchise.

The Politics of War Play

The impact that the *Star Wars* figures had on the toy industry was phenomenal, as evidenced by the fact that "in 1978 Kenner sold over 26 million figures; by 1985, 250 million." Profits from the toys, figures, lunchboxes, and video games eventually totaled $2.5 billion by the end of the first three films (Engelhardt 269). This was in addition to the huge takings at the box-office, where *A New Hope* (1977) would follow Steven Spielberg's lead with *Jaws* (1975) and *Close Encounters of the Third Kind* (1977) and achieve blockbuster status. *A New Hope*, which only cost $11 million to make, "began as a summer movie, ran continuously into 1978, and was re-released in 1979." It earned "over $190 million in U.S. rentals and about $250 million worldwide, on total ticket sales of over $500 million" (Thompson and Bordwell 522). It is no secret that Lucas kept the rights to the merchandise in order to recover the investment in the film, and no doubt he has been smiling ever since. Yet the first movie's importance is that it helped to cement the summer blockbuster as part of American film culture and make merchandising an integral part of the Hollywood production plan.

Justin Wyatt sees *Star Wars* as a high concept franchise, the first to really approach toy merchandising with vigor and, as a result, increase its market appeal.[1] For Wyatt, the *high concept* movie was an important part of the New Hollywood film industry. *High concept* films are those that are conceived as highly marketable and therefore highly profitable, as well as being visually striking and stylistically innovative. Such films, for example, *A New Hope*, are different through their "emphasis on style in production and through the integration of the film with its marketing" (Wyatt 20). In terms of the *Star Wars* features, we can describe them as *high concept* since they are comprised of what Wyatt labels "the look, the hook, and the book": "The look of the images, the marketing hooks, and the reduced narratives" (22). The fictional world of *Star Wars* that had kept children engrossed for two hours also had underlying marketing advantages: "The film's novel environment and characters have been so striking that Kenner Toys has been able to go beyond the figures in the film by adding new characters to the *Star Wars* line in keeping with the film's mythological world" (Wyatt 153). The infinite potential for expansion kept the figures popular throughout the 1980s as children continued to watch and rewatch the movies and play with their own make-believe worlds.[2] While *Star Wars* was influencing children at play, it was also having a profound effect on American politics.

Star Wars has always held close links with contemporary American politics, and, as Peter Krämer points out, we can thank Ronald Reagan's March 23, 1983, televised speech asking support for the proposed increase to the defense budget for prompting people to associate the two. However, it was not Reagan who first used *Star Wars* to paint a picture of America's Strategic Defense Initiative (SDI): "When Senator Edward Kennedy first attached the 'Star Wars' label to the President's vision in comments made on the floor of the Senate the day after the speech, it was to accuse Reagan of 'misleading Red Scare tactics and reckless *Star Wars* schemes'" (46). Right-wing cold war politics were indelibly etched onto the characters and back-story that informed the *Star Wars* universe: Heroic rebels versus the Evil Empire became the United States against the Soviet Union.

Intriguingly, for those opposed to SDI, the rebellion in *Star Wars* could be seen as a metaphor for the Left's struggle against Reaganism and the politics of big business. Nevertheless, the politics surrounding the merchandise, particularly toys, echoed a different shift in national identity. For Tom Engelhardt the toys, and their subsequent popularity with children, usually boys, represented an end to what he terms "victory culture." Throughout its history, America has defined itself through war and its triumph over adversity. Its culture of victory has filtered down to the masses in many different forms; for example, we can see the humble children's game of cowboys and Indians as a toned-down, yet biased, retelling of America's so-called valiant march westward despite the Native American presence. Engelhardt sees America's involvement in Vietnam as the turning point where victory turned to defeat, and Americans had to cope with images of historic victories despite extreme losses being felt at home and abroad. He charts this development in the 1970s, beginning with the ultimate American toy: G.I. Joe.

G.I. Joe was created in 1964 by Hasbro, at a time when the U.S. military was suffering several public relations difficulties, and was meant to instill pride in children who could own a 12" version of their army heroes: "A friendly one-sixth replica of the soldiers he represented, G.I. Joe, like the celluloid heroes of so many Hollywood combat films, put a trustworthy, amiable, childlike face on the image of the U.S. military" (Hall 35). For the first three years, G.I. Joe was the most popular toy for boys, and the manufacturers created new versions, characters, and accessories to increase their market share.[3] Yet, as Karen Hall reminds us, after the 1968 Tet Offensive in Vietnam, Americans began to realize the country was stuck in stalemate, and military toys slumped in sales. G.I. Joe no longer represented an accurate depiction of America's tradition of war heroism (Hall 36). During the demise of the 12" soldier, children were beginning to learn about the multiple stories of people previously invisible in public school curricula: Native Americans, Chicanos, African Americans, and women. American history was no longer the story of a united people, but one that included oppression and violence against minorities. As those who were once invisible told their own histories and Vietnam finally ended in 1975, Engelhardt maintains that white Anglo-Saxon Protestant (WASP) "children, like adults existed in a remarkably storyless realm" (180). War was no longer something of which Anglo-America could boast, and its stories of heroism were hollow misrepresentations of an imagined past.

This imagined past is indicative of a cultural engagement with nostalgia so intimate and impervious that, as postmodern theorist Fredric Jameson has pointed out, "we are unable today to focus on our own present, as though we have become incapable of achieving aesthetic representations of our current experience" (117). Star Wars' use of nostalgia to convey the heroism of the past is an illustration of a regressive American yearning to return to more innocent times: the films and Saturday afternoon TV serials, such as Buck Rogers (1950–1951) and Flash Gordon (1954–1955) (Jameson 116). Engelhardt recognizes this yearning in the creation and development of the Kenner action figures of 1978 and argues that Lucas reconstituted "war play as a feel-good activity for children" (268). His new franchise reversed the feeling of loss after Vietnam and literally replaced it with A New Hope. The concerns over national politics, overpopulation, and energy shortages that had once weighed heavily on the films of the early 1970s (THX-1138 [1971], Soylent Green [1973], Rollerball [1975], and Logan's Run [1976], to name a few) had been forgotten as George Lucas and Steven Spielberg took moviegoers to another place. Their films rejected the earlier period's pessimism and suggested that the social problems of the decade could be solved. Many films conveyed a vision of hope, in which the future might become a technological paradise—complete with world peace. As a result, while *Star Wars* has been criticized for its affirmative visions and has often been associated with a conservative shift to Reaganite cinema (see Ryan and Kellner's analysis, for example), it is possible to see it differently.

The science fiction films of the early 1970s were unable to imagine the possibility of redemption and viewed humanity as simply doomed. Thus, while they have been seen as radical, they were also profoundly nihilistic, with no alternative to the decadent order of things. In contrast, *Star Wars* was concerned with the exact opposite, an attempt to imagine an alternative and establish a sense of hope. Kenner's decision to make the figures pocket size meant that children could carry these representations of a fictional future universe around and create their own make-believe world wherever they played. The futuristic looking aliens, creatures, and humans with a superior command of technology, both on screen and in toy form, reassured adults and children alike that America was on the right track. Throughout American history, technology has stood as a symbol of progress: For example, as America became more industrialized in the eighteenth century, the notion of technological improvement became important to national identity (Marx 197). Thus, the rhetoric of progress, tied in with technological advancement, has played a crucial part in the erroneous belief that America is an exceptional nation. The larger G.I. Joe figures represented an America, albeit more realistic, that was too hard to accept.

Evidence for the Kenner toys' impact can be seen in the proliferation of toys and cartoons created in the early 1980s modeled on the *Star Wars* theme of rebel heroes versus evil empire: Kenner's own M.A.S.K, Hasbro's Transformers, and Mattel's He-Man, to name a few (Kline 221). These new futuristic and fantastic worlds showed war without human loss, machines doing the fighting, and technology saving the day. *Star Wars*–size figures "were transported into millions of homes where new-style war scenarios could be played out" without acknowledging America's delicate position after Vietnam (Engelhardt 269). In 1982, even G.I. Joe had a makeover, with Hasbro rendering the figures 3 3/4" and deciding to create a new, faceless enemy (COBRA) for America's heroic fighting force. Each Joe would be an individual team member with his own identity and personality; as with *Star Wars* toys, children could collect and play with a range of figures that represented variations of good, evil, skill, and visual appeal. "War play on 'Earth,'" as opposed to the alien play of *Star Wars*, "would be in the reconstructionist mode" supported by collector's cards, TV cartoons, movies, video games, and comics. Children were now totally ensconced within a manufactured world, with war as the background and America still victorious (Kline 284).

Dan Fleming sees the popular effect of the *Star Wars* figures as being part of what he calls "narrativisation," whereby toy versions of TV and movie characters, such as the Lone Ranger and Tonto, representing both the specific series and familiar stories and relationships, informed playing with the toy: "Throughout the 1960s the toy industry became increasingly dependant on cinema and, especially, on television for play-worthy objects that could borrow the popularity of a screen character or story. Such objects then came with a narrative attached" (102). Kenner did not dare deviate from the narrative of the *Star Wars* universe for risk of alienating the children who had already become familiar with Lucas's imaginings and breaking the deal agreed with Lucas himself.

Narrativisation helps children interact with fictional reality, or make-believe, during play. This creates what Fleming terms "a semiotic space" (201) where toys can act as transitional tools allowing children to experiment with their own developing identities and understand the adult world (202). Unfortunately, as outlined in this section, the close attachment of *Star Wars* action figures to America's national condition in the late 1970s and early 1980s meant that war was the underlying theme of the toys and merchandise produced by Kenner. Consequently, war, or, more precisely, America's fascination with victory in war, was also central to the adult world that children identified with by playing with 3 3/4" Leias, Lukes, Darth Vaders, and Stormtroopers. However, as the next section shows, only when child play becomes disassociated from *Star Wars* toys do we see war and war play as less important to the continued success and popularity of the action figure. What is significant is the change in narrativisation of the toys, which moves from the politics of war play to the politics of self-identity and fan empowerment.

Toying with Identity

As already stated, *Star Wars* toys have been predictably linked with the social and political climate in America, although there can be cases made for the international aspects of war play, particularly when looking at Britain and its empire/war heritage. This section moves away from American national politics to look at the continuing international influences of the toys.

According to Kendall Walton, the appreciation of art, fiction, or music is similar to a child's devotion to playing in an imaginary world; paintings, novels, and plays are props in the relationship between the subject and the representational arts (11). As children grow up, their props within their fictional world of make-believe, dolls, hobbyhorses, toy trucks, and teddy bears are merely transformed as part of adult life: "The forms make-believe activities take do change significantly as we mature. They become more subtle, more sophisticated, less overt" (12). Although child play is described by Walton as less sophisticated, he acknowledges that examining the methods of creating imaginary worlds with the make-believe that children use during play is important in helping understand the relationships adults have with the real world, as well as with the various representations of reality seen in the visual and creative arts.

For children growing up imagining themselves part of the *Star Wars* universe, the toys are integral props in the make-believe relationship they have with that fictional world. Playing, and collecting the toys affirm and bring the *Star Wars* story to life. Consequently, as Walton suggests about make-believe in adulthood, those adults that used to play with the figures begin to have a more complex relationship with the toys and figures they collected as children. They are no longer seen as objects of play but as markers of personal identity, evoking memories of childhood, and as symbols of cultural capital, which can be bought and traded within a fan community. After all, as Roland Barthes observed in *S/Z* (1975) about the nature of the text,

> Rereading is no longer consumption, but play (that play which is the return of the different). If then, a deliberate contradiction in terms, we *immediately* reread the text, it is in order to obtain, as though under the effect of a drug (that of recommencement, of difference), not the *real* text, but a plural text: the same and the new. (16)

In other words, there are multiple readings to be made regarding the play with, and the collection of, *Star Wars* action figures—the most significant now being that adult fans of all nationalities are collecting them as part of their own search for personal identity. Art historian Michael Camille views collecting less as a pathology centered on economic consumption and more of "a socially creative and recuperative act," where the identity of the collector is self-fashioned through the accumulation of collectibles (qtd. in Staiger). For Jeremy Beckett, lifelong *Star Wars* fan and toy enthusiast, adults collect the action figures for one of three reasons: suffering the "Peter Pan Syndrome," recapturing one's youth, or getting involved in a phenomenon that "has encompassed hundreds of millions of people around the world." Whereas the first reason sees collectors returning to a nostalgic personal past where they played with toys and reenacted scenes from the movies, the second reason hinges on the collector never having experienced the thrill of the original toys or movies because they neither could afford nor have permission to buy them. Beckett's third reason for the popularity of *Star Wars* toys is the renewed interest in the franchise created by the prequels (4).

One of the most popular *Star Wars* figures to collect, the Stormtrooper, has gone through dramatic changes since first appearing as pioneers of the 3 3/4" market in 1978 (see fig. 5). The figure at the extreme left of figure 5 is from the original Kenner line, the two in the middle are part of the Kenner "Power of the Force" relaunch of figures which coincided with Lucas's digitally remastered films starting in 1997, and the final Clone Trooper is from the release of *Attack of the Clones* (2002). These new Stormtroopers, as revealed in the title, are the forebears of the Stormtroopers made famous in the first three movies.

Figure 5: These Stormtrooper action figures illustrate the evolution from the stiff early original to the more flexible and poseable figures of recent years – a feature that has enhanced their value as collector items that require special knowledge. Collection and photography: Lincoln Geraghty.

Visually, the toys differ quite acutely: The original figure has straightened limbs with little pose-ability; the two from 1997 are molded with more active stances, and their weapons and painted details enhance their play potential; and the Clone Trooper comes with accessories and color-coded insignia (replicating the clones in the film) and can be posed in a number of ways. As the characters develop on screen, the figures begin to show potential for expanded play; the various types, classifications, and colors of Clone Troopers that could be bought increased as they became central to both *Attack of the Clones'* plot and the then undisclosed plot of *Revenge of the Sith* (2005).[4] This point echoes Wyatt's assertion about the "mythological world" of the franchise and Fleming's analysis of "narrativisation." In sales, before the May 2005 release of *Revenge of the Sith*, the franchise had accumulated $9 billion for the merchandising (Abraham) and $3.4 billion in worldwide box office receipts (Crawford).

During the March run up to *Revenge of the Sith*, Krysten Crawford pointed out that Darth Vader was unsurprisingly the focal point to the merchandising tie-ins ("Jedi Jackpot").

For the prequels, the action figures and play sets were specifically targeted at two markets: the children's toy market and the adult collector. The latter was undeniably the one that the toy industry saw as the cash cow. According to Jim Silver, an industry expert on action figures, "*Star Wars* has the biggest collector base of any brand," and license holders have been able to bank on that base, no matter the age, buying the latest new release (qtd. in Crawford). However, for Jonathan David Tankel and Keith Murphy, collecting 'collectible' artifacts has become more than just trying to make money from the nostalgic yearnings of some die-hard fans: "For the fan, the potential for profit at some future date, while always present as in any economic transaction, is often overshadowed by the value created by the ownership of the artifact in the present" (56). John Fiske sees "the accumulation of both popular and official cultural capital," signaled through the fan collection (records, toys, books, etc.), as the "point where cultural and economic capital come together" (43). In other words, fans of popular culture, such as *Star Wars* or the Beatles, and avid buffs of official culture, such as opera or fine art, share the same desire both to know as much as they can about their subject and to collect as much physical material as they can (42–3).

A simple search on eBay notched up hundreds of potential purchases of both rare and common *Star Wars* action figures: I searched for Stormtroopers (seen in fig. 5) and had 218 hits ranging from an original priced at $2.75 to a "Power of the Force" version priced at $5.00, and ranging from a vintage reissue priced at $9.95 to a selection of original Stormtroopers, Biker Scouts (*Return of the Jedi*), and Snowtroopers (*The Empire Strikes Back* [1980]) that seemed overpriced at $69. There is obviously a fan market where profit is important; nevertheless, it seemed more significant that there was also a community where fans got together not only to trade, but also to discuss the implications of their passion for collecting the toys of their youth. Annette Kuhn's term "enduring fandom" fits here, although she defines it as "loyalty to a [film] star" throughout a fan's life "beyond the star's death" (135). It is quite clear that *Star Wars* fans are still loyal to their childhood plastic playmates even after they have reached adulthood. To this form of fandom and fan community, I turn—in conclusion—specifically to identify and examine the noticeable change in meaning the *Star Wars* toys have undergone.

In 2003, the official *Star Wars* fan club in Mexico put together a convention to celebrate twenty-five years of *Star Wars* toy collecting. Fans and collectors from all over the world gathered in Mexico City to see, trade, and talk about the latest toys as well as the classics: what conference attendee Dustin calls, in his conference diary, "*Star Wars* Collectors Convention in Mexico

City" (2003), "pure heaven." This convention attracted 'celebrity' collectors, described as "Super Collectors" by Dustin, who even signed autographs for fans eager to hear about their collecting and toy anecdotes. This particular revelation was interesting since it is well documented that fans have great admiration for the stars of their favorite films and programs, yet it slightly alters the fan/star relationship when the star is a collector like themselves.

Quite clearly, toy-collecting fans have created their own hierarchy of esteem that includes the actors and producers of *Star Wars* but also members of their own community. Those, like Joseph Iglesias, who have collected toys since childhood astounded Dustin because he was fascinated to hear about bootleg copies of his favorite figures: "From Brazilian figures made out of lead to the infamous Uzay 'Head Man' Joe [Joseph] seems to be on top of it all." *Star Wars* toy collecting has become a real universe within the fictional universe created by the franchise: Collector Joe can make his own Brazilian versions of famous figures, the Turkish company Uzay can make affordable bootleg figures to sell all over the world, and Kenner can produce an exclusive members-only "*Star Wars* Convention Exclusive Silver Boba Fett with Star Case" that was distributed in Mexico City, yet all are in great demand.[5] Furthermore, Joe's and Uzay's appropriation of what Engelhardt has described as a very American product is similar to the relationship scrutinized by some scholars between international women and the American Barbie doll.

Barbie was first released in 1959 and quickly became a homogenized American idol, but what is interesting for Pamela Thoma (1999) and J. Paige MacDougall (2003) in their studies of Barbie collecting around the world is that Barbie's meaning was changed and adapted to suit personal and international tastes. Thoma's study of beauty pageants argues that Asian American girls used Barbie's glamorous image as a template for their own "transnational feminism": in other words, gaining acceptance in a stereotypically white female environment.[6] MacDougall goes further and argues that appropriation of the Barbie doll in Mexico offered young girls a "local identity rather than emulating the meanings and values she was attributed by Mattel" (257). Through a process of "creolization," consumers in the Yucatan region of Mexico gave their Barbies new Mayan identities, complete with self-woven traditional dresses: "Overall, the creolization of Barbie dolls in this context demonstrates the power of consumer agency to contain global images within local systems of meaning" (273). Both of these studies, and the example of Joe from Brazil turning *Star Wars* figures into personalized bootlegged collectibles, follow David Hesmondhalgh's analysis of the cultural industries; he asserts that local markets can compete with the hegemonic forces of American cultural imperialism, as with the Latin American *telenovelas* (182–3). Local and personal identities act in contrary ways vis-à-vis the American meanings that Tom Engelhardt reads into children's war play with post-Vietnam *Star Wars* toys.

The fans at the Mexico City convention were working out a new identity in relation to their favorite collectibles, not one based on a particular political viewpoint, but one rooted in postmodern forms of self-identity and society. It is clearly ironic that collectors have chosen to use a licensed corporate product to define their identity; one might call it a form of surrender to the influences of American cultural hegemony. However, the fact that collectors also go beyond the boundaries set by Lucas and Kenner, creating their own versions of figures, buying and selling bootleg copies that are just as rare as official figures and revered in equal measure, signals that the hegemonic framework weakens when examined on a global scale. Collectors all over the world dip in and out of the imagined fantasy world of *Star Wars*, adding to and expanding the universe created by Lucas.

In his explorations of the dilemmas of modern selfhood, Anthony Giddens sees "What to do?", "How to act?", and "Who to be?" as the "focal questions for everyone living in circumstances of late modernity [the here and now]." As well as asking these questions, people try to answer them "either discursively or through day-to-day social behaviour" (70). In what Giddens calls "the trajectory of the self," people are constantly trying to define themselves and their self-identity through reflexive examination of their "life-cycle" (14). In the *Star Wars* fantasy world, the collector-fan's self-identity is in a constant state of reflexive examination as new films are released, toys are produced, and conventions are organized. Dustin, Joe, and all the "star collectors" adapt and change their lives as they interact with each other and with the new toys they collect. Joe makes new bootleg copies to sell and display at conventions, people like Todd Chamberlain give lectures on the art of making vintage display cases (qtd. in Dustin), and Dustin himself feels he "can hold [his] own now after hearing these guys talk about" collecting "Lili-Ledy" collectibles.

Star Wars toys, and all their related packaging and display paraphernalia, carry intensely individualized personal meanings that define who these fan collectors are and help guide their own "trajectory of the self." Cornel Sandvoss's recent study of fandom suggests that "the more that approaches to fandom emphasize the element of the reader's self in the construction of meaning" or, in terms of this study, their determination to collect all the figures and toys available, "the greater the degree of polysemy [multiple readings] they imply." Self-reflection in fandom has often been taken to mean that texts become a blank screen on which fans reflect their own self-image; they "are *poly*semic to a degree that they become *neutro*semic—in other words, carry no inherent meaning." Sandvoss asserts that "neutrosemy" is the "semiotic condition in which a text allows for so many divergent readings that, intersubjectively, it does not have any meaning at all" (126). *Star Wars* toys then do not carry inherent meanings; playing with and collecting them in pursuit of self-identity create the meaning.

Conclusion

This chapter has charted the various meanings *Star Wars* toys have assumed in the past twenty-seven years, from the action figure being part of America's tradition of war play to its representing the self-styled personalization of fans from all over the world. Through an analysis of *Star Wars* merchandise and the ideological implications of a pop culture phenomenon, I have attempted to understand the connection between cult fandom, national politics, and self-identity. Whereas scholars have previously placed *Star Wars* within its national contexts, myth (Galipeau), American society (Engelhardt), and the changing political landscape (Krämer) or studied the community of its more active fans (Brooker) within the confines of either textual poaching (Jenkins) or textual game keeping (Hills),[7] this study has linked the two independent strands together, examining the developing significance of the *Star Wars* action figure from imaginary child play to authentic adult collecting.

Star Wars has clearly affected the lives of millions who not only believed as children in the make-believe world of a "galaxy far, far away," but also see the products of a multibillion dollar merchandising campaign as integral components of their adult lives. *Star Wars* can no longer be analyzed solely on the basis of the changing American political landscape; the ideological contexts surrounding the production and release of the first three movies cannot fully explain the continued popularity of the toys for contemporary adult/child collectors. Those who collect the merchandise today do so because the act of collecting, playing, and recapturing one's youth is bound up in the modern desire to define oneself through symbolic possessions rather than through shared national beliefs. From a fixed and undeniable meaning established by Engelhardt, which hinged on the national psychology of America's "end of victory culture," to a multilayered and interchangeable framework that allowed for personal empowerment, *Star Wars* toys have not only been "played with" but have also been "played up" in the day-to-day lives of people growing older.

Notes for Chapter 13

1. Eric Greene notes that *Planet of the Apes* (1968) created a similar buzz around its toy and comic merchandise (164–9).

2. A contemporary franchise example is the animated series *Star Wars: Clone Wars* (2003–2005), which has produced its own brand image and tie-in products (*Clone Wars* action figures, DVDs, and books), becoming a diversification within diversification, a fictional universe within a fictional universe.

3. G.I. Joe was an international success too; under the name of "Action Man" he was popular in the United Kingdom (Fleming 97). When G.I. Joe was relaunched in 1984, as 3 3/4" action figures, British children knew them as "Action Force." The inevitable television animated series quickly followed.

4. We can see the same thing happening with the battle droids in *The Phantom Menace* (1999).

5. According to Jeremy Beckett, the "Turkish line of Uzay bootleg figures is without a doubt the most well-known line of *Star Wars* bootlegs in the world." The specific figure mentioned by Dustin, "Head Man," is an ultra rare figure based on the official Emperor's Royal Guard figure from *Revenge of the Sith* (2005) but with a chromed head and shield (Beckett 209). The "*Star Wars* Convention Exclusive Silver Boba Fett with Star Case" is also available online with Amazon.com if you live in the United States or Canada.

6. Ann DuCille has also looked at African American female identity of the Barbie doll and commented that black Barbie dolls have problematized race and racial issues in America: "The particulars of black Barbie illustrate the difficulties and dangers of treating race and gender differences as biological stigmata that can be fixed in plastic and mass-reproduced" (57).

7. "Textual poaching," Henry Jenkins's term, is derived from Michel de Certeau (1984) to describe the process by which fans embrace and transform the original text; in the case of *Star Wars*, the text becomes a catalyst for a network of new elaborate interpretations and meanings (24-7). "Textual gatekeeping" is explained by Matt Hills as the process through which "poacher" fans become legitimate producers and owners of cult texts—story writers, for example, within the "cultural parameters of niche marketing" and an "interpretive community" of fans (40).

Works Cited

Abraham, Kristin. "TD Monthly's Top 10 Most Wanted Action Figures." *TD Monthly: A Trade Magazine for the Toy, Hobby, Game & Gift Industry* May 2005. 12 July 2005 <http://www.toydirectory.com/monthly/article.asp?id=1336>.

Barthes, Roland. *S/Z*. Trans. Richard Miller. London: Jonathan Cape, 1975.

Beckett, Jeremy. *The Official Price Guide to* Star Wars™ *Memorabilia*. New York: House of Collectibles, 2005.

Brooker, Will. *Using the Force: Creativity, Community and* Star Wars *Fans*. New York: Continuum, 2002.

Crawford, Krysten. "The Jedi Jackpot." *CNN/Money.com* 31 Mar. 2005. 12 July 2005
<http://money.cnn.com/2005/03/31/news/newsmakers/starwars/>.

de Certeau, Michel. *The Practice of Everyday Life*. Berkeley: U of California P, 1984.

DuCille, Ann. *Skin Trade*. Cambridge, MA: Harvard UP, 1996.

Dustin. "*Star Wars* Collectors Convention in Mexico City." *Rebelscum.com*. 14 July 2003. 12 July 2005 <http://rebelscum.com/article.asp?i=43924>.

Engelhardt, Tom. *The End of Victory Culture: Cold War America and the Disillusioning of a Generation*. Amherst, MA: U of Massachusetts P, 1998.

Fiske, John. "The Cultural Economy of Fandom." *The Adoring Audience: Fan Culture and Popular Media*. Ed. Lisa A. Lewis. London: Routledge, 1992. 30-49.

Fleming, Dan. *Powerplay: Toys as Popular Culture*. Manchester: Manchester UP, 1996.

Galipeau, Steven A. *The Journey of Luke Skywalker: An Analysis of Modern Myth and Symbol*. Chicago: Open Court, 2001.

Giddens, Anthony. *Modernity and Self-Identity: Self and Society in the Late Modern Age*. Cambridge: Polity P, 1991.

Greene, Eric. *Planet of the Apes as American Myth: Race, Politics, and Popular Culture*. Hanover, NH: UP of New England, 1998.

Hall, Karen J. "A Soldier's Body: GI Joe, Hasbro's Great American Hero, and the Symptoms of Empire." *Journal of Popular Culture* 38.1 (2004): 34–54.

Hesmondhalgh, David. *The Cultural Industries*. London: Sage, 2002.

Hills, Matt. *Fan Cultures*. London: Routledge, 2002.

Jameson, Fredric. "Postmodernism and Consumer Society." *The Anti-Aesthetic: Essays on Postmodern Culture*. Ed. Hal Foster. Port Townsend, WA: Bay Press, 1983. 111–25.

Jenkins, Henry. *Textual Poachers: Television Fans & Participatory Culture*. New York: Routledge, 1992.

Kline, Stephen. *Out of the Garden: Toys and Children's Culture in the Age of TV Marketing*. London: Verso, 1993.

Krämer, Peter. "*Star Wars*." *The Movies as History: Visions of the Twentieth Century*. Ed. David W. Ellwood. Stroud: Sutton Publishing, 2000. 44–53.

Kuhn, Annette. "'That Day *Did* Last Me All My Life': Cinema Memory and Enduring Fandom." *Identifying Hollywood's Audiences: Cultural Identity and the Movies*. Ed. Melvyn Stokes and Richard Maltby. London: BFI, 1999. 135–46.

MacDougall, J. Paige. "Transnational Commodities as Local Cultural Icons: Barbie Dolls in Mexico." *Journal of Popular Culture* 37.2 (2003): 257–75.

Marx, Leo. *The Machine in the Garden: Technology and the Pastoral Ideal in America*. New York: Oxford UP, 1964.

Ryan, Michael, and Douglas Kellner. *Camera Politica: The Politics and Ideology of Contemporary Hollywood Film*. Bloomington, IN: Indiana UP, 1988.

Sandvoss, Cornel. *Fans: The Mirror of Consumption*. Cambridge: Polity P, 2005.

Staiger, Janet. "Cabinets of Transgression: Collecting and Arranging Hollywood Images." *Particip@tions* 1.3 (2005). 17 Feb. 2005.
<http://www.participations.org/volume%201/issue%203/1_03_staiger_article.htm>.

Tankel, Jonathan David, and Keith Murphy. "Collecting Comic Books: A Study of the Fan and Curatorial Consumption." *Theorizing Fandom: Fans, Subculture and Identity*. Ed. Cheryl Harris and Alison Alexander. Cresskill, NJ: Hampton P, 1998. 55–68.

Thoma, Pamela. "Of Beauty Pageants and Barbie: Theorizing Consumption in Asian American Transnational Feminism." *Genders* 29 (1999): 37 pars. 4 Mar. 2005.
<http://www.genders.org/g29/g29_thoma.html>.

Thompson, Kristin, and David Bordwell. *Film History: An Introduction*. 2nd ed. Boston: McGraw-Hill, 2003.

Walton, Kendall L. *Mimesis as Make-Believe: On the Foundations of the Representational Arts*. Cambridge, MA: Harvard UP, 1990.

Wyatt, Justin. *High Concept: Movies and Marketing in Hollywood*. Austin: U of Texas P, 1994.

Other Films Cited

Close Encounters of the Third Kind. Dir. Steven Spielberg. Columbia/EMI, 1977.

Jaws. Dir. Steven Spielberg. Universal, 1975.

Logan's Run. Dir. Michael Anderson. MGM, 1976.

Planet of the Apes. Dir. Franklin J. Schaffner. 20th Century Fox, 1968.

Rollerball. Dir. Norman Jewison. Algonquin, 1975

Soylent Green. Dir. Richard Fleischer. MGM, 1973.

THX–1138. Dir. George Lucas. Zoetrope Studios/Warner Bros., 1971.

Television Programs Cited

Buck Rogers. ABC. 1950–1951

Flash Gordon. 39 episodes. Syndicated. Intercontinental Film Productions. 1954–1955.

G.I. Joe. 95 episodes + movie. Syndicated. Hasbro Inc./Marvel Productions/Sunbow. 1983–1987.

He-Man and the Masters of the Universe. 330 episodes. Syndicated. Filmation Associates/Mattel Inc. 1983–1985.

M.A.S.K. 75 episodes. Syndicated. Kenner/Ashi Pro. 1985–1986.

Star Wars: Clone Wars. 20 episodes. Cartoon Network. 2003–2005.

The Transformers. 98 episodes + movie. Syndicated. Hasbro Inc./Marvel Productions/Sunbow/Akom. 1984–1987.

Toys Cited (Ephemeral URLs Omitted)

Star Wars Convention Exclusive Silver Boba Fett with Star Case. 2003. Brian's Toys. 12 July 2005 <http://www.amazon.com>.

Star Wars Original Stormtroopers, Snowtroopers, Bikers! 2005. Kenner. 12 July 2005 <http://www.ebay.com>.

Star Wars OTC Vintage Stormtrooper in Hard Case! Rare. 2005.

Star Wars The Power of the Force Stormtrooper. 2005. Kenner. 12 July 2005 <http://www.ebay.com>.

Vintage *Star Wars* Stormtrooper Complete C-9.5+. 2005. Kenner. 12 July 2005 <http://www.ebay.com>.

Evaluations

Blowing Stardust in Our Eyes: Digital Film Theory and Identification with Imaginary Cameras

Andrew Plemmons Pratt

One subtle way that movies create meaning is through the camera's position in each scene. Logically, camera position and movement determine how viewers see a film's action and, consequently, how they interpret what they see. Camera position creates meaning in the effects-laden Podracing scene in *The Phantom Menace* (1999) and is especially important for two reasons. First, the sophisticated computer-generated imagery (GCI)—the most sophisticated use of the technology seen yet in 1999—demands a rethinking of how cinematography uses visual cues familiar from popular culture to render as realistic images of things that are impossible to photograph. "CGI proper," writes film historian and critic Stephen Prince in his important "True Lies" essay of 1996, "refers to building models and animating them in the computer" (27–8). Prior to *TPM*, CGI appears primarily as an additive process; shots in *Jurassic Park* (1993) or *Terminator 2* (1991) capture pictures of real sets and actors and add to them animated models of dinosaurs or cyborgs. In the Podrace, realistic CGI begins literally from the ground up, as the camera follows real actors and digital characters through a digital landscape. Second, taking into account the digitally *rendered* (as opposed to merely *captured*) nature of images that make up the Podracing scene, we must consider how the ideology of a film narrative operates when the camera is not capturing images of real things and when the camera may be virtual—an imaginary concept in itself.

Critics and fans have had mixed opinions about digital effects in *TPM*, *Attack of the Clones* (2002), and *Revenge of the Sith* (2005). Prior to the release of the first three episodes, audiences got a taste of additive digital effects in the special editions of the original trilogy, which improved the picture and sound quality. The special editions also retained the altered scenes that appeared in the 1997 theatrical re-release of the movies: Digital alterations included flesh-ing out the backdrops of Mos Eisley and adding Jabba the Hutt and Anakin Skywalker (Hayden Christensen) to scenes where they had not previously ap-peared. For some, the effects are just inherent in the genre: Realistic sci-fi re-quires meticulously rendered visuals.

Others see the deluge of precision-crafted shots as a compensation for the weak scripts of the first three episodes. *Variety* magazine's reviewer Todd McCarthy picked up on the video game merchandizing potential of the effects, calling *TPM* "a fanciful and fun movie for young boys ... always visually divert-ing." He, like other critics, also lamented the plastic feeling that the effects lent to the most recent movies. "The new CGI characters are notably lacking in charm or interest other than on the design level ... they bring nothing new or special to Lucas' universe, and in a sense overpopulate it" (53). Jonathan Romney, writing in the British *New Statesman*, called *TPM*, "dull and distant ... too concerned with denying its own construction, with appearing seamless, which is why its castles seem built of air" (38). But critical concern for CGI's misapplication paled in comparison to the wrath of fans outraged by the criti-cal whipping boy of the movies: Jar Jar Binks. Fury over the bumbling Gungan brewed on Internet sites even before *TPM*'s theatrical release. The Sci-fi Movie Page Web site (<http://scifimoviepage.com>) has an entire page entitled "Jar Jar Binks Must Die!" It recalls the sentiments of fans in 1999: "By the time he opened his mouth to deliver only one line of dialogue in the full trailer, the newsgroups on the Internet were already abuzz with pure hatred for him" (O'Ehley). Jar Jar was just the most obvious target for the concern that the technical wizardry behind CGI characters outstripped their onscreen charisma. One disgruntled fan found Jar Jar's digital existence so pernicious that he re-edited a version of movie to remove most of the shots in which he appeared; the resulting *Phantom Edit* spread across the Internet and spawned similar ama-teur revision projects. (This story is told in Mark McDermott's chapter 15 in this volume.)

Most of these responses focus on the narrative results of digital effects, rather than on the conditions of film production that dictate how the effects can generate visual meaning. Much of the conversation about CGI in the *Star Wars* movies—and other films in general—revolves either around the technical innovations (cameras, computers, software, and animation) that enable digital cinematography or whether the resulting images add to the movie's quality. My intention is neither to catalogue the technical innovations of George Lucas's Industrial Light and Magic[1] nor to assess whether CGI makes *TPM*—or any *Star Wars* movie—a better film. My approach focuses on how CGI, which is central to Lucas's lifetime project, changes the way we have to think about the rela-tionship between movie imagery and our familiar modes of interpreting the visible world. How do we understand the movie's references to a world outside the film based on what is present on or absent from the screen? The Podrace scene from *TPM* on which I focus is a detailed example of the CGI methods used in the two movies that followed. Moreover, the film provides a useful transition from the traditional filmic work of the original trilogy to the wholly digital work of the final two films.

The Podrace brings together characters from across the spectrum of *Star Wars* humanoid races. The sheer variety of races is shorthand for the various cultures and ethnicities populating the world of Lucas's imagination. But despite the diversity of the characters in *TPM*, power ultimately lies in the hands of the white males, be they good or evil. This is no different from the three preceding episodes; the egalitarianism is ultimately superficial. This discussion tackles some of the cinematographic mechanics that construct that image of the dominant white male. Those visual mechanics are not the product of CGI innovations—they are the same codes found in traditional cinematography. If *TPM*—and the Podrace in particular—are so technically innovative, then we might ask the following question: Why are digitally constructed images chained to myopic ways of depicting the interaction of different races in a fantastic world?

Laying the Scene for *The Phantom Menace* **Podrace**

Vendors edge their way up and down the stairs, hawking overpriced refreshments. Pit crews scurry to make last-minute preparations. The commentators butter up the fans with banter—"we have perfect weather ... and a big turnout here, from all the Outer Rim territories"—and the crowd thunders as their favorite racers edge out onto the course.

The Podracing scene begins with an establishing long shot from high above the raceway. Below the camera is the starting line and the enormous grandstands filled with brown-clad spectators. A trumpet fanfare blares on the soundtrack. The camera spirals downward and into the sandy horseshoe-shaped structure. The next cut suspends the camera directly in front of the commentator's box.

This pair of shots takes only a few brief seconds but immediately establishes the way we see the entire scene. For anyone who has ever seen televised American sporting events, there are clear familiarities in this opening shot. Aerial shots like this first one are immediately recognizable to anyone who has seen televised broadcasts of sporting events. Imagine for a moment how a hypothetical average American would equate the film scene's formal elements with cues brought from American cultural texts. The *blimp shot* is a standard image from the opening of football games, baseball games, or NASCAR races. The camera recording the shot is suspended from a helicopter or a blimp, and trumpet-heavy music usually accompanies the scene. This shot establishes the lay of the physical space for the absent viewer. It allies the viewer with the spectators present at the event. Paradoxically, the "God's eye" perspective shows us the "everyman," the indistinguishable individual consuming this nugget of popular sporting culture. The movie doesn't dwell on the customs and traditions of frontier Tatooine, where the race is taking place, but the aerial shot establishes strong enough parallels to popular American sporting culture that the scene seems real as the opening moment of a high-profile race. A viewer familiar with the ways a television camera shows us a sporting event can anticipate overtones of machismo and masculine bravado, along with an air of nationalistic or regional pride.

The racing stadium is obviously a fictional place. It is, in fact, a miniature model overlaid with digital effects to create the convincing illusion of a real place. Visible from the air are thousands of small moving characters on the sand track and in the grandstands, many of them trotting around in perfectly realistic patterns. In long shots of the grandstand, most of these race fans are digital, their movement controlled by algorithms that allow them to wander up and down the stairs or even run to the bathroom (Robertson). Most of the hundreds of individual shots (many mere seconds long) that make up this racing scene are effects shots, meaning they contain at least some digitally rendered elements. Many shots of the race itself are entirely CGI. Stephen Prince's definition, referring "to building models and animating them in the computer," distinguishes this additive process from effects shots that merely alter existing film frames, for instance, to remove the safety wires used in dangerous stunts ("True Lies" 27–8). And, as Prince goes on to argue, the advent of the highly sophisticated digital cinematography developed in the 1990s demands a rethinking of how movies like *TPM*—which seamlessly weave live action actors and real sets with digitally rendered actors and sets—present images that appear realistic to audience members.

Prince's understanding of CGI's implications for film theory form a starting point for asking questions about how form relates to social function in effects-laden scenes like the Podrace, which use digital cinematography to create a particular ideological way of experiencing film narrative. By this, I mean that the way the camera works in the Podrace scene sets up certain relationships between groups of characters within the movie by visually borrowing images from the real world that determine relations between real groups of people. *Ideology* is a set of ideas that express a person's understanding of self as a function of the social conditions—educational, legal, religious, socioeconomic, etc.—that form the matrix for living. In this neutral sense, the terms *ideology* or *ideological* lack a pejorative flavor. The way we interpret any movie depends partially on our self-conception as members of a society. It follows that certain ideas resonate with our views or strike us as distasteful. But we are never outside our own inescapable ideology. Thus, because the camera has its way of representing social relations, those representations are necessarily ideological.

Film Theory and Digital Cinematography

"Creating credible photographic images of things which cannot be photographed—and the computer-imaging capabilities which lie behind it," writes Prince, "challenge[s] some of the traditional assumptions about realism and the cinema which are embedded in film theory" ("True Lies" 28). His argument takes as its starting point the celebrated digital effects used to create footage of Tom Hanks chatting with John Kennedy in *Forrest Gump* (1994), as well as the digital animation that brought to life the dinosaurs of *Jurassic Park* (1993). But the suspension of disbelief required for these movies, as well as for *TPM*, is fundamentally different from that required for the fantastic visual realities of animated movies or comic books, which do not strike the average viewer as incomprehensibly different from physical reality. In each of the latter, viewers can see images of objects, characters, and events that are not directly related to objects, persons, or events in real life. Film theory, Prince claims, "has construed realism solely as a matter of reference rather than as a matter of perception as well" ("True Lies" 28). He distinguishes between images that are "referentially real" and images that are "perceptually real."

Traditional film theory, Prince writes, "is rooted in the view that photographic images, unlike paintings or line drawings, are indexical signs: they are causally or existentially connected to their referents" ("True Lies" 28).[2] A photograph or a reel of movie film depicting a person is a sign that points to a tangible person separate from the image, but which still exists in physical reality. The image is not the thing itself but depends on the existence of the thing itself, because, without the person, the image could not exist. The term *sign* simply refers to a relationship between the picture that we see of something and the idea of that absent thing. Broken down, the sign has two parts: the *signifier*, which is the present image a viewer sees, and a *signified*, the absent thing to which the signifier points; together, these are the two halves of the *sign*. An animated movie or a painting contains images of objects that may very well have no tangible existence at all, but the framing and context of the image contain cues indicating that break from reality. Socially acclimated viewers understand these stylistic cues in *Beauty and the Beast* (1991), a Dali painting, or a *Batman* comic as indicating that what they are seeing is not meant to refer to things that are referentially real. But, Prince argues further, "Even unreal images can be perceptually realistic. Unreal images are those which are referentially fictional" ("True Lies" 32).

His revised definition of film realism complicates traditional definitions that understand cinema as a "recording medium" ("True Lies" 29). If we consider the opening shot of Tatooine's grandstands as an *indexical sign*, then it is simply an image of the miniature model built by the designers and photographed with a 35mm camera. Ignoring the digital spectators or matte background added to the shot in postproduction, the model part of the image has a real referent that is made of foam and paint. But that reality of the image is not the one intended for moviegoers to perceive. The scale and framing of the model against the background, along with the digital spectators, create an image that is "referentially unreal"—there obviously neither is nor ever was such a grandstand teeming with the inhabitants of an alien planet—but that is nonetheless "perceptually realistic." "A perceptually realistic image," in Prince's refined definition, "is one which structurally corresponds to the viewer's audiovisual experience of three-dimensional space. Perceptually realistic images correspond to this experience because film-makers build them to do so" (32). In the case of the opening sequence for the Podracing scene, this structural correspondence depends on a number of interlocking formal elements.

As described earlier, the aerial perspective of the "blimp shot" invites viewers to understand the scene within the familiar context of a massive televised sporting event. The coloration, perspective, and detail of the background environment correspond to recognizable images of desert environments found on Earth. The animated movements of the thousands of fictional spectators likewise mimic those of large crowds. Moreover, as the camera spirals downward, two massive sandstone columns bisect the frame, reinforcing the effect that viewers are looking from the perspective of a real camera moving through three-dimensional space that must navigate real obstacles in its path.

Cameras and Virtual Cameras

This question of the reality inherent in the camera's perspective is particularly interesting because, in effects-heavy scenes like the Podrace, it is not always obvious from shot to shot whether a real camera was involved in the creation of the image. We know from interviews with the effects production crew that the grandstand was a model, meaning—at minimum—that a 35mm camera captured pictures of a blank miniature against a blue screen (Robertson). Following this panoramic shot are dozens of closer shots containing live actors on real sets interacting with digitally animated characters. When the film cuts from shots like these to shots of the Podracers screaming through the desert at a simulated 600 miles per hour, it becomes less obvious that no camera actually captured the images of Sebulba or Anakin (Jake Loyd) flying through stone arches or of the other racers crashing as their engines shredded apart in smoke and flames. This juxtaposition of shots in which the viewer's perspective corresponds to that of a real camera in contrast to shots where the viewer's perspective corresponds to that of a virtual camera is a cinematographic trick creating perceptual realism as an effect of the shot's formal elements.

But the interchange of mixed shots and entirely CGI-rendered shots is only one cue enhancing perceptual realism. "At a visual level," Prince points out, "these cues include ways that photographic images and edited sequences are isomorphic with their corresponding real-world displays" ("True Lies" 31). That is, the images onscreen represent vantage points within the movie that would make sense to a real person moving around in the scene—if it were an actual place. He offers a few examples of such visual correspondences: "replication of edge and contour information and of monocular distance codes," as seen in the blurriness of rock formations in the deep background of the race-course; "in the case of moving pictures, replication of motion parallax," which pulls the desert ground past the Podracers at blisteringly fast speeds; "and in the case of continuity editing, the creation of a screen geography with coherent coordinates through the projective geometry of successive camera positions," meaning that a shot from Anakin's perspective looking out of his cockpit at Sebulba logically precedes a medium shot from the side of both Podracers or a full-on shot looking backward at both Podracers. Further technical manipulation ensured that even the subtlest details of the computer animations looked as similar to the 35mm live action shots as possible. Tim Alexander, an effects supervisor for *TPM* reported that,

> special software ... compensated for the idiosyncrasies of the wide-angle lens used in the live-action shots. For example ... on the live action plates, the color at the edges around people and objects split the red and blue, so he added that aberration to the CG characters. All the CG elements were rendered in sharp focus; the compositors added film grain, rack focus, and depth of field. (Robertson)

The realism of these images results from both intense attention to physical detail and calculated correspondence to familiar visual cues. Before production of the Podrace even began, George Lucas had a reference tape made that demonstrated how he wanted the crashes to look. Included in this tape were "real shots of wild crashes from F1 & NASCAR between animatics [animated sequences]. Apart from their visceral impact, they showed that cars simply don't crash and explode into fireballs as per the *Star Wars* convention. [Viewers] actually saw them break up, metal shredding" (Williams). Viewers are supposed to delight in the visual carnage of the other racers. Like a NASCAR race, we are watching for the crashes, which, in the context of the Podrace, are not just entertaining—they are one cue among many lending perceptual realism to the fantastic elements of the scene.

In each of these examples from the purely CGI shots of the Podracers out on the course, motion parallax—the sensation that objects close to a moving body appear to move more quickly than those further away—is a particularly important cue lending credibility to the realism of the image. The scale and distance of the desert rock formations mean that viewers never have to see them up close in detail. Furthermore, the Podracers are in constant motion relative to one another, sometimes swept up in clouds of dust or exhaust, but likewise never still. Viewers familiar with everyday highway travel are used to this lack of visible detail when moving briskly through an environment.

Simply put, CGI animation looks more believable the faster the objects in the frame are moving or the further away they are. This is why these shots of the race are more perceptually realistic than many shots of Jar Jar Binks, who is a marvel of character animation but is nonetheless often up for close, detailed scrutiny, which inevitably reveals his shortcomings as a realistic living creature, be it the texture of his clothing or his lack of sweat glands. "Cinematic realism," writes Prince, "is seen as an *effect* produced by the apparatus or by spectators positioned within the Lacanian Imaginary. Cinematic realism is viewed as a discourse *coded* for transparency such that the indexicality of photographic realism is replaced by a view of the 'reality-effect' produced by codes and discourse" ("True Lies" 31). In the next section, I explain the "Lacanian Imaginary" to which Prince refers and elucidate how the sum of these "reality-effects" places viewers in a specifically designed position from which to understand the narrative.

Identification *with* versus Identification *as*

Even if there are certain digital tricks that blur or mystify distinctions between indexically real and perceptually real images, those rendered shots still encourage viewers to identify with the camera's perspective. Such identification, in turn, locks viewers into a coded way of seeing the narrative within the scene. The assumed hypothetical American viewer identifies with the white male hero of the scene, while antagonists and bystanders alike are cast as *other*. These others are in a position that does not give them the power to represent themselves through looking—instead, the camera represents them by looking *at* them. This particular way of formally presenting male human characters for viewers to *identify as* dovetails with larger arcs of the *TPM* narrative that cast racially othered antagonists in a reductive light. Parsing out the theoretical mechanics of identification with the camera is important in this case: Just as the perceptual reality of an image is an *effect*, the result of visual cues correlating to physical reality, so too the perspective of the viewer is an *effect* of the cinematography. And just as there is an ideology to the way of looking at shots of real objects and persons, there is also an ideology to the way of looking at virtual objects and persons.

Consider the first shots we see of Anakin preparing his Podracer at the starting line. His mother, Shmi (Pernilla August), comes over to tell him to be safe. Ironically, Sebulba covertly sabotages Anakin's vehicle, then comes over to taunt the boy: "You won't walk away from this one, you slave scum," he says. Anakin holds his own, retorting, "Don't count on it, slime ball." A moment later, Qui-Gon (Liam Neeson) arrives to offer Jedi advice on following his instincts. Each interaction centers on Anakin, and, aside from the exchange with Qui-Gon, each is shot at a low angle roughly corresponding to Anakin's eye level. Each conversation builds tension, because a viewer can imagine that he or she is in Anakin's position, with a difficult task and several people's welfare in jeopardy. This first type of identification at work in the movie is *identification with*, and I want to contrast it with *identification as*.

In addition to *identification with* the characters, a viewer participates in another sort of identification. A viewer makes sense of the dramatic situation and the tension over Anakin's task from within a particular ideology. According to theorist Louis Althusser, "Ideology represents the imaginary relationship of individuals to their real conditions of existence." In this situation, ideology refers not only to the familiar narratives that allow viewers to understand Anakin as a messianic figure in a struggle for freedom, but also to the understanding of those cultural texts (mass commercial sporting events) that correspond to the realistic visual codes of the scene. In Althusser's conception of ideology, these narratives are part of an apparatus that forms an imaginary link between a person's sense of self and his or her political situation. Depending on a viewer's ideological relation to the narrative of *TPM*, he or she can (or can fail to) *identify as* a person for whom this narrative makes sense as a description of his or her relationship to the "real conditions of existence" (36). Althusser terms this process of identifying oneself within an ideological framework "interpellation."

He proposes that "*All ideology hails or interpellates concrete individuals as concrete subjects.*" In his scenario, ideology "recruits" individuals as subjects through "*interpellation* or hailing," as when the police call out to someone on the street, "Hey, you there" (48). Hearing this call elicits from most any citizen a bodily reaction—an about-face turn to face the speaker, an authority figure. This reaction stems from the individual's realization that it really was him or her to whom the address was directed and that the proper reaction to such an address is a physical recognition of himself or herself as subject to that authority. An individual realizes his or her subject status under the law just as one recognizes his or her own identity. This effect of "hailing" is ideological, and "the existence of ideology and the hailing or interpellation of individuals as subjects," Althusser explains, "are one and the same thing" (49). Ideological apparatuses like the call of the police provide a subject status for individuals and a framework for understanding one's relation to the "real conditions of existence."

Althusser treats the policeman's call as shorthand for those functions he labels "ideological state apparatuses," or ISAs. ISAs are social institutions—the legislative and judicial systems, education, religion, and culture, etc.—that hail people within ideology, offering them a framework in which to recognize their subjectivity (17). It is useful to understand filmic narratives and their cameras as subfunctionaries of the cultural ISA, because they have the potential to hail viewers into an ideology of a particular culture. Specifically, the camera—be it real or virtual—is an apparatus that uses certain visual cues that reinforce for the viewer an ideology that lies behind the creation of the scene.

Interpellation into a particular way of looking at the race is another cue lending perceptual reality to the scene. The scene seems more realistic because it addresses those hypothetical American viewers within the context of their culture and within the narrative and visual codes bound up with correlating cultural texts. Although not always immediately apparent, part of a viewer's understanding of a cinematic narrative comes from the perspective granted to the viewer by the camera. To clarify this point, a short diversion into psycho-analytic film theory is necessary.

Jacques Lacan, a psychoanalytic theorist, proposed a theoretical "mirror stage" scenario that imagines an infant in front of a reflective glass. Before arriving in front of this mirror, the infant has no conception of its disparate flailing body parts (head, arms, and legs) as a *whole body* connected to the concept of a *whole person* and his or her ego. The infant lacks a conception of himself or herself as a virtual (thought-having) and material (bodily) being. In this situation, the mirror is a tool that provides the infant with visual feedback relating internal decisions to move body parts to the external results of moving around in the world of objects. "The *mirror stage* is a drama ... which manufactures for the subject, caught up in the lure of spatial identification, the succession of phantasies that extends from a fragmented body-image to a form of its totality ... and ... to the assumption of the armour of an alienating identity" (Lacan 4). In front of a mirror, the infant can observe its own body moving in response to its own thoughts and consequently can identify with this reflection, a self that is simultaneously *not* itself.

The reflection creates this conception of a unified self but is divorced from that actual self—a reflected image helps us understand ourselves but is also obviously *not* us. "The child's ego is formed by identification with its like," film theorist Christian Metz explains, "the other human being who is in the glass, the own reflection which is and is not the body, which is like it. The child identifies with itself as an object" (45). The infant is obviously not an object, but seeing the relation between internal thoughts and external movement depends upon the image in the mirror. The mirror only has the power to reflect objects; it obviously cannot show the infant its complex identity as a thought-having person in the material world. But, in Lacan's hypothesis, part of our understanding of ourselves as *individuals* in the world emerges from this image of ourselves as *objects* within the world. It shows us the part of ourselves that is outside of ourselves, and that image contributes to our personal identity.

Metz expands this conception, casting the cinema as a perceptual mirror that reflects objects in the world—not just images of those objects, but their sounds and their position in moving space. Whereas a mirror presents a more or less flat image of what stands before it, the camera (and, here, he is talking about a *real* camera) can move through locations and around objects and people, adding depth and dimensionality to what it reflects. "But the perceived is not really the object," he points out; "it is its shade, its phantom, its double, its *replica* in a new kind of mirror" (45). This new mirror can reflect anything in the world for the viewer to perceive, and, while the images to which Metz refers are pictures of real things, the images are simply signifiers (like photographs) pointing to the real things that previously stood in front of the camera. "The unique position of the cinema lies in this dual character of its signifier: unaccustomed perceptual wealth, but at the same time stamped with unreality to an unusual degree" (Metz 45). Films show us in great depth and detail images and sounds that engage our perception, but those sights and sounds are simultaneously unreal because they signify in their very absence. The things we see on screen are phantoms like the reflection of the infant in the mirror, but, whereas the mirror reflects a body present in front of it, cinematic signifiers (images) point to absent signifieds (real objects that are not actually present).

The cinema "differs from the primordial mirror in one essential point," because while the mirror can reflect anything, "there is one thing and one thing only that is never reflected in [the cinema]: the spectator's own body" (Metz 45). Metz claims that "what *makes possible* the spectator's absence from the screen—or rather the intelligible unfolding of the film despite that absence" is that previous internalization of the mirror stage wherein the viewer is "able to constitute a world of objects without having first to recognize himself [or herself] within it" (46). For Metz, the opportunity viewers have to identify with the characters within film narratives is obvious. This type of identification with characters is not particularly different from identification with characters in a literary or dramatic work.

Unlike a literary experience, we identify by *seeing* those characters, and unlike a dramatic identification, film narratives can be composed of long sequences without any human being in them with whom to identify (47). "The spectator is absent from the screen: contrary to the child in the mirror, he cannot identify with himself as an object, but only with objects that are there without him" (48). Whereas the mirror stage identification provides for identification with a nonidentical possible self, a viewer aware of his or her absence from the screen identifies with the possible selves that are the characters on the screen. This preconceived understanding of the mirror stage allows the viewer to understand that the film narrative is a reflection of a world of objects *of which the viewer is not a part.* Therefore, instead of identifying with his or her own reflection in a mirror, the viewer can identify with—imagine himself or herself as—the characters on screen and, in doing so, make logical sense of the narrative world.

These are the mechanics of how viewers can identify *with* characters on screen. But looking even more closely at the starting line conversations in the stadium, we can observe how the camera's perspective corresponds with Anakin's. The camera's "ideology" helps us identify *as* Anakin and *as* a particular type of viewer watching Anakin. During the course of the race, the only forward-facing, first-person perspective granted to viewers is from Anakin's vantage point in his cockpit. When we see him revving his engines on the starting line, the camera looks at him head-on, then cuts to a first-person shot; shots of other drivers have no corresponding first-person cut. Moreover, language distances us from other characters. Few of the other racers speak, and the primary one that does, Sebulba, does not speak English—he reaches viewers through the yellow veil of subtitles for expressions such as "Ni chuba ya?"

This process of *identification as* a particular character or type of spectator is the same as the process of *interpellation* explained above; the two terms are synonymous. *Identification with* and *identification as* (*interpellation*) thus operate simultaneously. Both facilitate a hypothetical viewer's comprehension of the narrative; the former allows the viewer to understand the imaginary world on the screen; the latter connects the story of that world to social frameworks in the real world. Based on Metz's understanding of how the camera shows us people who are outside our immediate presence, viewers can identify *with* any character on the screen. But, paradoxically, the cinematography of the Podrace ushers viewers toward identifying both *as* Anakin and *as* the viewer of a sporting event corresponding roughly to those commonly found on American television.

It seems painfully ironic that the movie maps a particular sort of American narrative—the heroic wager made in order to escape from slavery—onto a cute sandy-haired white boy. Whether or not Lucas gave any thought to the cultural correspondences of slavery does not really matter. What does matter is that, within the context of the story, slavery operates as an instrument of racial equality. Deliberately counter to historical American slavery, the two white characters living on Tatooine are instead subject to the power of a nonwhite (indeed, nonhuman) master, Watto, who won Anakin and his mother, Shmi, from one of the Hutts that wield economic and martial control over the region. But despite the equalizing narrative effect of placing the white characters in a subject position, the visual elements I discussed earlier still work to *other* the alien characters, maintaining a racial distance.

In the end, the actual political effect of the ideological vantage point is muddled. Anakin's story and conditions of existence are Americanized, despite their lack of actual congruency to American culture. His story is just the typical story of the white male overcoming adversity in the face of others unlike him. Simultaneously, the viewer looks at the race like a TV sports fan, participating in the collective fan identity by rallying around the hero—someone who both has solidarity with the American ideals of the conquering white male and the underdog pulling himself up by the bootstraps.

Conclusion: Digital Content and Social Form

Lucas made a radical cinematic choice to shoot both *Attack of the Clones* and *Revenge of the Sith* in high-definition digital format, rather than on the traditional 35mm film used for *TPM*. Most of the visual differences between 35mm film and digital video are negligible for viewers; they concern how 35mm film captures motion more cleanly and how digital video is crisp compared to the slight grain in any 35mm image (Prince, "Emergence of Filmic Artifacts" 31). Regardless, the more recent installments avoided sequences of CGI fireworks quite as self-consciously brazen as the Podrace. Digital rendering continued to expand the possibilities for presenting sweeping visuals like the cityscape on Coruscant and the limitless battalions of the clone armies. In terms of environmental rendering, the climactic *Revenge of the Sith* battle between Anakin (Hayden Christensen) and Obi-Wan (Ewan McGregor) puts viewers in a situation not unlike the Podrace. As Anthony Lane of the *New Yorker* put it in his excoriating review, "*Revenge of the Sith* is a zoo of rampant storyboards. Why show a pond when CGI can deliver a lake that gleams to the far horizon? Why set a paltry house on fire when you can stage your final showdown on an entire planet that streams with ruddy, gulping lava?" (94). Realism in the scene rests in part on constant motion that prevents scrutiny of small details, as well as referential cues pointing to documentary footage (from whence some viewers would presumably get their basic understanding of lava flows). Moreover, cues encouraging identification with the camera in such scenes emphasize the idea that, within the context of realistic digital filmmaking, "we now need to think of cinematography, and even directing, as *image-capture* processes" (Prince, "Emergence of Filmic Artifacts" 30).

Pointing the camera at indexically real people or objects becomes one small piece in the construction of a realistic set of images. Lane's point is worth focusing on because it emphasizes the *constructedness* not just of the scene, but of the *way of looking* at the scene. Digital moviemaking expands the possibilities for what visual signifiers can appear within the frame of the screen, but it is still limited by the familiar ways that a real or virtual camera can frame those elements. Digitally woven movies like *Episodes I* through *III* may be menageries of storyboards; they may be something more. But the intense attention to detail in their construction can teach us a good deal about how we perceive digital movies in relation to the real and, in turn, how any image addresses us through its form, in addition to its content. Having spent some time examining the technical and imaginative wizardry that goes into creating realistic fantastic cinematography, we might return to the question of race raised early in this discussion. *Star Wars* CGI demonstrates the virtually limitless possibilities for the content of the images in a movie. But it seems obvious that the form of these images is trapped in an ideology that simply reproduces the narrative dominance of the white male. Nothing inherent in the technology necessitates this complicity. New social lenses for CGI can still emerge, but not in Lucas's world.

Notes for Chapter 14

1. Industrial Light and Magic has laid out the timeline at its corporate Web site. <http://www.ilm.com/inside_timeline.html>.

2. Prince draws this model from film theorist Peter Wollen's discussion of philosopher Charles Peirce in Wollen's *Signs and Meaning in the Cinema* (122-4). Peirce, in turn, worked with Ferdinand de Saussure's model of the sign (articulated in his *Course in General Linguistics*). Peirce subdivided signs into icons, indices, and symbols. In his system, icons resemble the objects to which they point. "The portrait of a man resembles him," writes Wollen, although a portrait need not resemble a real person. "An index," Wollen explains, "is a sign by virtue of an existential bond between itself and its object" (122). Thus, the photographic images pertinent to this discussion are indexes. Finally, symbols have an arbitrary link to their corresponding objects or concepts. A written word is a symbol because it has "neither [a] resemblance to its object nor any existential bond with it" (123).

Works Cited

Althusser, Louis. "Ideology and Ideological State Apparatuses (Notes Towards an Investigation)." *Essays on Ideology*. London: Verso, 1984.

Kraus, Daniel. "The Phantom Edit." *Salon* 5 Nov 2001. 12 Sept. 2005 <http://www.salon.com>.

Lacan, Jacques. "The Mirror Stage as Formative of the Function of the I as Revealed in Psychoanalytic Experience." *Ecrits*. Trans. Alan Sheridan. New York: W.W. Norton & Company, 1977.

Lane, Anthony. "Space Case, *Star Wars: Episode III*." *New Yorker* 23 May 2005: 94.

McCarthy, Todd. "*Star Wars: Episode I–The Phantom Menace*." *Variety* 17 May 1999: 53.

Metz, Christian. "Identification, Mirror." *The Imaginary Signifier: Psychoanalysis and the Cinema*. Trans. Celia Britton, Annwyl Williams, Ben Brewster, and Alfred Guzzetti. Bloomington: Indiana UP, 1982.

O'Ehley, James. "Jar Jar Binks Must Die." *SciFi Movie Page*. 12 Sept. 2005 <www.scifimoviepage.com/jarjar.html>.

Prince, Stephen. "The Emergence of Filmic Artifacts: Cinema and Cinematography in the Digital Era Source." *Film Quarterly* 57.3 (2004): 24–33.

———. "True Lies: Perceptual Realism, Digital Images, and Film Theory." *Film Quarterly* 49.3 (Spring 1996): 27–37.

Robertson, Barbara. "Star Wars = Four New Digital Stars." *Computer Graphics World* June 1999. 12 July 2005 <http://cgw.pennnet.com/Articles/Article_Display.cfm? Section=Archives& Subsection=Display&ARTICLE_ID=50438&KEYWORD=barbara%20robertson%20star %20wars>.

Romney, Jonathan. "Cause and Effects—Science Fiction Films with Computer Generated Imagery." *New Statesman* 12 July 1999: 38.

Williams, David. "John Knoll—Visual Effects Supervisor." *aussie short films.* 12 July 2005 <http://www.aussieshortfilms.com.au/asfcustom.php?Item=swsem4.html>

Wollen, Peter. *Signs and Meaning in the Cinema.* London: Secker & Warburg, 1969.

Other Films Cited

Beauty and the Beast. Dir. Gary Trousdale and Kirk Wise. Disney, 1991.

Forrest Gump. Dir. Robert Zemeckis. Paramount, 1994.

Jurassic Park. Dir. Steven Spielberg. Universal/Amblin, 1993.

Terminator 2: Judgement Day. Dir. James Cameron. Carolco/Le Studio Canal, 1991.

CHAPTER 15

The Menace of the Fans
to the Franchise

Mark McDermott

That *The Phantom Menace* (1999) disappointed *Star Wars* fans is a cultural commonplace. Yet the critical failure of the first prequel trilogy film has been belied by the movie's actual box-office performance. Each of the latest three *Star Wars* movies has grossed over $300 million in U.S. box-office receipts, already surpassing *The Empire Strikes Back* (1980) and *Return of the Jedi* (1983). As of September 30, 2005, the *Exhibitor Relations* list of all-time box-office leaders had *TPM* at #5, just $30 million behind *A New Hope* (1977) at #2. A quarter century of movie ticket inflation had long ago knocked *ANH* off its perch as the all-time box-office leader, but its 1997 "Special Edition" release allowed it to gain new momentum behind the reigning champ, *Titanic* (1997).[1]

It is notable that the fans of the original franchise have been the most vocal critics of the new films. Will Brooker's study, *Using the Force: Creativity, Community and* Star Wars *Fans* (2002), detailed the split on Internet bulletin boards between "Bashers," who saw *TPM* as failed kiddie entertainment by an auteur who had lost his storytelling skills, and "Gushers," who, even as they stood up for Lucas's vision, admitted to being troubled by some of its aspects— but more often than not would return to the theatre to seek something else to make them believe in the message of the franchise (91–3). The worldwide popularity of the *Star Wars* franchise has assured that criticism of *TPM* and later, *Attack of the Clones* (2002), would expand beyond the purview of nitpicky fans and affect the public at large.

How did the vocal *Star Wars* fans engage the issue of the apparent decline of their beloved franchise? Here I examine three forms of creative public expression that reflect their dissatisfactions. First is the commentary on the movie series from current creators of cultural texts, many of whom had identified the *Star Wars* movies as an influence in their own lives. Second, there are the efforts of current dedicated *Star Wars* fans who have communicated their feelings about the franchise at the same creative plane as the movies them-selves: by making their own short films for the *Star Wars* Fan Film Awards (SWFFAs) and for any other forum that will allow them to exhibit their efforts or spare the bandwidth to host their films over the Internet. Third is the small number of fans whose commentary on the films has taken the form of re-editing the movies themselves, giving rise to the first of what is likely to be-come a succession of "Phantom Edits" of popular films.

Surprisingly, many of the source materials cited in this essay have not only described some disappointment at Lucas's direction with the franchise, but they have also implied a form of direct action in taking back *Star Wars*. Some of these works figuratively wrestled the film itself from Lucas's hands. Others hijacked the films by creating new versions that attempted to better fit the temperament of the adult fan.

"Alternate Ending: Luke's Father is Chewbacca": The Popular Media Responds

Unlike movies whose failure among critics and at the theatres provided much fodder for late-night talk show monologues, *Waterworld* (1995) or *Gigli* (2003) being examples, nearly everyone with an opinion on *TPM* or *AOTC* can be presumed to have at least seen the movies. Yet the perceived artistic failure of the first films in the prequel trilogy has been set in the public mind. Much of this perception seems to have stemmed from the influence of other creators of popular culture texts. Nearly all of the current generation of Hollywood crea-tors, popular writers, and artists can trace their desire to work in their fields to the influence of the original *Star Wars* trilogy. It was many of these who said publicly that they felt let down by the prequel trilogy, and they expressed their feelings through their creative output.

Among the first creators to "break bad" over *TPM* was Aaron McGruder, author of the comic strip *Boondocks* and an admitted "near-fanatical *Star Wars* enthusiast" (Templeton). During May of 1999, before *TPM*'s opening, the strip's protagonist, a politically radical African American youngster named Huey Freeman, had several encounters with the "Psycho *Star Wars* Guy." Though portrayed as a young white male who was never seen without an Obi-Wan Kenobi hood and who waited in line at the theater weeks before the opening of *TPM*, Psycho *Star Wars* Guy seemed to be drawn from McGruder's own love of the series. Huey's only beef with the movie before its opening was tied to his happiness that Lucas had cast African American actor Samuel L. Jackson as the Jedi Mace Windu. After pondering for a moment, Huey de-clared, "he had BETTER not be the first one to die." (May 9, 1999). But in strips running the week of July 5 through 10, after *TPM* had made its mark on the moviegoer, McGruder's characters are seen working through their disappointment with the movie, as Huey and his brother Riley tried to bring Psycho *Star Wars* Guy out of his denial and admit that it was a bad film. (A year later, the strip showed Psycho *Star Wars* Guy acting on Huey's off-hand remark and kicking Lucas in the rear on national television.) The main source of McGruder's anger with the movie appeared in the July 4th Sunday strip, which started with a caption reading that *Boondocks* had been replaced with a new comic, "Wacky Fun with Jar Jar Binks." This strip showed Jar Jar reprising many of his speech patterns and actions that had earned him comparisons with minstrel stereotypes, ending with the signoff "Oh-Tay!" that mimicked Buckwheat of the Little Rascals series. After seeing AOTC, McGruder admitted that it was a slightly better movie, which was damning by faint praise. However, as with *TPM*, the movie was far too long, spent too much time rehashing plot points and making "Mission Statements," and gave too little time to action. "There are 40 Jedi with light sabers in that scene," he says, "and for some reason I'm looking at C3PO acting silly. Get the robot off the screen and show me a Jedi knight killing something. Or like, Mace Windu is about to go head to head with the bad guy—and here comes this alien bull creature. I don't want to see a bull right now. There are important things happening" (qtd. in Templeton).

Bill Amend's strip *Fox Trot* features a character, Jason Fox, who represents all the characteristics of a comics/movies fanboy, and has provided running commentary on many aspects of the *Star Wars* films. In a Sunday strip of April 2005, Jason and his friend Marcus are using action figures to act out what could motivate Anakin Skywalker to turn to the Dark Side: In one panel, Jar Jar announces "Meesa gonna be your Padawan!" Another has Anakin being assigned the lightsaber with the pink blade. The final straw comes when Palpatine assures him, "I promise to never call you 'Ani'."

The writing staff of the *Simpsons* shot several succinct barbs at Lucas but, in many cases, long after the movies had come out. The many *Star Wars* references in the show, from the first season on, had been duly noted by the *Star Wars* community. An article in *Star Wars Insider* quotes Bill Morrison, editor of the *Simpsons* comic books: "Most of us working not only on the show, but also on the *Simpsons* comic grew up with *Star Wars* [ANH] ... [which] came out the year I graduated high school, and I didn't have a summer job, so I ended up seeing *Star Wars* 25 times" (qtd. in Chernoff). This mutual admiration from both camps turned concrete with the 1994 episode "Burns' Heir." With the family seated in Springfield's Aztec Theatre to watch "Siskel & Ebert: The Movie," the entire audience gets blown out their seats by a parody of the THX "the audience is listening" promo. Lucas himself apparently liked the parody so much that he had Lucasfilm, creator of the THX standard, commission a wide screen remake of the animated gag to show as the real THX trailer that summer (Chernoff).

That the *Simpsons* was always prepared to bite the hand that feeds them Butterfingers (despite what one of Bart's blackboard gags reads) has long been apparent in their repeated pokes at Rupert Murdoch and Fox. Yet, it took three years for the show to finally comment directly on *TPM*: In the 2002 episode, "Half-Decent Proposal," the story opens on a montage of Springfield denizens asleep in their beds. The camera wanders into the bedroom of "Comic Book Guy," adorned with an array of *Star Wars* posters. As the camera zooms in to Comic Book Guy, sleeping beneath *Star Wars* bedding in Chewbacca pajamas, he is clutching a Jar Jar Binks doll and murmuring "Oh Jar Jar, everyone hates you but me." The 2003 episode, "C.E. D'oh," featured Homer's coworkers Lenny and Carl fighting each other, using plutonium rods as lightsabers, with Lenny arguing, *"The Phantom Menace* sucked more!" and Carl claiming, *"Attack of the Clones* sucked more!" Oddly, the *Simpsons'* most direct criticism of Lucas required the use of pseudonymous characters. The 2004 episode, "Co-Dependent's Day," sees Bart and Lisa going to the long-awaited latest movie in the "Cosmic Wars" series: "The Gathering Shadow."

The movie turns out to be a long drone about galactic economics, echoing science fiction writer David Brin's *Salon* (<http://www.salon.com>) complaint that the only plot device in *TPM* that wasn't a recycled cliché was the movie's opening crawl setup: "A sci-fi action movie whose premise is based on taxation of trade routes and negotiations over tariff treaties? Now that ... (yawn) ... is something ... I've ... never ... (snore)" (1999). The new movie offers none of the exciting action sequences of the previous entries and has a tiresome comedy relief character named Jim-Jam Banks. When their complaint letter to the film's creator, "Randall Curtis," elicits a form letter response, Bart and Lisa confront Curtis personally at his northern California ranch. Curtis is drawn to exactly resemble George Lucas, and, in his home, we clearly recognize *Star Wars* props, such as Yoda and Stormtrooper statues, C-3PO, and R2-D2. Here, Curtis/Lucas actually acknowledges the weaknesses in his film and, as consolation, offers the children boxes of Jim-Jam Cereal ("It's just Alpha Bits with extra J's.") before riding off on a Tauntaun.

Another prominent jab, this one at both Lucas and Steven Spielberg's habit of altering their films for re-release and home video, occurred in the 2002 *South Park* episode "Free Hat." The boys are alarmed to see a trailer for the re-release of *E.T. The Extra Terrestrial,* in which all the guns had been digitally changed to walkie-talkies. Following this was a trailer for a fictional re-release of *Saving Private Ryan,* again with guns changed to walkie-talkies and the word "Nazis" replaced with "persons with political differences." The feature turns out to be a re-re-re-release of *The Empire Strikes Back* with all the characters digitally replaced by Ewoks. This leads Stan and Kyle to start the "Save Films from Their Own Directors" club. But the club's appearance on ABC's *Nightline* only inspires Spielberg and Lucas to re-edit *Raiders of the Lost Ark.* To save the only negative of the film, the boys break into Skywalker Ranch and find themselves amid props from *Star Wars* and *Raiders* and a glass case displaying a *Howard the Duck* costume. Intercepted by Lucas as they try to make off with *Raiders'* film cans, the boys make one final appeal:

> KYLE. You yourself led the campaign against the colorization of films. You understand why films shouldn't be changed.
>
> GEORGE LUCAS. M-that's different. These are my movies. I made them, and I have the right to do whatever I want with them
>
> STAN. You're wrong, Mr. Lucas. They're not your movies. They're ours. All of ours. We paid to go see them, and they're just as much a part of our lives as they are of yours.
>
> KYLE. When an artist creates, whatever they create belongs to society.

Lucas and Spielberg go ahead with the re-edit anyway, and they premier it in a familiar desert canyon. Stan, Kyle, Cartman, and Tweek (Kenny having remained dead for that entire season) have been tied to posts by walkie-talkie toting guards. As the directors, joined by their partner in revisionism, Francis Ford Coppola, start the movie, Stan quotes Indiana Jones in warning his friends: "Close your eyes.... Don't watch the movie, you guys. It'll be terrible. Close your eyes!" Sure enough, the new version is so bad that it kills all of the audience and melts the directors' faces just as in the original *Raiders*.

Creators Matt Stone and Trey Parker have claimed credit for the decision by Lucas and Spielberg that they would not alter the *Indiana Jones* movies for DVD release, a decision announced shortly after the *South Park* episode aired (yet, the release re-titled the first movie as *Indiana Jones and the Raiders of the Lost Ark*) (Hill).

Brooker also notes a BBC television comedy called *Spaced*, whose protagonist, a comic book artist, is still dealing with his disappointment over *TPM* eighteen months after its release and who loses his job at a comic book shop when he bawls out a young customer for wanting to buy a Jar Jar Binks doll (79–81). Regrettably, this comedy has not yet made its U.S. run on BBC America.

The creators of these entertainments no doubt either remember the first time they saw *Star Wars* in the theatre—before it was saddled with the *A New Hope* episode header—or else the franchise has simply always been a part of their lives. They grew from adolescence to adulthood with the movies available for repeated viewing, each time reinterpreting the text of the film according to their maturing expectations. Those who wished to explore the franchise *Expanded Universe* could choose hundreds of books and comics appropriate to their changing worldview. But even as far back as *ROTJ* (1983), the movies seemed to be directed to an increasingly juvenile audience: *ROTJ* with its overly cute Ewoks knocking off the Empire with rocks and sticks (and spinning off into a cartoon series and TV special) and *TPM* with the ten-year-old Anakin Skywalker, building his own droid and Podracer with innate technical skills unmatched even by Jimmy Neutron, and the childlike Jar Jar Binks.

"Controlsa-Altsa-Deletesa": The Fan Film Competitions

Fans of popular movies or television shows have long sought ways to interact with the universe created by these entertainments and to create their own experiences in these universes. Genre fan culture has a history almost as old as any given genre itself. The Wikipedia entry on *fan fiction* notes that reference to original popular texts as *canon* originated with the Baker Street Irregulars ("Fan Fiction"). The first science fiction fanzine, the *Comet*, was published in 1930 by the Science Correspondence Club in Chicago, the Superman character first appeared in 1932 in Jerry Siegel and Joe Shuster's *Science Fiction* fanzine, and the World Science Fiction Convention began meeting in 1939. Filking, or folk singing based on science fiction works, became popular in the 1950s.

The spread of fan culture was limited by available technology and the attendant cost of production and distribution. Early fanzines were carefully typed to hectograph masters that might yield up to a hundred copies. No doubt, many 8-mm film reels of *Flash Gordon* pastiches were shot by enthusiastic fans over the years, with no means to duplicate copies. But the growing audiences at science fiction and comics conventions, and at campus film screenings in the 1970s, topped by *Star Wars'* popularity, finally made fan films a viable means of expression.

The best-known early *Star Wars* pastiche was *Hardware Wars* (1977). It was not so much a fan film, but more a *Cracked* magazine style lampoon that wasted no opportunity for a gag, from the brown Cookie Monster Muppet as "Chewchilla the Wookiee Monster" to the pastries forming "Princess Ann Droid's" hairstyle. Paul Frees, who narrated the first *Star Wars* teaser, was also hired for this film, intoning, "You'll laugh! You'll cry! You'll kiss three bucks goodbye!" The short reveled in its cheapness, especially in the "blaster fire" created by simply scratching the film, and is said to be one of the most profitable short films of all time. Director Ernie Fosselius later produced the Coppola parody *Porklips Now* (1980), and can be heard on *ROTJ* performing the sobs of the Rancor Keeper after Luke Skywalker kills his beloved pet ("Ernie Fosselius").

The directory of films on the fan site TheForce.Net (<http://www. theforce.net>) (TFN) lists the oldest fan film as *"The Empire Strikes Quack"* (1991). John Hudgens synchronized clips from the original trilogy to the audio track of the Warner Brothers cartoon *Duck Dodgers in the 24½th Century* (1953), with Luke Skywalker reading Daffy Duck's lines, C-3PO as Porky Pig, and Darth Vader as Marvin the Martian. The film was wildly popular on the convention circuit, but Hudgens has not transferred it to any electronic format since the film was technically illegal. He went on to create a humorous music video using footage from the TV series *Babylon 5* and was hired by that series' creator Joe Straczynski to create more videos for the convention circuit ("Dragon*Con").

The short that really fired up the current fad in fan films seems to have been *Troops* (1998). Director Kevin Rubio created a crossover parody with the television show *Cops,* following the mundane routine of the Imperial Stormtroopers on Tatooine as they investigated a report of two stolen droids, and ended up showing what *really* happened to the Jawas and to Owen and Beru in *ANH.* The ten-minute movie featured quality special effects, re-created *Star Wars* props and costumes (The Stormtroopers were fans wearing their homemade armor while waiting in line for a showing of one of the Special Edition films. Rubio spotted them as they were being interviewed on TV.) George Lucas called the production "lost footage from *Star Wars*" (Trivia for Troops).

Troops' popularity in the fan community, tied to the general anticipation over the promise of new *Star Wars* movies, helped launch a wave of fan films for *Star Wars* and for many other popular fictions. Since fan films by definition appropriate the intellectual property of another creator, they could never be exhibited or sold for profit. But by the late 1990s, advancing computer technology allowed filmmakers to shoot on digital video and edit on home computers or create animated shorts using Macromedia Flash and Shockwave, and other tools. This brought film production into the realm of the hobbyist, a reasonable expense for most dedicated fans.

The Internet was, of course, a major shaping influence on the fan film community. Sites and discussion forums traded information on creating special effects (a proper lightsaber glow is an absolute must), sounds, props, or costumes. Producers could locate fans willing to lend or rent their recreated sets or X-wing starfighters. Distribution of the end product could be limited only by bandwidth.

I surveyed films from two sites: the SWFFAs on AtomFilms (<http://www.atomfilms.com/af/spotlight/collections/starwars/>) and the "Fan Films" section of the fan-run site TFN. The SWFFAs are operated in partnership with Lucasfilm and offer prizes, including a George Lucas Selects award and possible commercial distribution—a group of SWFFA selections was shown at the 2005 Cannes Film Festival, in concert with *Revenge of the Sith's* out-of-competition showing. AtomFilms accepts submissions over a period of several months and chooses selections to be posted on its Web site and voted on by surfers. The competition has a set of rules for competing films: Films must be under ten minutes in length, and subjects are to cover "parodies of the existing *Star Wars* universe" or "documentaries of the fan experience" but not fan fiction that expands the existing *Star Wars* universe. Action figures, books, and other licensed products could be shown, but not music, video, or still images from the *Star Wars* movies. The site offers official sound effects for download ("SWFFA Terms").

The TFN Fan Films are reviewed and posted on a continuous basis. They have fewer restrictions on content, allowing for stories "in-universe," and hosting non–*Star Wars* topics as well (*Batman* and *The Matrix* are popular). TFN requests, but does not demand, exclusive online distribution for the films and will also post information on and links to popular fan films that they are not hosting, such as the forty-five-minute *Expanded Universe* opus, *Star Wars: Revelations* (2005). Both sites use a review process to decide which films are hosted, implying a responsibility on the part of their reviewers to assure fan appeal, and with an eye toward standards for family entertainment, and, even for TFN Fan Films, the tacit approval of Lucasfilm and its legal department.

Not surprisingly, many of the films on both sites are crossover parodies in the vein of *Troops*. *Escape from Tatooine* blends in elements of *Planet of the Apes* (1968/2001), while the animated *Dark Side Switch Campaign* features Anakin in a parody of the Apple Computers commercials; *Sith Apprentice* (2005), directed by John Hudgens, has the tag line, "With 'The Emperor,' 'you're fired' takes on a whole new meaning." And no explanation of the inspiration for *Anakin Dynamite* should be required.

But films starring the fans themselves can offer an interesting look into the relationship between the fans and their beloved source material. In *For Love of the Film* (2005), the theatre's projector breaks down at a showing of the 1997 Special Edition of *ANH*. When the theatre manager cannot calm the unhappy patrons, he offers a line of Obi-Wan Kenobi's dialogue from the movie. The fans immediately pick up on the cue, and end up re-enacting the entire movie, with an emotional climax worthy of a DeBeers diamond commercial. This film won the George Lucas Selects award at the 2005 SWFFA. Within the warm fuzzies evoked by this film, there is a subtext that the fans are indeed the true guardians of the *Star Wars* canon, and they are prepared to take over the narrative if need be. The Web site for Atom Films (see fig. 6) celebrates this protective role.

Confiscation of the narrative is the theme of the TFN Fan Film *Fanboys* (2003). Set in the year 1999, the film has a *Star Wars* fan approached by a group of strangers claiming to be with the so-called "real" Rebellion. They claim to be fighting the Empire everywhere else in the galaxy and that the *Star Wars* films are actually their propaganda to prepare uncontacted worlds to take their part in the rebellion. But the Earth's edition of the trilogies was sabotaged by the Empire; instead of going on indefinitely, the series ended with

ROTJ showing the Empire easily conquered by "a bunch of teddy bears," making it seem like the Empire is not a threat. And, the Rebel agents explain, the new *TPM* is another Imperial ruse to turn Earth fans to the Dark Side, which has the cool double-bladed lightsabers and droid armies. One of the rebels holds up a picture of Jar Jar, explaining that the audience will "want to be on the side that's killing him!" The fan is recruited to steal a preview copy of *TPM* so it can be re-altered. The so-called "rebels," however, are merely movie pirates trying to steal a film print. One pirate is a mole in Lucas' employ, who secures the movie, leaving the real pirates to discover they've stolen a copy of the 1978 *Star Wars Holiday Special.*

Figure 6: The home page on the Internet for Atom Films, a fan site, permits visitors to videostream into their computer screens *For the Love of the Film*, a mere five minutes and twenty-five seconds.

Where fan films take a critical look at the canon, Jar Jar has usually served as the convenient whipping boy. In a SWFFA selection, *Star Wars: The Phantom Menace Prologue* (2002), it's "Darth Jar Jar" who dispatches a trio of Jedi Knights investigating reports of a new hidden evil on the planet Naboo. That the three Jedi are played for laughs, behaving somewhat like argumentative fans, suggests that it was indeed Jar Jar who destroyed the fans' ability to enjoy the prequel movies.

Ultimately, the popularity of *Jar Jar's Walking Papers* (2002) suggests a desire by fandom assembled that Lucas would admit his mistakes and move on. This short, chosen as Best Animation at the 2002 SWFFAs, used stylish hand-drawn animation to show Lucas giving Jar Jar the bad news at a Bennigan's. The cartoon Lucas explains that Jar Jar was originally expected to become the Christ figure of the *Star Wars* stories. "Are you at all familiar with the Christ story?" he asks. "A lot of it hinges on the fact that He was ... uh, He was a well-liked guy. I mean people just liked Him. He wasn't spazzy or irritating in any way." After deflecting Jar Jar's objections ("Oooh! Meestah Lucas! I could growsa beardsa!" and "Ooh! Ooh! Waitsa! Waitsa Mr. Lucasa! C3PO! He's irritating!"), Lucas opens a laptop computer: "The guys wrote down the keystrokes for me here. Oh, that's funny. (Jar Jar: 'Whatsa?') The keystrokes. See, it's kind of cute. It's 'Controlsa-Altsa-Deletesa.'" And Jar Jar disappears.

Such criticism of Lucas' creative decisions is interesting in that it is found in fan films hosted on a site with Lucas's participation. The implicit acceptance of this criticism by Lucasfilm should justify the subjective choice of films discussed in this section. And while those who have a beef against the prequel trilogy can enumerate many faults beyond the presence of Jar Jar Binks, the character seems to have become the primary icon representing fan dissatisfaction with *TPM*.[2] It is worth noting that the Gungan's role has diminished in the remaining two prequel movies, with C-3PO taking on the duties of intrusive comedy relief in *Revenge of the Sith*.

The "Phantom Edits" and the Future of Fan Interaction

For all the clever parodies and critical subtext of the fan films, they still cannot engage their source texts on an equal footing. Film producers may be able to duplicate costumes and sets, make use of John Williams' soundtrack music, and download authentic sound effects, but without access to the original canon—the films themselves—most fan films can engage the viewer only at the same level as any cleverly written fan fiction. But the advance of consumer technology has made it possible for some fans to take control of the original canon by appropriating the original films themselves.

It already seems oddly nostalgic to recall that *TPM* was released to home video on VHS in 2000, a full year before the DVD edition. By summer 2001, however, *Star Wars* fan boards and newsgroups were discussing digital copies of the movie that had appeared on file sharing networks, in comics stores, or at conventions in VHS and Video CD formats. By this time, it was already possible to import a VHS video into a computer with applications like Apple's iMovie, making simple edits and burning a disc with the result. But these movies weren't just dubs; they were re-edited in an attempt to smooth many flaws fans had found with the Lucas product. One of these re-edits included a new version of the famous opening crawl:

Episode I.I: THE PHANTOM EDIT

Anticipating the arrival of the newest Star Wars film, some fans, like myself, were extremely disappointed by the finished product.

So being someone of the "George Lucas Generation," I have re-edited a standard VHS version of "The Phantom Menace" into what I believe is a much stronger film by relieving the viewer of as much story redundancy, pointless Anakin actions and dialogue, and Jar Jar Binks, as possible.

I created this version to bring new hope to a large group of Star Wars fans that felt unsatisfied by the seemingly misguided theatrical release of, "The Phantom Menace." [sic]

To Mr. Lucas and those that I may offend with this re-edit, I am sorry :(

–THE PHANTOM EDITOR
thephantomedit@hotmail.com

Thus the term *Phantom Edit* has come to be applied to any similar fan project. Other edited versions circulated with their own fixes. Mainstream critics like the *Chicago Tribune's* Michael Wilmington reviewed it. The "signed" version was called the "West Coast Version" by *Film Threat's* Chris Gore.

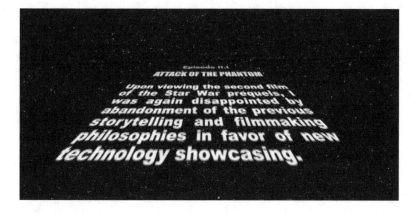

Figure 7: The opening crawl for *Star Wars: Episode II.I – Attack of the Phantom* (2003) reads: "Upon viewing the second film of the Star War (sic) prequels, I was again disappointed by abandonment of the previous story telling and filmmaking philosophies in favor of new technology showcasing."

Most fans were simply pleased by this version's attempts to reduce Jar Jar's involvement as much as possible, especially his poop and fart gags. Much of young Anakin Skywalker's dialogue was trimmed, especially his shouts of "Yippie!" The entire scene of Jar Jar, Qui-Gon, and Obi-Wan traveling through the water-filled core of Naboo was dropped as well. Redundant discussions of midi-chlorians were also dropped. The final result ended up at 120 minutes, twenty minutes less than the original. What was called the "East Coast Version" ran shorter at 112 minutes but did not cut Jar Jar's scenes. Instead, Jar Jar and the other Gungans' dialogue was scrambled to sound like alien language, while subtitles beneath the widescreen picture gave Jar Jar aphorisms like "Pride will blind you to the truth."

Most attention fell on the West Coast Version, since it included a name and e-mail address and, later, a Web site (<http://www.thephantomeditor. com>). Some guessed that the director was Kevin Smith—another avowed *Star Wars* fan—or perhaps disgruntled Lucasfilm employees. The *Washington Post* contacted the Phantom and he agreed to out himself as a freelance film editor in Santa Clarita, California (Greenberg). I too have corresponded with the Phantom while researching this paper, and he requested that I continue to refer to him by his *nom de Moviola*, leaving the curious to look up his real identity in the Wikipedia.[3] His Web site lists a background as a video store clerk and cable access TV host in Aurora, Illinois (long after *Wayne's World*). The Phantom reworked his re-edit once the *TPM* DVD was released, using a stock Apple Macintosh G4 and its Final Cut Pro video-editing suite. The new *Phantom Edit* DVD, now titled *Episode I.II*, offered a commentary track, which, the Phantom noted, was recorded using the microphone that came with the Mac, attached to an ironing board in his apartment.

The DVD included two extras cobbled from the deleted scenes in the original DVD: One scene showed the Gungan bongo craft surfacing at the Naboo capital city, then getting carried over a waterfall with Qui-Gon, Obi Wan, and Jar Jar barely swimming to safety. The Phantom version left Jar Jar in the bongo, screaming as he fell to his death. The other scene has Qui-Gon first encountering Anakin in a Mos Eisley street, fighting with a Rodian who may have been young Greedo. After the fight ends, the Rodian runs to a parent, whose alien words of comfort were resubtitled, "You're always starting trouble, Greedo. Everyone knows that YOU shouldn't attack someone first."

The commentary track allowed the Phantom to point out many edits he had made and to explain his motivations. By this time, he had heard from fans who were disappointed that he hadn't removed Jar Jar completely from the VHS version of the edit: "He has a purpose in the story, and it is his link to the Gungans that provides them with an army at the end of the movie. He has a couple other purposes, one of which doesn't quite hit his mark, to be comic relief. And so to remove him entirely from the story, it just wouldn't work."

It's Jar Jar who warns Qui-Gon in the Gungan Red Council chamber not to trust Boss Nass. Later, the Phantom compliments Lucas's characterization of Queen Amidala. After the Senate refused to offer military assistance to Naboo, Jar Jar asks Amidala, "People gonna die?" The Phantom notes,

> When Jar Jar says that they're not giving up without a fight, they have a grand army … the cut is actually full on her looking. That way, it's implying that she's hearing him say that they [the Gungan] have a grand army, registering in her head; maybe making a calculation in her head that his alliance with this army will actually be what will save them at the end of this movie, and she makes note of that…. It'll be very effective in the very next scene where they [Senator Palpatine and staff] tell her "We don't have an army; we can't fight a war for you." And she looks over to Jar Jar Binks, with everyone else seeming somewhat oblivious, and she says "I need your help." That's a characteristic of leadership. (*Star Wars: Episode I.II*).

Despite Jar Jar's importance to the story, the Phantom deleted the scene in the Battle of Naboo in which he is the first to surrender to the droid army. "If that [surrender scene] stays in, even with his accidental heroics, what business does he have being accorded a hero's welcome afterward?" the Phantom asks. Overall, Jar Jar spends much of the movie looking oddly to the left and right, but generally comports himself with more dignity—except that the painful energy discharge he receives from Anakin's Podracer is left intact in the re-edit.

It's also during a decisive battle that Anakin Skywalker has scenes and lines cut. Anakin impulsively leapt into a starfighter, managing to infiltrate and destroy the Trade Federation's Droid Control Ship, but completely by accident. The re-edit cut Anakin's cries of "Oops!" and his "Did I do that?" reaction shots to suggest guidance by the Force rather than happy accident. Earlier in the film, many more of Jake Lloyd's lines as Anakin were cut, leaving him with silent reaction shots that the Phantom claimed were more effective. Also stricken was much of the discussion of Anakin's midi-chlorian levels, an editing decision that favored fans upset that communion with the Force now depended more on one's bloodstream than one's religion.

The Phantom's commentary also pointed out many of the more technical aspects of his work. He tightened the narrative by cutting the long rising and falling action in many scenes and dropped dialogue in which characters merely described what happened in preceding scenes. To recreate Lucas's famous "window-shade" wipes, he had to alter the video's frame rate when trimming a scene to make the wipe as smooth as the movie. And a few scenes revealed continuity errors: During Qui-Gon's funeral, Obi-Wan looks over at Anakin, who in turn looks at him; then the next angle shows Anakin not looking at Obi-Wan, so the Phantom went so far as to rotoscope the characters so their actions matched.

Even without Jar Jar's active participation in AOTC, the Phantom describes the movie's "point of failure" as coming just after the beginning. On the commentary track to his *Episode II.1–Attack of the Phantom* DVD, he pointed out that Anakin failed to establish himself as a sympathetic character or someone whom we want to see get together with Amidala. Some of this failure of characterization is driven by the audience's foreknowledge that the relationship is doomed, even if the two will conceive the heroes of the first trilogy.

The Phantom also declared that any chance Lucas had to make the audience invest emotionally in his story was lost in the opening scene: Amidala's starship makes a risky trip to Coruscant; upon landing, the pilots express relief that they've survived a dangerous trip ... and the ship blows up. He compared this scene to the false suspense of the *Friday the 13th* horror series, where the endangered teenagers appear to have killed Jason Vorhees; then a character pauses by a picture window ... through which Jason crashes to kill her. "They always make the audience aware that danger is about to happen," he says, so now the audience knows more than the characters. An Easter egg on the DVD drives the point home by showing illustrative clips from the *Friday the 13th* films (*Star Wars: Episode I.II*).

Ultimately, the Phantom reveals himself as not merely a fan, but as someone who was inspired by Lucas's filmmaking vision to attempt to work in Hollywood himself. The Phantom Edit was originally a side project, perhaps a calling card, whose effect went far beyond the creator's intent. The Phantom's Web site details that Lucas himself requested a copy of the VHS version at the 2001 MTV Music Awards. Since other creators of fan films ended up working for Lucasfilm, it could have been a positive step. But in the June/July 2002 issue of *Film Comment*, Lucas, interviewed by editor Gavin Smith, said, "The Phantom Edit was fine until they started selling it. Once they started selling it became a piracy issue" ("Message").

From that point, the Phantom made many more media appearances to reiterate the fact that he had never sold copies of *The Phantom Edit*. He allowed himself to be interviewed by *Access Hollywood* for a segment to air June 27, 2001. After promoting the interview in the previous day's episode and continuing to billboard it up to two hours before broadcast time, when the episode aired, the interview was never mentioned; instead, *Access Hollywood* suddenly had an exclusive preview from next year's AOTC. The Phantom wrote that he realized he had never even been asked to sign a release form for the interview and suspected he was used as a bargaining chip to get the previews from Lucasfilm ("How *Not* to Reveal").

The Phantom Edits have been possible because of the confluence of trends in computer technology. Fans have attempted to remix their favorite cultural texts the best way that current technology and economy would allow. *Star Trek* scriptwriter David Gerrold described the case of a "sweet little old lady from Southern California who has tape-recorded every single *Star Trek* episode—for the express purpose of later dubbing in her own voice over the leading lady's" (108–9).[4] It has already been a generation since the rock band Yes brought digital sampling into the mainstream with "Owner of a Lonely Heart" (1983). Elvis Presley gained his biggest posthumous hit in 2002 when RCA authorized Dutch electronica project Junkie XL's underground remix of "A Little Less Conversation" for a Nike commercial. Although DJ Danger Mouse had complied with a cease-and-desist order from EMI records to stop distributing his mash-up *The Grey Album*, this fusion of The Beatles' *White Album* with vocals from Jay-Z's *Black Album* continued to propagate unchecked among Internet file sharing servers. By 2004, underground video distribution was such that a pirate could surreptitiously tape the first showing of *Spider-Man 2* in a Manhattan theatre at 12:01 a.m. on June 30, 2004, put a copy on the Internet within four hours, and authorities could find counterfeit copies on sale in the Philippines that morning (Healey and Philips). Each year the cost of entry into the realm of digital production has gone down, and the learning curve to proficiency has smoothed out.

It should not be surprising that there are re-edits of wildly popular movies. A cinematic remix is an easy beginner's exercise or after-hours project in film schools. Considering the copious time and effort that fans can expend making films, building spaceship sets, or tailoring costumes, it was inevitable that what's considered a flawed movie would go under an amateur editor's knife. The Phantom Edits succeeded because the editor was both a fan and a professional. So far, it is uncertain whether re-edits of *Revenge of the Sith* will be appearing soon, but the widespread distribution of the existing re-edits suggests they filled a need by fans to take control of their canon. To them, perhaps, George Lucas abrogated his responsibility to the franchise by waiting too long to extend the canon and by refusing to match the prequel to the expectations of an adult audience that grew up on the original films. Lucas deflected fan criticism of *TPM* by claiming it was intended for younger audiences, yet, in *ROTS*, the juvenile hero would end up turning to the Dark Side, killing all the younglings in the Jedi Academy, getting his legs chopped off by Obi-Wan, and being left to die in a magma flow until his rescue by the presumptive Emperor Palpatine. If Lucas would not cater to the tastes of fans that had grown up with the franchise, it was up to the fans to remake the prequel trilogy according to their own expectations.

As a reconstructed Trekkie myself, I could recognize the feelings of possession held by *Star Wars* fans, who felt they had carried the flame for Lucas's universe during the decade-and-change that Lucas had apparently abandoned it. Gerrold said as much about *Star Trek* fans' trepidations over the plot turns of the first *Trek* theatricals, because, "Indeed, it is the fans who act as if they are the actual owners of the show." Gerrold cited Howard Zimmerman, editor of *Starlog* magazine, who concurred:

> Oh yes—they think they own the show because for a very long time they were the only
> ones keeping it alive. Paramount didn't seem to care, Paramount wasn't bringing the
> show back, so Paramount was the enemy. Now … the fans resent it that Paramount
> has taken it away from them. They resent the studio, the producers—anyone who
> violates what they think *Star Trek* should be. (Gerrold 119)

Some twenty years later, Lucasfilm's head of fan relations, Stephen J. Sansweet, acknowledged the same for their franchise; noting, "*Star Wars* fans really have a sense of ownership about *Star Wars*" (Evangelista E1).

For the *Star Wars* fans, it was not a soulless corporate movie studio that had taken the franchise out of their hands—and fans could not have asked for a better villain than Fox's media robber baron, Rupert Murdoch—but instead the creator of *Star Wars* himself. It was Lucas, not Fox, who expended the resources to preserve the film elements of the original trilogy, then went on to add more visual clutter for the 1997 Special Edition re-releases. It was Lucas, not a studio censor, who twice reworked Han Solo's confrontation with Greedo to make it plain that Greedo shot first. And it was Lucas who decreed that the first trilogy would never be presented the way that fans saw when they first encountered *Star Wars*, but that the changes to the DVD release would be the final word. It seemed a final thumb of the nose that the Special Edition ending of *ROTJ*, with its scenes of simultaneous galaxy-wide celebration over the fall of the Empire, had a further change for the DVD: a shot of humans and Gungans on Naboo celebrating, with a distinctive voice calling out "Weesa free!"

The massive promotional effort aimed at pushing each movie in the prequel trilogy seemed off-putting to anyone who had first discovered *Star Wars*, like myself, from the May 30, 1977, *Time* magazine with the corner cover blurb, "Inside: The Year's Best Movie." Computer-generated aliens in Pepsi commercial tie-ins to *TPM* spent more time gushing over the movie than the product they were hyping. Later, Yoda himself would be pimping Pepsi, while Chewbacca was recording cell phone ring tones for Cingular Wireless. But the disaffected productions from a large core of fans would not have been enough to promulgate the perception of artistic failure for *TPM* and, to a lesser extent, *AOTC*. That took the work of many influential Hollywood creators for whom *Star Wars* had been an important touchstone in their lives. When Johnny Carson ruled late-night TV, other comedy writers concerned whether a joke about the entertainment industry was too inside would find out whether Carson's monologue had already joked about the topic (Evanier 30). Somewhere there was a similar tipping point at which writers or producers authorized themselves to let their inner fanboys describe their disappointment with the prequels to the rest of America.

Like the creators of most popular fictions with fanatical followings, Lucas has had to seek a medium between protecting the *Star Wars* brand and encouraging fan support by indulging their creativity in its support. The universe created in *Star Wars* has proven to be sufficiently big and adventurous to inspire fans to chronicle their participation in that universe, either as participants in it or as fans of it. One aspect of that participation has included chronicling their feelings that Lucas has led his creation astray or left the original fans in the dust while pursuing a more lucrative younger generation. Thus, the *South Park* boys and the characters in *Fanboys* attempt to literally take back the film reels of Lucas's creations. Even *For Love of the Film*, a Lucas favorite, shows fans taking over the presentation of *ANH* in a theatre. Compare the long-interrupted official narratives of *Star Wars* and *Star Trek* with other entertainment franchises with large fan bases: *Buffy the Vampire Slayer*, *The X-Files*, and *Xena: Warrior Princess* remained under the guidance of creators who recognized and encouraged their fan followings and were able to end their narratives at a time of their choosing.

Fan films and Phantom Edits seem to have a growing role in the interplay between fans of popular entertainments and their creators. Paramount has given its imprimatur to *Star Trek–New Voyages*, a fan film series set in year four of Kirk and Spock's first five-year mission. Though all the familiar roles are being played by fan actors, the series has attracted the participation of Walter Koenig and original series scriptwriter D. C. Fontana. The students of the Digital Animation & Visual Effects School at Universal Studios Florida created a fan film, *Batman: New Times*, told with computer-generated Lego figures and with Adam West reprising his TV Batman role and Mark Hamill playing the Joker. All of the fan films cited here have entries on the Internet Movie Database, further implying some permission from the owners of the source texts.

The issue of Phantom Edits may remain a thorny one for some time. It's unlikely that every fan favorite will be fan edited with a critical eye. *TPM* lent itself easily to this process simply by the fact that there was so much footage in the commercial DVD release that could be removed. Still, there are other films with a critical fan base that may be ready for the Phantom treatment. There exists a "Purist Edit" of *The Lord of the Rings: The Two Towers*, which reverses the changes made by Peter Jackson to Tolkien's original narrative, including the presence of Elves at Helm's Deep. The Superman Home Page (<http://www.supermanhomepage.com>) offers a scene-by-scene review of the "Restored International Cut" of *Superman II* (1980), which tracks down scenes filmed by original director Richard Donner before he was fired in favor of Richard Lester. Efforts by Warner Bros. to shut down sales of the cut have resulted in its becoming more available as a free download.

The creators of cultural texts have traditionally operated with the assurance that the process of creation is a one-way street: They publish or broadcast, and the fans consume. The producers of genre texts such as science fiction or comics have come to enjoy the support of a fan base, but only on a subservient basis: Fandom and fan writing were essentially the rookie leagues from which a Roy Thomas or a Kevin Smith might one day graduate to the big show. And any problems a bunch of fanboy geeks might have with a new movie or TV spin-off was unlikely to bother the greater viewing public.

But too many of these have indeed become producers of entertainment themselves. They've taken *Star Wars* and other favorites as their inspiration for joining the entertainment world, and they now have a soapbox to proclaim their dissatisfaction with dilutions to their favored texts. And a general public that follows the weekend movie box office like a baseball box score is listening. Even those that have remained at the fan level have taken advantage of new technology and the connected fan community to engage the studios on their own level.

Notes for Chapter 15

1. The "All-Time USA Boxoffice" chart, viewable at the Internet Movie Database, shows the following figures as of October 31, 2005:

Rank	Title	USA Box Office
1.	*Titanic* (1997)	$600,779,824
2.	*Star Wars* (1977)	$460,935,665
5.	*Episode I–The Phantom Menace* (1999)	$431,065,444
7.	*Episode III–Revenge of the Sith* (2005)	$380,262,555
18.	*Episode II–Attack of the Clones* (2002)	$310,675,583
19.	*Episode VI–Return of the Jedi* (1983)	$309,125,409
23.	*Episode V–The Empire Strikes Back* (1980)	$290,158,751

2. I would also note a well-reasoned defense by Chris Aylott of Jar Jar as *TPM*'s hero in the Joseph Campbell mold: "Jar Jar, Hidden Jedi?"

3. He also has an entry under his real name on the Internet Movie Database for his legitimate work, from which the "Trivia" item about having been the Phantom Editor was removed.

4. Gerrold's original 1973 edition, which noted the existence of K/S (Kirk/Spock) stories (120), was possibly the first mainstream book to describe fan *slash* fiction. It thus predated most academic recognition of the origins of fan-written slash fiction. For further details on the *slash* phenomenon, as well as an excellent introduction to fandom generally, see Penley.

Works Cited

"All-Time USA Boxoffice." *Internet Movie Database.* 31 Oct. 2005 <http://www.imdb.com/boxoffice/alltimegross>.

Amend, Bill. *FoxTrot.* 17 April 2005. 31 January 2006. United Press Syndicate: <http://www.mycomicspage.com/member/feature?fc=ft&uc_full_date=20050417>.

AtomFilms (home page). 3 March 2006. <http://www.atomfilms.com/af/content/love_of_the_film>.

Aylott, Chris. "Jar Jar, Hidden Jedi?" 14 Apr. 2000. 30 Oct. 2005 <http://www.space.com/sciencefiction/movies/jar_jar_holy_fool_000414.html>.

Bridges, Jeffrey. "*Superman II–Restored International Cut* Reviewed." *Superman Home Page.* 30 Oct. 2005 <http://www.supermanhomepage.com/movies/movies.php?topic=sup2-RIC-review>.

Brin, David. "What's Wrong (and Right) with *The Phantom Menace.*" *Salon* 15 June 1999. 27 Jan. 2005 <http://www.salon.com/ent/movies/feature/1999/06/15/brin_side>.

Brooker, Will. *Using the Force: Creativity, Community and* Star Wars *Fans.* New York: Continuum, 2002.

Chernoff, Scott. "I Bent My Wookiee! Celebrating the *Star Wars/Simpsons* Connection." *Star Wars Insider* 38 (June/July 1998). 30 Sept. 2005 <http://www.fortunecity.com/lavendar/tarantino/370/simpsons.html>.

"Dragon*Con Biography: John Hudgens." *Dragon*Con 2006 Web Site.* 24 Oct. 2005 <http://www.dragoncon.org/people/hudgenj.html>.

"Ernie Fosselius." *Internet Movie Database.* 24 Oct. 2005 <http://www.imdb.com/name/nm0287629/>.

Evanier, Mark. "Show Biz." Comic. *Hollywood Superstars* Feb. 1991: 30.

Evangelista, Benny. "Lights, Sabers, Action! *Star Wars* Fan Films out of this World Thanks to Cheaper, Powerful Technology." *San Francisco Chronicle* 9 May 2005: E1.

"Fan Fiction." *Wikipedia: The Free Encyclopedia.* 24 Oct. 2005 <http://en.wikipedia.org/wiki/Fan_fiction>.

Gerrold, David. *The World of* Star Trek. Rev. ed. New York: Bluejay, 1984.

Gore, Chris. "*Star Wars Episode 1.1: The Phantom Edit* (West Coast Version)." *Film Threat* 8 May 2002. 20 Sept. 2005 <http://filmthreat.com/Reviews.asp?Id=2130>.

——. "*Star Wars Episode 1.2: The Phantom Edit* (East Coast Version)." *Film Threat* 8 May 2002. 20 Sept. 2005 <http://filmthreat.com/Reviews.asp?Id=2131>.

Greenberg, Daniel. "Thumbs Down? Re-Edit the Flick Yourself." *Washington Post* 7 Sept. 2001: E01.

Healey, Jon, and Chuck Philips. "Security, Raids Can't Sink Pirates." *Chicago Tribune* 15 Oct. 2005: B3.

Hill, Jim. "Did Stan, Kyle and Cartman Really Save *Raiders of the Lost Ark?*" *Jim Hill Media.* 21 Oct. 2003. 24 Oct. 2005 <http://jimhillmedia.com/mb/articles/showarticle.php?ID=253>.

"How *Not* to Reveal Your Secret Identity." *Phantom Editor Web Site.* 30 Oct. 2005 <http://www.thephantomeditor.com/episode6.html>.

McGruder, Aaron. *Boondocks.* 11 May 2000. 31 Jan 2006. United Press Syndicate: <http://www.mycomicspage.com/member/feature?fc=bo&uc_full_date=20000511>.

"A Message from a Phantom Editor." *Phantom Editor Web Site.* 30 Oct. 2005 <http://www.thephantomeditor.com/legal.html>.

Penley, Constance. *Nasa/Trek: Popular Science and Sex in America.* New York, Verso 1997.

Phantom Editor. Letter to the author. 29 July 2005.

Star Trek—New Voyages *Web Site.* 30 Oct. 2005 <http://www.newvoyages.com>.

"SWFFA Terms and Conditions." *AtomFilms.* 28 Oct. 2005 <http://www.atomfilms.com/af/spotlight/collections/starwars/rules.html>.

Templeton, David. "Jedi Revolution: '*Boondocks*' Cartoonist Aaron McGruder Strikes back at *Star Wars* and George Lucas." *North Bay Bohemian* 30 May–5 June 2002. 8 Oct. 2005 <http://www.metroactive.com/papers/sonoma/05.30.02/talk-pix-0222.html>.

Wilmington, Michael. Rev. of *The Phantom Edit. Chicago Tribune* 22 June 2001. 16 Oct. 2005 <http://www.zap2it.com/movies/movies/spotlight/story/0,1259,7141,00.html>.

Other Films and Television Programs Cited

Batman: New Times. Dir. William Vaughan and Jeff Scheetz. 2005. 17 Sept. 2005 <http://daveschool.com/MoviePages/Batman/Screen_Batman.html>.

Beauty and the Beast. Dir. Gary Trousdale and Kirk Wise. Disney, 1991.

"Burns' Heir." *The Simpsons.* Dir. Mark Kirkland. Writ. Jack Richdale. Fox. WFLD, Chicago. 14 Apr. 1994.

"C.E. D'oh!" *The Simpsons.* Dir. Mike B. Anderson. Writ. Dana Gould. Fox. WFLD, Chicago. 16 Mar. 2003

"Co-Dependent's Day." *The Simpsons.* Dir. Bob Anderson. Writ. Matt Warburton. Fox. WFLD, Chicago. 21 Mar. 2004.

Fanboys. Dir. Pater Haynes. Prod. Haynes Film, 2003. <http://theforce.net/fanfilms/shortfilms/fanboys/>.

For Love of the Film. Dir. Barry Curtis. 2005. 17 Oct. 2005 <http://www.atomfilms.com/af/content/love_of_the_film>.

Forrest Gump. Dir. Robert Zemeckis. Paramount, 1994.

"Free Hat." *South Park.* Dir. Toni Nugnes. Writ. Trey Parker and Matt Stone. Comedy Central. 10 July 2002.

"Half-Decent Proposal." *The Simpsons.* Dir. Lauren MacMullen. Writ. Tim Long. Fox. WFLD, Chicago. 10 Feb. 2002.

Hardware Wars. Dir. Ernie Fosselius. Pyramid Films, 1977.

Jar Jar's Walking Papers. Dir. Joe Fournier. 2002. 17 Oct. 2005 <http://www.atomfilms.com/af/content/jar_jar>.

Jurassic Park. Dir. Steven Spielberg. Universal/Amblin, 1993.

Sith Apprentice. Dir. John E. Hudgens. Prod. Z-Team. 2005. <http://www.atomfilms.com/af/content/sith_apprentice>.

Star Wars: Episode I.II–The Phantom Edit. DVD-ROM edition with audio commentary. 2001.

Star Wars: Episode II.I–Attack of the Phantom. DVD-ROM edition with audio commentary. 2003.

Star Wars: Revelations. Dir. Shane Felux. Panic Struck Productions, 2005. 28 Oct. 2005 <http://www.panicstruckpro.com>.

Starwars: The Phantom Menace Prologue. Dir. Neil A. Wentworth. 2002. <http://www.atomfilms.com/af/content/starwars_prologue>.

Terminator 2: Judgement Day. Dir. James Cameron. Carolco/Le Studio Canal, 1991.

Trivia for Troops (1988). *Internet Movie Database.* 31 Jan. 2006. <http://www.imdb.com/title/tt0153301/trivia>.

CHAPTER 16

A Survey of Popular and Scholarly Receptions of the *Star Wars* Franchise

Bruce Isaacs

How has *Star Wars* been received by critics? The scope of this question eludes any comprehensive answer. Yet the summary of reviews and their tendencies offers a useful guide to scholarly investigations of the *Star Wars* franchise. It will also interest fans, reviewers, students of contemporary film and culture, and anyone else who is curious about the way contemporary culture engages with a set of films, its merchandise, and its other cultural legacies. The franchise is a significant cultural artifact, able to overcome a plethora of negative media reviews (particularly of *Episodes I, II,* and *VI*) while establishing a cult following in the midst of popular culture.

Sources and Arrangement

The critical material on the franchise (particularly *Episodes IV, V,* and *VI*) is seemingly inexhaustible. I have provided an overview that emphasizes widely read, influential expressions of taste. The reader's task is to determine how various approaches might be compared, contrasted, or otherwise reconciled.

I survey major U.S. newspapers and magazines for responses to the films and their perceived cultural impact. The emphasis on U.S. sources is necessary: The franchise found a foothold in film culture through its national reception. The international media reception to the franchise is less substantial. Perhaps what can be said is that the *Star Wars* franchise (particularly *Episodes IV, V,* and *VI*) simply did not mean as much to European and Asian audiences as it did to American audiences in the late 1970s and early 1980s.

While this compilation sometimes felt laborious, the results were often surprising and thought provoking. Surveying the sources comparatively proved unwieldy and led to a general lack of coherence. For this reason, I deal with each newspaper and magazine separately, at the risk of repetition; this piece is, after all, a research aid. I separate what I consider popular/mainstream reviews and the elite/influential U.S. media. This is less a value judgment of the opinions offered than an attempt to address various approaches within the U.S. media to the franchise and, perhaps more broadly, popular American cinema. For clarity and coherence, I have fashioned the body of scholarly work into three thematic subsections: Cultures and Industries, Politics and Ideology, and Mythologies. This approach seemed the most logical and user friendly.

Elite and Influential U.S. Media

New York Times

The *New York Times* is the most influential and highly regarded U.S. newspaper—at least this is the perception of a non-American writer. The condensed opinions of Janet Maslin and A. O. Scott frequently appear on billboards and advertising posters. While neither Maslin nor Scott have the stature of Pauline Kael (*New Yorker*) or Vincent Canby (*New York Times* critic from 1965–1993), they are central to the U.S. film review establishment.

Vincent Canby's review of *A New Hope* acknowledges it as "the most elaborate, most expensive, most beautiful movie serial ever made" ("*Star Wars*"). There is a sense in which he considers the film *merely that*, which is to say, less than art. But "*Star Wars* is good enough to convince the most skeptical eight-year-old sci-fi buff, who is the toughest critic." However, *Empire Strikes Back* is proof that "more nonsense [is] being written, spoken and rumored about movies today than about any of the other so-called popular arts except rock music. The Force is with us, indeed, and a lot of it is hot air" ("'Empire Strikes Back'" D25). His review is noteworthy for its negative evaluation of the franchise's most strongly reviewed film, as well as his allusion to the vacuousness of popular culture and art. By the time of *Return of the Jedi*, "the magic has gone" ("Force is with Them" H16). But again, it seems that Canby is at pains to demonstrate the film's formal incompatibility with his viewing sensibility: "I seldom have any idea where things are happening"; "I began to feel a profound sense of dislocation" ("Force is with Them" H16).

For Janet Maslin, *The Phantom Menace* sustains the "gee-whiz" spirit of the series. She mentions the controversy about villainous Asian stereotypes that hampered the film shortly after its release (see also Leo, "Fu Manchoo on Naboo," and Williams, "Racial Ventriloquism"). She also makes the comparison with *The Matrix* (1999), echoing both Ebert and Ansen that *TPM* is "sweetly, unfashionably benign."

A. O. Scott suggests of *Attack of the Clones* that it is little more than "a two-hour-and-12-minute action-figure commercial." "Lucas ... is, at best, a haphazard storyteller. He also has lost either the will or the ability to connect with actors." For Scott, *AOTC* is little more than a film processed as a mass culture product ("Kicking up Cosmic Dust" E1).

Scott's review of *Revenge of the Sith* is noteworthy, not least because he deems the film "better than 'Star Wars'," a courageous assessment in light of the legacy of *ANH* and *ESB* ("Some Surprises" E1). "The sheer beauty, energy and visual coherence of 'Revenge of the Sith' is nothing short of breathtaking." He claims that Lucas has "surpassed Peter Jackson and Steven Spielberg in his exploitation of the new technology's aesthetic potential." He acknowledges that this billion-dollar franchise, in *ROTS*, must culminate "against the optimistic grain of blockbuster Hollywood" ("Some Surprises" E1). Each claim, in my opinion, provides a significant point of departure.

New Yorker

Pauline Kael, the *New Yorker's* chief film reviewer from 1968 to 1991, is simply the most influential voice in film reviewing in the United States. Though she died in 2001, her impressive corpus of film writings constitutes a veritable barometer of the New York zeitgeist in the decades in which American film flourished in alternative and mainstream cultural arenas. For this reason, her reviews of the *Star Wars* franchise make for fascinating and essential reading.

The *New Yorker's* original review of *ANH* is written by Penelope Gilliat, who suggests that the film is both "amazing and familiar" (70). The notion of this aesthetic duality recurs in reviews and scholarly work, though few writers venture to conceptualize the familiar as enervating (see Copeland for precisely such a reading). For Gilliat, *ANH* is "exuberantly entertaining" (71). Pauline Kael's delayed review of *ANH* in September 1977, which reads like an indignant corrective of Gilliat's more favorable review, is surprisingly brief, though it is often cited: "The loudness, the smash-and-grab editing, the relentless pacing drive every idea from your head" ("The Current Cinema: Contrasts" 123). Whereas Roger Ebert finds the reservation of his "analytic self" ("*Star Wars*") conducive to the reception of spectacular fantasy, Kael intends something different here. *ANH* is merely a mass audience vehicle. "It's an epic without a dream"—this is resonant in light of Ebert's conclusion that it is an epic with precisely a dream and a sense of wonder. For Kael, "it's probably the absence of wonder that accounts for the film's special, huge success" ("Current Cinema: Contrasts" 123).

Roger Angell assesses *ESB* in much the same terms as Gilliat and Kael did with *ANH*: "I felt stretched and terrifically entertained—and convinced, as I was at 'Star Wars,' that I was watching a first class kids' movie" (123). He acknowledges a "pseudo-Sophoclean, outer-Freudian turn of events," but adds, "I don't think this movie odyssey needs to be significant in every possible way" (123). It is ultimately, as *ANH* was for Gilliat, a pure entertainment. Kael's review of *ESB*, anthologized in Kael, *5001 Nights at the Movies*, views the film, as most other critics did, as "by far the most imaginative part of the *Star Wars* trilogy" and appreciates "the love of movie magic that went into its cascading imagery" ("*Empire Strikes Back*" 217). Her review of *ROTJ* attacks the film on formal grounds—"there doesn't seem to be enough light, the editing isn't crisp" ("Current Cinema: Fun Machines" 88)—and for its lackluster approach to the material. In the last paragraph of her review, Kael prefigures David Thomson's attack of Lucas's *Star Wars* (*ANH*), describing it as "a film so successful that it turned the whole industry around and put it on a retrograde course" (Kael, "Current Cinema: Fun Machines" 88).

Anthony Lane's review of *TPM* accords with much of the mainstream criticism of the film, though he manages an elitist slant: "It is of course profoundly gratifying that 'The Phantom Menace' should emerge as a work of almost unrelieved awfulness" ("Current Cinema: Star Bores" 81). David Denby's review of *AOTC* is refreshingly restrained, valuing the film's visual grandeur, though remarking on its "lack of emotional impact" (114). Lane's review of *ROTS* is merely a reprise of his hyperbolic review of *TPM*, lacking specificity, detail, or much value: "Sith. What kind of a word is that? Sith" ("Current Cinema: Space Case" 94). What kind of opening is that?

Village Voice

Andrew Sarris is a significant voice in film criticism and history, most notably for his introduction of French auteur theory to the United States in the 1960s. While Coppola, Scorsese, and Altman were America's equivalent of Godard and Truffaut, he views Lucas and Spielberg as "harbingers of hope" and *ANH* as an "essentially faith-healing experience" ("10 Best"). The implication is that the film does not deal with real life but projects the individual and collective fantasy of the viewer back onto herself; in this sense, it is wish-fulfillment cinema. Tom Allen's review of *ESB* is decidedly and surprisingly negative, suggesting a number of slippages from *ANH*, "none of which favorably reflect on Lucas as preserver of the *Star Wars* mythos" (51). Sarris, in his review of *ROTJ*, writes "I have surrendered to the Force emanating from the myth-making factory of Big Brother George Lucas" ("Who Am I to Doubt"). Interestingly, unlike almost every other major U.S. review, he views *ROTJ* as a success in light of the "turgid" failure of *ESB*. In Sarris's opinion, the film appeals more to "the children in the audience" and "in all of us" ("Who Am I to Doubt").

J. Hoberman views *TPM* as a "dreary recap" of *ANH* ("All Droid up" 125). His review is one of the very few that suggests the presence of cost-free violence and militarism, without the "extended carnage" apparent in films such as *Starship Troopers*. Michael Atkinson views *AOTC* as a "nominal improvement" on *TPM*, suggesting that Lucas's vision has fragmented into a "gnat-swarm of design clutter" (126). This view echoes Kael's and Sarris's reviews of *ANH*, particularly in his description of *AOTC* as "a marathon of irrelevant, preadolescent dreaming." His conclusion is especially provocative: "*Attack of the Clones* is a golden calf, worshipped not out of primitive fear but populist groupthink" (126). Ed Halter's review of *ROTS* concludes that it "is an underachievement of escapist entertainment" (C63).

Time

The potential cultural resonance of *ANH* was immediately recognized by *Time*, which ran a feature on May 30, 1977. *ANH* is described as "a grand and glorious film" ("*Star Wars*: The Year's Best Movie" 40). The author (anonymous) acknowledges its recycling of myths and classic films as a form of cinematic invention: "The result is a remarkable confection: a subliminal history of the movies" (41). Gerald Clarke's review of *ESB* praises its "artful and meticulous detail," suggesting that the film overcomes the "sequel handicap" and "is, in some ways, a richer film" ("*Empire Strikes Back!*" 66). Interestingly, the increase in complexity, subtlety, and detail renders the film for Clarke less memorable than *ANH*. In the same issue, Clarke offers a brief biography of Lucas, suggesting that he is a storyteller in the traditional mode ("In the Footsteps of Ulysses"). Clarke favors *ROTJ* over *ESB* for what he considers a more coherent narrative. This piece is particularly interesting for excerpts from an interview with director Richard Marquand, who paints an unfavorable portrait of Irvin Kershner, director of *ESB*, and a statement from Spielberg claiming that "*Jedi* is the best *Star Wars* movie ever made" ("Great Galloping Galaxies!").

Richard Corliss, the influential and long-serving *Time* critic, indicts *TPM* for its lack of humanity and feeble acting: "One suspects that Lucas was more interested in the aliens than the humans" ("Phantom Movie"). He regards *AOTC* as a marked improvement on *TPM*, rejecting the spate of poor reviews that preceded the film's release: "There's nothing deep or emotionally grand about this enterprise, but *Star Wars* never occupied that part of the cinema spectrum" ("Let the Battle Begin" 80). Corliss dismisses the clichéd dialogue and wooden acting for the film's ultimate payoff, the saber duel between Yoda and Count Dooku (Christopher Lee), affirming the faith in the franchise's "movie magic." His review of *ROTS* echoes many of the sentiments of the mainstream press, suggesting a return to the spirit and elegance of *Episodes IV, V,* and *VI.* He cites Ian McDiarmid's Emperor as a "starmaking turn." The conclusion is particularly resonant: "Lucas found the skill to make a grave and vigorous popular entertainment, a picture that regains and sustains the filmic Force he dreamed up a long time ago, in a movie industry that seems far, far away. Because he, irrevocably, changed it" ("Dark Side Rising" 52).

Popular and Mainstream U.S. Media

Chicago Sun-Times (Roger Ebert)

Roger Ebert is an icon of the American film review scene. He has maintained both an air of authority and of being one of the people. It is then not surprising that he regards the franchise as *affective*, less significant for what it says than for what it *does to you*. Of ANH, he writes, "I lose my detachment, my analytical reserve. The movie's happening, and it's happening to me" ("*Star Wars*"). Though he considers *ESB* darker in tone, it still manages to create a "sense of wonder" ("*Empire Strikes Back*"). The story of the franchise, though "familiar," is a "less crucial element as time goes by," and, ultimately, the first trilogy is "fun, magnificent fun" ("*Return of the Jedi*"). The wonder of the first trilogy is transposed onto *TPM.* While it "tells a good story," "what he [Lucas] does have, in abundance, is exhilaration." What distinguishes *Star Wars* and Lucas's sensibilities from *The Matrix* and *Dark City* is that "[Lucas's] film's energy level is more cheerful; he doesn't share the prevailing view that the future is a dark and lonely place" ("*Star Wars–Episode I*"). Worth noting here is Ebert's ready acceptance of the franchise as popular and nostalgic mythology, a vision of a better time and place, and something akin to what Lucas envisioned (see Harmetz, "Burden of Dreams").

Ebert criticizes AOTC for its verbosity: "They [the characters] talk and talk and talk. And their talk is in a flat utilitarian style." The love story is viewed as "romantic cliché." He alludes intriguingly to the blandness of the visual effects and the lack of visual acuity in the imagery. This leads to a brief discussion of the relative merits of film (35 mm) and digital imaging, a topic at the forefront of contemporary cinema (particularly after the innovations of Lars Von Trier and the Dogma group, who championed stylistic and thematic realism in cinema in the 1990s). Essentially, for Ebert, AOTC falls flat because of poor dialogue, narrative clichés, and a whole that "lacks juice and delight" ("*Star Wars–Episode II*"). *ROTS* is a "return to the classic opera style that launched the series.*" Interestingly, though Ebert criticizes the credibility of a number of sequences and finds that the "saber fights go on forever," he concludes that these are "more observations than criticisms" and acknowledges that " [Lucas's] 'Star Wars' movies are among the most influential, both technically and commercially, ever made. And they are fun" ("*Star Wars–Episode III*").

Newsweek (David Ansen)

David Ansen's response to *ESB* correlates neatly with Ebert's and offers some evidence toward a broad-based conclusion about the reception of at least *Episodes IV* and *V* in the United States: "The novelty, of course, is gone, but the 'gee-whiz' spirit lives on." Ansen recognizes the Freudian subtext with "all these caves and swamps of the unconscious." Interestingly, his reservation to the franchise lies in its lack of "story (as opposed to action), characters (as opposed to cartoon figures) and any real emotional resonance" ("Force is Back").

Ansen's response to *TPM* accords with Travers (see Travers below) rather than Ebert in both its evaluation of the film and its cynicism about the franchise's cultural pervasiveness: "The movie is a disappointment. A big one. Will you take my word for it? Of course not. This massively marketed movie is virtually critic-proof." He finds Jake Lloyd's Anakin "adorable" but that he "looks like he should be hawking cereal on TV commercials." He offers an intriguing intimation that Lucas's worldview is incompatible with contemporary culture: "And in the year of 'The Matrix,' which offers a new style of special effects and a dystopian fantasy that hits closer to home, Lucas's childlike vision is beginning to look merely childish" ("Star Wars: The Phantom Movie" 56). Recall that Ebert said precisely the opposite of *TPM* in his review, citing *The Matrix*.

For Ansen, *AOTC* has lost the first trilogy's "mythic undertones" and is "just for kids," redeemed only by a rousing final act in which special effects and inventive visuals dominate ("Attack of the Groans" 64). His review of *ROTS* exemplifies the mainstream reception but observes that the plot familiarity works to Lucas's advantage: "When that massive, menacing black Vader helmet clamps down on the deformed head of the boy we used to know as Anakin, the *frisson* has a mythic kick." Ansen also draws a comparison between the story and the current political climate of the United States, in which it is "hard not to feel that Lucas's engagement with this story has a contemporary urgency." Like Ebert and Travers, he salutes the franchise despite its flaws and acknowledges its cultural significance: "What you can't argue with is that he's [Lucas] stayed true to his vision, and that that vision has changed the cultural landscape irrevocably" ("End of the Empire" 62).

Rolling Stone (Peter Travers)

Travers and *Rolling Stone* have a special place in popular culture, traversing the divide between music, art, film, celebrity, and other privileged cultural arenas. He is noteworthy also because he is a respected voice in contemporary mainstream and alternative cinema. His commentary on the *Reservoir Dogs* Special Edition DVD is indicative of this stature.

His review of *TPM* is exemplary of its mainstream reception. "There's a less fancy explanation for why Phantom Menace will inspire fetishistic worship: it's loaded with cool stuff and reasonable facsimiles thereof are on sale at your local Force emporium." "In terms of visual sophistication ... Lucas ranks with the masters." But he chides Lucas for his dialogue, as did most other reviewers (though Ebert overlooked this in *TPM*). The conclusion to the review is cynical: People will think what they think. "I'll take *The Godfather* when it comes to film franchises, but it's Lucas ... who knows how to make audiences an offer they can't refuse" ("*Star Wars–Episode I*").

In his lukewarm review of *AOTC*, Travers alludes to a "Freudian subtext [as] a huge improvement over the Jar Jar juvenilia that blighted 1999's *Phantom Menace*." However, he shares Ebert's aggravation at the script's talkiness, and complains, "Lucas still can't write dialogue that doesn't induce projectile vomiting." *AOTC* "reminds us of the dark power *Star Wars* exerted before it became a franchise" ("*Star Wars–Episode II*"). Most remarkable in Travers's review of *ROTS* is a brutal attack on what he considers an enfranchised product that has blindsided "several critics" (in fact, *ROTS* has been reviewed more strongly than any of the films since the 1980s *ESB*) ("*Star Wars–Episode III*"). While *Episodes IV, V,* and *VI* belong in Travers's "personal time capsule," *Episodes I, II,* and *III* are merely aberrations. In light of the obvious distinction of *ROTS* over *TPM* and *AOTC* (narratively, thematically, and visually), in my opinion, it is a case of the reviewer protesting too much.

The Scholarly Reception of the Franchise

Cultures and Industries

I take the phrase "cultures and industries" from the classic formulation of Horkheimer and Adorno in *Dialectic of Enlightenment* (120–67). I suggest the following sources criticize the franchise for exemplifying a prevailing mode of passivity in popular culture.

David Thomson's "Who Killed the Movies?" is an oft-cited *Esquire* article that charts the transformation of a vital and creative Hollywood (Coppola, Scorsese, Altman, etc.) into an industry producing only franchise cinema and tie-in merchandise. This is a clear, lucid piece that takes as its point of departure the notion that the *Star Wars* franchise privileges fantasy and self-delusion over the introspective and political investigation of reality: prior to the "blockbuster phenomenon" (57) cinema was anchored in a sense of reality, social conditions, and, equally, a sense of the artistry of cinema. He challenges Lucas as a producer rather than a director (for a seminal analysis of the production aesthetic in Hollywood, consult Schatz 652-4) and sees the Lucas/Spielberg legacy in what he considers their protégés, Robert Zemekis, Roland Emmerich, and Michael Bay (60-1). For a more rigorous analysis of the Hollywood culture industry written in the same spirit, see Thomson, *The Whole Equation: A History of Hollywood* (2004) (particularly 332-72, where the argument encompasses the invasion of computer-generated imagery and digital cinema). As a useful summation on Lucas as filmmaker in his *Biographical Dictionary* (1995), Thomson offers, "he testifies to the principle that American pictures are produced, not directed.... Above all, *Star Wars* and the Lucas Empire raise the worry that brilliant film students know too little about life, and are then protected from learning more by their outlandish success" (457).

Salon's Charles Taylor picks up this argument in "How 'Star Wars' Ruined American Movies": "With 'Star Wars,' director George Lucas didn't completely kill off American movies, but he did manage to cripple them badly." Jon Lewis offers a historical approach to Lucas and Spielberg as New Hollywood exemplars in "The Perfect Money Machine(s)." Lewis makes the observation that box-office interest is a relatively recent phenomenon (2). He cites approvingly Thomson's "Who Ruined the Movies?" and suggests that the "New Auteurism" is founded on "high concept entertainment," embracing "simple, striking narratives—narratives that support mass marketability" (4). He concludes provocatively by suggesting that the Lucas/Spielberg films have "less to do with form and style than with the large and more complex interactions between the films and the film-going, video- and merchandise-buying public" (8) and the cultural style of the Ronald Reagan years. For an oft-cited and influential piece that attempts to build the cultural bridge between film and politics, see Robin Wood, "Papering the Cracks: Fantasy and Ideology in the Reagan Era." A complex understanding of the passive consumer-citizens in Reaganite society can be found in Britton, "Blissing Out: The Politics of Reaganite Entertainment." Britton conceives of a Reaganite culture industry via Frankfurt School theory (Adorno, Marcuse) and, in the process, formulates a negative-utopian aesthetic in which an artwork must engage "with a feeling of tragic loss or a context of struggle or protest" (8). Rather than engaging with the inherent tragedy of material reality, Britton suggests that *Star Wars* reverts to wish fulfillment (8-10). He treads much the same territory as Thomson and Lewis. Suffice it to say that *Star Wars* is devalued. He also connects the Lucas/Spielberg aesthetic with late capitalism (Britton 13-4), drawing on the influential Marxist-aesthetic work of Frederic Jameson's *The Cultural Turn* (particularly chapter 1, "Postmodernism and Consumer Society"). For similar readings, less reliant on Frankfurt School aesthetic theory, see Rosenbaum's oft-cited "The Solitary Pleasures of STAR WARS" and "Excessive Use of the Force": "The nub of Lucas's postmodernism was to retain the kinetic pleasure of those clips [aerial fight scenes] and remove everything that might suggest human devastation or historical nuance, turning it all into a giddy fireworks display" ("Excessive Use").

Roger Copeland's oft-cited piece, "When Films 'Quote' Films, They Create a New Mythology," views *ANH* as a "world 'mediated' through other movies." Copeland is one of the first to recognize the quotation of John Ford's *The Searchers* when Luke finds his aunt and uncle murdered by Stormtroopers. He is also a very early exponent of cinematic quotation as a new kind of film sensibility. Interestingly, he reads the Riefenstahl quotation of *Triumph of the Will* (1935) in the medal ceremony of *ANH* as a warning not to "surrender ourselves totally to 'The Force'" (Copeland 71). See Lubow, "The *Star Wars* War I: A Space Iliad," for an early recognition of the visual borrowing.

For a superb response to the perceived "industrialization" of the Lucas aesthetic and the ruination of the movies, see Tara Brabazon, "We'll *Always* Have Tatooine? *Star Wars* and Writing Popular Memory." Brabazon claims that *"The Phantom Menace* is not only a marketing creation, it is an affective phenomenon, an historical moment over-stuffed with memory and emotion. No article, academic, or journalist has conveyed this story. It is simpler to decry the hype, rather than to evaluate collective memory" (8).

Politics and Ideology

Dan Rubey's "Not so Long Ago, Not so Far Away" approaches the fantasy of *ANH* as ideological, suggesting that "Myths and fantasies are not eternal: they are historical" (5). An "implicit conservative, reactionary strain is present in STAR WARS and undercuts the film's tone of youthful rebelliousness" (5). Unlike Copeland, Rubey views the obvious quotation of *Triumph of the Will* as one of the "totalitarian, fascist overtones [that] grows so naturally out of the rest of the film's fantasies and images" (6). For a similar reading of the Riefenstahl quote in Lucas, see Lawrence and Jewett (275). According to Rubey, *ANH*'s conservatism can be traced to its emphasis on natural and hereditary privilege (6) that filters into racist and sexist relationships between the individuated Luke and the rest of the characters, who are merely instrumental to the expression of hereditary and yet personally attained individualism (7). For an entertaining (and, to my mind, wholly perverse) piece on the racism of *Star Wars,* see Clyde Taylor, "The Master Text," in which "The mystical mumbo-jumbo about 'the Force' reveals the Jeddi [sic] knights to be the Knights of the Ku Klux Klan updated" (100) and the battle walkers on Hoth in *ESB* "nothing less than mechanized camels. Camels? Then Arabs" (104). Rubey's conclusion is provocative: "The film pretends to depict the struggle of good against evil, but in fact the evil exists in order to allow the good characters to act violently" (10). In this sense, it is a fantasy in which "Everything is a visual trip, an aesthetic experience" (3), including violence and the expression of power. Kuiper treads much the same path, suggesting that "The *Star Wars* trilogy [*Episodes IV, V,* and *VI*] creates and recreates imperial myths which serve to sustain an imperial culture" (77). These myths include the "nuclear family which is the social unit on which an empire is based" (79), the irrationality of decisions in which "the Force flows unobstructed" (80), and the clear distinction between good and evil (82). In this sense, *Star Wars* espouses as imperialistic an ideology as that depicted in its own "evil Empire."

Peter Lev offers a lucid account of the differences in politics and ideology of three significant, and relatively contemporary, science fiction films, *Star Wars, Alien* (1979), and *Blade Runner* (1982). His piece is particularly useful in considering Lucas's mythical ideology alongside Ridley Scott's dystopian realism. Robert G. Pielke offers a comparison of the respective futures of *ANH* and Kubrick's *2001: A Space Odyssey*, tracing various thematic and formal similarities and dissimilarities. Unfortunately, he offers a somewhat superficial reading of both films. For a more adequate reading of the convergences of the *Star Wars* franchise mythology, the Reagan mythology, and the development of the Strategic Defense Initiative (SDI, later dubbed 'Star Wars'), see Peter Kramer.

John Shelton Lawrence and Robert Jewett trace a form of the American monomyth and its unsettling similarities to European fascism in the *Star Wars* franchise (275–77). Religious idealism and hereditary monarchy are present both in the *Star Wars* universe and fascist discourse. Critically, for Lawrence and Jewett, "the notion that all of life resolves into clear-cut battles between good and evil is itself antithetical to the democratic understanding of governance" (278). See also Terry Curtis Fox for a reading of *ANH* as affirmation of "at best a parliamentary monarchy" (23). He veers close to Lawrence and Jewett's reading of fascism in the franchise by acknowledging the Riefenstahl quote in *ANH*'s concluding scene. Arthur Lubow also criticizes *ANH* for the celebration of mysticism over science and views this as a profoundly ideological choice: "What are we to make of this mumbo-jumbo? Is it significant that beneath this film's futuristic skin there beats an unregenerate reactionary heart?... STAR WARS is a paean to mysticism and an attack on modern science" (21). Jacobson sees *Star Wars*' fascination with technology as part of the "romanticization of the military in American films" (10), which he connects with a form of "cultural imperialism" (10). For a contrary and lucid reading of *Star Wars* as *anti-militaristic*, see David S. Meyer. For an impassioned attack on fascist and/or racist readings of *ANH*, see Denis Wood, "The Stars in Our Hearts—A Critical Commentary on George Lucas' *Star Wars*."

Mythologies

In this section, I focus on two writers for their numerous and often interconnected pieces on the franchise. Andrew Gordon has written widely on popular culture and myth (see his more recent work on *The Matrix* in *"The Matrix*: Paradigm of Post-Modernism or Intellectual Poseur? (Part II)"). Anne Lancashire's three pieces on *ESB*, *ROTJ*, and *TPM* offer a very useful structural overview of the plots, narratives, and themes of the six films.

Gordon's seminal piece, "*Star Wars*: A Myth for Our Time" suggests that *ANH* "is a masterpiece of synthesis ... demonstrating how the old may be new again. Lucas has raided the junkyards of our popular culture and rigged a working myth out of scrap" (315). The essay traces this intertextual aesthetic (of heroic fantasy, Edgar Rice Burroughs's adventure stories, *The Wizard of Oz*, *Forbidden Planet*, and *Flash Gordon*) out of which Lucas "constructs a coherent myth" (319). (Todd H. Sammons surveys and analyzes the intertextual connections between *Star Wars* and the classic epic form.) Gordon offers a detailed analysis of *ANH*'s narrative framed by Campbell's *Hero of a Thousand Faces*, a source subsequently acknowledged by George Lucas. Gordon's analysis, alongside numerous others, is perhaps the most precise and detailed in charting the mythic archetypes. See also Miller and Sprich for an "Archetypal-Psychoanalytic" reading of *ANH*. For an overview of Lucas's interests in Campbell's mythologies, see Coralee Grebe.

Critically, for Gordon, "Lucas attempts to make this essentially Oedipal fable guilt-free" ("*Star Wars*" 323). The resonant conclusion—"Viewers recognize that *Star Wars* has no direct relation to external reality, but it does relate to our dreams of how we would *like* reality to be" (325)—implicitly rejects the reading of *ANH* as militaristic (Rubey, Kuiper, etc.). Like other writers (notably Lancashire), Gordon reads *ESB* as stressing "the price of independence from the parents, the pain caused by the necessary death of the old self in the course of initiation" ("*Empire Strikes Back*" 314). He also traces the significance of the "primal anxieties" in *ESB* that were not explicit in *ANH*: being eaten alive, suffocation, and fear of falling (316). Less impressed with *ROTJ*, he aligns himself with Robin Wood, Britton, and others: "*Jedi* is a Reaganesque-era movie: a slick, sentimental, derivative Hollywood product, hollow at the core" ("*Return of the Jedi*" 45). The film fails on two fronts: "The *spectacular* degenerates into mere *spectacle*" (46), and it fails to carry forward the mythical coherence and continuity from the first two films. Lucas does not engage with the complexity of the maturation process for the hero, "avoiding powerful parricidal and incestuous impulses" (49). "Therefore the series is suffused with violence and castration anxiety" (52). *ROTJ* is corrupted by a "kind of affectlessness" (52). Gordon offers a reading of sexuality in *Episodes IV, V,* and *VI,* addressing the wish-fulfillment impulse of the spectator and popular cinema ("Power of the Force"). He concludes that the trilogy "provides something for everyone, on one psychosexual level or another" (205). It satisfies an erotic yearning for "action and speed" and "allows the viewer to triumph vicariously over fears of incest [Luke/Leia], castration [Luke/Vader], and homosexuality [the Emperor]" (205). His article, "You'll Never Get out of Bedford Falls: The Inescapable Fantasy in American Science Fiction and Fantasy Films," traces the centrality of the home and family in American popular cinema through Frank Capra, *The Wizard of Oz* (1939), *Star Wars,* and the *Back to the Future* trilogy (1985, 1989, 1990). He implies that there is an essential conservatism in the ideology of mainstream U.S. cinema.

Lane Roth and James Curtis separately offer analyses of *Star Wars* as Western genre and, in a broader sense, of reflecting on traditional myths and texts. For Roth, "films like *Star Wars* and its successors are, like Westerns, essentially romances" (184). Curtis is one of the few writers who explores themes common to *American Graffiti* (1973) and *Star Wars.* In concluding that the two films issue from a similar aesthetic wellspring, he makes the profound observation that "George Lucas is the first major American director whose aesthetic sense was formed by television and rock 'n roll" (598).

Anne Lancashire's three pieces on *ESB, ROTJ,* and *TPM* read the franchise as forming a coherent and complex whole founded on a detailed mythological structure, as well as a visually spectacular continuity. Unlike Gordon, she views the first trilogy as concluding appropriately with the hero's maturation: "Luke finally chooses, as not in *Empire's* duel, love over destruction or escape" ("*Return of the Jedi*" 62). The "structural and thematic unity" of the trilogy (55) foregrounds a "world in which men grow and acquire new, complex perspectives on human existence as they move from innocence through experience to maturity" (63), which "is popular art at its creative best" ("*Return of the Jedi*" 63). Lancashire's most interesting and innovative observation comes in her piece on *TPM,* "*The Phantom Menace:* Repetition, Variation, Integration," in which she suggests that a reading of the franchise requires an integration of a structural unity rather than a conventional appraisal of a single film. She addresses Campbell's mythology as central to Anakin's maturation, which parallels the same process in the first trilogy. "The films together move, for the integrating spectator, towards an increasingly complex view of human experience" (52).

Terry Dowling draws on Jungian archetypes to locate the significance and cultural resonance of *Star Wars:* "Just as Obi-Wan tells Luke that he has taken his first step into 'a larger world,' this is precisely what such a film allows us to do, and one can't help but feel that Jung would have approved wholeheartedly.

It is a 'healing' film" (8). In this sense, myth is regenerative and restorative, achieving what Lucas intended (see Aljean Harmetz, "Burden of Dreams"). Denis Wood traces mythical and narrative patterns in *Star Wars*, White's *The Book of Merlyn*, and Tolkien's *Lord of the Rings* and *The Hobbit* ("Growing Up among the Stars"). The significance of this piece lies in its convincing account of the central features of these narratives and their centrality to Western culture. In this sense, Daniel Mackay's notion that *Star Wars* has been wrongly elevated to the status of myth because "its message about the human spirit is assembled from the remnants of the old mythologies—mythologies that no longer carry weight in the way we live our lives today" (74) fails to appreciate the ontology of contemporary cultural myth. However, in his defense, he does place a very strict definition on mythology, which he draws from Campbell.

The response to *The Star Wars* franchise has been rich and varied. Indeed, the categorization of a massive body of work has proved as energizing as the engagement with the material surveyed. Perhaps, in conclusion, what remains to be said is that the franchise eludes simplistic critical models and finds favor with critics of astonishingly varied political, ideological, and cultural persuasions. It is therefore a cultural artifact that will continue to bear critical scrutiny and sustained scholarly analysis.

Works Cited

Allen, Tom. "What Empire?" *Village Voice* 26 May 1980: 50-2.

Angell, Roger. "The Current Cinema: Cheers and Whimpers." *New Yorker* 26 May 1980: 123-5.

Ansen, David. "Attack of the Groans." *Newsweek* 20 May 2002: 64.

——. "*The Empire Strikes Back*." *Newsweek* 19 May 1980: 105.

——. "The End of the Empire." *Newsweek* 16 May 2005: 62.

——. "The Force is Back with Us." *Newsweek* 19 May 1980: 49-50.

——. "*Star Wars*: The Phantom Movie." *Newsweek* 17 May 1999: 56.

Atkinson, Michael. "Reproductive Rites." *Village Voice* 21 May 2002: 126.

Brabazon, Tara. "We'll *Always* Have Tatooine? *Star Wars* and Writing a Popular Memory." *Australian Journal of Communication* 26.2 (1999): 1-10.

Britton, Andrew. "Blissing Out: The Politics of Reaganite Entertainment." *Movie* 31/32 (1986): 1-42.

Canby, Vincent. "'The Empire Strikes Back' Strikes a Bland Note." *New York Times* 15 June 1980: D25.

——. "The Force Is with Them, but the Magic Is Gone." *New York Times* 29 May 1983: H16.

——. "*Star Wars*—A Trip to a Far Away Galaxy That's Fun and Funny." *New York Times* 26 May 1977.

Clarke, Gerald. "*The Empire Strikes Back!*" *Time* 19 May 1980: 66.

——. "Great Galloping Galaxies!" *Time* 23 May 1983: 62+.

——. "In the Footsteps of Ulysses." *Time* 19 May 1980: 62-3.

Copeland, Roger. "When Films 'Quote' Films, They Create a New Mythology." *New York Times* 25 Sep. 1977: 71.

Corliss, Richard. "Dark Side Rising." *Time* 9 May 2005: 52.

——. "Let the Battle Begin!" *Time* 20 May 2002: 80.

——. "The Phantom Movie." *Time* 17 May 1999: 80+.

Curtis, James M. "From *American Graffiti* to *Star Wars*." *Journal of Popular Culture* 13.4 (1980): 590-601.

Denby, David. "The Current Cinema: Star Struck." *New Yorker* 20 May 2002: 114-5.

Dowling, Terry. "The 'Man' with the Off-White Light-Sabre." *Science Fiction* 1.3 (1978): 4-9.

Ebert, Roger. "*The Empire Strikes Back*: Special Edition Release." *Chicago Sun-Times* 21 Feb. 1997.

——. "*Return of the Jedi*." *Chicago Sun-Times* 25 May 1983.

——. "*Star Wars*." *Chicago Sun-Times* 1977.

——. "*Star Wars–Episode I: The Phantom Menace*." *Chicago Sun-Times* 17 May 1999.

——. "*Star Wars–Episode II: Attack of the Clones*." *Chicago Sun-Times* 10 May 2002.

——. "*Star Wars–Episode III: Revenge of the Sith*." *Chicago Sun-Times* 16 May 2005.

Fox, Terry Curtis. "The *Star Wars* War: II: Star Drek." *Film Comment* 13.4 (1977): 23.

Gilliat, Penelope. "The Current Cinema: Galaxy Crisis." *New Yorker* 13 June 1977: 69-70.

Gordon, Andrew. "*The Empire Strikes Back*: Monsters from the Id." *Science-Fiction Studies* 7 (1980): 313-8.

——. "*The Matrix*: Paradigm of Post-Modernism or Intellectual Poseur? (Part II)." *Taking the Red Pill: Science, Philosophy and Religion in* The Matrix. Ed. Glenn Yeffeth. Dallas: Benballa, 2003. 85-102.

——. "The Power of the Force: Sex in the *Star Wars* Trilogy." *Eros in the Mind's Eye.* Ed. Donald Palumbo. New York: Greenwood P, 1986. 93-207.

——. "*Return of the Jedi*: The End of the Myth." *Film Criticism* 8.2 (1984): 45-54.

——. "*Star Wars*: A Myth for Our Time." *Literature/Film Quarterly* 6.4 (1978): 314-26.

——. "You'll Never Get Out of Bedford Falls: The Inescapable Family in American Science Fiction and Fantasy Films." *Journal of Popular Film & Television* 20.2 (1992): 2-8.

Grebe, Coralee. "Raiders of the Myths: Lucas and Spielberg Borrow From Campbell." *Cinemafantastique* 19.4 (1989): 7, 58.

Halter, Ed. "May the Force Be Over." *Village Voice* 18-24 May 2005: C63.

Harmetz, Aljean. "Burden of Dreams: George Lucas." *American Film* (June 1983): 30-6.

Hoberman, J. "All Droid up." *Village Voice* 25 May 1999: 125.

——. "The Force Will Always Be with Us." *Village Voice* 18 May 1999.

——. "I Oughta Be in the Pictures." *New York Times Magazine* 15 July 2001: 13-4.

Horkheimer, Max, and Theodore W. Adorno. *Dialectic of Enlightenment.* Trans. John Cumming. New York: Continuum, 1991.

Jacobson, Harlan, "Thunder on the Right." *Film Comment* 19.4 (1983): 9+.

Jameson, Frederic. *The Cultural Turn: Selected Writings on the Postmodern, 1983–1998.* London: Verso, 1998.

Kael, Pauline. "The Current Cinema: Contrasts." *New Yorker* 26 Sep. 1977: 123.

——. "The Current Cinema: Fun Machines." *New Yorker* 30 May 1983: 88-90.

——. "*The Empire Strikes Back*." *5001 Nights at the Movies.* Pauline Kael. New York: Henry Holt, 1991. 217-8.

Kramer, Peter. "Star Wars." History Today 49.3 (1999): 41-7.

Kuiper, Koenraad. "Star Wars: An Imperial Myth." Journal of Popular Culture 21.4 (1988): 77-86.

Lancashire, Anne. "Complex Design in 'Empire Strikes Back.'" Film Criticism 5.3 (1981): 38-52.

——. "The Phantom Menace: Repetition, Variation, Integration." Film Criticism 24.3 (2000): 23-44.

——. "Return of the Jedi: Once More with Feeling." Film Criticism 8.2 (1984): 55-66.

Lane, Anthony. "The Current Cinema: Space Case." New Yorker 23 May 2005: 94.

——. "The Current Cinema: Star Bores." New Yorker 24 May 1999: 80-2.

Lawrence, John Shelton, and Robert Jewett. The Myth of the American Superhero. Grand Rapids, MI: W. B. Eerdmans, 2002.

Leo, John. "Fu Manchu on Naboo." U.S. News & World Report 12 July 1999: 14.

Lev, Peter. "Whose Future? Star Wars, Alien, and Blade Runner." Literature/Film Quarterly 26.1 (1998): 30-7.

Lewis, Jon. "The Perfect Money Machine(s): George Lucas, Steven Spielberg and Auteurism in the New Hollywood." Film International 1 (2003). 30 June 2005: 1-12. <http://www.filmint.nu/pdf/english/perfectmoneymachine.pdf.>.

Lubow, Arthur. "The Star Wars War I: A Space Iliad." Film Comment 13.4 (1977): 20-1.

Mackay, Daniel. "Star Wars: The Magic of the Anti-Myth." Foundation 76 (1999): 63-75.

Maslin, Janet. "The Phantom Menace: In the Beginning, the Future." New York Times 19 May 1999.

Meyer, David S. "Star Wars, Star Wars, and American Political Culture." Journal of Popular Culture 26.2 (1992): 99-115.

Miller, Martin, and Robert Sprich. "The Appeal of Star Wars: An Archetypal-Psychoanalytic View." American Imago 38.2 (1981): 203-20.

Pielke, Robert G. "Star Wars vs. 2001: A Question of Identity." Extrapolation 24.2 (1983): 143-55.

Rosenbaum, Jonathan. "Excessive Use of the Force." Chicago Reader 7 May 2005. 31 June 2005 <http://www.chicagoreader.com/movies/archives/0197/01317.html>.

——. "The Solitary Pleasures of STAR WARS." Sight and Sound 46.4 (1977): 208-09.

Roth, Lane. "Vraisemblance and the Western Setting in Contemporary Science Fiction Film." Literature/Film Quarterly 13.3 (1985): 180-6.

Rubey, Dan. "Not So Long Ago, Not So Far Away." Jump Cut 41 (1997): 2-12, 130.

Sammons, Todd H. "Return of the Jedi: Epic Graffiti." Science-Fiction Studies 14 (1987): 355-70.

Sarris, Andrew. "The 10 Best, and All the Rest." Village Voice 2 Jan. 1978: 41-2.

——. "Who Am I to Doubt a Jedi?" Village Voice 31 May 1983.

Schatz, Thomas. "The Whole Equation of Pictures." Film Theory and Criticism: Introductory Readings. Ed. Leo Braudy and Marshall Cohen. Oxford: Oxford UP, 2004: 652-56.

Scott, A. O. "Kicking up Cosmic Dust." New York Times 10 May 2002: E1+.

——. "Some Surprises in That Galaxy Far Away." New York Times 16 May 2005: E1.

"Star Wars: The Year's Best Movie." Time 30 May 1977: 40-4.

Taylor, Charles. "How 'Star Wars' Ruined American Movies." Salon 27 Jan. 1997. 31 June 2005 <http://dir.salon.com/jan97/starwars970127.html>.

Taylor, Clyde. "The Master Text and the Jeddi [sic] Doctrine." Screen 29.4 (1988): 96-104.

Thomson, David. A Biographical Dictionary of Film. London: Deutsch, 1995.

——. "Who Killed the Movies?" *Esquire* Dec. 1996: 56–62.

——. *The Whole Equation: A History of Hollywood.* New York: Alfred Knopf, 2005.

Travers, Peter. "*Star Wars–Episode I: The Phantom Menace.*" *Rolling Stone* 10 June 1999: 135–6.

——. "*Star Wars–Episode II: Attack of the Clones.*" *Rolling Stone* 6 June 2002: 83–4.

——. "*Star Wars–Episode III: Revenge of the Sith.*" *Rolling Stone* 2 June 2005: 87.

Williams, Patricia. "Racial Ventriloquism: Racial Stereotypes in *The Phantom Menace.*" *Nation* 5 July 1999: 9+.

Wood, Denis. "Growing Up among the Stars." *Literature/Film Quarterly* 6.4 (1978): 327–41.

——. "The Stars in Our Hearts—A Critical Commentary on George Lucas' *Star Wars.*" *Journal of Popular Film* 6.3 (1978): 262–79.

Wood, Robin. "Papering the Cracks: Fantasy and Ideology in the Reagan Era." *Movies and Mass Culture.* Ed. John Belton. New Brunswick: Rutgers UP, 1996. 203–28.

Other Films Cited

Dark City. Dir. Alex Proyas. Mystery Clock Cinema/New Line Cinema, 1998.

The Matrix. Dir. Andy and Larry Wachowski. Groucho II Film Partnership/Silver Pictures/Village Roadshow Pictures, 1999.

Starship Troopers. Dir. Paul Verhoeven. Big Bug, Tristar, Touchstone Pictures, 1997.

The Triumph of the Will. (orig. *Triumph des Willens*) Dir. Leni Riefenstahl. Leni Riefenstahl-Produktion/NSDAP-Reichsleitung, 1935.

CHAPTER 17

Conclusion: Finding Myth in the History of Your Own Time[1]

Matthew Wilhelm Kapell

Minerva, the Roman goddess, is said to have sprung fully formed from the head of her father, Jupiter, after he suffered a severe headache (Guerber 39–40). In much the same way, *Star Wars* seemed born from the aching and questing mind of George Lucas when it was first released in 1977. Its rapid success made him seem like a latter-day god.

The people of the Roman Republic and Empire, in various places and times, attributed different abilities and skills to Minerva. She was occasionally a goddess of wisdom and, in Italy proper, the goddess of warriors. She was also a goddess of crafts and, in the later Roman Empire, a goddess of poetry. Though the story of Minerva's birth from the head of Jupiter suggests a newly formed goddess, she was actually a recycled goddess from the Greek goddess Pallas Athena. Athena, a goddess of war and wisdom for the Greeks, was born from her father's head as well, the major difference of birth being that her father was Zeus. It remains a central aspect of myth that cultures actively reuse the mythology of their own past. And, of course, Lucas's story too had its long history, since he had worked intensely for several years on his script, building a complete back story, rewriting what would become the draft of the original *Star Wars* multiple times. As Minerva was once Athena, Luke Skywalker (Mark Hamill) began his existence as Luke Starkiller.[2] With both Minerva and Athena, the Romans and Greeks reimagined and reworked the stories around these goddesses to fit their own dispositions to explain their worlds and to frame their own existential issues of meaning. The journey of the Skywalker family is a reworking of many mythological structures, and that reworking was conscious both on the part of Lucas and on the part of the viewers of the *Star Wars* films.

It is clear that *Star Wars* was not born wholly new from the mind of Lucas. Not only did he write and rewrite his drafts and notes, he also included stories and ideas from the hands of others that seemed to resonate with viewers. Some, like the obvious archetypes from the work of mythographer Joseph Campbell, mentioned by John Shelton Lawrence in both his chapters here, were intentional on the part of Lucas. Other ideas and other ideologies found their way to the story in less conscious ways. Cultural ideas and ideals about gender and sexuality, violence, good and evil, and innate and learned abilities were all expressed in particular ways in *Star Wars*—but with a degree of intentionality that remains difficult to estimate. Lucas the storyteller tried to write a new kind of myth, but, in doing so, he reinforced many cultural norms from his own life and, indeed, the lives of his viewers. It is the purpose of this book to examine those cultural norms, to think about the issues that a viewer finds reinforced within the texts of the *Star Wars* narratives. It is the retelling and recycling of earlier stories that make *Star Wars* such a potent imaginary world to consider from the perspectives of our own shared and continually recycled culture.

The best received stories of the present—be they a film or television show, a novel or video game—often achieve their popularity by retelling past stories, myths, and histories. The *Lord of the Rings* and *Matrix* film trilogies each paint their stories with broad strokes of our collective myth and history. The quest of Frodo Baggins mirrors the quest narratives throughout many cultures, while Neo's path in the *Matrix* films recapitulates multiple stories of the apotheosis of humans into god-like forms. The *Harry Potter* novels and films rework similar narratives/tales of quest and transformation, and Harry's special powers recount not only the abilities of mythological figures like Minerva, but also the abilities of more recent fictional heroes like those of the Skywalker family.[3]

There is no doubt that the sprawling narrative of *Star Wars* is rich in cultural expression. Like the myths of gods and goddesses among the Greeks and Romans, *Star Wars* has been continually reworked and reimagined. Many loyal fans of the first trilogy of films (1977–1983) were aghast when Lucas used computer-generated imaging to expand and rework those films in the late 1990s. He had dared to tinker with his own sacred canon. Yet there is very little difference between this reworking and the reworkings of the Romans, who would add poetry to the exhaustive list of Minerva's abilities. As Andrew Plemmons Pratt and Mark McDermott note in their essays here, the reworking of a film's text is a part of the reimagining of a story for a contemporary audience. The rapid advances in digital technology made by Lucas's own Industrial Light and Magic made it irresistible to tinker with what seemed flawed to him on its initial release. Lucas reworked his already recycled narratives, and viewers were, at the same time, busy doing the same.

And like the Greeks and Romans before them, the consumers of *Star Wars* narratives see within their texts abundant examples of issues so important that they crave additional embodiments for further imaginative play. As a result, the *Star Wars* texts that are canonical to the series—the films, the official novels, and the video games—have been expanded in many non-canonical texts. These new narratives include fan Web pages, alternate stories written by both fan and professional writers, and the creation—based on Lucas's own prodigious back story of the entire franchise—of a huge "history" of a galaxy far, far away.

Myth, History, and Religion: *Star Wars* As a Story for Our Times

The historian Richard J. Evans has said that much of history writing is an attempt merely to account for "political or social movements in the present" (128). By this he means that the purpose of professional historians is often not the representation of the past, so much as it is to justify a particular aspect of the present. Myth works in a similar fashion. As the mythographer William G. Doty notes, myth "provides information about the structure of society ... in a narrative form" (14). Myths, like history, are more than the simple stories we tell ourselves about the past, they are ways of imagining "the possible new presents and futures that we have only begun to anticipate" (Doty 68). In other words, the usual distinction between myth and history is quite blurred, and never more so than when a galaxy's "history" is far, far away. Certainly, the galactic history in *Star Wars* is not "true" in the sense that any part of it really occurred.

But the *Star Wars* stories tell us about ourselves, and our own past and present, and may even help shape our future in ways about which we can only begin to speculate. This is precisely what Jess C. Horsley does when he works within the community of *Star Wars* collectors: He uses the *Star Wars* narrative to take a place within his culture. As he notes, he is forming notions of cultural reality, emphasizing in his collecting those aspects of the *Star Wars* narratives that most appeal to him as a member of his culture. Of course such play is by no means limited to collecting action figures and other memorabilia. Lincoln Geraghty and John Panton describe how playing within the *Star Wars* world reinforces gender roles and power relationships, how it informs both childhood and adult understanding of what kinds of behaviors are acceptable, and how the toys help to establish an adult identity—long after the childish play with them is past. This play is a kind of myth creation itself. Knowing the behavior of the various characters within the *Star Wars* universe allows both children and adults to rework important ideological positions within their own culture. Be it the heterosexual relationships of Padmé (Natalie Portman) and Anakin (Hayden Christensen) or Leia (Carrie Fisher) and Han (Harrison Ford), which Philip L. Simpson sees as problematic in his analysis, or the underlying male homosexual relationships that Roger Kaufman explores in his own essay, love relationships are explored in ways that Lucas might never have realized while writing his expansive story. This kind of myth creation is interlaced with individuals thinking about their positions within the social and public spheres in which they move. On the surface, Star Wars may be a story about the rise and fall of an Empire, but important issues of very real love relationships remain central to that story in ways that all viewers should consider.

Of course Star Wars is not real. But, in another fashion, as a set of images that is emotionally compelling, Star Wars is very real. There are no (or very, very few) people today who worship the goddess Minerva as though she were as real as the moon. Yet, to viewers of Star Wars the Jedi, the Sith, Han Solo, and Padmé are real in the sense that they have inhabited viewers' imaginations. But, more importantly, they are real in that they also affirm ideas about our selves, our societies, our history, and our culture within their narrative. One method of affirmation from the franchise side is to offer symbols that resonate within existing religious systems, as Jonathan L. Bowen and Rachel Wagner suggest in their essay. Jennifer E. Porter amplifies by explaining how those existing connections can be expanded to consider what is, for some tongue in cheek, a new religion of Jediism. In both cases, the myth creation argues for the impact of Lucas's narrative in the wider culture.

So Star Wars is not history, but, at the same time, Star Wars is a cultural history of our times and a vector leading to new futures that continue to contain it. As much as a novel, or a photograph, Star Wars is something that we must wonder about. Lynn Hunt, the cultural historian, frames the issue in provocative terms. For Hunt, a cultural historian must ask, "What does a picture or novel [or film] do? How does it do it? What is the relationship between the picture or novel and the world it purports to represent?" (17). While the "history" of the Star Wars universe is not "true," the events of the Star Wars narrative have a truth for us, its viewers. And although the representation of that history—of the droids, of the heroes, of the villains—is unreal, it possesses a hyper-reality that seizes our minds more fully than many items of everyday experience. Michelle J. Kinnucan's examination of the cultural significance of redemptive violence offers a way to examine both the Star Wars story and our own desire to defeat the so-called bad guy, whoever the bad guy might be in any given year. Stephanie J. Wilhelm also explores this destruction of evil, the privileged position of the good guy with the good culture, so important to understanding Western culture, in her essay. For Wilhelm, it is a tradition as old as Rome—and thus Minerva—in which the dominant power exerts that power over those without voice or agency, and, usually, those lacking agency are also set aside by their perceived race or gender.

As much as Athena is a prototype of Minerva, Athena, too, has her own cultural precursors. The mythographer Merlin Stone has traced Athena's archetypes to earlier cultures in Crete, Egypt, and elsewhere. In Stone's analysis, these earlier goddesses were far more dominant and important within their cultures than either Athena or Minerva would be in later epochs (9-29). Riane Eisler has argued these feminist precursors are the reason Athena and Minerva retain within their skills those of knowledge and wisdom (113). To understand Minerva, one must understand her own back story, both the specific kind created by the likes of Virgil and the cultural kind created by all those individuals who found resonance in the Minerva stories.

The monumental backstory Lucas has developed is also full of precursors, both conscious and unconscious, and similar cultural sea changes abound. My own essay on racism and the eugenics movement traces these notions of a select superior few, be they European "whites" of the nineteenth and twentieth centuries on Earth or the gifted Jedi of *Star Wars*. Biological notions of a more advanced group who redeem the Republic reflect this older legacy of blood-based superiority.

Kevin Smith Strikes Back!

The use of a traditional and canonical work for a new end is a standard procedure in literature. As Minerva is a culturally reshaped Athena—who is herself a re-imagined goddess from earlier forms—so too is Virgil's *Aeneid* an expansion and reuse of Homer's *Iliad* and *Odyssey*. In the *Aeneid*, a lone survivor of the siege of Troy, Aeneas, flees and eventually founds the city of Rome. Where the poems of Homer are, in the terms used by the historian Dean A. Miller, almost romances in their "complex" and "sentimental" tones, the *Aeneid* of Virgil as "nationalistic" fits in a more "epic category" (43-4), almost a "Latin propaganda piece" (158). These distinctions also help describe the differences between the original *Star Wars* trilogy's romantic tones for the destruction of the galactic Empire and the prequel trilogy's nationalistic and more epochal description of the rise of that Empire. As Stephen McVeigh makes clear in his essay, the entire *Star Wars* narrative is structured not only around the rebellion depicted in the films but also around wars of our own history and present. Thus, watching George Lucas's films, we cannot help but see them through a lens of our own experiences, recasting the narrative within our own personal and societal stories.

Interpreting a story like that of *Star Wars* through our own cultural experiences is what all viewers do. Fans just do it more intensely. Perhaps the most famous fan of the *Star Wars* films is the independent director of the films *Clerks* (1994), *Chasing Amy* (1997), and *Dogma* (1999), Kevin Smith. Smith, a Virgil to George Lucas's Homer, wears his fandom on his sleeve and is never afraid to insert references to his favorite *Star Wars* moments into the dialogue of his films. He does, however, rework Lucas's narrative for his own ends. This use of another story within the narrative of his own scripts has been called "textual poaching" by Henry Jenkins. Smith makes use of the *Star Wars* universe less in tribute than in expanding his own ideas about how Americans experience popular culture.

In *Clerks*, two characters, Dante (Brian O'Halloran) and Randall (Jeff Anderson) discuss the ramifications of the destruction of the second Death Star in *Return of the Jedi*. It is troubling to Randall that the second incarnation of the ultimate battle station is not yet fully constructed. Thus, when it is destroyed, it must have been full of independent contractors, just trying to "make a living." What moral justice could possibly lie in that? For the characters in *Clerks*, this changes the way they view the destruction of the second Death Star and, indeed, the entire structure of the original trilogy. This change in the conception of the narrative is common in myth as well. In Homer's *Iliad*, Aeneas is a secondary character at best, but, in Virgil's *Aeneid*, he is central to the entire narrative. For Kevin Smith's characters in *Clerks*, the "independent contractors" become central to an understanding of the narrative of *ROTJ* and recenter our understanding of the victory of the Rebel Alliance. As much as a reading of Virgil's epic requires a new understanding of Homer, watching the prequel trilogy recenters the earlier film's narrative on Darth Vader. Kevin Smith's probing fandom also restructures the *Star Wars* narratives, raising a moral question that the auteurs of *ROTJ* likely overlooked.

In Smith's film *Chasing Amy*, the gay, African American comic book artist Hooper X (Dwight Ewell) sees the entire arc of Darth Vader's redemption in the original trilogy in terms of racist stereotypes. Hooper sees the uniformed Vader as a black "Nubian God" and the removal of his helmet in *ROTJ* as proof that the trilogies message to African Americans is that "deep down, inside, we's all wants to be white!" For Hooper, the original *Star Wars* trilogy reinforces a mythical "whiteness" and is, as a result, problematic. On a larger scale, though, this kind of interpretation is what all viewers undertake, consciously or not, when watching, talking about, and thinking about a cultural product.

What Kevin Smith did through his own films is merely a very public example of each viewer's cultural interpretation. He has even been able to form an entire film around his own interpretations of *Star Wars*. His *Jay and Silent Bob Strike Back!* (2001) uses the quest theme of myth to humorously poke fun at not only the *Star Wars* stories, but also the entire panoply of things at which Smith often pokes fun. These include concepts of gender, sexuality, race, class, and American culture in general. This book, an attempt to find the force in the *Star Wars* franchise, is an example of that kind of interpretation—albeit a far more serious kind. Our contributors have specifically centered their essays on notions of gender and sexuality, religion and culture, and politics and science, because these issues are important not only to the films, but also to the wider culture of the viewers. As much as *Star Wars* is a story about a galaxy far,

far away, it is also a story about ourselves and about our place in our current world.

The Used and Recycled Past

The stories we tell, and the stories we choose to experience together, are continually reworked and reinvented as new myth or new history. This is done by storytellers, George Lucas surely included, but also by those who listen, who watch, and who experience those stories. The psychologist Clarissa Pinkola Estés has argued that storytelling is the art of "bringing up, hauling up" and "not an idle practice" (463). The purpose of storytelling for Estés is not something to passively experience, but something that must "happen to you" (464). Each viewer of a *Star Wars* film, each reader of one of the novels or player of one of the games, enters an interpretive universe—becoming not only the passive receptor of their media, but a part of the story encountered. It happens *to* us and *with* us. We become not just those who experience the story, we become part of the story itself. The Romans did precisely this when they reenvisioned the goddess Athena as their own goddess Minerva. A goddess of the home, Minerva served a central position in the Roman pantheon. Most importantly, she was a goddess who used her power for knowledge and, in times of conflict, for defensive warfare exclusively. As Yoda tells Luke in *The Empire Strikes Back*, "A Jedi uses the Force for knowledge and defense, never for attack." So perhaps it is time to reimagine Minerva for our own time—as a Jedi! Then again, in George Lucas's expansive universe of stories, perhaps that is precisely what we—all of us!—have already done and what each contributor to this volume has also done.

Notes for Chapter 17

1. William G. Doty, John Shelton Lawrence, Celia Teil, and Stephanie J. Wilhelm each read and made substantive comments on this conclusion. Each has my thanks.
2. The STARKILLER Web site ("Adventures") provides many of the early scripts from "The Adventures of Luke Starkiller," Lucas's many early drafts leading to the original film. The link to the fourth draft of the early scripts provides the first reference to Luke Starkiller.
3. For *The Lord of the Rings*, Anne C. Petty provides excellent insight on the mythological foundations used by Tolkien; *The Matrix* films are explored similarly in Kapell and Doty; Elizabeth Heilman provides similar insight into the mythology in Harry Potter. John Shelton Lawrence and Robert Jewett examine the specifics of such remything in their work, paying attention to both popular sacred and secular mass culture with excellent examples of specific cases.

Works Cited

Doty, William G. *Mythography: The Study of Myth and Symbols*. Tuscaloosa, AL: U of Alabama P, 2002.

Eisler, Riane. *The Chalice and the Blade: Our History, Our Future*. New York: HarperCollins, 1987.

Estés, Clarissa Pinkola. *Women Who Run with the Wolves: Myths and Stories of the Wild Woman Archetype*. New York: Ballantine, 1992.

Evans, Richard J. *In Defense of History*. New York: W.W. Norton, 1999.

Guerber, H. A. *The Myths of Greece and Rome*. 1907. New York: Dover, 1993.

Heilman, Elizabeth. *Harry Potter's World*. London: Falmer, 2002.

Homer. *The Iliad*. 1934. Trans. W. H. D. Rouse. New York: Mentor, 1950.

——. *The Odyssey of Homer*. Trans. S. H. Butcher and A. Lang. New York: P.F. Collier, 1909.

Hunt, Lynn. "Introduction: History, Culture, Text." *The New Cultural History*. Ed. Lynn Hunt. Berkeley, CA: U of California P, 1989. 1-24.

Jenkins, Henry. *Textual Poachers: Television Fans and Participatory Culture*. New York: Routledge, 1992.

Kapell, Matthew, and William G. Doty, eds. *Jacking in to the Matrix Franchise: Cultural Reception and Interpretation*. New York: Continuum, 2004.

Lawrence, John Shelton, and Robert Jewett. *The Myth of the American Superhero*. Grand Rapids, MI: Eerdmans, 2002.

Miller, Dean A. *The Epic Hero*. Baltimore: The Johns Hopkins UP, 2000.

Petty, Anne C. *Tolkien in the Land of Heroes: Discovering the Human Spirit*. New York: Cold Spring Press, 2003.

Stone, Merlin. *When God Was a Woman*. New York: Harcourt Brace Jovanovich, 1976.

Virgil. *The Aeneid*. Trans. John Dryden. New York: P.F. Collier, 1909.

Films and Other Media Cited

"Adventures of Luke Starkiller." Rev. 4th draft. *STARKILLER–The Jedi Bendu Script Site*. 28 Oct. 2005 <http://www.starwarz.com/starkiller/scripts/thestarwars_revised_fourth_draft_mar. htm>.

Chasing Amy. Dir. Kevin Smith. Too Askew/View Askew, 1997.

Clerks. Dir. Kevin Smith. Miramax/View Askew, 1994.

Jay and Silent Bob Strike Back. Dir. Kevin Smith. Miramax/View Askew, 2001.

Star Wars Filmography

Principal Films in Chronological Order

Star Wars: Episode IV – A New Hope. Dir. George Lucas. Production: Lucasfilm, Ltd. Dist. 20th Century Fox, 1977. 121 min./125 min. in Special Edition of 1997.

Star Wars: Episode V – The Empire Strikes Back. Dir. Irvin Kershner. Production: Lucasfilm, Ltd. Dist. 20th Century Fox, 1980. 124 min./129 min. in Special Edition of 1997

Star Wars: Episode VI – Return of the Jedi. Dir. Richard Marquand. Production: Lucasfilm, Ltd. Dist. 20th Century Fox, 1983. 134 min./136 min. in Special Edition of 1997.

Star Wars: Episode I – The Phantom Menace. Dir. George Lucas. Production: Lucasfilm, Ltd. Dist. 20th Century Fox, 1999. 133 min.

Star Wars: Episode II – Attack of the Clones. Dir. George Lucas. Production: Lucasfilm, Ltd. Dist. 20th Century Fox, 2002. 142 min.

Star Wars: Episode III – Revenge of the Sith. Dir. George Lucas. Production: Lucasfilm, Ltd. Dist. 20th Century Fox, 2005. 140 min.

The Story of Star Wars (two compilation videos narrated by C-3PO). "The Story of Anakin Skywalker" (narrated clips from *ANH*, *ESB* and *ROTJ*). "The Story of Anakin Skywalker (narrated clips from *TPM* and *AOTC*). Production: Lucasfilm, Ltd., 2005. 60 min. (2x30 min.)

Abundant details regarding actors, musical scores, and technical personnel for the films are available at Internet Movie Database <http://www.imdb.com> and at <http://www.starwars.com>. The Starwars.com Website offers numerous featurettes, some in streaming video.

Principal Documentaries

Empire of Dreams: The Story of the Star Wars Trilogy. Dirs. Kevin Becker and Edith Burns. Production: Lucas Film Ltd./Fox Television Network/Prometheus Entertainment, 2004. 120 min. (contained in the *Star Wars Trilogy* Bonus Material DVD)

From Puppets to Pixels: Digital Characters in Episode II. Dir. John Shenk. Production: Lucasfilm Ltd., 2002. 52 min. (contained in Disc 2 of *Attack of the Clones* DVD release of 2002)

The Beginning: The Making of Episode I. Dir. John Shenk. Lucasfilm, Ltd., 2001. 60 min. (contained in Disc 2 of *The Phantom Menace* DVD release of 2001)

State of the Art: The Previsualization of Episode II. Producer Gary Lera. Lucasfilm, Ltd., 2002. 23 min. (contained in Disc 2 of *Attack of the Clones* DVD release of 2002)

The Mythology of Star Wars (with George Lucas and Bill Moyers). Videocassette. Dir. Pamela Mason Wagner. Production: Films for the Humanities, 1999. 57 min.

Within a Minute: The Making of Episode III. Dir. Tippi Bushkin. Narrated by Rick McCallum. Production: Lucasfilm, Ltd., 2005. 78 min. (contained in Disc 2 of *Revenge of the Sith* DVD release of 2005).

Contributors

Jonathan L. Bowen is a graduate of Oregon State University's philosophy department. He is a life-long *Star Wars* fan and the author of a nonfiction book titled *Anticipation: The Real Life Story of Star Wars: Episode I–The Phantom Menace*, which looks at the unprecedented media coverage and cultural impact of the first prequel and its place in film history. Bowen also runs a critical review Web site at <http://orbitalreviews.com>. In his free time, Bowen enjoys adding to his massive *Star Wars* collection and discussing the movies with other fans online.

Lincoln Geraghty is Senior Lecturer in Film Studies in the School of Creative Arts, Film, and Media at the University of Portsmouth, with a PhD in American studies from the University of Nottingham. His work has been published in the *European Journal of American Culture*, *Extrapolation*, *US Studies Online*, *The Journal of Popular Culture*, *Literature/Film Quarterly*, *Refractory: A Journal of Entertainment Media*, *Scope: An Online Journal of Film Studies* and *Reconstruction*. He is currently working on several books—*Living with* Star Trek: *American Culture and* Star Trek *Fandom* (forthcoming), an edited collection entitled *The* Star Trek *Effect*, and a third a collection entitled *Generic Canons: Genre, History, Memory*. He wishes his mum and aunt had listened to him as a child and kept the *Star Wars* toy packaging—"Rubbish," they said, "who would want that in the future?"

Jess C. Horsley, like Luke, grew up on a farm and dreamt of escaping his small-town life to travel other worlds. After enlisting in the United States Marine Corps as an infantryman, he realized this dream. A decorated combat veteran, Horsley is currently at work on a memoir of his experiences as a grunt in Iraq. Now an English education and writing major at Morningside College in Sioux City, Iowa, Horsley works as contributing editor to <http://www.figures.com>, the Internet's number-one action figure Web site. Supported by his beautiful wife Shelly, this avid pop culture fan continues to collect action figures and has over 2,000 pieces in his collection. Most of them are from *Star Wars*.

Bruce Isaacs is putting the finishing touches on a doctoral thesis in the English Department of the University of Sydney, Australia. His work looks at film aesthetics, popular culture, and the idea of spectacle cinema. He has published on *The Matrix* in Kapell and Doty's *Jacking in to The Matrix Franchise* (2004) and on narrative theory in *New Punk Cinema* (2005). He has published a short story entitled "The Sound of the Fury of Walter Wishwell" in *New Writing* (London). He is currently working on a screenplay that is indebted to Jean Luc Godard's *Breathless,* a film that embodies everything that is cool about the movies.

Matthew Wilhelm Kapell edited, with William G. Doty, *Jacking in to the Matrix Franchise: Cultural Reception and Interpretation* (2004). Holding an MA in anthropology, he is a PhD student in American history at Wayne State University in the highly underrated and not overly violent city of Detroit, Michigan. He has published in multiple disciplines, including work on the genetics of human growth, the effects of poverty on childhood, Holocaustal images in *Star Trek,* utopian thought, and Christian romance fiction. He has taught anthropology, history, sociology, Africana, and women's studies at the University of Michigan-Dearborn, Wayne State University, Michigan State University, and Lawrence Technological University. His essay here is drawn from his previous work in human genetics and the history of eugenics in North America and Europe. His daughter, Zoe, owns both a green lightsaber and a red lightsaber and powerful with the Force she is. Due to his short stature and general level of hairiness, his wife has frequently referred to him as an Ewok.

Roger Kaufman is a licensed, gay-centered psychotherapist with a private practice in Hollywood, California, specializing in Jungian and psychoanalytic depth work with gay men and lesbians. His previous writing on gay archetypal psychology and film has been published in the *Los Angeles Times,* the *White Crane Journal,* and the *Gay & Lesbian Review Worldwide.* He has provided training lectures for psychotherapy with gay men at many clinics in the area, as well as the California State University at Northridge. He also lectures for the general public and is the continuing education coordinator for the Institute for Contemporary Uranian Psychoanalysis, an organization dedicated to fostering an integrative gay-centered psychology. He received his MA in clinical psychology from Antioch University and his BA in history from Brown University. Roger's office is strategically located on Hollywood Boulevard, just two blocks from Graumann's Chinese Theater, making it easy for him to worship frequently at the historic site of so many *Star Wars* premieres.

Michelle J. Kinnucan is a National Science Foundation Graduate Research Fellow and an editor of and contributor to *Critical Moment.* Her writing has appeared in *PS: Political Science and Politics, Agenda,* <http://commondreams. org>, *Nonviolent Resister,* and *The Record.* Her 2004 article on the Global

Intelligence Working Group is featured in *Censored 2005: The Top 25 Censored Stories*. She struggles against the Force—both sides—from her Life Star in Ann Arbor. She has previously written about *Star Wars* for <http://commondreams.org>. She may be contacted at haymarketgal@yahoo.com.

John Shelton Lawrence is Professor of Philosophy, Emeritus, at Morningside College in Iowa. His rookie editing years were spent with the undergraduate *Sequoia Literary Magazine* at Stanford in the 1950s. With Robert Jewett, he authored *The American Monomyth* (1977, 1988), *The Myth of the American Superhero* (2002—Winner of the John Cawelti Award for the Best Book on American Culture), and *Captain America and the Crusade against Evil* (2003). He prepared a presidential filmography for *Hollywood's White House* (2003) and a Western filmography for *Hollywood's West* (2005). He developed his first interest in George Lucas when two friends and their father acted the courtroom scene in *THX-1138*—becoming very excited about the stylish visualizations but unsure of what it all meant. Among the authors of this book, he is the one who most looks like Yoda but doesn't feel half as wise or weary.

Mark McDermott received a Master of Arts degree in popular culture from Bowling Green State University. Mark has contributed several articles to *The Guide to U.S. Popular Culture* (Ray B. and Pat Browne, eds.) and the *Encyclopedia of Television* (Horace Newcomb, ed.). He has also increased humanity's store of knowledge by kicking in entries to Roger Ebert's *Little Movie Glossary* and the Internet Movie Database. His knowledge about everything but the *Titanic* made him the second person in history to blow the $500,000 question on *Who Wants to Be a Millionaire* but he still has the laurels of his undefeated 1988 run on *Jeopardy!* to rest on. Mark first understood the appeal of *Star Wars* during his Christmas season retail job in 1977, when he tried to at least rack the first *Star Wars* action figures before anxious shoppers could snatch them away. He remains convinced that *Star Wars* is a better film when Han shot first. During his summer as a movie extra, he sat behind Ned Beatty and Patty Duke in *Prelude to a Kiss* and was in the stands at Wrigley Field when John Goodman enacted the "called shot" in *The Babe*. He currently works as a Prepress desktop specialist at RR Donnelley's Downers Grove, IL, office, raises the World's Cutest Boy with his wife, and brews beer at home.

Stephen P. McVeigh is a lecturer in the Department of American Studies at the University of Wales Swansea where he also serves as Academic Director of the War and Society programs. His book, *The American Western*, will be published in 2006. His essays on cultural history, literature, and cinema have been published in books such as *The Mediated Presidency* (2006) and *Clint Eastwood: Actor/Director* (2006). He also contributes the section "American

Literature 1900–1945" in *The Year's Work in English Studies* for Oxford University Press (2003–2005). He is currently working on a book examining the World War II films, mainstream and propaganda, of American directors such as John Sturges, John Ford, and John Huston. Stephen wholeheartedly subscribes to the belief that "hokey religions and ancient weapons are no match for a good blaster at your side, kid."

John Panton received a Master of Arts degree in European film studies from Exeter University, England. He is a lecturer currently teaching film and media studies in Devon, England. His interest in science fiction has been the focal point of much of his academic study from university onward, with a particular focus on 1970s American dystopian film and European science fiction in general. This has often led to suggestions from peers that he "really should get out more."

Andrew Plemmons Pratt is currently in the MA program in the Department of English Language and Literature at the University of Virginia. He received a Bachelor of Arts degree from the University of Virginia in English language and literature and American studies in 2005. His undergraduate work focused on issues of art and politics, digital humanities, and visual culture, and his undergraduate thesis focused on the relation of ACT-UP AIDS activist graphics to advertising. In his spare time, he wears overalls.

Jennifer E. Porter is Associate Professor of Religion and Modern Culture in the Religious Studies Department at Memorial University of Newfoundland, Canada. She began her career by studying nonmainstream contemporary religious movements and later combined this interest with a love of science fiction and popular culture by looking at the religious dimensions of *Star Trek* and *Star Trek* fandom. She is the coeditor (with Darcee McLaren) of *Star Trek and Sacred Ground: Explorations of Star Trek, Religion and American Culture* (2000) and is the author of various other articles on *Star Trek* and religion, among other things. With the release of the 2001 Jedi census information, she found herself sucked through a wormhole into the alternate universe of *Star Wars* fandom and began to research the influence of *Star Wars* on the spirituality of fans. She hopes to publish a book on the Jedi path at some point in the near future.

Philip L. Simpson is Professor of Communications and Humanities at Brevard Community College/Palm Bay campus in Florida where he serves as Academic Dean of Behavioral/Social Sciences and Humanities. He has written a book, *Psycho Paths: Tracking the Serial Killer through Contemporary American Film* *and Fiction* (2000), and essays in journals, such as *Cineaction, Paradoxa, Clues,* and *Notes on Contemporary Literature.* Encyclopedia entries have appeared in *Twenty-First Century British and Irish Novelists* (2003), *The Guide to United States Popular Culture* (2001), *War and American Popular Culture* (1999), and *The Encyclopedia of Novels into Film* (1998), and book chapters have appeared in *Horror Film: Creating and Marketing Film* (2004), *The Terministic Screen: Rhetorical Perspectives on Film* (2003), *Car Crash Culture* (2002), *Jack Nicholson: Movie Top Ten* (2000), and *Mythologies of Violence in Postmodern Media* (1999). Now that he serves as an academic administrator, his colleagues are fond of saying he has "turned to the Dark Side."

Rachel Wagner is the Hundere Teaching Fellow of Religion and Culture at Oregon State University in Corvallis, Oregon. In fifth grade, Wagner brought her R2-D2 action figure to school every day until it fell apart. In her early adolescence, she wore her long brown hair in twisted braids, earning her the nickname "Princess Leah." Now an adult with no R2-D2 and no long braids, Wagner still loves to think about film and other media and how they shape our lives. She has written several book chapters and essays about *The Matrix* franchise and representations of violence with religious ideology and was interviewed for the Warner Bros. documentary "Roots of the Matrix" for the Ultimate Matrix Collection. When not writing, teaching, watching films, or playing very average over-the-hill soccer, Wagner spends time with her amazing twelve-year-old son Isaac, admiring his skill in programming robots, playing the saxophone, and mastering ever more brilliant feats of creative engineering and programming.

Stephanie J. Wilhelm specializes in African-American history and literature and has multiple contributions in the forthcoming multi-volume Oxford African-American Reference Encyclopedia. She also cowrote an essay for *Jacking in to the Matrix Franchise* (2004) examining the *Matrix* films from the perspective of Cornel West's prophetic pragmatism. As this essay enters publication, she will be considering doctoral programs in African-American history or literature after the completion of her MA in literature at Wayne State University. She is currently finalizing her own encyclopedia project on African-American slave narratives, to be edited with Paul Finkelman. She lives in a household of four cats, three birds, two ferrets and two other Jedi. The birds and cats all carry either Russian or Cuban revolutionary names, suggesting both her political leanings and her opinion of the Rebellion in *Star Wars.*

Index

N

M

O

X

Y

Z